# DAVID SUZUKI
# HOLLY DRESSEL

# GOOD NEWS

## FOR A CHANGE

### HOW EVERYDAY PEOPLE ARE HELPING THE PLANET

GREYSTONE BOOKS

Douglas & McIntyre Publishing Group
Vancouver/Toronto/New York

David
Suzuki
Foundation

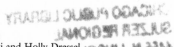

04 05 06 07  5 4 3

Greystone Books
A division of Douglas & McIntyre Ltd.
2323 Quebec Street, Suite 201
Vancouver, British Columbia
Canada V5T 4S7
www.greystonebooks.com

David Suzuki Foundation
2211 West 4th Avenue, Suite 219
Vancouver, British Columbia
Canada V6K 4S2

First published in 2002 by Stoddart Publishing Co. Limited, Toronto, Ontario

*National Library of Canada Cataloguing in Publication Data*
Suzuki, David, 1936–
Good news for a change: how everyday people are helping the planet/
David Suzuki and Holly Dressel.

Co-published by: David Suzuki Foundation.
Includes bibliographical references and index.
Previous ed. has title: Good news for a change: hope for a troubled planet.
ISBN 1-55054-926-X

1. Environmentalism. 2. Environmental degradation. 3 Sustainable development.
1. Dressel, Holly Jewell. II. David Suzuki Foundation. III. Title.
GF75.S993 2003   363.7   C2003-910055-3

Library of Congress information is available.

Cover design by Bill Douglas @ The Bang
Text design and typesetting by Tannice Goddard, Soul Oasis Networking
Printed and bound in Canada by Friesens
Distributed in the U.S. by Publishers Group West

Greystone Books is committed to reducing the consumption of old-growth forests in
the books it publishes. This book is one step towards that goal. It is printed on acid-free paper
that is 100% ancient-forest-free, and it has been processed chlorine-free.

We gratefully acknowledge the financial support of the Canada Council for the Arts, the British
Columbia Arts Council, and the Government of Canada through the Book Publishing Industry
Development Program (BPIDP) for our publishing activities.

*To our grandchildren:*
*Tamo Campos, Midori Campos, Jonathan Suzuki-Cook*
*and Parker Toole*

# CONTENTS

# ACKNOWLEDGMENTS

As usual with such efforts, so many people helped us that we cannot thank them all. We have had to single out those who have worked above and beyond the call of duty. Besides David's secretary, Lisa Hayden, who provided a consistently cheerful link between the authors, we want to thank Joel Silverstein for transcribing tapes that were often poorly recorded because of difficult field conditions. We would also like to thank Angel Guerra, Jennifer Glossop, Jim Gifford and Jane McWhinney for the many extra duties they performed and for their sincere interest in making this a better book. Christine and Ernst von Weizsacker provided warm hospitality as well as much-needed rest and advice in the middle of Holly's travels. Vandana Shiva and Elizabeth May gave enormous amounts of their time and encouragement, as did David and Fran Korten. We are truly in the debt of Dick and Jeanne Roy, who so unselfishly helped with research around the Pacific Northwest. We wish to acknowledge Beth Burrows and Helmut Meyer, who were unfailing in providing fast information about agricultural, scientific and justice issues. Holly was particularly inspired by Jerry Mander, and also wishes to express her gratitude for the honest critiques provided by Jim Latteier.

We regret not being able to use many of the wonderful stories provided to us, especially those shared by Mike Green and Fred Gallagher. Gerry Scott, Roberta Martell and Tara Cullis of the DSF generously gave of their time to help us with several issues. We very much want to thank the many readers of our last book, *From Naked Ape to Superspecies*, which became a bestseller, for making this book possible. We would like to thank our children, and we especially thank our grandchildren for being the physical reminders of why each generation needs to work so hard to prepare and conserve the world for the next.

# INTRODUCTION
## So What's the Good News?

### The Revolution's Here

*Until we have a reasonable idea of where we want to go,*
*we are unlikely to get there.*
— DAVID KORTEN, *THE POST-CORPORATE WORLD*

We, the authors of this book, have been involved in environmental battles for decades. Both of us have often viewed the escalating environmental crisis as a kind of war. As in a war, there have been defeats and victories. We've witnessed ecological and social atrocities, but we've also had the privilege of working with people who are among the most creative and courageous on earth. Many moments have come when we found it difficult to envision a time of peace. In our efforts to save this forest or that species, we sometimes lost sight of the real goal — resolution and balance. So we decided we'd written enough about contentious opposition. It was time to do a book about dynamic equilibrium; we needed to determine whether there existed practical ways by which humans could support themselves without despoiling the planet.

Once we began to look into it, we made some astonishing discoveries about ourselves as well as about the world. For example, we now realize that we shared a common attitude: that fighting for the environment is self-sacrificing and austere, and that concerned people have to don the hair shirt of discipline and control in order to conserve and protect the natural systems around us. To "save the planet" we would have to give up things like eating meat, drinking coffee or taking trips. In short, we believed that having cleaner air and water and preserving our plants, soils and animal species meant human lives would have to be less fun, with fewer opportunities for personal satisfaction. Only as we began to research this book did we comprehend that we had it all wrong.

As seasoned activists, we had also thought we were somehow immune to a pernicious philosophy underlying our modern culture, which implies that the fulfillment of personal, individual desire is the basis of human happiness; that life on this planet would be unbearable without an escalating level of material comforts; and that self-indulgence and self-realization are the same thing. In fact, we had completely internalized these cultural teachings. The process of trying to find workable solutions to the fundamental environmental and social problems facing the world today forced us to step back and question our personal assumptions about life. We met people striving to find solutions, and as they talked about the way they lived and their most fundamental visions for the future, we had to reflect on what had brought each of us the most personal happiness in the past. This exercise made us realize that, beyond very basic levels, our separate experiences of satisfaction, contentment and joy had very little to do with material consumption and comforts. They had more to do with connecting with others, with feeling useful and, amazingly enough, with sharing everything — from food and feelings to ideas and beliefs.

If we're pretty typical of most humans, and sharing, connecting and being useful are what really make us happy, how did we fall so deeply for a culture that tells us that selling our life's labor for fancy toys like SUVs and airplane rides, enormous houses, clothes, drugs, cosmetics, and enough food to make a majority of us actually obese, will bring joy and fulfillment? Many books have analyzed the relatively innocent way our current economic dogma, often expressed by the terms "globalization" or "neo-liberalism," developed after the Great Depression. It was designed to enlarge and spread wealth by increasing consumer desires and therefore industrial productivity and employment. But it has gradually turned into a tool used by groups of the already wealthy to subdue and plunder every natural resource and every human culture left on the planet. Those who need this historical background will find some of the best resources on the subject in the bibliography at the end of this book.

We wanted to create another kind of resource, one that would help the people who have already accepted that we've taken a wrong turn figure out, not what happened in the past, but where to go next. *Good News for a Change* gives readers some simple, workable and practical ideas about how to get out of a cultural and economic bind that many people now realize is rapidly leading us away from everything we really want out of life. To our amazement, we've learned that we don't have to give up our dearest desires to live sustainably; in fact, we can very often have our cake and eat it too. We discovered that living in harmony with the earth's natural systems almost always brings what we term "double dividends." There are ways for humans and for all the other animals and living things that support the entire web of life on earth to survive and thrive together. As we find methods to reduce pollution, waste, disease and loneliness, we can gain more forests, more birds, wildflowers and predators; as we grow more sustainable and more delicious foods, we can also create increasing numbers of better jobs that will bring us more free time. It is entirely possible for our restored natural systems to surround closer and more prosperous communities, populated with healthy people who are enjoying life.

After many years of recognizing and publicizing the enormous dimensions of the global eco-crisis, we certainly didn't expect all that. Actually, when we first began writing, we were worried we wouldn't be able to find truly sustainable solutions for more than a very few of the problems afflicting the natural world. But as we traveled over three continents, interviewed hundreds of people and pored over thousands of pages of research, we discovered what we had hardly dared hope for: not just isolated or individual solutions and technologies, but a vibrant and interwoven movement for a systemic cultural change from consumption to sustainability. We found it among many individuals, groups and even governments around the world.

Progressive governments in Europe, for example, are often able to work towards sustainability objectives, but in places where governments aren't responsive, people have simply started their own organizations to achieve their goals. Whether we found national policies or neighborhood and individual initiatives, however, all the movements we describe are groping towards something they term "sustainability." That means they're trying to understand the physical and biological limits of the planet and how we, as natives of this place, can learn to live within those limits. Even people working in the belly of the beast, in the hearts of large corporations and economic institutions like the World Bank, are beginning to raise questions about the efficacy of mainstream business and management methods that preach unending growth on a finite planet. They are starting, as we show in chapters two and eight, to help in the work of defining how much humans can take, and how much we have to conserve or create, to maintain a productive natural world.

This overriding idea of sustainability takes into account an equitable way of sharing the earth's productivity, as well as the amount and the types of human activities that can be maintained over the long term. Those working to define sustainability were also motivated by a very profound goal: if our activities are *not* sustainable, we're dooming our children and grandchildren to disease, misery and unbearable levels of social inequality. So wherever we went, whether the people we met were individuals, members of a co-op, a community, an NGO or a government agency, they were focusing on long-term goals of sustainability and equity with the kind of energy and commitment that most people display when protecting their children. As they've developed the sustainability ideal for their children's future, they've also discovered new and better ways to live right now.

While raising better beef and lamb in the American West, for example, ranchers are learning to bring drought-stricken, marginal land back to life and are making their family farms thrive. Their remarkable production methods, detailed in chapter three, achieve higher quality and greater market stability by protecting wild predators like mountain lions and coyotes! And these methods also encourage the reappearance of wild plants and flowers — the restoration of the entire ecosystem. In chapter six, in the key environmental field of forest management, we show how both native groups and big landowners have discovered practices that provide lumber while conserving bear and salmon, birds and huckleberries. Chapter five discusses agriculture and illustrates that even in desperately poor countries like India, small farmers have, on their own, developed methods of crop production that can feed the hungry indefinitely without destroying soil or water resources or reducing people to dependence on outside food sources. In chapter four, we describe desertified areas around the world where villagers are learning how to bring dry riverbeds back to life. When they do, they're also helping their small communities win the right to local, democratic control of their resources.

Although they're not well publicized, incredible new technologies, detailed in chapter eight, have the potential to replace, control and even eliminate almost every form of pollution and toxin, so that people no longer have to live in fear of leaks, spills or contamination. In the same chapter, we visit big, modern cities like Chicago, Berlin, Portland and Bogotá, which are experimenting with revolutionary urban designs that increase human fulfillment while conserving natural resources. And in chapter nine, we introduce a few pioneering educators who are learning how to teach students to really *think*, and are even curing them of learning disorders and reducing their social confusion and alienation.

One of our first discoveries was how the groups offering this good news to the rest of us tend to mirror the fact that natural systems, such as habitats, watersheds and species composition, change every few miles or so on this planet. Groups working on sustainability seldom conform to large constructs like nation-states or global marketing groups. They are nearly always locally based or else working in close contact with local people. This makes them diverse, in a state of constant flux, even messy — exactly what large governments find difficult to manage and attempt to stamp out. Our research showed again and again that the people in a position to know what will really work over the long term in a given area — and also the only ones who have a clear self-interest in making sure the area remains healthy — are locals committed to one place, people who have no plans to move away. The quintessential "locals" are aboriginal groups who still live in territories they've inhabited for millennia. Considering how few of these groups are left, a remarkable number of solutions, or patterns for solutions, are coming from them. But we also discovered that as soon as people make that local commitment — that they aren't going anywhere and they want to stay and leave something for their families — the sustainability concepts begin to roll out of their brains pretty quickly.

This local focus brings out the other key element that movements towards sustainability have in common: they are inherently egalitarian and democratic. It has been amply proven over the years that without general consensus among the people affected, any method of managing natural systems — whether planting trees, introducing soil conservation or implementing animal protection programs — won't function over the long term. But if there is broad-based consensus among local users, ecosystems can be managed to produce indefinitely, as we'll show in the terraces of Bali and the fisheries of Louisiana and India, in mixed organic agricultural systems around the world, and in locally managed businesses like the Collins Pine company in northern California. These examples make the fact increasingly clear that natural resources need to be protected from outsiders who have no attachment or commitment to an area and whose only real interest is ever-higher profits. Every group involved in this revolution is trying to move towards arrangements that benefit not short-term outside interests (the industrial pattern most common today), but local, long-term users. This pattern also protects small, local communities from being overwhelmed and impoverished by financial and cultural forces working on the global level. Too often such outsiders take away everything the local groups had built up over centuries, leaving them with little to do but abandon their homes or resort to violence.

We discovered that all the groups working towards sustainability use similar methods. They create a positive, almost idyllic vision of where they want to go and how they want life to be, not just in the next quarter, as our industries generally do, but many years down the road. They imagine everything they want to have — happy children, big parks, clean water, lots of wildlife, standing forests, good jobs — and they work towards those things. Our current industrial management paradigm identifies negative areas like unemployment, pollution sites or teenage pregnancy and concentrates on trying to deal with each problem separately. This new, positive approach not only keeps people energized and focused, but has greater success in actually finding solutions to individual problems.

The programs and methodologies that we look at in this book are extremely varied and flexible, but if one word had to describe them all, it would be "humble." Allan Savory's Holistic Management methods, which we visit in detail in chapter three, are a good example. They evolved to assist pasture and animal management, and under this system's guidelines for making changes in water or stock management are the words "assume wrong." The people who work with entire systems have realized that even though humans can split the atom and clone sheep, they still don't understand all the intricacies of a complex, interwoven natural system.

The mainstream method of managing a natural system is to send off for experts. These are people who have generally spent a certain number of years working not in the local ecosystem, but reading books or conducting laboratory experiments somewhere far away. We then slavishly apply their commands; for example, adding chemical fertilizers to farmland. If that method doesn't work after a time, we never question the original assumptions; we just intensify what we're doing. We add more fertilizer and we get hardpan and destroyed watercourses. When that approach impoverishes the land, we turn to more experts, who may suggest a chemical water-treatment plant and genetically engineered seeds that don't mind salinization or a lot of nitrogen. Then we repeat the whole pattern. Without the ability to *stand back and reassess* our management strategies and the value systems that underlie them, we're doomed to keep on making these kinds of mistakes.

By always remaining humble and flexible, whole-system managers monitor the effects of their methods not after something goes wrong, but from their very inception, and they pull back and think things over at the very first sign of ecosystem disturbance. They even have a different value system for judging what's going wrong. For instance, holistic ranchers don't just look at yields per acre or grazing capacities. Because they've learned that grass won't grow properly in a damaged, incomplete ecosystem, if they notice the loss of *any* plants or animals, including insects, "weeds" and predators, they reassess all their methods. By treading lightly on the earth and trying to learn from natural systems, holistic methods are far more successful at reforesting land, bringing dying watercourses back to life and enabling local communities to make a living again than any technical quick-fix. And they also help people regain confidence in their own abilities and have pride in their traditions.

Two fascinating qualities about the movements we encountered are first of all that most of them are completely ignorant that anyone else is doing the same thing. The second is that nearly all are spontaneous and come from the bottom up, not the top down. It appears to be primarily the people who know an ecosystem, a town or an industry who are getting these creative ideas about how to make them viable, productive and nonpoisonous over the long term. Chefs and restaurateurs, small business entrepreneurs, even big corporations like Nike, Ford and Ikea, are becoming increasingly responsive to suggestions not from on high, but from within their ranks, on how to provide products and services without damaging the earth and our collective human future. It's not too much to say that even in the business world we encountered a small but growing revolution towards sustainability that ranges from product quality, ecological design and capacities for recycling, all the way to how profits are distributed and employees are treated.

This new movement works by consensus — in other words, it takes a good deal of time for the practitioners to work out and agree upon which way they want to go. But when they do, they are unstoppable, because they are basing their methods on deeply felt and democratically agreed-upon values. These new methods and attitudes don't come from government or religious edicts, political or social fashion, or appeals to the more base and selfish sides of our natures that are typical of advertising. Each person involved has had to examine his or her own most deeply held values in order to decide what is the best way for all of us to prosper and to share on a finite planet. These shared values come from individual brains and hearts, but as we discovered, whether they're popping up in Africa, India, Germany or Canada, they are remarkably in accord. They have even started to come together to create concrete templates that enable us to see what kind of world we'd be living in if it were run sustainably.

In the early part of this book, we look carefully at economics — whether a different way of dealing with the material world could support us all. Our shock was considerable when we found out that sustainable methods not only could support us all longer, but the vast majority of us would be better off. Then we examine our society's obsession with constantly growing economies, globalized trade and GDPs, and compare their long-term effects to those that accompany bottom-up sustainability. This is a method that makes the dangers and advantages of each approach abundantly clear. The new revolution in values and management centers around long-term, general productivity instead of short-term, individual gain. Instead of determining "acceptable" levels of carcinogens or toxins, the new revolution is proceeding directly to phasing out all dangerous petrochemicals and wasteful processes. It doesn't subscribe to values based on individual materialism or anxieties about personal security imposed from above by industry and government. Such values have to be held in place by constant media discussion, advertising and political persuasion. These new forms of management encourage people to unearth their individual and community's creativity in order to realize their deepest values, counting on human contact and common sense, not television and experts, to spread the desired goals.

By going deep into their souls, people are discovering how alike most of these human values really are — and from that beginning, they are evolving new ways to live. Those new ways can be seriously delayed without widespread social and political support of the population, however, and those working on sustainability can always use some help. For anyone who wants to get involved, we have provided a short list of web sites and addresses at the end of the book.

As far as this book is concerned, another bit of good news is that we found publishers and readers were more than ready for us. The proof of that is that the first edition of this book hit not only the best-seller list in Canada within four weeks of its release, but it became number one. The reviews were almost universally glowing; several university courses, both in Canada and the United States, have already been built around it; and despite the loss of our first publisher, we are bringing out a paperback edition in record time. The moment really has come to talk about the good news — for a change.

CHAPTER 1

# MAKING MONEY LIKE THE BEE
## Doing Business Without Doing Harm

*The wise and moral man*
*Shines like a flower on a hilltop,*
*Making money like the bee*
*Who does not hurt the flower.*
— *THE PALI CANON* (500 BC)

It seems to be a fact of life that we can only survive by using up and destroying things, if only the food we consume. So perhaps it's impossible to do no harm on a material level. Nevertheless, most of us would prefer not to destroy things or harm others while we're trying to support ourselves and survive on this planet. In fact, we would like to leave the world a better place than we found it. And yet many of our most recent efforts to improve our world and better our lives — building highways to allow cars to bring people closer together, dams and power plants to get them lights at night, housing tracts, convention centers and shopping malls to serve their needs — have also brought a lot of harm: global warming, habitat destruction, toxic waste and resource depletion. It's beginning to seem impossible to live in a complex, urban economy without participating in this kind of destruction.

So how can we make a living like the bee that doesn't hurt the flower? The State of the World Forum held in New York in September of 2000 investigated this very question. It was attended by corporate and environmental leaders, scientists, academics and spiritual leaders from all over the world — from anthropologist Jane Goodall and environmentalist Vandana Shiva to philanthropist George Soros and guru Deepak Chopra. Among the many workshops was one called "The Emergence of a New Paradigm of Business." The panelists were Amory and Hunter Lovins, the famous eco-inventors of Rocky Mountain Institute, Anita Roddick, the charismatic founder of the Body Shop, and Elizabet Sahtouris, evolutionary biologist and co-author (with Sidney Liebes and Brian Swimme) of *A Walk Through Time*. The audience was unusually expressive and intelligent. The moderator asked how many in the room considered themselves "business people"; almost everyone held up their hands. Then he asked how many were directors, CEOs or owners of their own businesses, and almost as many held up their hands again. The discussion was riveting and ranged from the corporate behavior of Shell Oil to the principles of Natural Capitalism. Then a woman of about fifty with a mane of snow-white hair stood up and described a sign she keeps in her bedroom closet, so she'll see it first thing every day. It says, "Good Morning, Beautiful Business!" It reminds her of how grateful she is for her business, because it's the way she believes she can make a difference while she's here on earth.

"That's the beauty of business," she said. "You can offer your best possible service, be the best you are. Young people might think that businesses just exist for getting rich. But small businesses are one of the planet's most wonderful means of *serving* and doing good." The woman was Judy Wicks, and the audience's response to her was remarkable; a palpable sense of approval swept over the crowd, a feeling of gratitude for her statement. This is not what we thought "business leaders" were like; the room got positively misty with emotion. Those of us working on environmental issues don't always know what's going on in the business world. It turns out there's a very quiet but extremely thorough revolution underway, and Judy Wicks is one of its main practitioners. She's the operator-owner of a restaurant in Philadelphia called the White Dog Café, which grosses over $5 million a year, and performs every kind of social and environmental outreach imaginable, functioning more like a foundation than a business. She's also the current president of the Social Venture Network headquartered in San Francisco, a whole movement of like-minded people[1] who are committed to creating a more just and sustainable, more environmentally and socially conscious world, through business.

Judy Wicks's White Dog Café is a full-service restaurant in the tree-shaded university district of Philadelphia, open seven days a week. They do a great salmon with sorrel sauce and fresh corn cakes. They make sweet-sour pork medallions, mammoth salads, honey-glazed ducks, and a famous chocolate pie layered with caramel and whipped cream. They use only cruelty-free meats, and as much organically raised produce and meat as they can get. They do all they can to keep genetically engineered food out of their kitchen, seeking out non-GE soy and corn oils. But most of their customers don't come in for these reasons; they come because it tastes so good. Wicks jokes, "I use food to lure innocent customers into social activism." But she adds, more seriously, "If you're gathering people together to eat, why not talk too?"

White Dog has offered Table Talks on the War on Drugs, the Supreme Court's decision to elect George Bush, the genetic engineering debate, and much more. They help organize rides to rallies and marches; they sponsor trips abroad to the many "sister restaurants" that Wicks has linked up with in the Third World. They give inner-city tours, like their child-watch tour, a real outreach in dangerous Philadelphia, designed, as she puts it, "so that upper and upper middle-class people can actually see the way children's lives are led in the inner city, both the good and the bad. We visit model programs, as well as ones that need help. We usually have a theme; if it's juvenile justice, we visit the court system — or it might be education, health care, recreation. We visit different institutions and then have a talk on it." The tours tempt local residents with a continental breakfast at the café, then after the tour and lunch, the speaker solicits questions from the group. "We do a tour of community wall murals, community gardens; we do an eco-tour every spring. We went to see a solar house and we rode in an electric car. Last year it was on urban sprawl, so we went out into the countryside to view development that was taking over the family farms." During the year, White Dog gets local residents involved with big community draws like the Farmer Sunday Supper and The Dance of the Ripe Tomato. They also take interested customers on tours of the farms that supply them. "We really are just a popular, trendy restaurant, known for good food," Wicks says. "A lot of people who come don't know anything about our politics or philosophies. That gives us a constant supply of folks ripe for education."

The White Dog Café has a mentoring program for inner-city high school kids, which has been going on for the last decade. Judy says, "Tenth-graders from West Philadelphia High School who are interested in the restaurant business come and do shadowing days with our staff. They get two days in the kitchen, two days in the dining room, a day in the office and a day in the retail store. Six to eight kids come through for six days each, and at the end of the year we have an event, like a dinner-dance called the Hip Hop, which the kids put on with the help of our staff." Their program provides even more opportunities: "After they finish the mentoring, we try to provide jobs for the ones who are the most interested, as busboys or prep people. One young man has become a line cook for us. We also provide a scholarship for one person who wants to go on to culinary school. It's only $1,000 a year, but the third student is about to finish his four years, and then we'll be choosing another." They even have a Workplace Giving Program, so that employees can contribute to more "progressive charities," as Wicks puts it. A couple of years ago she began her living wage program, where business people pledge to pay salaries well above the minimum wage, no matter how menial the job. "I was delighted," she says, "when one of my dishwashers started becoming a philanthropist, and even that you can *be* a philanthropist when you're making $8 an hour. He has a dollar taken out of his paycheck each week. That's $50 a year or so. He also has signed up for our 401k Program, which means that if he puts $50 in the Black United Fund, we match it. So he's actually contributing $100 a year to this charity, which will make a difference to them."

Most of us would find it hard enough just to create a successful business, and Judy Wicks admits: "For the first five years of my restaurant's existence, I did nothing but business, because I had to. And I'd drop into bed exhausted." When she first opened the White Dog, which started as a coffee and muffin take-out, she still thought, like so many of us, that business and money had to be kept separate from love and service. But, as she says, she lived above the store. Even today, when the business has spread to cover five contiguous Victorian townhouses, Wicks still lives on the upper floors of one of them. "My first kitchen was an outdoor charcoal grill in the backyard, because I couldn't afford to put the exhaust system up through the house. I just gradually built it up. It was a labor of love. I built it with the intention of having it be my life's work. I didn't create a business to sell for profit. I created a business to be my life; to be the environment in which I wanted to live and raise my children. Since then I've realized that I literally live above the store. That's the old-fashioned way of doing business . . . living upstairs. You know, whether it's the tailor shop or the corner grocery store or the family inn or the family farm, you raise your family right in the same place where you do business."

That's not the way businesses are typically run any more, and that fact may explain a lot. As Wicks says, "People are now more able to compartmentalize their lives, so that they can have different values at home than they do at work. Business schools teach you to leave your values at home when you go to work. That's the way 'sound business practices' are actually taught to young business students. I think socially responsible business was that way by nature in the old days, simply because business people were part of the community. They naturally wanted to do well within it. As corporations have gotten larger, their leaders and owners are no longer living in the same community as their customers, so there's more opportunity to compartmentalize values."

Wicks wanted to do things differently. "Our mission statement is to be fully of service in four different areas: in serving our customers, which is logical; in serving our community; in serving each other, as employees; and in serving our natural world. So at the White Dog, we have different programs in all four of those areas. And profit, to me, is simply what fuels the company in order to fulfill our mission." That's not to say the business isn't viable, or that the people involved in it aren't doing just fine. Yearly profits out of the $5 million (U.S.) gross are as much as $300,000. Of that, Wicks takes between $65,000 and $100,000. That's a fine and comfortable living for a single parent with two college-age children. "I don't want to be a wealthy person. I have no interest in that whatsoever, even if it were handed to me. But of course I don't want to be poor. It's just that you get to a point when you realize you don't need any more stuff. I don't have any interest in accumulating a great deal of wealth to leave to my children, either. I'm already going to leave them a house and a business, which is more than I inherited. I wouldn't want to leave them more than that because that would probably just mess them up."

So what does Wicks do with the "extra" money? Exactly what good businesses always have done: she pays her employees more, increases the quality of the product, and contributes to the community. She also makes her employees feel they have a long-term stake in the whole operation. Her seventy-five full-time and twenty-five part-time staff members have a great deal of autonomy. The chef makes as much as she does, and controls the inflow of food and the outflow of recycling. She says it was hard at first to delegate control as she expanded the business into other realms, but she did it by trusting and involving the others. By refusing to believe in the typical business paradigm — that her income had to match that of others in the same situation, that her business had to make higher profits to be worthwhile, or even that she had to be always in charge, doing better than her own employees — she became free to follow her dream. "The idea that good business is actually cooperative, as opposed to competitive, is something I really believe. If we really do care about the world and about people, the concept of cooperation in the business world is much more important than competition, more important than having more or being 'better' than others at any level."

One of the first causes that took her beyond just taking care of business was humane treatment of farm animals. Back in the 1980s, when she first learned about the cruelty involved in most industrial pork farming, she had a decision to make. "I was just appalled," she says. "And at first I thought, 'What am I going to do? I'm in the restaurant business. This is where my meat comes from. Am I going to have to go out of business? Am I going to have to become a vegetarian restaurant?' My customer base is not vegetarian! So at first I just kind of hid from the issue. I'm a real animal nut; the thought of it just made me cringe. But then I came to a turning point where I just said, 'I don't want to be in the restaurant business if it means being a part of a system where animals suffer. Just take pork off the menu — bacon, ham, pork chops — I don't want it until we find a place where we can get humanely raised pigs.'"

It wasn't easy. It took months of research, looking for local farms, figuring out delivery systems and so on. They found that they couldn't buy by the cut or the pound; they had to take the whole pig or cow and find a use for every part. But as Wicks says, "That's also a very ecologically sound way of doing business, rather than just taking the prime cut. Make hamburger with the rest, or make shanks, sweetbreads, and all those kinds of interesting dishes. Luckily I have a chef, Kevin von Klaus, who's become a partner and who, once he was exposed to these issues, embraced them as well. And he's the one who has to juggle all twenty-five or so of the different farmers we buy from." Instead of just picking up the phone and ordering all their produce from one place and then phoning again to order all their meat from another, they've evolved a very complicated ordering system. One farmer may bring in berries, another the lettuces, and yet another, a pig or some free-range chickens. "We seat 200, so we go through a lot of food. We had to get another walk-in cooler just to take care of the fresh produce that we have to store. Just now I'm lending one of the farmers who brings me local food $30,000 to buy a new truck, so getting stuff to me is more viable in that he can deliver to more restaurants when he comes in from Lancaster County. This is a service I want to do, because I really want to build up a local economy. Since I believe in small business and living above the shop, I also believe in buying locally, and using my purchasing dollar to advance my own local community."

Wicks even formed the local chapter of Chefs' Collaborative 2000, a national group that encourages members to buy directly from local farms. She's trying to get her competitors to join up. "If I can talk them into buying local produce, the guy buying a truck with my loan is going to start delivering his vegetables to my competitors. So at first I thought, 'gee, is this a smart thing to do?' But then I realized that if I really care about the pigs that are being brutalized in this world, if I really care about what it's doing to our soils not to grow organically, I've got to bite the bullet. This organic, cruelty-free thing is not my personal invention, my 'market niche.' I want it to be what everyone does, including the other restaurants competing for my customers."

A lot of people go public and expand their businesses away from this local ideal and become unwieldy corporations, Wicks explains, simply because they get bored. They have other interests they want to pursue, and they decide to compartmentalize their business, so it will provide the money to enable them to realize their other life goals, like collecting old books or race cars, or even, say, helping inner-city children. "Rather than starting another restaurant when I got bored," she says, "I just went deeper into what I had. I started doing these programs because they were issues that interested me. And I discovered that I really could address every single subject I was interested in, through my business."

## Business in Revolution

*The return from your work must be the satisfaction that work brings you and the world's need of that work. With this, life is heaven, or as near heaven as you can get.*
— W.E.B. DU BOIS

People working with the erosion of the environmental and social quality of life in the modern world talk a lot about "sustainability." They're trying to figure out how we can continue to make a living and support our families without using up what the planet produces so quickly that we don't leave any productive base for the generations that will follow us. When the concept has been used in terms like "sustainable development," and especially as "sustainable logging" or "sustainable mining," its meaning has often been twisted to let industries get away with merely planting a few seedlings or paying lip service to the concept by some slight slowing of the pace of extraction that still does not provide serious security for the future. In fact, everyone does know what this word means; it's just that no one knows exactly what it looks like in practice. People working to establish environmentally and socially sustainable businesses and livelihoods today all admit they don't know if what they're doing is exactly right. They're feeling their way, slowly, carefully, and with a lot of self-examination, humility and flexibility. And the more they hear about what seems to be working for others, the closer the entire process comes to establishing a consensus about what sustainability really is.[2]

Collins Pine is a timber company that often turns up in discussions about what sustainability might look like. They own what has been called the finest privately owned industrial forest in the U.S., and their practices have been praised by everyone from the Rainforest Action Network and the Sierra Club to the *Washington Post* and the *Christian Science Monitor*. Collins Pine is the White Dog Café writ large and 150 years down the road. It employs 7,500 people directly, and grosses about $250 million (U.S.) a year in plywood, hardwood and softwood lumber, oil and gas. The business was started in 1855 by the present owner's grandfather-in-law in Pennsylvania, where they still hold 51,000 hectares (126,000 acres). And this family still lives above the store. At the age of 86, Mary Beth Collins is still the key shareholder and guiding light of all their practices. One son, Terry, lives in the remote village of Chester, California, with his wife and two home-schooled sons, where he manages the sawmill and oversees forest operations. Another son, Truman Jr., does not work in the business, but maintains a lively interest. The day we visited their big operation in Chester, on the gala occasion of cutting the two-billionth board-foot out of this thriving, diverse, sweet-scented forest, three of Mary Beth's children were in attendance. Truman and Mary Beth Collins live in Portland, Oregon, where the family, staunch Methodists, have funded everything from libraries and scholarships to church construction and foreign aid programs. What's most remarkable is the mission of their company. They have formally pledged to do three things: maintain the health of the total forest ecosystem; support the production of wood on a sustained, renewable basis; and provide social and economic benefits to the surrounding areas and communities.

The proof that they mean it lies in two bottom lines: money and certification. Collins Pine makes smaller profits than its publicly traded competitors simply because its owners aren't greedy. Wade Mosby, vice president of marketing at Collins Pine, is a walking encyclopedia of company and local history. He says, "We're losing 25 percent of the kind of profit other outfits get with our more long-term method. For example, the way we use natural tree regeneration means the forest matures at a more normal rate. The usual, even-age tree farm monoculture management style is 25 percent more lucrative over the short term. So we 'lose' hundreds of thousands of dollars that way. And for that reason alone, if we had a different family running things, we'd be long gone."

Ironically, Collins Pine also takes a hit from government regulators, precisely because its forests are more ecologically rich. "Because we're good managers and have more species, we get more stringent regulations on our lands to protect the fish and game species we've managed to bring back. You'd think that kind of practice would earn a company tax rebates or some other kind of encouragement, but it's just the opposite. You have to shoulder economic and regulatory liabilities if you also want to protect the resource for the future." Mosby has a lot more to say about the perverse subsidies and regulatory practices that favor destructive companies over companies like Collins Pine. The U.S. Forest Service, for example, was at that moment cutting a firebreak just inside their property line, because a well-managed, mature forest tends to stop burns. He says, "They cut the firebreak swath *inside* our trees because they know fire won't get any further. When you're only ten percent of a watershed, and your neighbors all clearcut, the forest service ends up letting the likes of MacMillan Bloedel overcut, and then we're not allowed to take any more ourselves in the state-allowable cut, because of their poor practices. That's the kind of thing that shows that all the rules are increasingly written for big, publicly owned transnationals."

Barry Ford, Collins Pine's head forester at the Alameda forest, concurs. "We have the great gray owl feeding in our meadows. There are only 100 pairs left in California; we're the southern end of their range, and because of that, the regulations stipulate that we have to leave a 182-meter (600-foot) wide strip of trees around all the meadows. In order to have those trees available for our use, I could have said there were no owls, and frankly I haven't seen any. But I know that's the right habitat, so I say yes because they could be there now, or if we save the place, they could be coming." Collins Pine employees like Ford don't mind the lower profits or even the stiffer regulations; the Collins family takes low enough profits that they can provide decent, secure livings for all their employees. But the main thing they like is the way they feel about what they do. "Beavers have probably doubled here since I came in twelve years ago," says Ford proudly. When I asked Mosby about his professional life, he agreed. "Going to work feels real good. We may not have made as much money, but we've changed a whole industry. Money isn't everything. The satisfaction of knowing you've improved things is pretty important, too. Four generations of my family worked in the woods. I saw my dad clearcutting these forests, destroying the places he loved, that he depended on for a future. I waited for years for a chance to work at Collins Pine. That's typical of many of the people who work here. And, you know, we're still learning, all the time."

The attitude reflected in this last statement was most revealing and very often repeated within the company. It surfaced most dramatically when it came to their second bottom line: certification. Certification means inviting an outside agency in to determine if a company's practices are truly sustainable, so that the lumber can become "certified," that is, bear a consumer label stating that it is cut within the renewable limits of that forest. Everyone I spoke to admitted they had at first been reluctant to apply for certification. They were worried about potential loss of control, having somebody from the labeling body come in and tell them what to do. Their former chief forester, Bill Howe, resisted certification because he figured it would only bring outside interference and more paper work. He underwent a change of heart and eventually embraced it, not only because it solidifies the market, but because it inspires everyone to greater heights. Terry Collins, the family son running the show in Chester, says, "Collins Pine was getting maybe a little complacent. We thought we knew all there was to know about sustainable forestry. But as we went through the certification process, we found ourselves being asked some challenging questions by a third party. Then we started to realize we could do better. It's really revitalized our practices."

Bill Howe concurs: "For my part, you know, I wanted the market to control this process, not state legislation. But I found out you end up doing more than you might have without certification. Not that there are so many benefits in doing it, mind you; you don't get some big acknowledgment or prize for doing good." He laughs. "It forced me to rub elbows with environmentalists working on this mutual goal of sustainability; it expanded both our understandings of each other. At the internal meeting of the Forest Stewardship Council, who are the certification folks, I sat across the table with the co-founder of Greenpeace. I never would've done that! Neither would he! But that way, we were forced to listen to each other. If people talk face to face, it's amazing what they can agree on. Any kind of dialogue generates some level of trust. You have to vent back and forth, but you learn."

## First Steps

*In order for a society to be sustainable, Nature's functions and diversity must not be systematically impoverished by physical displacement, over-harvesting or other forms of ecosystem manipulation.*
— THIRD SYSTEMS CONDITION OF THE NATURAL STEP

All around the world, but especially in Europe and the Pacific Northwest, businesses are finding inspirational and organizational help from The Natural Step, or TNS, which began in Sweden about ten years ago. It is not a religion, a management fad, a touchy-feely marketing strategy or even a philosophy. It's not quite like any of the usual buzzwords and fashionable belief systems that usually afflict the ethos and organization of business. It's more like a set of observations.

Back in the 1980s, Dr. Karl-Henrik Robèrt, a Swedish doctor specializing in cancer in children, realized he was seeing a significant increase in cases of childhood leukemia. He traced the cause to increasing toxins in the environment due to industrial pollution. He persuaded fifty other Swedish scientists to help him draft a consensus document that describes our basic knowledge of the biosphere's functions and the way humans interact with them. This document was edited twenty-one times before it was sent to every household and school in Sweden. Then, in the early 1990s, Robèrt worked with physicist John Holmberg to define a set of systems conditions for determining sustainability, basing them on the laws of thermodynamics and natural cycles. The original consensus document and the four systems conditions they developed are now the foundation of The Natural Step. They can be summarized as follows: In order for a society to be sustainable, nature's functions and diversity are not systematically 1: subject to increasing concentrations of substances extracted from the earth's crust; 2: subject to increasing concentrations of substances produced by society; 3: impoverished by physical displacement, over-harvesting or other forms of ecosystem manipulation. 4: In a sustainable society, resources are used fairly and efficiently in order to meet basic human needs globally.[3]

Sweden was the right place and the 1990s was the right time to unveil this new way of analyzing human and planetary interaction, and many business and political leaders, including King Gustav of Sweden, got involved. Today more than seventy Swedish municipalities have adopted The Natural Step methodology, as have sixty corporations, including IKEA,

Scandic Hotels, Electrolux and Swedish McDonald's. Less than five years later, The Natural Step had spread to North America, with Paul Hawken, the founder of Smith & Hawken Garden Supplies and author of *The Ecology of Commerce*, as the North American chair. The main office is in California, but it's in the Pacific Northwest, specifically Portland, Oregon, that the TNS tenets have really taken root and borne fruit.

The four tenets of The Natural Step basically set up the bottom-line conditions under which a society can be sustainable. The first one, for example, advises against subjecting natural systems to "increasing concentrations of substances extracted from the earth's crust." This is a very basic tenet, since almost everything we extract from beneath the earth turns out to be poisonous to the living creatures living on the surface. The four systems conditions include particular examples, such as "In practical terms, the first condition requires society to implement comprehensive metal and mineral recycling programs, and decrease economic dependence on fossil fuels."

The four conditions are remarkable in that in less than two pages of print they outline what sustainability is, and how we can recognize when we are exceeding its limits. They are founded on the basic laws of physics, four principles that are derived from the First and Second Laws of Thermodynamics: "Nothing disappears. Everything spreads. There is value in order. Structure and order are created by plants using energy from sunlight." Then the TNS organization tries to help interested parties learn how to achieve sustainability in their everyday businesses, on the basis of a deep understanding of the inescapable facts on which life is based. TNS is not judgmental or frighteningly demanding. For example, one key aspect of the four tenets is the advice that "Organizations are not expected to achieve long-term goals immediately. On the contrary, they are . . . encouraged to start with the 'low-hanging fruit,' those steps that are easiest to take and will help move an organization closer to its goals."

The Natural Step has been taught at lunch meetings to more than 800 Collins Pine employees to date. The middle management of Nike and many other Portland-based businesses, like the Norm Thompson clothes catalogue, have adopted TNS principles and instituted admirable environmental strategies in their daily work. Much of this flowering of activity is due to Dick and Jeanne Roy, a husband and wife team who head up both the Northwest Earth Institute and the Oregon Natural Step Network in Portland. Dick Roy was trained at Harvard Law School; his career as a corporate lawyer was not only lucrative, it was illustrious enough to get him listed in *Best Lawyers in America*. In 1993, however, he left his job with the biggest law firm in the Northwest to devote the rest of his life to being, as he calls it, "a volunteer for the Earth." Jeanne Roy had always made sure their six-figure income was an "externality" to their lives, not its determining factor. So they've lived in the same modest ranch house in a wooded suburb of Portland for thirty years; they generate less than two bags of garbage a year, own one small car and rarely buy new clothes. Their three children got homemade sandwiches and cookies wrapped in waxed paper used again and again in their lunches, because their mother was also writing a weekly "Reduce, Reuse and Recycle" column and heading up Portland's Recycling Advocates, which have helped make that city a national model.

By the time Dick left corporate law, he had won the respect of many local business and government leaders, not only for his business acumen, but, as one colleague says, for "really walking his talk." He realized these leaders might listen to what he had to offer, so he and Jeanne began working out a two-pronged approach to environmental education on the local level. Their Northwest Earth Institute (NWEI) offers a variety of simply designed, oddly stimulating courses on four subjects: Discovering a Sense of Place, Choices for Sustainable Living, Globalization, and Deep Ecology. The courses are conducted during corporate lunch hours and government conferences, church socials and neighborhood get-togethers. The Roys themselves get things started, but then the participants take over, with remarkable results. The Oregon Natural Step Network is a project of the NWEI, and the two in concert have spread the four systems conditions throughout the Pacific Northwest, making it arguably one of the most ecologically sustainable places on the continent. These simple, non-invasive, non-judgmental courses have been influential in ways that even the Roys could not have imagined.

For example, Nike is no longer using PVCs (polyvinyl chlorides), a chemical allegedly linked to hormone mimicry and sexual deformities and malfunctions in humans, in any of their products. They're buying up vast amounts of organic cotton, and are trying to get every trace of greenhouse gas out of the airsoles in their shoes. Neil Kelly, a large local furniture company, has moved aggressively to create home cabinetry aligned with the four system conditions, and is marketing it in partnership with Collins Pine and Environmental Building Supplies. Boora Architects, a middle-of-the road architectural firm before taking the Roys' courses a mere four years ago, now specializes in sustainably designed buildings. They concentrate on cost-effective means of using less electricity and fuel, more natural light and heat, and reused or otherwise ecologically sensitive materials, and they try to retain as much of the natural world around each site as possible.

The staff of 105 at Boora are mostly in their late twenties and thirties; they make for an unusually happy and buoyant office atmosphere. After all, they're successful and well paid, they're doing creative work, and they're also able to see themselves as helping the earth. Clackamas High School, for example, which was under construction by Boora when we visited, takes account of prevailing winds and seasonal sun angles, uses the nearby wetlands to provide cooling, and has views from every single window. Boora's construction materials are low-toxicity, low-maintenance and long-life. The principles they operate on were all derived from the four Natural Step Systems Conditions, and they have paid unexpected dividends. Eighty percent of the time, the new, green school building will need neither furnace heating nor air conditioning, saving the school board $50,000 a year, forty percent of its existing maintenance costs. So even though the revolutionary design will cost a little more up front, it will pay for itself in only eighteen months.

That's one of the most important things about TNS; possibly because its principles are in line with the natural, physical laws of the planet, they have often proven to increase the long-term profitability of anything they're applied to, through increased efficiency and decreased waste. Boora had originally protested that they could not make any special green designs because they had to stay competitive, and schools in particular have tight construction budgets. But the way The Natural Step courses and principles are presented is so friendly and non-threatening that the architects were able to forget their defensive posture; individuals in the firm began thinking about TNS principles in their specific design contexts. Slowly but surely, they came up with an idea here and an idea there that has changed the entire direction of their business and has made them more, rather than less, desirable to their clients.

It's the economic dividends that are bringing in the heavy-hitters like Nike and IKEA as well, although multinational corporate involvement differs from that of smaller, local, generally privately owned firms like Boora or Collins Pine in fundamental ways that we'll investigate further on. The impetus for their participation comes from the savings in waste and improved public relations. Dick Roy calls it "a middle management revolution," and indeed, it's interesting that at Nike the green initiative is coming not from the CEOs and presidents or from the unions and workers, but from vice presidents, marketing heads, engineers and transportation coordinators. Sarah Severn, a pretty blond woman with a light English accent who came to Nike's big Portland office five years ago, says, "I was brought over here to help bring a European perspective to a U.S.-based company, because there was emerging legislation in Europe beginning to look at the impact of all sorts of chemicals in products." Today Severn is the director of Sustainable Development for all of Nike, seen by many in the company as the instigator of an entire new ethos.

At that early point in her Nike involvement, Severn found out about TNS and she also read Paul Hawken's seminal book *The Ecology of Commerce*. "That was really the wake-up call that helped explain all the issues very dramatically." Phil Berry, today in charge of Footwear Sustainability, was brought in to work on pollution prevention. Nike labs were given the goal of replacing inorganic solvents with water-based adhesives, cleaners and primers. "And that's been an incredible success," Severn says. "But it hasn't been easy. There's been a lot of research that didn't pan out. People were very committed; they kept trying." She says the key is a forward-looking approach: "You can't just beat yourself up when you find out how dangerous some material you've been using is." She says the goals are to substitute positive materials for hazardous ones and to produce things that can be safely returned to the earth. As TNS suggests, whatever can't be absorbed into the earth, like lead or certain plastics, needs to remain within the manufacturing process and be used over and over again. She says, "That's obviously a challenge when you have a very broad-spread consumer-based business."

This is very expensive work, and it doesn't always generate positive public-relations reactions. When Nike jubilantly announced they'd found alternatives to PVCs in a joint ad with Greenpeace, Severn says, "The vinyl industry came after us with a vengeance! In hindsight, we should have just quietly said we're phasing out PVCs. But we had a torrent of e-mails complaining that our decisions were biased by Greenpeace, that we were just being a pawn in this game and were falling into the Greenpeace agenda. And we were told we had no basis for our decision-making. It was a well-orchestrated industry campaign, with letters to board directors and so on. In the end we responded, 'We've based our decisions not on Greenpeace, but on The Natural Step framework. And that's non-negotiable.' We opened up a dialogue with the industry around the potential for making PVCs sustainable. You know, from our point of view, if you could make it sustainable then we could use it. But currently, in that particular framework, we just can't."

Nike is far from unsympathetic to other industries. Severn says, "I can see the predicament for them. It's tough because their whole industry is affected; they've got jobs they want to conserve, and economic and supply structures they can't suddenly change overnight. And they pointed out, quite rightly, that many other materials we were using don't pass those definitions for sustainability. And we said, 'Yes. But PVC is probably the one that violates pretty much every single systems condition, and we have to start somewhere. So we're sorry, but that's it.'" As at Boora Architects, being modern and innovative means money and survival over the long term. So for now, Severn and her colleagues have executive and shareholder support, and they've taken off. We met with Dave Buchanan and Dave Newman, two members of an eighty-member team who are figuring out, among other things, how much $CO_2$ the company is generating by shipping its shoes all over the world, and how they can get this amount down by encouraging better-built transports and sourcing more materials locally. Chemist Louie Labonté is working on getting carcinogenic phthalates out of all the inks; Phil Berry is coordinating an effort to make a totally recyclable shoe, with uppers and lowers that can be easily separated and recycled into other products — everything from more shoes to basketball court pads and volleyballs.

These are expensive, long-term research projects, and they have tremendous spin-offs. The fact that Nike is now using a mere 3 percent of organic cotton in their products, globally, has been, as Sarah Severn says, "a huge boost to the organic cotton industry . . . because we're just such an enormous buyer." Of course, this is exactly how dangerous chemicals and other new, man-made materials got where they are today. Huge companies spent research funds to develop them and then they were used; that brought costs down and made the new chemicals desirable for others. That strategy can work both ways.

But all this begs the question to some extent. Nike never did very much manufacturing. Like so many other brand-name corporations, they are primarily a design company, selling an image. Most of Nike's corporate funds are spent on advertising and distribution. They out-source the actual manufacture to other companies, which is one reason they were caught with their pants down when the inhumane conditions in some of the nameless factories making their products were revealed. And one big reason for the disconnect between miserable sweatshops and fine, sincere people like Severn is that decisions about manufacturing and pay-rates are not reached around the kitchen table above the shop, as at the White Dog Café or Collins Pine. They are made in boardrooms far away from the workers, and they are cold-blooded, mathematical calculations based on what country or factory offers the cheapest labor. The results have been human misery and public embarrassment for many companies. Like Nike, IKEA also became environmentally and socially sensitive only *after* it had earned itself a bad reputation, in the latter case, for the lavish use of carcinogenic solvents and varnishes.

Sustainability often begins as a marketing decision, but it's one that has cultural repercussions throughout a company. Nike middle managers currently have big budgets and considerable autonomy to work on fascinating scientific questions that may help save the earth for their children; so they're really happy and motivated. They're so motivated that some even end up leaving the company to work for non-profits, as their vision of their goals becomes clearer. As Dick Roy says, "In a situation like the one at Nike, those of us concerned about the environment can't lose. They're pushing the envelope of what you can do for sustainability within the corporate structure."

## God Is an Environmentalist

*You have to take your values from your customers, your designs from nature, and your discipline from the marketplace.*
— HUNTER LOVINS, OF THE ROCKY MOUNTAIN INSTITUTE

Other big corporations are getting on the sustainability bandwagon, and using TNS is not the only strategy available. People like Amory and Hunter Lovins of the Rocky Mountain Institute, inventors of those long-lasting, funny-looking neon light bulbs, the hyper-car and many other innovations, have concentrated on the principles contained in Paul Hawken's book *Natural Capitalism*. They say that TNS defines sustainability and shows the goal, but Natural Capitalism gives templates for how to get there. Amory and his ex-wife and still friend and partner, Hunter Lovins, are techies and futurists. They don't worry about ethos; they invent the methods and machines that we'll all use in a sustainable society. So they don't go to any of their clients, who include Ford Motor Company and Shell Oil, "and argue with them about values or philosophy, or even ecology," says Hunter. She is small and wiry, and generally sports a cowboy hat to go with her strong western drawl and her part-time job as a volunteer firefighter. "We talk about the bottom line and technology that will meet their objectives in a way that'll increase their profits. That tends to get them interested." Neither Amory nor Hunter Lovins sees any percentage in worrying about a corporation's past history. "Nobody likes being told they're a bad person," says Hunter. "It just makes them stop listening. But if we can show them technologies where they can do what it is that they're about more cheaply, more profitably, it moves the debate to a different space."

Hunter claims to be seeing the same kind of systemic change in multinationals that we saw among private business people at the State of the World Forum. She mentioned a powerful CEO whose name she didn't want to divulge. "Increasingly these guys see sustainability as a competitive advantage. So much so, they don't want their competitors to know what they're doing. It's an interesting turn-around. Companies are investing a lot of money in these systems and they're saying things like, 'Even if in the short term it costs more, it's an investment in the viability of my company for the future.'" Hunter likes to quote from the ultimate environmental corporation, Interface Carpet, run by CEO Ray Anderson. Interface was the first big company to publicly embrace TNS, Natural Capitalism and sustainability. As one of the main consultants on their projects, Hunter likes to explain how they did it. Once Interface Carpet had decided to commit to sustainability, they literally looked at what nature uses to cover surfaces, things like moss and humus. Interface's designer Joseph Okey spent a lot of time with Janine Benyus, forester and author of the best-selling book *Biomimicry*, thinking through how these substances work in nature to keep that "floor" sustainably covered.

"Clearly one of the things nature doesn't do," Hunter continues, "is make persistent toxins. Nature recycles everything, genuinely recycles it. So Okey said, 'Right. Carpet at the moment can't be recycled. We don't have a way of getting the nylon face off the backing. Some companies chop it all up and make nylon and backing into new backing; downcycling, which is better than nothing. But it's not recycling. Clearly we have to get the nylon into new nylon; the backing into new backing. Which means it has to be separable.' So this is the sort of mental process they went through to invent the product Solenium. When Okey presented it to a bunch of us — his eyes were *this* big! He said, 'God must be an environmentalist. I didn't think it could be done. I told Ray I didn't think it could be done.' "

The reason Okey described God as an environmentalist is that the product he had invented to mimic nature was also better for Interface, in every way. Hunter says, "It's cheaper to make; it's four times as durable; it requires 35 percent less materials; and if you couple that with all the other steps Interface takes, you wind up with a carpet that needs 97 to 99 percent fewer materials to manufacture, and still delivers the service to the customer. That's almost a 100-percent increase in resource productivity — just because Interface asked the right questions in an honest and searching fashion, coming out of a conversation with sustainability experts." She points out that she and Amory and the other scientists working at the Rocky Mountain Institute are not carpet experts. "That's *their* job. We can help clients ask the right questions, in an honest and scientific process. And this is the kind of thing that happens."

Interface Carpet funds its ongoing sustainability programs out of the money it saves by *not* generating waste and by using materials to their full potential, which is exactly why Shell Oil and Nike are also interested in the process. CEO Ray Anderson says, "We have inventoried every single waste outfall; that means we have examined how much and where we're dumping any wastes, whether into the air, the water or on the land. We are systematically eliminating all of it. Our goal is zero waste, because waste is unmarketable production. If we make it, we're paying for it . . . and we can't sell it. So we're trying not to make it in the first place."

## Racing to the Top

*Some people would say that the strict German ratings and calls for bans on certain chemicals are interfering with Third World attempts to start a business or get a better life. But that is no reason not to do what you know is right; and you know it's right for them, in the long run, as well as yourself.*
— PETER SIEBER, DIRECTOR OF STIFTUNG WARENTEST

In Germany, thousands of big manufacturers and multinational corporations have been forced by legislation and by consumer watchdogs to prove just how creative and flexible they can be, not in pursuing higher dividends, but in meeting standards to deal with wastes and toxins that will allow them to stay in the market. Stiftung Warentest (SW) is a consumer watchdog foundation originally funded by the state. It assesses products — everything from sausages and medicines to cell phones and vehicles — for economy, safety, and something our consumer watchdogs don't pay much attention to: environmental sustainability. It assesses about 2,200 products every year in stringent tests, and prints the results in monthly publications that cost less than $5 and are read by nearly 700,000 people each month. Stiftung Warentest has a lot of power. Its director, Dr. Peter Sieber, says, "A product with a minus or 'unsatisfactory' rating is off the market in a very few months' time." Besides publishing its results, SW also releases certain ratings to broadcasters. There are about 2,500 TV spots a year dealing with their test results; that's seven or eight a day! Sieber estimates that their test results reach about 45 to 50 million Germans a month (out of a possible total of 80 million). Polls show that more than 70 percent of Germans follow SW's advice when making a purchase.

Since it can't advertise, Stiftung Warentest receives some federal money to make up the shortfall between what it needs and the DEM 85 million it gets from its publications. Its advisory council, which sets the standards and determines the tests, is composed of six consumer reps, six trade and industry reps, and six independents, including environmental NGOs. Stiftung Warentest has avoided the kind of coziness that has grown up between North American agencies and the chemical and manufacturing industries by adhering to strict statutes about organizational privacy, non-fraternization with anyone standing to gain from their ratings, and non-acceptance of any gifts, on pain of immediate dismissal. And unlike Agriculture and Agri-Food Canada, as well as the USDA and the EPA in the U.S., they have come out firmly against genetically engineered foods and virtually all pesticides, in complete support of organic food. This fact alone has given them credibility over the last few years of Europe's continuing genetic contamination, Mad Cow and Foot-and-Mouth Disease crises.

Stiftung Warentest judges products by four criteria:

*Resource conservation.* They ask whether the product uses renewable energy and materials, reduces varieties of material so as to be recyclable, uses recycled material, consumes water heavily or requires a lot of energy to operate. The European Community invented an energy label a few years ago rating these categories from A to G, A being the highest. Manufacturers are allowed to set their own rating, but SW tests and competing manufacturers keep them honest.

*Quality of product.* This is normal consumer protection, but it considers factors like clothing with toxic chemicals used as sizing, or appliances that still consume electricity while "off," as being products of "poor quality."

*Minimal use of toxic materials.* Does the product create toxins or non-recoverable materials? Sieber says, "This is a very important criterion which has led to fewer and fewer dangerous chemicals in the German product environment."

*Additional environmental criteria.* These are issues that would fall through the cracks: the use of oil furnaces as compared to gas and solar, things like the efficiency of insulation and the cost ratio of natural gas and electric clothes dryers. In other words, they rate long-term performance, economy and durability, not just price.

At Stiftung Warentest, environmental concerns are supposed to be only 15 percent of a product's overall rating, but as Sieber says, "If there's a really big environmental problem, the use of heavy metals or some such, then it takes over and can by itself give the product a minus. Manufacturers know this and avoid toxins. For example, there might be a really good deodorant propelled by CFCs; it will get a minus rating, even though the same product in a pump dispenser will get a good one." Under the toxic substances criteria, SW looks at what they call "the prevention of critical products," that is, keeping heavy metals and dangerous carcinogens like PCBs out of the environment. Sieber gives the example of cadmium: "An intense yellow color shows that products such as plastics or paints may contain cadmium. One plastic housing on a vacuum cleaner was full of cadmium, and it wrecked the rating of the whole product, which went back up when the manufacturer changed it. That's an example of an extremely bad environmental component messing up the whole product. Another example is the minus rating we gave to all TVs using lead and cadmium in their glass tubes, which is not necessary to the product's performance. Now none of them do, and since German brands serve an international market, everyone benefits." Of course, SW can't check all brands; some cheap portables from other countries being sold in Germany may be full of lead and cadmium.

Since SW has the time and budget to test only major brands and products, it needs help. "That's why we appreciate the role of watchdogs like Greenpeace, that will pinpoint troublesome products from time to time," explains Sieber. "They're not always systematic of course, or even that scientific, but they can get public attention, which will then allow SW and others to concentrate on the problem." He was thinking about polyvinyl chlorides in baby toys, recently exposed by Greenpeace and the Sierra Club, or the new concern about phthalates. Although Stiftung Warentest is the biggest environmental and consumer watchdog in Germany, it only tests the final product, and doesn't investigate methods of production. In the case of aluminum, for example, that limitation ignores a crucial part of the picture, because it's wasteful electrical consumption and poisoning of water during smelting that makes the final product unsustainable. Sieber says they are now doing work on the whole life cycle of a product, from inception to reuse, the Nike method. They're asking: How recyclable is the product? How separable are the components? Is there product responsibility in place? But the *way* Nike is making the gases in the shoe or, for instance, electroplating steel or lacquering things — the possible destructiveness of such processes in various industries is not yet being systematically explored. "We would need a lot more science," Sieber says, "and we don't have it yet."

Still, SW is going a long way to initiate an ongoing process. The purity and safety of food was very much on everyone's mind when we were in Germany, and the subject of genetic engineering is a very hot one in northern Europe. So many people oppose such foods that GE test-plots in Germany have to be guarded or the plants will be pulled up by irate locals. Germans want to know what comes in with imported food as well. Sieber says, "We tested and found Genetically Modified Organisms (GMOs) in over 30 percent of prepared breads, cakes, desserts, tofu, chips, sweets. And we gave them minus ratings. We effectively condemned those brands." When we asked why they'd give a minus to GMOs — after all, the research isn't all in — he said, "In fields of uncertainty we follow the basic rules of the precautionary principle. Avoid what is avoidable and suspicious, and await more science. Things with problematic ingredients may be out there labeled 'safe,' and maybe some of them are — but how about all together? They can add up. If 1 percent is allowable, and 2 percent is bad, what about consuming 0.01 percent here and 0.09 percent there? We have to make sure people realize that they're consuming many things with problematic ingredients. If there are alternatives, they should take them."

Sieber emphasizes that a consumer group like his is just one part of the equation. "Environmental organizations can go further in smaller areas. Government policy has to get involved too. We all know that politicians only act when there is pressure. The consumer has to be convinced to make that pressure and he has to convince the politicians to make legislation. This chain of activity or influences sometimes has weak, sometimes strong links. We're just one of them, trying to make it hold together." Another link is the corporations themselves. Not all of them oppose environmentally friendly policies. German appliances are already under national product responsibility legislation. That means that the manufacturers have to take back every single component of the products that they make. In order for that to be economically viable, that means they have to make fridges, stoves and washers — and as of 2002, even cars — out of materials that can either go back to the earth or be reused in the industrial stream. And they're doing it, with barely a whimper.

Europe also has organizations of green entrepreneurs who have banded together to accelerate this process. One example is BAUM, headquartered in its own architect-designed green building in Hamburg. We met with project manager Mathias Weiss, who looks like a Dürer portrait of a young man, thin-cheeked, with a jutting chin, curling dark hair and a gentle manner. The organization's acronym stands for Bundesdeutscher Arbeitskreis für Umweltbewusstes Management eV, roughly translated as "environmentally friendly business entrepreneurs." The word "Baum" itself translates as "tree," and BAUM has branches in Hamburg, Munich, Leipzig and Hamm, employing about sixty people full time. BAUM is financed by member fees at DEM 6,000 per year for companies with more than 500 employees. We met in the office kitchen, a very large and breezy space with an open window, a garden view and friendly people offering coffee and biscuits.

We talked about the tiny cars that one sees in all German cities: the Lupo from VW, the A-Class from Chrysler and the Smart Car from MCC. These vehicles get about 33 km per litre of gas (over 78 miles to the gallon!). They do it by weight and efficiency (they're not even battery hybrids like Toyota's Prius), and although mysteriously unavailable in North America, they are proliferating abroad. Besides their obvious economic advantage, these little runabouts can also be completely recycled, because the new EC regulations state that, beginning in 2002, European manufacturers will have to take their cars back for recycling. How do you recycle a whole car? Mathias said, "One way to achieve that is to use only one kind of plastic in the car's construction, instead of four or five. BAUM has one as their company car. I, too, thought it might be dangerous . . . so tiny and light! But statistics show no more injuries or deaths in accidents than normal cars, even on high-speed German highways, so now I'm relaxed when I drive it. They have carbon bodies, which are far lighter, yet even less likely to injure passengers in a collision."

## Show Us the Money

*It is high time the ideal of success should be replaced with the ideal of service.*
— ALBERT EINSTEIN

Many entrepreneurs would like to found their own decent, sustainable business on the standards that BAUM, SW and Judy Wicks are using — or improve the business they've got. But they don't think they'll ever be able to find the capital to do so. Non-profit daycares, housing for seniors and the handicapped, and inner-city co-ops, for example, are not always able to find government or charitable funding. Families or small groups that want to start a new initiative like an organic farm or dairy, a retail outlet for earth-friendly merchandise, a recycled-fiber clothing manufacturing business, or the construction of green buildings — in short, almost anyone who wants their business to reflect their values — will have trouble being recognized as "serious" and "businesslike" by most banks and financial institutions. But such people need to know that there are banks out there, real banks, whose mandate is not to amass money, but to help socially and environmentally sustainable businesses get off the ground. The GLS Bank in Bochum, Germany, is only one of a handful of such financial institutions sprinkled around the globe that have been founded to provide capital for enterprises that don't have the same look and feel as those set up for profit and profit only.

The GLS Gemeinschaftsbank, a large, airy building on a busy corner in the industrial city of Bochum in central Germany, extends credit and financing to "social, ecological or cultural enterprises." It was founded by the famous Waldorf Schools twenty-five years ago when the schools needed funding for their own projects. At first, the new bank concentrated on helping schools, local health clinics and other social non-profits. Over the last decade, however, it has expanded into ecologically friendly businesses. Anyone who is trying to fund the marketing of organic food products or ecologically made handicrafts, a wind or biomass energy utility, a sustainable tree plantation, what have you, has a decent chance of getting start-up or support funding at 4.5 to 6.5 percent interest rates from the GLS. Cornelia

Roekl, one of their credit managers, says, "We prefer to loan to a group. If several people have gotten together and they want to get funding for something like an environmentally sound housing co-op, to refurbish the building in sustainable ways, we're interested. A single person trying to start up, say, an organic bakery, will have more trouble. Things can happen to just one person — health problems, a divorce, any kind of set-back — that may cause them to give up on their new business, and put our loan at risk. But if you've got even a small group of four or five people, we've found that someone else can shoulder the load, and the business or non-profit venture tends to work out."

Since the GLS bank has assets of over DEM 300 million, they can help a lot of businesses get a start. In the last eight years, they've grown in size and assets at an average of 10 percent a year. And they've got company. The Triodos Bank, a similar institution with branches in Holland, Belgium and the UK, is experiencing the same kind of success; their growth, for 1999 alone, was 37 percent, and their net worth is £404 million, well over $800 million. All the branches practice what they preach, working out of green buildings, making sure their own workers and communities are treated the way their mandate demands. The Holland branch has provided funds for the expansion of a professional daycare center, as well as a company that not only recycles old appliances and household equipment, but also provides re-entry jobs for the unemployed. In these days of Mad Cow and GMOs, they're also helping a large, established feed company open a branch that will process and distribute all-organic feed.

Triodos money helped set up the Essential Trading Co-operative, one of the largest worker-owned co-ops in Britain, which imports fair-trade goods and wholesales organic foods to 600 retailers around the UK. Triodos Belgium provided a large loan for the construction of a huge eco-building that houses the Oxfam World Shops in Ghent. In Breda, Netherlands, consumers now have a new natural-foods supermarket chain that's going national; the Dutch branch of Triodos provided the funding for the pilot project. They are also providing money for solar energy systems in many towns across the country, systems that will provide about 60 percent of the energy required to run each home. There are many other bank services available, such as the Triodos Dairy Conversion Loan in England, which supports dairy farmers while they convert their herds to organic feeds. The Triodos Solar Investment Fund finances solar energy projects in developing countries, and their most brilliant venture, Triodos Match, Ltd., acts as a match-maker to pair up social and environmental businesses that need capital with people who have capital — and frequently relevant skills and experience as well. These investment "marriages" typically work for businesses trying to raise between £20,000 and £500,000. Triodos currently has investment suitors with more than £4 million, just waiting for their environmental love matches. Besides all this, Triodos offers normal banking services such as personal checking and savings accounts, and they are active in outreach projects such as forgiving Third World debt and supporting organizations like the Environmental Law Foundation. They give a lot of their profits to charities. They're definitely not the kind of bank we're used to.

North America, especially Canada, is lagging behind in creating such wonders, but there are two similar financial institutions in the States. The Shorebank in Chicago was founded in 1973 mainly to help entrepreneurs in inner-city neighborhoods get the start-up funding they need to take control of their lives. So far they've sent out $600 million in loans to help revitalize the lives of 13,000 families and businesses in the tough south and west sides of Chicago. That completely social mandate expanded with the founding of their affiliate, Shorebank Pacific, in Portland, Oregon, whose focus is environmentally sustainable and community development projects. Shorebank Pacific has provided start-up funds for such businesses as a furniture manufacturer who uses sustainably harvested alderwood and recycles waste into new products, an affordable housing rehab project that uses sustainably harvested or recycled materials, and a septic treatment company that makes sure sewage doesn't harm sensitive ecosystems.

## Speak Softly; Carry a Big Stick

> *Credibility with consumers is at the core of our success . . . While we aspire to create marketplace rewards for responsible producers, we make it pretty tough for them to earn our seal of approval.*
> — DEBORAH KANE, DIRECTOR OF THE FOOD ALLIANCE

Not only is it possible to get the money to start socially and environmentally sustainable businesses; it's happening all over the place. But once a business that makes money like the bee gets going, who will make sure it doesn't hurt the flower? Who's making sure that the organic milk in the new dairy really is pure, that 10 percent of the profits really are going to charity, and that nobody's dumping anything down the storm drains? That's being taken care of as well. All kinds of certification agencies are popping up, with a mandate to inspect business products and processes and make sure they're living up to their claims. They even certify the eco-banks.

The ISO system is part of the International Organization for Standardization established back in 1947, and 14001 is their environmental standards certificate. Triodos is one of the first banks to secure an ISO 14001 certificate for its environmental management systems, one of the few such regulatory systems that's internationally recognized. The ISO conducts audits to make sure that stated mandates, like an environmental management policy, are being practiced on the shop floor and actually produce the desired results. They help an organization make sure that its own monitoring and evaluation systems are adequate, and they check back every year. Every three years they completely re-assess the operation before issuing a new certificate.

In addition to the Forest Stewardship Council mentioned earlier, which is also international, there are local organizations like The Food Alliance (TFA) in Oregon, a group of farmers, consumers, scientists, grocers, processors, distributors, farm worker representatives and environmentalists all working together to make sure that food can be identified according to its components and production processes. Like the ISO, they also audit food producers to see if their food is all they claim it to be; they analyze foods for traces of contaminants like pesticides or GMOs, and they even make sure the people working for the company are properly treated, something that's very unusual in the agriculture business. Therefore, the TFA-Approved label, now becoming used across the Pacific Northwest, ensures consumers that high standards have been met in pest and disease management, soil and water conservation, and human resource development.

In addition to these groups that help bee-and-flower businesses thrive and let consumers know who's walking their talk, there are other ways to ride herd on the really big players. In Frankfurt, for example, city manager Klaus Weichert controls a $200 million budget in the city's environment department, which shares a green building with several environmental NGOs. He is responsible for water management, green spaces, public transit, brownfields (the term for former industrial sites) and toxic dumps. Frankfurt has one of the largest green belts surrounding its urban area in all of Europe. Some of the land the city owns is rented out to farmers who are willing to grow only organic crops, and business is good because the city helps them market the vegetables and high quality wheat they produce.

Frankfurt also works on sustainability programs with its extensive industrial and banking base. The Deutsche Bank, for example, which is headquartered in Frankfurt, Germany's largest city, has sustainability criteria for loans. Before it gives an industrial loan, its risk assessment includes whether or not a business will be creating brownfields or using large amounts of land or water. But as Weichert says, "The municipal government's specific instrument is environmental liability legislation. Because their insurance costs will be higher if they engage in environmentally dangerous practices, businesses have to pay attention to these things. And they do, because this is the kind of financial pressure that they understand."

There are good reasons for businesses to carry liability insurance in Germany. Here, national laws freeze high-flying multinationals into one place and one time; they give them an identity that can be affected by local laws, something that multinational corporations usually don't have to deal with. German liability law also gives them a face, so they can be prosecuted for wrong-doing just as individual citizens can. In Germany, businesses, no matter how large, no matter where they're headquartered, can be held liable for their own products, both in terms of the production process and in terms of product use. "Before these laws," Weichert says, "the person who suffered from a hazardous product had to prove how the business had injured them. Now it's the opposite; the company has to prove its product could not have done the injury — to the person's health, or to the soil water or air."

Weichert cites a recent example. "We had conflicts around some toxic wood protectors that were accused of being the cause of severe health problems. The company had to prove they did every kind of test to make sure the product was benign, they had to prove they had done all they could to avoid these problems." But how do you allocate responsibility within a huge, amorphous corporation? "Simple," says Weichert. "At each level of management, one individual is identified as having financial responsibility for his or her department, so they are also personally financially responsible for its mistakes. And we will take it up to the very highest level, the CEO, the members of the board, if necessary. A person is identified, and that person, not the corporation, will be sued, and they'll have to prove beyond a shadow of a doubt that they took every precaution to make sure the product was safe to people's health, and to the environment." Laws like this would make short work of disasters like Union Carbide's gas leak in Bhopal, India, the Firestone tire scandal in the United States, or genetic engineering everywhere. In most countries, no one can be held accountable and a corporation can just dissolve and re-form even if it does get fined. These laws exist right now in Germany and are undoubtedly one of the main reasons why Germany has a much better handle on food purity, toxic waste and environmentally polluting energy systems than does most of the rest of the world.

Advocates for big corporations would claim that such laws would paralyze investment and make it impossible for businesses to function; and they'd resort to their biggest threat — that "the economy will suffer." But in fact, Germany has been using these laws for six years now, and it remains one of the most business-attractive, prosperous nations in the world. When they understand the parameters, even corporations like the Union Carbides, Shells and Firestones can watch their liability bottom line. As Weichert says, "financial risks are something they understand, and can include in their business plans. It's part of their culture."

## Really Good Jobs

*The end product of our work is jobs. We decided to make this a financially viable system, based in the marketplace, using technology which is carefully designed not to be destructive to the environment, or to communities. We're not always successful — but we have more examples of things that work than most.*
— ASHOK KHOSLA, FOUNDER OF DEVELOPMENT ALTERNATIVES

Are organic foods, high sustainability standards and government watchdogs all luxuries only the rich can aspire to? When taken to task for locating their non-unionized, unsafe sweatshops and steel mills in Third World countries, multinational corporations like to say that these countries are in such bad shape that even a job chained to a chair making designer jeans for $2 a day is better than starving in a drought-stricken village. Most of the time that's debatable, but it may occasionally be true. Still, a lot of people in the Third World would like a better choice than just being caught between a rock and a hard place. Organizations like Ashok Khosla's Development Alternatives are trying to provide options that won't make them slaves to a multinational, won't turn them into mindless consumers, and won't trash the ecosystems that are their only hope for a future.

Khosla is a physicist educated at Harvard and Cambridge who set up India's first environmental policy bureau back in 1972. Since then, he has been director of the United Nations Environment Programme, vice president of the Club of Rome, councillor to the World Conservation Union and chairman of the NGO Global Forum at the Earth Summit in Rio in 1992. When he left the UN, his goal was to create one million decent, sustainable jobs in India over the next ten to twelve years; and amazingly, he's on track. It's been seven years, and his own NGOs, Development Alternatives (DA) and Technology and Action for Rural Advancement (TARA), have already created over 400,000 jobs.

India's needs are different from those of Germany or North America. For one thing, 65 percent of the population still lives on the land, and the country desperately needs rural jobs, so that people aren't forced to migrate to the already overcrowded, overwhelmed cities. But the options currently available to people in the Indian countryside are very limited and they tend to destroy the land on which they depend. Development Alternatives is trying to tackle these immense problems. Khosla says, "We're trying to create sustainable livelihoods in a manner that is replicable on a large scale, that will create lifestyles that potentially don't destroy the environment. We try to work primarily on the basis of what seems to be needed by people, perceived by them as important. Sometimes we come in and say, 'Here's a good idea. You might like it.' And that can work. But more often, they tell us what they'd like, and we try to do that." Development Alternatives, although non-profit itself, aims to teach people how to be self-supporting entrepreneurs. "We decided early in the game that if you're going to create a change on a market scale, it couldn't be on the basis of a do-good, bleeding-heart approach. There are millions of good pilot projects done, but then they die, because ultimately, they have to be self-supporting."

"For us," Khosla explains, "the goal of providing sustainable livelihoods has four or five basic components. One is simply to come up with jobs in the first place. Two is that those jobs provide a reasonable income that would be comparable to what an industrial worker in a slum, say, in Bombay, might make, so that people won't be tempted to leave their families to go there. It should also provide meaning and dignity in life, and a way of establishing all the things that honorable work does for people — self-respect . . . stability. We're not always successful in all that, but we try. Not only do these livelihoods have to refrain from destroying the environment, they must actually regenerate it. Here the idea of not destroying the earth is moot, because in most of central India, the forests are gone. There's no water . . . no rivers. The soils are like concrete, or they've washed out to sea. There are no functioning ecosystems left. So this sustainable work has to help restore the environment, or it won't be able to carry on into the future. And finally, these livelihoods must create goods and services for local economies. It is simply not sustainable to work for the export market to meet the goals of globalization. None of these criteria are rigid, of course. I have no problem with sending out some of our best fruit or handicrafts to generate a cash flow for people to be able to then buy bicycles or televisions or whatever. But by and large, the primary loop that has to be served is the local economy." Development Alternatives is socially as well as environmentally ambitious. "For us," says Khosla, "a sustainable livelihood is a particularly appropriate concept for the marginalized, the people who are getting left behind: women, tribal people, the poor. People who don't really have options the way things are currently set up. So we target them first and foremost."

Ashok Khosla's two organizations, DA and TARA, are headquartered on an acre or so (half a hectare) of landscaped grounds in a section of Delhi stiff with government offices and bounded by a huge and beautiful park. The building itself is all mud-brick, made by a innovative process they discovered that is providing an exemplary livelihood in seven centers across India. The brick-making method saved about half a hectare (one acre) of forest just in the construction of this building, because the bricks are compressed, not fired. Walls made from them are so thick that they eliminate the need for air conditioning, a horribly unsustainable practice in Delhi, where the temperature is above 30°C (86°F) at least nine months of the year. The resulting structure is a beautiful dark, earthy red, with barrel-vaulted ceilings. In its mysterious little courtyards and landscaped grounds you can sip chai or lassi while gazing at the arched alcoves and bright cupolas.

The Delhi DA office may be beautiful, but it also bustles with activity; there's a big library and many offices overflowing with paperwork, where researchers, interns and managers toil through most weekends to make sure the enterprises they've founded actually function. We spent an afternoon there, and then went out to Jhansi, a central Indian city of about a million people 480 km (300 miles) to the east, to see their work in the field. In the countryside outside the city, DA has established its main center, TARA, where they manufacture the compressed, non-fired bricks, as well as stone-dust roofing tiles, another of their successes. Jhansi is in a quarry area, and the air and vegetation for miles around are white with dust blown from the tailings. Instead of letting the powdered stone continue contaminating the air and water, Tara is collecting it for reuse. At a spacious factory that also produces hand-made paper, workers vibrate the stone dust and compress it into moulds to come up with extremely functional gray roofing tiles. Since the tiles are as cheap as traditional fired ones and last twice as long, they can even compete with thatch in price, so the poorest family can afford them. As we traveled around the district, we noticed them on every type of structure, including a tribal snake temple.

There are now 300 such factories spread all over India, creating about 3,000 truly sustainable jobs, mostly for women, at better rates of pay than they could ever hope to make elsewhere. Studies have shown that the tribal women trained to work for DA and TARA also have smaller families than their village counterparts. Moreover, once they've seen such initiatives in place, people are setting up their own little enterprises based on the same model. TARA itself is a model for a self-supporting sustainable industry. They got the water and power they needed — and also restored the surrounding ecosystem — by building a small, earthen "check" dam across a seasonal riverbed on their land. They put up a biomass-fed power station that is fuelled by burning the ubiquitous and damaging exotic plants like *lantana* that infest central India. They then set up their factory, which, besides providing scores of jobs, has its own restaurant, garden and daycare. It wasn't hard to attract workers, Khosla says. "Unlike most normal jobs, our recruitment is based on need rather than skill or ability. Many of the people were taken on simply because they desperately needed a job — widows, who are particularly unprovided for in the rural economy, and women whose husbands are not helping support them. Anybody can be trained to make these tiles or the handmade paper. They just have to want to do it."

Development Alternatives doesn't want to be just an educational facility or an employer. They want to give people a ladder out of the hole. In the area between the city of Jhansi and the beautiful temple and palace town of Orchha, TARA-made products are widely advertised on billboards and housings, and in the popular press; and the company has a very good reputation among the locals. Development Alternatives doesn't try to make profits, but they also can't allow themselves to lose money. To them, that would mean that whatever they're doing isn't going to work for people in the long run. So, in addition to helping make a good product, they also help find markets. Khosla says, "We've been developing essentially a franchising approach, so that we provide the support systems for a small enterprise to grow. We find people who have some entrepreneurial skills, put them through a battery of tests and figure out whether they are able to run a business. We train them, provide them with equipment. We demonstrate good business practices, like maintenance, payroll, inventories. We get statistics from them, so we can try to understand how to improve things. What are the failure rates? Have they properly targeted their market? We even give them a brand image, do advertising and artwork, and offer ideas for brochures. We become a marketer. But honestly, we're not that good at it. Basically, we do come from non-marketing backgrounds. So we're just learning how to do that."

Khosla, like so many people working toward sustainability, is disarmingly hesitant and deprecatory about what he does. It's a real sign of the methodology. In fact, DA breaks even on their beautiful rag papers and bags, they're doing extremely well with the compressed brick and roofing tile factories, which are continuously expanding, and they've opened up a dozen vertical-kiln factories across India, which employ hundreds of men at good wages. These kilns for fired brick use a simple technology developed in China, which emits less than half the carbon and sulphur dioxide of existing brick works. Besides all this, DA is tackling the loss of forests and of rivers, the two main causes of the ghastly air and water quality in north-central India. (Their remarkable ability to bring back perennial sources of water cheaply and almost at will is described later in the book.) But what DA's tens of thousands of useful, sustainable jobs clearly demonstrate is that job creation efforts play out very differently according to the values on which they're based. New businesses whose goal is local social and environmental sustainability, not profit for a distant multinational, are starting to be a force for good all over the world. They're proving that even the poorest of the poor do not have to sacrifice their natural resources or become slaves in a sweatshop just to survive.

## Live and Let Re-Live

*Let's not mistake capitalism for democracy.*
— GEORGE SOROS

Privately owned businesses and publicly traded ones are not the only way to make money like the bee. Maybe one of the best methods of all to make long-term honey is through a non-profit, or a co-operative owned by its employees. These two similar business structures are also growing by leaps and bounds across the world. We went to see one in Portland, Oregon, the Recycling Center, which is on the tough side of town. Shane Endicott, its director and founder, is a long-time resident of the poor, mostly black neighborhood on the northeast side of Portland in which he established the Center. He's in his mid-thirties, but looks younger. As in most such vibrant, revolutionary organizations, one person got it going, but many more have shouldered the burden, so that it likely could run well — though not with as much electricity — without him. The Center is a perfect example of the kind of non-profit, or even for-profit, business that can be adopted all over the world as a way to live like a bee, in every sense of the term.

Endicott started this business while he was still working at the St. Vincent de Paul charity center in Salem, Oregon. For more than two years, he and a friend, Jim Prindahl, spent their spare time doing in-depth research all over the country, from L.A. to Philadelphia, from D.C. to Nova Scotia. They liked carpentry, and they wanted to start some kind of a building center, ideally one that would recycle almost everything. Eventually they got a $15,000 loan from an individual and started their operations out of a driveway. All they had was the research, a business plan and a volunteer base. A month later they already could afford four full-time employees. Now they have an enormous building more than half a city block long, filled with windows and doors of all sizes, toilets, pipes and electrical equipment, with its extensive yards piled with old sinks, windows, lumber, nails, bathtubs — you name it. At first glance, it looks like debris, but it is actually very carefully graded and organized, and it's constantly being purchased. In the back there are large workshops where value-added work is done, where everything from broken doors to lamps is repaired, so it won't be wasted in a market where buyers may not know how to restore old plaster molding or have the time to find matching stained glass.

A year ago, only six or eight months after start-up, they had twelve or thirteen paid workers, and now, after not quite two years of existence, they have thirty-six full-time employees, as well as a few part-time workers and volunteers. They thought they'd pay back the initial loan in a year or so, maybe start grossing around $200,000 in a couple years; they made that much and paid the loan back in the first year, and they're now grossing over a million dollars U.S. a year. Entry-level jobs shifting bricks or pulling nails out of two-by-fours pay $10 U.S. an hour, which is about four dollars over the minimum, with full medical and dental coverage for the worker and about 80 percent for their families. Within six months, workers generally get a dollar an hour wage hike, and are quickly making $15. Needless to say, there's very little turnover, and the last offer for one job attracted 76 applicants. Eighty percent of the staff is taken from the disadvantaged neighborhood they're in, and the Center facilitates home ownership for their workers in a variety of ways, from loans to special prices on materials and help with construction. The neighborhood paper calls them "the anchor that's revitalizing the community." Top administrators like Endicott, who probably works a sixty-hour week, get $40,000, but it's set up so there can never be huge salary gaps between administration and workers. Many, like Jim Prindahl and Bill Welch, are experts who came from much better-paying jobs because they were attracted by the possibility of putting their hearts into something and still being able to support themselves.

This building recycling center works the same way Interface Carpets does. It makes an asset out of waste, and refuses to let there be any. Endicott says, "The usual 'crunch and dump' demolition and salvage companies that operate in any city were high-grading, taking the occasional beautiful door or mantel and selling it for plenty to rich people, but doing very little to help reduce the overall waste stream or increase the availability of recycled materials to middle and lower income people. I believe *everything* should be recycled, down to a two-foot length of nail-studded two-by-four, or some partly broken gyprock. That's what we do." The Recycling Center makes sure what they sell is at least 50 percent below the retail price, and they make enough on select items like pretty windows to deal with the piles of what looks like broken bits. And although they've become so successful they could ship these products and materials to other markets and expand their operation, they won't go out of state because they don't want to burn fuel and add more carbon dioxide to the atmosphere.

The reason they're competitive as a business and cheaper than other "deconstruction" services, is that they do everything by hand, so there are no heavy machinery costs. Moreover, they employ four to six workers for every one in comparable companies, and they still pay much higher wages! We automatically think that human labor, even at low salaries, cannot possibly be cheaper than mechanization, but Endicott's team looked into that and discovered that in their industry, human labor is much cheaper than machines, which have not only enormous initial costs, but a constant thirst for fuel and repairs. Most telling of all, the Recycling Center doesn't need to show a profit; like Development Alternatives, all they're trying to do is meet their costs, which is a huge advantage. Endicott says, "We've benefited by two progressive laws in the area: high dumping fees of about $17 a ton, a cost to customers that is simply eliminated by the Center. We just come and take it all away. Owners of demolished or refurbished buildings also benefit from a tax break for 'donating' their material to a non-profit. So all you have do is call us up — less mess, less cost. Naturally we're popular."

What the Center is doing is about more than just sustainability and the environment, although that's a big part of it. Endicott says, "I'm not an environmentalist. I just think that if people are healthy, living healthy lives in healthy places, they'll do things that are right for all the systems. We have every walk of life working and buying at the Center. We don't talk politics or 'the environment.' If we took on that role, we wouldn't be able to integrate and do so well in this community. Everyone can come in here, Republicans, Democrats, whatever." Endicott gets very serious when he talks about the calories that come from the planet's real energy source, the sun. He calls them BTUs, and he says, "Normally our society spends thousands of BTUs on fossil fuels, steel, supporting these huge machines to crunch and dump the BTUs of things that could be saved. Then they have to go out and crunch up more forest BTUs, wasting new growth, and then going through the same cycle, over and over. We break that cycle. My hair stands up when I think about it! Look!" He showed an arm that was indeed a mass of goose-bumps in the warm room. "It gets to me, because I realize that we're *recognizing* that energy, continuing its life, employing people — and by doing that, capturing that energy into their lives, so it just keeps on living. And so do the trees, and so do we!"

The business co-op idea is a mighty good one, because, after all, how many of us want to work all our lives so that already rich shareholders can get richer? We just want to make a decent salary. This type of business can take many forms, many of which have no particular environmental or social mandate, and aren't even non-profits. In Quebec, a popular game preserve, Parc Safari Africain, and Schwartz's, a classic Montreal eatery, are both employee-owned co-ops. Even if they don't directly try to save the earth, they tend to hurt the flowers a lot less. They're worth looking into. And they're proliferating all across the world.

## Avoiding the Octopus

*This obsession for maximizing profits to shareholders has got to be seen as abusive, as dangerous, and as one of the most appalling situations on this planet. Because it makes for criminal behavior.*
— ANITA RODDICK, FOUNDER OF THE BODY SHOP

If it's profitable to be environmentally sound, even on a small scale, even in the Third World, why aren't the big guns going for it and expanding the market for more green buildings, green cars and green jobs? Well, some of them are — or so they would like us to believe. BP says its letters don't stand for "British Petroleum" anymore but for "Beyond Petroleum," and they're investing heavily in new solar and hydrogen-based technologies. Toyota has come out with the Prius, a hybrid battery and gasoline car. Since they're the first with the prototype, they look very progressive indeed. Shell Oil has established Shell International Renewables, with $500 million committed to developing solar, biomass and wind energy.

These are very hopeful trends, and yet — BP, Shell, Mobil, Chevron and many other big oil companies are actually *increasing* their exploration and drilling operations.[4] The big talk at the FTAA meeting in Quebec in 2001 was about how Canada could help quench the U.S. thirst for yet more oil by developing its tar sands deposits, as well as sending the U.S. more of everything already being pumped. Millions of barrels of crude were recently been discovered just off the coast of Nigeria, and one of Bill Clinton's last acts as president was to go to that country and cozy up to the present regime. For years, the people of the Niger Delta have begged Shell to stop burning its excess gas off in flares, a practice that's largely illegal in North America because of the pollution that comes down from the continuous smoke. But now the oil companies are planning to flare the offshore wells. As Owens Wiwa, part of the opposition to drilling expansion in the country, points out, "If they finally do close down their flaring in the Delta but then start flaring offshore, the world's atmosphere won't see any net difference."

We see the same behavioral dichotomy with companies like Ford and Toyota. A new son of the family, Bill Ford, is talking green enough to make any environmentalist's mouth water. But even he has admitted that his company cannot phase out his most gas-guzzling models as long as they're selling well. So without new government standards, it will take many, many years for the company's green incentives to make any impact on our atmosphere.[5] Toyota's Prius would also mean a lot more if the company as a whole were more like Interface, Collins Pine, or the White Dog Café — really committed to a principle. But at the moment it is happily manufacturing some of the largest SUVs on the market and seemingly has no plans to get rid of them to concentrate more intensely on making battery-powered cars. It's important that these new technologies be developed, and these days only corporations have the necessary wealth to do so; but until the old practices are statistically overwhelmed by the new, such innovations will hardly make a dent in the amount of poison enveloping the planet.

On the plus side, of course, thanks in part to the very corporations that poison the planet, we now know that we can do it: we can make efficient cars, build green, substitute for toxins, reuse and conserve, save the world's resources for the use of future generations. So the question still remains: Why don't we? Shell ran a touching ad in a recent *National Geographic*: "Wish upon a star . . . with real goals and investment, energy from the sun can be more than just a daydream." Behind this message was a beautiful sunset on a pristine ocean shore. If you set this image against the thousands of people still suffering and dying in Nigeria, the indigenous groups even now being displaced by Chevron and Mobil in South America,[6] and the threats against the Arctic Refuge in Alaska — all in order to extract a few months' more toxic, global warming, resource-destroying oil — you sense a pretty serious disconnect. Although corporations themselves are capable of helping a great deal, they are still a very, very large part of the problem. Many of them seem to have two different faces. We decided to talk to a famous CEO whose business has been green from inception to find out why that is.

Anita Roddick founded and helped run one of the world's best-known publicly traded corporations, the Body Shop. Like Ben and Jerry's Ice Cream, Patagonia Clothing or Interface Carpet, the Body Shop is known for its light step on the earth, for claiming to adhere to standards of social justice and environmental responsibility. But corporations like Nike, Shell Oil, Dupont and British Petroleum make exactly the same claims. How can we tell who's really walking the talk? They all have a lot of money to spend on PR. And it's easy to be fooled if you've never been to Nigeria, a Body Shop herbal collection point or a Nike sweatshop. Not only has Roddick visited such places, she's organized trips for other leaders to go and see for themselves what all these companies' policies actually do. Following praise of Shell's new green image at the State of the World Forum business workshop in New York, she stood up and said, "Ferocious criminal acts are being perpetrated by business in the name of trade." She went on to describe suffering in the Nile Delta's makeshift hospitals due to a lack of medication and government help, traceable to, she says, the region's resistance to more drilling by Royal Dutch Shell and other companies.[7] "And Shell isn't breaking any law, because there's no code of global governance." How did someone who feels so passionately about social and environmental justice become the millionaire queen of a huge multinational corporation, which many say is not so perfect itself?

In a way, Roddick is the proverbial bird in a gilded cage, a very good person caught in a very bad system. She says, "Ben and Jerry's, Patagonia, the Body Shop — we thought business was more than profit: joy, wonderment, gaining a livelihood honorably. But small groups of stockholders who spend little time in a company can change all that. We need to realize that stockholder votes aren't the only way to run business." What she was talking about was the basic difference between a private business, like the White Dog Café or Collins Pine, and a publicly traded corporation. What a business person gets when she "goes public" is a great deal of capital to expand. What she loses is control. As strangers buy up stock, they become "shareholders." That means they have a say in how the company is run. It's a rare company founder who is able to hold on to a truly controlling share of the stock in their own creation. And the newcomers very often vote the founder out, simply because what they have invested in the business is not their time, passion or ideals, but their money, and that's the only thing they want out of it. In fact, under current corporate law, a business corporation is not allowed to use its assets for anything that cannot be proven to make it more money.

Corporate charities have to prove they have PR or tax abatement goals, with the intent to increase profits. If the managers want to do more, they have to form separate, charitable foundations. So Judy Wicks's dinner talks and inner-city outreach, Collins Pine's decision to spare old growth and keep owls in the woods, even Sarah Severn's attempts to get all the greenhouse gases out of Nike airsoles — none of these initiatives will stand the proverbial snowball's chance in hell if they ever run up against the bottom line in a publicly traded corporation. It is only because the first two businesses are privately owned that they can do such things. If Nike ever cuts back on $CO_2$ emissions enough to affect the bottom line, these policies will most likely be history.

Like Judy Wicks, Anita Roddick and her husband, Gordon, founded the Body Shop both to make a living and to be their life's work, to reflect and promote values that were firmly earth-centered. "Our vision was never bigness," she says. "It was cheekiness; it was having an idea, and just seeing how far it goes." Like the devoted middle management pushing the envelope at Nike, it seems strange that the people who are so successful at business often don't think about the implications of how it's all set up. It never occurred to Roddick, as it apparently didn't occur to Ben Cohen of Ben and Jerry's, what it really meant to go public. "It was such fun," she says. "We were getting so many more shops! We needed to have more retail spaces, and we weren't being taken seriously by the real estate groups. That was one of the reasons we decided to go public, to get the money for that kind of expansion, and to build a manufacturing plant. We wanted to control everything, like the extrusion of all our plastics; we wanted to make sure they were environmental. We wanted to be able to bring back the bottles and recycle them. We didn't believe anybody was going to put in the standards we wanted. And we decided going public, on the market, was the way to get the money to have that control."

Like Ben and Jerry's, which introduced all kinds of non-corporate behavior into their business, making sure no one in the lower ranks was paid obscenely less than people on the top, making sure 7.5 percent of pre-profit revenue went to charities, refusing to buy milk with the genetically engineered hormone rBGH in it, the Body Shop initially got away with their cheeky nonconformity. At first no one, not their lending institutions or shareholders or boards, interfered. "They left us alone," says Roddick. "They never hindered what we were doing because our profits were just celestial. We were going like this — straight up! And they never were a problem, back then."

The expansion itself backfired, especially in the United States. "We came in with all the grand hoo-ha of this new concept. Within five years we had thirty competitors, all in the same genre, with the same ideas. But only one consideration was missing. They didn't have the values. They didn't have the issue on animal testing. They didn't have the community trade, the environmental standards. And the American public didn't give a toss, as long as it smelled good, and there were fifteen flavors of bubble bath. We should never have gone into the malls of America. We should have stayed in urban core areas where we were seen as idiosyncratic." There is a note of serious regret in Roddick's lament, and that's because once the stock price started going down, she discovered what her core values really meant to her fellow stockholders: absolutely nothing. By 1998, Roddick had been kicked out by her own board. She still owns 30 percent of the stock and she's still respected as the founder. But like so many before her, she's discovered that your whole life's efforts can be taken away in a second, if you don't deliver those quarterly increases.

In a way, this multi-millionaire, world-famous author of a best-selling book, very much wants to "express all her interests through her business" in the same way Judy Wicks does. She helped fund the anti-globalization protest in Seattle. She longs to keep her "thumbprint" on the business. "But you know," she says, "I'm getting so bloody radical as I'm getting older, I wonder, 'am I dysfunctional in this company? Am I being too anarchic?' I mean, I want to go to Nicaragua, I want to expose sweatshops." But she can't. Not in the company she founded; it's too big. Ben and Jerry's, after a valiant behind-the-scenes battle, was taken over by the food giant Unilever. Their other ice creams, like Häagen-Dazs, routinely use rBGH-treated cows' milk. The umbrella company certainly doesn't contribute money to charity until it hurts, and they don't limit their CEO's salary to a certain multiple of the wage of the kid who's scooping the ice cream, like Ben and Jerry's used to do.

Roddick says, "We were simply used, to imply that the market was freer than it actually is. And we didn't really change things, because we were so idiosyncratic." She's wrong; they did change things. Their fall is just as instructive as their rise. For a while, big business could say that moral, socially responsible multinationals were very rare, but they were possible. And now that the people who formed the value base of Ben and Jerry's and the Body Shop have been thrown out, it's obvious that they're not. It's the same for the brave people reforming away in the bowels of Nike. As Dick Roy says, "Nike is an experiment in a publicly traded monster. The psyche is changed here in the head office, so far — but it's all product in the final analysis, and margins and profits — not values."

So there seem to be two options if you want to do business. You can stay private and retain control, and, like Judy Wicks, create a truly "beautiful business" that you can pass on through the generations, the way Mary Beth Collins did. If you go that way, you'll probably never get the capital to expand or become really influential in your country and make a difference with the real movers and shakers. Or you can think big and go public. After all, a major player like Roddick gets the chance to meet presidents and prime ministers and tell them what she thinks. And an even bigger one, like Nike, can afford to do research that can revolutionize our most necessary products, or create a market for organics. As a consumer, if you like the idea of a chain hotel you can depend on around the world or you truly love your Starbucks mocha, then you might want to do what Roddick suggests.

"Everything is possible. I mean, businesses are not found in nature. They're not ordained by the Almighty. They're made by men and women; and therefore they can be subject to change . . . We have to redefine the notion of profit. Who should profit? Is it just the small group of people that have invested in a company? Or is it the bigger society? Is it employees? Is it community? Is it suppliers? Is it the environment?" Roddick's vision is not unlike some of the laws and social obligations that already exist in countries like Germany. Roddick says, "I believe there's got to be regulations on business! I believe there's got to be penalties. There's got to be a corporate code of governors that penalizes you. Not just the sort of little thing like the Valdez Principles that you sign up with and do nothing. You've got to have solid penalties. Corporate pollution has got to be seen as a criminal act. They're always saying that businesses are made of people. If that's the case and you can't sue a business for what it does, then you must have the power to sue the people. And as a business person myself, if I made a mess and I wasn't seen to be responsibly dealing with the problem in a heartfelt way, I would want to be penalized and publicly shamed."

"Thanks to the unelected folks at the World Trade Organization," Roddick adds, "society can't get at these groups for penalties." And in fact it would even be hard to get national laws like Germany's over here, given the current political climate. But it was hard in Europe, too; that's no reason not to try. Anita Roddick agrees that when Shell and Toyota make the right noises they should be publicly and loudly thanked. "But what the world needs is not these huge kinds of global trade and World Bank initiatives, but *small*-scale economic initiatives. The poor must be allowed to tell *us* what they need, not vice-versa. Businesses like ours should be seeing how many community initiatives we can encourage — local work on AIDS, health, the environment . . . grassroots stuff. We forget that the only good thing about wealth is that it allows you to be generous. Otherwise, you diminish the human spirit and the resources of the planet by holding onto it."

CHAPTER 2
# WITHDRAWING CONSENT
## Practicing Democracy

### Controlling Predation

> *I am certain of only one thing: business as we know it is*
> *destroying the Earth, including all cultures and living systems.*
> *Never before has there been a system so ubiquitous, so destructive,*
> *and so well managed. It is our creation.*
> — PAUL HAWKEN[1]

Really big businesses, the publicly traded, multinational corporations, are, as we saw in chapter one, the predators of the business ecosystem, what you might call its foxes, wolves and sharks. As environmentalists, we'd never suggest getting rid of all the predators in nature; an ecosystem isn't healthy without a little of everything. But predators have big teeth and rapacious appetites, so the whole system has to keep them under control, by constricting their habitat, the way product and personal responsibility laws do, and by limiting their food supply, the way public awareness and consumer revolt can. Natural predators are held in check by the physical reality of the planet: ecosystems are not infinite, and endless growth is not possible. These are the simple laws of nature, and if our economic system were also rooted in the laws of physics and thermodynamics, we wouldn't be having an environmental crisis now. Many of the people grappling with that disconnect have concluded that if we were to stop creating human fantasies and start applying the principles of physics to our economic system, we might discover that we *can* have it all — publicly traded corporations whose habitat and diet are properly controlled, large and small private businesses that are both regulated and encouraged to have ethics, all kinds of government development and research institutions, non-profits, volunteer organizations, worker-owned co-ops and large numbers of socially useful institutions like schools, hospitals and parks, entirely supported by communal funds.

Only by having a society that supports all these ways of making money and distributing real wealth will we have a balanced economic ecosystem. By allowing one social entity, the publicly traded corporation, to absorb nearly all our political power and natural wealth, we've put our entire economic, political and ecological structure at risk. The business structures we discussed in chapter one — like the Social Ventures Network, the Triodos Bank, Collins Pine, the Recycling Center, and Stiftung Warentest — are prospering and expanding because more and more people are realizing that we have to get some diversity back in our business culture. But these initiatives are delicate. They can be wiped out by a few pro-corporate laws and the kinds of rulings that regularly come out of economic trade bodies like NAFTA and the WTO. We need to fight for business and economic diversity. All over the world this battle is being engaged, and it's not just a confrontation between large and small, international and local. It's an actual process of determining what is really valuable in human life, of evaluating what kinds of riches will make us happy and protect our children into the future. There are thousands of examples of this interface between the old economic mainstream and the new attempt to create sustainable values, but the best way to see how these things work on the ground is to tell a particular story.

## Beautiful Blue Lagoon

*[This] is the last undisturbed gray whale breeding and calving area on earth, and for that reason may be of unique importance for the survival of that species.*
— SCIENTISTS' STATEMENT TO URGE MITSUBISHI TO ABANDON SALTWORKS AT LAGUNA SAN IGNACIO[2]

Baja California is a narrow peninsula of the Sonoran desert that runs off the bottom of California. In this barren, underpopulated Mexican province, a remarkable story has been playing out over the past six years. It all began back in the early 1950s, when one of the three largest multinational corporations in the world, Mitsubishi, established a massive saltworks on the Ojo de Liebre or Scammon's Lagoon, a dent in the eastern coastline of the great

Baja peninsula. The company pumped thousands of gallons of water a day out of the lagoon to evaporate in salt pans that covered miles of the desert land, took it out on barges to the only deep port in the area, an island 64 km (40 miles) off the coast, and then loaded it on tankers to be shipped to Japan for more processing. Over the course of thirty years these industrial activities produced seven million tons of salt annually, provided around 800 jobs, and were the main reason a tiny desert settlement of fifty people, Guerrero Negro, has mushroomed to a population of 12,000. It was, in short, the typical story of a modern, extractive industry, controlled by a multinational corporation, creating salaried jobs in a remote area, while exploiting an "unused" natural resource.

Meanwhile, about 120 km (80 miles) south in the same ecosystem, a similar lagoon was coming under the influence of another kind of "development," and an entirely different way of valuing wealth. In 1948, a group of fishermen who used to come across the gulf to catch turtles on the shores of this smaller lagoon, San Ignacio, decided to settle in the area permanently. The turtles went into decline almost at once, which made the new settlers think about what they were doing. For reasons that had as much to do with loving the place they lived as with making a living, they took on the local mentality we described in the introduction and started to ask themselves what kind of life they wanted for their families over the long term. The original three fishermen founded the Cooperativa Pesquera de Punta Abreojos in their new town of Punta Abreojos as a way of taking control of their still-thriving abalone and lobster fishery and making sure it didn't go the same way as the turtles. The co-op rapidly became a marketing as well as a resource tool and found stable Asian markets for the community's fish. Javier Vallavicencio and Isidro Arce, grandsons of the original founders, are still community spokespeople.

Today, this is not a typical poor, resource-based Mexican town; co-op members gross $2 to $3 million (U.S.) a year and they have their own cannery to maximize profits. Their population of 3,000 boasts a number of fisheries technicians, two or three doctors and other college graduates. The co-op polices its members; anyone caught with a turtle or found to be infringing on their sustainable fishing practices is not allowed to fish for three months. And although they know the lagoon better than anyone on earth, they are humble enough to have hired university researchers to come and monitor their fishing methods. This was how they learned that their practice of using gill nets off-season was scraping the lobster and abalone seedbeds and causing populations to decline. They've made that practice illegal.

The townspeople of Punta Abreojos were not the only ones to place a non-industrial value on the resources and beauties of Laguna San Ignacio. The desert around it is home to saguaro forests and succulents, five kinds of cacti, coyotes, elf owls, eagles, hawks, vultures, ospreys and pelicans, and all the normal desert fauna of gila monsters, rattle and coral snakes, tarantulas and horned toads. There is also the tiny barrendo, an endangered pronghorn antelope, and a slow rain cycle to keep everything alive. The natives explain the rains are "regular," meaning they can absolutely count on one or two days of rain — every three years! Every fifty years, however, there is a cloudburst and the arroyos fill up; even the huge saguaros, together with tons of desert soil and brush, flood down to the sea to replenish the lagoon's nutrients.

The lagoon dazzles like a giant sapphire from the desert shore, but its smooth surface is deceptive. Besides the lobster and abalone populations that make up the fishery, it is home to thirty other commercially viable fish species, three species of endangered sea turtles, as well as clams, sharks and rays. But its most remarkable native is one of the largest mammals on earth — the Pacific gray whale. There are only three places left on earth where this endangered whale can breed, and this tiny lagoon is the only one, the very last that is uncorrupted by industry or pollution. After journeys of thousands of miles, hundreds of pregnant mothers and young whales arrive at this last sanctuary, to give birth and recover from a journey that has taken them past admirers crowded along the shores from Alaska, all down California, to this tip of Mexican desert.

A few co-op members participate in a carefully controlled eco-tourism business off one side of the lagoon, where boats take people out to wait a stipulated 100 meters (328 feet) from the whales. Ari Hershowitz, a chemist who works with the Natural Resources Defense Council, an American environmental group whose most visible leader is Bobby Kennedy, Jr., has seen them many times. He says, "You push out from the hot desert into the open water, and in the distance, you see a puff of vapor, the whale's breath. If you're lucky, and you usually are, they'll come straight towards you. The moms seem to be just as excited as you are. They rush over to introduce you to their newborns. They'll push the babies towards the boat with their noses, and play with you for ten or fifteen minutes at a time. They don't mistake the boats for whales — they look you in the eye, they spray and then roll over to peer at the result, whack their tails, act amused when you get wet. They'll let you stroke them, put your hand in their mouths; they'll even hold the boats on their bellies to keep you from leaving! It's an unforgettable experience. It's such a magical place."

It's so magical, in fact, that it now enjoys every level of government protection imaginable. As early as 1979, Mexico designated the lagoon a whale sanctuary. Ten years later, it became part of the El Vizcaino Biosphere Reserve, the largest protected natural area in Latin America. And in 1993, it was granted the highest honor in our current regime of valuing natural systems: it joined just 140 other areas on the whole planet, including Yellowstone Park and the Great Pyramids of Egypt, and was named a World Heritage Site by the United Nations. Besides all this, the lagoon area is also a state bird sanctuary, and a reserve for the turtles and for the antelope. As Hershowitz says, "It is supposed to have five levels of protection, to keep it safe." Obviously, in terms of non-monetary, non-industrial values, this lagoon is one of the places we cherish most on earth, according it our highest official attention and our pledge of eternal protection.

What happened next is probably not a surprise to anyone who understands how modern industrial society and its most recent extension, the globalization of economic trade, have their own ways of valuing real estate and natural resources. In the early 1990s, Mitsubishi, in a joint venture with the Mexican government's Exportadora del Sal, S.A. (ESSA), decided to close the saltworks in Ojo de Liebre lagoon and build a bigger and better one at San Ignacio. It would have a slightly larger capacity (8 instead of 7 million tons a year) and be almost entirely mechanized. It would have a pier, so salt tankers could come in and out of the lagoon and not waste time and money going out to the island, a plan that would require some dredging. Mitsubishi and the Mexican government maintained that the project would not have any effect on the ecosystem — even though the new facility would cover 30,000 hectares (116 square miles); that is, twice the land area of Washington, D.C. and more than twice the size of the lagoon itself.

Water would be pumped out of the lagoon at a rate of an Olympic-sized swimming pool every two seconds, to fill evaporation ponds secured from the elements — including the once-every-fifty-year cloudbursts — by simple earthen dikes. The remaining liquid, called bittern brine waste, contains toxins like boron, iodine, bromine, potassium chloride and magnesium sulfate, all proven deadly to marine life. It would be pumped back into the mouth of the bay at a rate of 22,000 tons a day. A pier over a mile long would be built in the pathway of the migrating whales, on top of the abalone and lobster fishery. Besides these effects on the lagoon, surrounding tidal flats, wetlands, succulent ecosystems and estuaries, the saltworks would also have brought in thousands of construction workers and truck traffic, spilling oil and diesel fuel. After construction, mechanization would eliminate 600 of the 800 jobs, thus impoverishing Guerrero Negro, the town that had sprung up to service the original saltworks.

Mexicans who knew about the parks and were proud of the World Heritage status began to mount opposition, but their Secretary of Commerce, who was also the chairman of ESSA's board of directors, argued that in these days of global competitiveness, Mexico simply could not afford to pass up the $120 million (U.S.) in foreign investment to construct the facility, to say nothing of the $80 million a year in revenues it expected from the operational plant. And, of course, there was a big rush; this facility had to be created as fast as possible, so that the money could start rolling in, too fast for there to be exhaustive environmental studies. Basically, what he was reiterating was the depressing fact that most people have noticed about modern society: under our present economic value system, factories, however dirty, and jobs, however few, must always be assigned a higher value than animals, parks or natural resources, however unique or beautiful.

An active Mexican environmental organization, the Grupo de los Cien, didn't agree with this set of priorities and began to fight for environmental evaluations, but they realized they couldn't do it alone. They contacted the Natural Resources Defense Council in Washington, and in May of 1995 the two groups threw down the gauntlet by taking out an ad in the *New York Times* outlining the Laguna San Ignacio situation. This was the beginning of an international campaign to put pressure on the Mexican government and Mitsubishi. The community and the environmentalists also enlisted a powerful ally, the International Fund for Animal Welfare (IFAW), which has a long history of whale advocacy. Movie stars Pierce Brosnan and Glenn Close, international investment houses and trade unions joined the struggle. An e-mail campaign for adults and a poster, postcard and letter-writing campaign for children inundated Mitsubishi with requests to leave; more petitions found their way to the World Heritage Committee of UNESCO. The European Union threatened trade problems if the Mexican government did not withdraw its support for the saltworks "without delay."[3] The NRDC and IFAW went to Japan, and were touched and surprised by the warmth of Japanese consumer support for their campaign. And they published an unimpeachable scientific statement that was endorsed by thirty-four of the world's most respected scientists, including nine Nobel Prize winners. It pointed out that this project would be "contrary to the principles and values that sanctuaries, biosphere reserves and World Heritage Sites were created to uphold."

Mitsubishi had published a rebuttal in an American newspaper, saying that its Ojo de Liebre saltworks north of the new site had "operated in harmony with nature for more than 40 years." They insisted that any decision on their new saltworks be "based on science," which would be independent of what they termed "the external considerations" of "judgments and values." No one had ever actually studied what was happening up north in remote Ojo de Liebre, and when the Mexican environmental department did, the first thing they discovered was nearly a hundred endangered sea turtles dead on the lagoon shores; subsequent legal suits uncovered 298 separate violations of Mexican environmental law at the saltworks. In 1999, the NRDC had enough steam behind it to call a boycott with the slogan: "Mitsubishi: Don't Buy It." They concentrated on California, and there, Mitsubishi car dealers and appliance salesmen suddenly began receiving irate e-mails. By October, fifteen global mutual funds handling billions in investments announced their refusal to buy Mitsubishi stock until the company abandoned the saltworks. Even the UN's World Heritage Committee released a report signaling deep concern for the whales and the site in general.

On March 2, 2000, then-Mexican President Zedillo announced that the government still deemed the project both economically and environmentally feasible, but nonetheless it was being canceled, and funds would be provided to help the people of the region find sustainable alternative livelihoods. It was an exciting moment for the campaigners. But although it was wonderful to save the world's last gray whale nursery, there really were some industrial values to consider. Given that human beings need salt to live, where would the 8 million tons a year that Mitsubishi was going to provide come from now? The answer, as it turns out, was that Mitsubishi wasn't mining salt to flavor corn on the cob. The San Ignacio saltworks would have given them the cheapest facility on earth for making one of the most egregious chemicals known, the primary hormone-disrupter implicated in the increasing numbers of little girls experiencing menarch at the age of eight, or little boys born with small or deformed penises: polyvinyl chlorides, or PVCs.

The salts recovered from the San Ignacio Lagoon would have been broken down to sodium hydroxide, then chloride, to make a substance that many companies are desperately trying to get out of their products to meet anti-pollution norms. At the costs that Mitsubishi expected to experience — with its many subsidies and tax rebates from its friends in the Mexican government, its lowered labor costs and its complete lack of responsibility for waste treatment or site clean-up — Mexico's share of the deal would not even have equaled what it spent to attract the industry in the first place. What Mitsubishi would have had, and what it probably doesn't need very desperately, is a profit of nearly twenty times the expenses it would have incurred in building the facility.

This story illustrates a simple fact about what is happening around the world. More and more people are trying to base their lives, not upon short-term monetary gain, but upon deeply held human values that transcend political borders. They are all part of a positive globalization movement. But the local co-op members are the ones who will have to make the greatest adjustments and sacrifices in their way of life if the lagoon is to remain pristine over the long term. The outsiders, the NGOs, the scientists, the supporters, even the movie stars, have realized that nobody can just come in and tell people dependent on a resource to stop using it without providing some economic alternatives. So the movement to save Laguna San Ignacio is not over, but just beginning.

These days, the co-op members are looking for more ways to lessen their impact on the ecosystem, and they're getting help from the people they met during the campaign. The NRDC, the University of Toronto and the Institute for Electricity Studies in Mexico are helping the fishworkers of San Ignacio free themselves from their dependency on diesel fuel. It was costing them $10,000 (U.S.) a month to buy gas and oil to power their desalinization and packing plants, as well as their boats and homes. They will now be using both wind and solar technologies that will reduce expenses and spare the environment, thanks to outside grants and expertise. They've also hired a water keeper from Long Island to help them raise oyster seed to increase the profitability of their current small oyster aquaculture business. They figure that spending less on fuel and having a sustainable oyster fishery will enable them to husband the abalone and lobster over a much longer period of time. In short, they're finding alternatives to our usual methods of extracting maximum amounts of resources at top speed; and they're still making a good living.

No one involved in the fight to save the whales of San Ignacio accepted the normal compromises that our current economic system demands. They didn't agree that their only choice was between jobs and the environment; they also didn't look for compromises that would have allowed "some" brine release and "acceptable" amounts of whale and lobster decline, in exchange for a few jobs. They looked to their deepest values, and never considered our twentieth-century economic paradigm's prime directive of money and jobs in the same breath as the long-term value of the whales and a functioning natural system. They showed their humility by mimicking nature the way forestry managers do at Collins Pine. By keeping their interference and extraction to a minimum, instead of a maximum, they are trying to make sure the natural system can go on taking care of whales, lobsters and antelope in the intricate and mysterious way it always has. They are already reaping the multiple rewards of living within the planet's physical laws; thousands of enjoyable, long-term jobs instead of hundreds of destructive ones, and surroundings that are the envy of every visitor. All stakeholders involved did this together. From German mutual fund investors and Japanese consumers to the environmental groups in northern cities and the co-op fishers of Punta Abreojos, everyone recognized that for the survival of the world at large, it is becoming increasingly dangerous to be bound by this rush to create cash that typifies the primary system of values that has been proliferating in our society since the First Industrial Revolution.

## The Value of Money

*Money is like an iron ring we've put through our noses. We've forgotten that we designed it, and now it's leading us around.*
— BERNARD LIETAER, BELGIAN CURRENCY EXPERT[4]

One of the reasons we've gotten into the habit of managing all our resources for the short-term, all across the planet, is that it pays a lot better. The rewards our economy gives to people for using up the planet's natural resources as quickly as possible have increased exponentially in the past two or three hundred years. If we want to try to figure out if that's a healthy trend, we have to understand how it developed. David Korten, now a well-known economic and business expert and author of the influential book *When Corporations Rule the World*, was posted to different parts of the world back in the fifties and sixties. His experiences working for the U.S. Agency for International Development and the Rockefeller and Ford

Foundations made him realize that most of us labor under a fundamental confusion about the very definition of what is valuable.

"Wealth," he says, "is something that has real value in terms of meeting our needs and fulfilling our wants: the natural productive systems of the planet and physical things like factories, homes, farms, stores, actual transportation and communications facilities, as well as the people who work to produce the goods and services that sustain us. Modern money is only a number on a piece of paper or an electronic trace in a computer, that by social convention gives its holder a claim on that real wealth. In our confusion, we've concentrated on the money, to the neglect of those things that actually sustain a good life."

In order to illustrate what he means, Korten suggests that we "think of a modern money economy as containing two related subsystems. One creates wealth," that is, it builds those factories, stores and farms, employs people and uses the extra production of nature in the form of plants, sunlight or water at the same rate that it can be renewed. This can be also termed living off of nature's interest while conserving its capital for future generations. "This is how people have lived on the planet for many centuries in the past," Korten says. "The other subsystem is money; a convenient mechanism for allocating wealth. In a healthy economy, the money system is a servant of wealth creation, allocating real capital to productive investment, and rewarding those who do productive work in relation to their contribution."

Korten points out that money should never be the only or even the dominant medium of exchange. "One of the most important indicators of economic health is the presence of an active economy of affection and reciprocity, in which people do a great many useful things for one another with no expectation of financial gain." Anyone who has ever spent time in poorer countries, in rural areas or in small towns knows exactly what this means. Korten adds, "Pathology enters the economic system when money, once convenient as a means of facilitating commerce, comes to define the life purpose of individuals and society." We can tell when a system has become pathological quite easily, he says. "When financial assets and transactions grow faster than growth in the output of real wealth, [that's] a strong indication that the global economy is getting sick."[5]

Bernard Lietaer, author of *The Future of Money* who also helped design the Euro, points out that "Today's official monetary system has almost nothing to do with real wealth. Just to give you an idea, 1995 statistics indicate that the volume of currency exchanged on the global level is $1.3

trillion U.S. per day. This is *thirty times* more than the daily gross domestic product (GDP) of all the developed countries of the world put together."[6] In other words, this money is almost fully decoupled from any measurable physical wealth. Lietaer adds, "Of all that volume, only 2 to 3 percent has to do with real trade or investment; the remainder takes place in the speculative global cyber-casino; currency trading and speculation, for example. This means that the real economy has become relegated to a mere frosting on the speculative cake, an exact reversal of how it was just two decades ago." One reason this happened is that during the Nixon administration the United States decoupled paper money from gold because they found pegging imaginary wealth to something physical was too limiting. Today, a few countries still maintain a 10 percent reserve of deposits, which prevents the banking system from creating more than 10 times as much currency; but as Korten says, "Today most money is created by borrowing. When a bank decides to grant a loan, they create that money out of nothing; but it still represents a claim on the real wealth of anyone who wasn't given a loan."

A given individual or corporate group, say, Bill Gates or Microsoft, can, under our current system, apply to a bank for a $2 billion loan for various kinds of business development. The bank grants the loan, which means they create that $2 billion out of thin air, and by social convention, agree that it is now in the hands of the corporation. So with that money, the corporation can go off to Saudi Arabia, Peru or even Saskatchewan or Indiana, and buy up mines, forests, factories — entire towns if they want — since they have a new money power against which the locals, who used to have tenure over such things, simply can't compete. This means, says Korten, that "increasingly, your money supply is being controlled by outsiders, by the banks. They're creating the money and they're taking the profits out of [a given] country or place, essentially for simply renting that money to some group or corporation when they made out the loan." To put it crudely, it's a system of pretend money. We make it up, then we give it to certain groups, like investment banks or dot-com start-ups, but not to others, like disabled children or unemployed fishermen. But there is no reason why we can't use the pretend money any way we want. Only real wealth is limited by reality.

We've known for a very long time that all the energy on this planet, and all true wealth, ultimately comes from our one energy source: the sun. Its calories are stored in plants, in animals, and in organic materials like oil and gas. We can take them out and spend them like interest on a bank investment, but if we use them faster than they can be replaced, faster, for example, than forests or crops or fish can grow, then we destroy the systems that produced them in the first place. This means that instead of living on the interest from that energy, we've begun to live off the capital. Many of the people who are assessing our core values and searching for a new way to manage the world understand that the fantasy economy we created based on "pretend" money is running up against the brick wall of a finite, physical world. The enormous disconnect between the rates at which we want to increase money and the rates at which true wealth can be produced is eating away the earth's capital, and therefore its ability to provide wealth, not just in a faraway future, but in an increasingly immediate one. Many people are trying to set up new systems of living on the planet that value the actual physical wealth that supports us. They use what they term a "holistic" approach, which looks at the entire context of society and wealth, and recognizes the fundamental difference between wealth and money. Not only does this system favor the wise use and increase of true wealth, it acknowledges something greater than both: the ancient cultural values of sharing, cooperating and seeking to live in harmony with natural law.

## The Second Industrial Revolution

*We will make sustainable use of renewable natural resources such as water, souls and forests. We will conserve nonrenewable resources through efficient use and careful planning.*
— NUMBER TWO OF THE CERES PRINCIPLES FOR BUSINESS[7]

Architect and designer Bill McDonough, the dean of architecture at the University of Virginia, will be heard from several times in this book. He is one of the many people who are re-examining the core values and beliefs of Western culture. He says that in the West we've now had two Industrial Revolutions. The first was about resource extraction and money. The second is happening now, and it's about resource conservation and values. McDonough says that if you were to articulate the First Industrial Revolution as a design assignment to a class of students, you'd have to say something like: "Please design a system that pollutes the soil, air and water; that measures productivity by how few people are working; that measures prosperity by how much natural capital you can dig up, bury, burn or otherwise destroy; that measures progress by the number of smokestacks you have; that requires thousands of complex regulations to keep people from killing themselves too quickly; that destroys biodiversity and cultural diversity; and that produces things that are so highly toxic they require thousands of generations maintaining constant vigil, while living in terror."[8]

This is undoubtedly not the system that the people working toward the First Industrial Revolution at the end of the eighteenth century meant to create, but it's a pretty good description of the one we got. McDonough says an industrial system is now being designed on the basis of a new paradigm, and he can describe how it will work: "The New Industrial Revolution introduces no hazardous materials into the ecosystem; it measures prosperity by how much natural capital is being accrued in productive ways; it measures productivity by how many people are gainfully and meaningfully employed; it measures progress by how many buildings have no smokestacks or dangerous effluents; it does not require regulations whose purpose is to prevent us from killing ourselves; it produces nothing that will require the vigilance of future generations; and it celebrates biological and cultural diversity and solar, not paper, income." It all sounds too good to be true; but he's far from being alone in this holistic goal. This is a description of the very revolution we discovered while researching this book, and it's taking place all around us. It marks a real, systemic change in every level of society, all over the world.

In our current system, we are typically required to make hard, "either-or" choices: a new factory and the jobs it will provide, or a clean river? Parks and bike trails to make a rundown neighborhood more livable, or a new hospital? Grazing land for ranchers or local tribes, or habitat for wolves and tigers? Or, as at San Ignacio, $80 million for the government and some jobs, or pristine habitat for some whales? We get very depressed when we notice that the immediate and human needs, particularly the economic ones, win out every time. The result has been, all over the world, dirtier rivers, lousier neighborhoods and dwindling numbers of wild animals, especially predators. These purely economic considerations — the bias to create factory jobs and manage nature for immediate, short-term benefit — have preoccupied us ever since the First Industrial Revolution, when we first began to slice nature into its component parts and to see it as a machine to be managed piecemeal for human use. We also came to view our survival in terms of money from jobs in manufacturing and technology, as opposed to our old, non-cash sources of wealth, like fish or apples.

It's true that throughout the long human past it has been insecure and frightening to depend entirely on nature's erratic bounty; but it's also no coincidence that we've done more damage to natural ecosystems in the past

200 years than we did in the preceding 100,000. So, given that we have managed to subdue nature quite effectively, the question people are asking themselves now is whether it might be possible to have some of *both*: a fair number of paying, secure jobs and industries *and* a decent base of natural systems to support them, instead of all one or all the other. This attempt to combine our technical gifts with our expanding knowledge of how the planet really works is what the Second Industrial Revolution is all about.

## Double Indemnities, Double Dividends

*Companies that pursue these natural principles are not only more profitable, they're more fun. All of a sudden they have intellectual challenges again, [and they're] rewarding employees who eliminate waste, empowering their workers to be responsible.*
— HUNTER LOVINS

We are used to the fact that the infrastructures that support First Industrial Revolution technologies, like developing harbor or airport facilities in the Third World, using chemicals in industrial agriculture, damming up rivers for power and irrigation purposes, building highways and so on, will need heavy outside investment. We assume such projects will require expensive technologies and machinery, and that they'll also need public funding in the form of subsidies, tax breaks, continuing grants and rebates. But in the New Industrial Revolution, we're learning that when something works in harmony with our planet's natural cycles and systems, it doesn't need such a heavy capital investment or constant artificial support. It also doesn't have hidden liabilities that dump pollution and energy costs on society at large, greatly increasing the original capital expenditure that has to be made by people who may not even share in the benefits. Most interesting of all, when technologies and practices work in concert with physical reality, they nearly always provide more than one benefit, as we will see again and again. Coming to a decision to save watercourses, for example, by raising hogs in a sustainable, organic manner, will not only prevent cancers and contamination in water, soil and meat. As we'll see in chapter five, it will also return pasture land to a greater state of diversity, enabling it to support greater numbers of animals, and it will provide a stable, long-term income for more people than our current mechanized industrial feeding operations can.

Our current system of meat and poultry production, run on the old industrial paradigm, has hidden pollution, water, transportation and labor costs. Big operations, for example, operate with a skeleton crew of perhaps four people in charge of producing 50,000 pigs a year: the pigs are overcrowded, undercared for and must be fed hormones and antibiotics in such an environment, or the overcrowding and stress will cause infections and keep them from eating properly. This causes a serious rise in costs for society, in terms of increased cancers and other diseases in a human population that ingests the hormones and antibiotics that are fed to the pigs. It also leads to the contamination of rural soil and watercourses by the high concentrations of manure and the undesirable chemicals in the manure. Almost none of the expenses such practices entail are reflected in the producers' costs or the final consumer price. That means, for example, that pork produced in eastern Canada and the United States, which is habitually sold overseas to Asian markets, is subsidized not just by national governments, but by cash-strapped rural taxpayers in Quebec, Alberta, North Carolina, Georgia or anywhere else there is a concentration of industrial hog farms. If the true costs were added, no producer could afford to shoulder them and continue to raise meat in such an environmentally damaging way. They would have to adapt existing, healthy methods that make the meat somewhat more expensive but a lot less dangerous, provide more rural jobs and have an actual moral base. This is just one example of the double indemnity/double dividend contrast between the two industrial revolutions that is so upsetting in the present but so encouraging for our future.

Conversely, many of the practices derived from First Industrial Revolution thinking — biologically engineered food crops, for example, which may at first seem to be revolutionary and progressive — on careful inspection turn out to have multiple indemnities. We found that this is one of the best ways to distinguish something truly sustainable from something that is not. As we will see in chapter five, genetically manipulated hybrid crops are delicate, and for optimum results need a strict regime that requires even more water than usual and carefully spaced doses of expensive pesticides, herbicides and fertilizers. Most of these crops are in fact unsuitable for many of the countries they are claimed to benefit, because they need such a high capital investment and because their use of chemicals destroys delicate tropical soils.[9]

Ironically, like so many other First Industrial Revolution technologies, biotech could not exist at all without billions of dollars of public money. Such technologies generally get enormous grants and gain access to publicly funded research at the development stage. They're given tax relief from factory construction on through subsidized fuel and national marketing support. They even benefit from the many international trade deals that favor the use of heavy industrial methods and which sometimes actually outlaw local seeds and agricultural practices. In fact, institutions like NAFTA and the WTO do everything in their power to help chemical companies like Dow and Monsanto transport and sell their seeds and industrial inputs around the world. As we describe in chapter five, if that tax money were used differently, agriculture would be not only safer and far cheaper to maintain over the long term; it would actually be more productive, and much more economically viable for local farmers.[10]

Besides providing double dividends and avoiding indemnities, the New Industrial Revolution mimics nature rather than basing its methodologies on man-made machines. Architect Bill McDonough says we need to ground ourselves in hard science, that is, in the measurable reality of how natural systems work on this planet, if we want to survive here. Earth itself, he says, "represents chemistry; and the sun, physics. When the two get together, an energy source is created — water and soil under the solar flux, creating a kind of photosynthetic energy cell." This physical/chemical energy generates plants and animals on the surface of the earth — what is termed "solar income" — in such incredible diversity and fecundity that it produces more than the overall system needs. Solar interest is the excess fruit that feeds massive numbers of insects, the birds that eat the excess insects, or the millions of fish fry that nourish other fish. That excess can be harvested by humans for food energy of various kinds without harming the ability of the solar system to keep on producing. But if we take one fish or tree species, for example, faster than it can reproduce its numbers, then we aren't living on solar interest, but on solar capital. We're depleting the capital we should be keeping in the "bank," which will produce the income needed to support our children in the future.

McDonough puts the second part of how to pattern our industries on nature, what is termed "biomimicry," very simply. He says, "waste is food." Whatever you can't use in any manufacturing or energy-creating industry has to go back into natural or industrial systems to feed them; otherwise it's proof you're losing part of your investment and are causing damage to natural systems. So, if we produce wastes like toxic chemicals or heavy metals that cannot be reabsorbed by natural systems as "food," like leaves or any other biodegradable material, then we're not only costing ourselves money by producing something we can't use; we're destroying the ability of the natural systems we dump the wastes on from producing other products for us in the future. Obviously, multiplied over space and time, this is a process humans cannot continue. The repercussions of the First Industrial Revolution system have become very dangerous to our long-term survival simply because it is living off too much solar capital instead of just solar interest.[11]

The Rocky Mountain Institute in Colorado is a remarkable think-tank that has spent the last thirty years grinding out the nuts and bolts of the New Industrial Revolution, the super-efficient light bulbs, solar panels and cars that are entering the mainstream market today. The Institute's founders, the lawyer/inventor team of Hunter and Amory Lovins we met back in chapter one, have been able to illustrate very clearly what they call the "diseconomies" of large scale energy, food and industrial production. By mimicking nature, which works in multiple ways on small, extremely varied scales, people like McDonough and the Lovinses have been able to evolve whole new technologies: ways to make cars and machinery that use silica and carbon, nature's non-toxic building materials, and more ways to use clean and renewable solar and hydrogen power.

The elimination of all wastes is a goal common to the people trying to attain social and economic sustainability. If waste isn't biodegradable, it will have to be recycled back into the industrial system, as we saw with the processes used by Interface Carpet. As we also saw in chapter one, this idea is not some far-off pipe dream; it is actually law in much of Europe. Since there is no such thing as waste in nature, there can be no such thing in sustainable industry and its production methods either. Examples of using waste as food abound in the chapters ahead. Most importantly, we have also learned to mimic where nature gets its energy in the first places, by going to the same sustainable sources — the wind and the sun.

The First Industrial Revolution not only "externalized" its many costs, like waste and pollution; it also attempted to deny any intrinsic connection between economics and human morality. The mechanistic method of manipulating the world was set in motion by Sir Isaac Newton almost three hundred years ago. He felt science should view the cosmos as a giant mechanical construct, and like a machine its parts should be isolated and examined one by one to be understood. Under Newtonian science, things were separated, not united; genes were separated from organisms, and values were excised from science. Concepts like morality, happiness and sharing were put into a box marked "ethics," and quickly came to be considered, like poisonous wastes and by-products, "externalities" to the more vital functions of economics and science. As science gradually attained an almost religious status in human society, those things lying outside it gradually lost their value. In the Western world especially, over time, the economy and the creation of money have been gradually elevated until, during the past few decades, they are now seen as being one of humanity's highest goals. And yet, this money value system has become a global force only recently. A revolution against it has developed very quickly, at least partly because mainstream science and economics do not reflect the latest findings of modern physics: that relationships between components are the key to understanding their functions, and that a whole is a great deal more than the sum of its parts. In short, as we learn to clone humans, insert the genetic make-up of animals, plants and viruses into one organism or create uncontrollable poisons like nuclear waste, many people are recognizing the fact that using science and economics outside the context of human values and ethics is becoming not just morally questionable but very dangerous to our survival.

In reality, values are not an externality to most people. We seem to need morality, ethics and spirituality as much as we need jobs and money. At any rate, we become unhappy and seriously disoriented without them. The practitioners of the Second Industrial Revolution realize that fact and always consider higher human aspirations as they develop ways to feed livestock or build cars. This is why they try to incorporate in their vision of long-term goals questions like: Are the jobs their industries provide both lasting and fulfilling? Are the animals they are raising enjoying their lives? Are the food they produce so pure and wholesome that the farmers are proud of it? And do the cities that boast high average incomes have it distributed equitably enough to be pleasant to live in? These are the values that underlie another recent phenomenon: hundreds of thousands of comfortable, middle-class Westerners risking tear gas, beatings and arrests in order to protest the monetary values and goals of mainstream economics.

## Withdrawing Consent

*Most economists simply have no tools for thinking about the issues people are out on the streets protesting. They think their institutions protect the market, and they think we have a market economy. They even think of the corporation as a market institution. But the global corporation is an instrument of monopoly capitalism, geared to defeating every one of the principles of a [true] market economy.*
— DAVID KORTEN

As Ari Hershowitz of the NRDC points out, "If our society no longer allows us to protect a place like San Ignacio, then nothing can be protected. If the promises all these governments have made to value such things aren't honored, what in heaven's name is?" It's a good question. Our current global value system has made it necessary for thousands of people to expend extraordinary amounts of energy, time and money to save something that was supposed to be massively protected from industrial development in the first place. And it might easily have been worse. Currently, under the laws of the NAFTA U.S./Mexico/Canada trade agreement, had Mitsubishi been an American or Canadian company, they could have sued the Mexican government for millions of dollars for the revenue they *would* have made if they hadn't been compelled to leave. And in that case, the government probably would have caved in. It's just a stroke of luck that the World Trade Organization, of which both Mexico and Japan are members, hasn't yet been able to push through its Multilateral Agreement on Investment (the temporarily derailed MAI), which would have permitted such corporate lawsuits against governments worldwide, instead of just between Canada, Mexico and the United States.

Even as things stand, the United States has been forced to abandon its efforts to protect endangered turtles from being caught in fishing nets. Simple and cheap turtle extruder nets were ruled a "restraint of trade" by the WTO after Mexico complained, which is why so many anti-globalization protesters dressed as turtles in Seattle. A ruling under the infamous Chapter 11 of NAFTA has forced Canada to add to all its gasoline a possibly harmful manganese additive manufactured by Ethyl Corporation, the same company that invented lead additives. Even though the additive is banned in most American states, the Canadian government has also been forced to pay Ethyl $13 million and make a public apology for the loss to their reputation suffered when the possible neurological problems associated with the product were openly discussed in federal Parliament. And most recently, a tiny town, Guadalcazar in the state of San Luis Potosi, Mexico, has been denied the right to zone against a toxic waste dump operated by the U.S. corporation Metalclad, on the grounds that their attempt to protect their children from dangerous chemicals is a breach of trade rules. They can ban the dump, of course, say the trade judges; but only if they find $16 million to compensate the company for all its present and future revenues.[12]

It is becoming clear that if the value system that has grown up in the shadow of the First Industrial Revolution continues to be humanity's main

goal, we will find it increasingly difficult to protect any of the basic require-
ments of civilized life. These trade rulings, as well as the lack of any
mechanism for democratic input into the treaties in the first place, are the
reasons why, in the late 1990s and early 2000s, so many people have risked
going out on the streets demanding that we start working towards other
goals. As one of the most vocal Canadian anti-globalization activists, Jaggi
Singh, says, "The gains we enjoy in the North, like public health care,
resource protection and education, are becoming illegal under our system of
trade rules. The agreements used to make them illegal don't use that word.
They say they are 'unfair trade practices,' they're 'trade barriers' or 'discrimination against foreign companies,' all words we don't want to be associated
with: discrimination, being unfair. The PR firms selling these agreements and
their ideology have been doing a great job of making them seem natural,
making them seem fair, making them seem logical. But of course there's
nothing logical about claiming that a community that wants to protect its
resources or assure equitable medical care is indulging in 'unfair trade.'"

Nearly all the exciting solutions we outlined in the introduction to this
book rely heavily on local, municipal, state or national organizations, laws
and agreements for their functioning and support. What everyone working
towards sustainability has to face at the outset is the fact that, as matters
stand, nearly every strategy or idea for a sustainable future that we can think
of can be overturned by the world trade agreements our governments have
already signed — NAFTA, the coming FTAA, the WTO, APEC and many
others. When people take the time to read them, if they look on the Internet
to see the appeals now being fought, they quickly understand what we
mean. They should also begin to realize why the sight of hundreds of thousands of people at trade negotiations barricades is itself another form
of very good news. It's a recent and remarkable development in the exercise
of democratic rights; but now, that good news is also threatened by the
specter of terrorism. Conservative and corporate influences in government
are increasingly equating patriotism with the enthusiastic acceptance of
a loss of civil liberties. The radical fundamentalist groups accused of the
terrorist attacks promote an extremely oppressive society that also does
not tolerate dissent. Bills such as C-38, which makes Western societies more
repressive and less democratic, may end up being not so much a hindrance
to terrorists as a way of helping them out.

The growing numbers of people joining the anti-globalization protests
are in danger of being accused of sympathy with terrorist goals; the irony, of

course, is that in many ways, freedom of dissent is the clearest antidote to terrorism. These protests began among disadvantaged people in the Third World; half a million poor Indians rallied to protest the precursor to the WTO, the Uruguay Round of the GATT, in 1993. Still more Mexican farmers turned out to protest the effects of NAFTA in Mexico City in 1999, and in Geneva back in 1998, thousands of increasingly middle-class anti–G-7 protesters were gassed from helicopters. The protests have spread so widely today that even the mainstream media has to admit that the huge majority of people attending them are normal, hard-working, non-violent people exercising their rights of assembly and free speech.

The 70,000 demonstrators in Seattle who stopped the millennium round of the WTO, the 20,000 in Washington who protested the World Bank and the IMF, the 50,000 in Quebec City and the amazing 150,000 in Genoa protesting the G-8, forced people like President Jacques Chirac of France to pay lip service to issues like democracy and poverty, forced the publication of the text of the FTAA, and got the big trade institutions to start talking about debt relief, cheaper pharmaceuticals for countries stricken by AIDS and help for starving women and children. In other words, dissent is beginning to force the democratization and humanization of the trade institutions — the exact opposite of the goal of a terrorist attack, which is confusion and the brutal polarization of opinion that supports retaliation.

The huge turn-outs for demonstrations and marches in the countries that have been the greatest beneficiaries of the values of the First Industrial Revolution also show that the fight against globalization is not a radical, fringe movement, but a public expression of dissent by ordinary people who simply do not agree with the way things are being valued at a basic, systemic level. Like the people who fought for the Laguna San Ignacio, these protesters are demanding not adjustments and mitigations, but real change. They recognize that our economic and science-based industrial system, which once seemed so exciting and liberating, has turned out to be unacceptably damaging to the natural systems we depend on for survival. It is now so all-encompassing that it threatens human freedom, happiness and basic social values. It has created a chasm between rich and poor, haves and have-nots, so wide that most analysts agree that the increasingly unfair distribution of global wealth and the continuing dependence upon oil as a fuel has been instrumental in leading to social destabilization, epitomized by the attacks on the World Trade Center.

The people we are meeting in this book, however, are trying to work out ways to defuse extreme feelings of disempowerment, as well as developing more long-term, independent sources of energy and real wealth for everyone.

## History Shows the Way

*[The Bretton Woods Institutions] were supposed to help national governments regulate trade in a way that would strengthen their domestic economies and maintain balance in the global system.*
— DAVID KORTEN

Few people, even those protesting in the streets, believe that we do not need some kind of global institutions that can oversee financial transactions, regulate trade and even trace corporate wrong-doing. It's the undemocratic way those institutions are set up, the lack of public input or accountability that has pushed people out on the barricades. Maude Barlow is the author of *Global Showdown* and head of the Council of Canadians, an NGO that has analyzed global trade policies since the 1980s. She points out that John Maynard Keynes, the brilliant architect of what is termed "the Bretton Woods Institutions" (named after the place where they were negotiated) set them up "to be threefold: the World Bank, the IMF and the ITO, the International Trade Organization. All of them were supposed to be democratically overseen by the UN, and all were supposed to regulate trade while incorporating all the basic UN covenants, [like] freedom of movement and assembly, housing, education, health and medical care, full and decent employment, membership in unions, asylum and so on."[13]

The ITO, in particular, would have been the trade watchdog of today's globalization protesters' dreams. "[It had] rules against dumping of commodities and toxins, rules to stop global monopolies, and provisions to put a stop to anti-competitive corporate practices. It would even have allowed a country to maintain its independence and expropriate the assets of a foreign company for reasons of national economic sovereignty, if this were necessary to maintain the goals of full employment and social security."[14] And it would all have been administered by democratically elected representatives who had to answer to an electorate.

However, as part of their war effort, the United States had built up the world's most highly industrialized infrastructure, producing more goods than they could possibly consume, even more than could be absorbed by a recovering Europe. The threat of communism was very vivid in the national consciousness, along with the fear of yet another war, if the industrial machine could not keep humming, creating jobs. An ideology took hold which, fifty years later, was termed "the Washington Consensus." It was a kind of economic monotheism, a belief that neo-liberal market economics ("neo" because they go back to the liberalization theories of *laissez-faire* capitalism that brought widespread social unrest back in the early nineteenth century) should be the economic model for all countries, regardless of resources, history or culture. A certain amount of nobility, as well as profit, lay in making sure this belief system spread all around the world. Under intense pressure from the United States, therefore, and without a General Assembly vote, says Barlow, "the U.S. killed the ITO in a single Council vote, creating the GATT (General Agreement on Tariffs and Trade) in its place, and it then removed all three [Institutions] from UN control, basically making them arms of the U.S. Treasury Board." Today, the only trade body that is democratically run, is transparent and which tries to adhere to a code of labor, social and environmental ethics, is the European Union. But APEC, NAFTA, the Asian Development Bank, the FTAA and of course the IMF, the World Bank and the WTO, operate much differently than John Maynard Keynes intended.

To most people, official descriptions of these institutions sound much more like John Maynard Keynes's vision of a true market economy than the unequal and undemocratic institutions they actually are. For these reasons, many defenders of the present system are perplexed and offended to see that so many people want to change it. They accuse the protesters of being uninformed or confused, and think they are people who want to return to a lost era of "separation, localization, and relentless autarky," in the words of the Nobel Prize–winning economist Amartya Sen. David Korten says, "Even somebody with the credentials of Dr. Sen clearly hasn't a clue. He seems to think that those who are out on the streets are against trade, against communication, against the exchange of culture and ideas; which is absurd. These are among the most internationalist people on the planet."

### We Are in Serious Trouble
*(Placard carried by a young protester, Seattle, 1999)*

> *I think humanity is generally good, and capable*
> *of tremendous good.*
> — JAGGI SINGH, ANTI-GLOBALIZATION ACTIVIST

Canada's pre-eminent anti-globalization figure is Jaggi Singh, a twenty-eight-year-old activist with a soft-spoken, self-deprecating manner and a dry sense of humor. He currently faces trial in Canadian federal court, accused of inciting a crowd to riot, and is one of the first test cases for the tightening of Canadian civil liberties following September 11. He contends that he should have the names or at least the identification numbers of the plain-clothes police who grabbed him in the spring of 2001 in Montreal and who later, in Quebec City, kidnapped him, spiriting him away in an unmarked van in front of a shocked crowd. The Crown contends that his right as a citizen to be able to identify the police would "compromise national security."[15]

Are Singh and his fellow activists really a danger to their fellow citizens, conspiring to bring back the bygone days of local isolationism and violent socialist revolution? Not according to him. He explains in his quick voice that what he's involved in is a revolution to create, not the old goals of a different means of production or ownership, but "a new system of values." "I think our movement has values," he says, "of solidarity, mutual aid, direct, participatory democracy, self-determination on a group and an individual level, respect for ecology and the environment, and that we're trying to develop systems that live by those values." By contrast, he says, "Our current system's values are based on greed, on profit, on competition. A friend of mine likes to say it's a society that 'looks like Disney, tastes like Coke and smells like shit.' It's superficial, it's crass, it's depressing — but it presents itself as new and exciting."

Like so many people in this book, including the activists who saved the whales of San Ignacio, Singh and his friends try to keep their eyes on the prize. An equitable and democratic society with no daily compromises of a "little bit" of corruption, a "low level" of toxins, a "few" badly paid workers — that's what they're aiming for. Singh and the vast majority of his fellow protesters aim for the highest ideals and are resolutely non-violent — ready to put their own bodies on the line, but no one else's. They do, however, believe in a diversity of approaches. "We have to use popular education," he says. "We have to use protest, we have to use creative interventions like theater, we have to use the threat of a positive example; but we also have to use the threat of threats, of people confronting power and getting in the way and challenging authority by marching in rich areas or outside conventions and making people uncomfortable. There's a whole toolbox, a friend of mine likes to say, of struggle, and you have to use all those means. Everyone gets reached in different ways."

In fact, violent aggression is not much use to activists like Singh, and they know it. They know they can't rely on physical power and that their real strength lies in their numbers. The more of them there are, the less a government can claim it represents its people; and the more they stick together, the less the authorities can pick out and isolate "radicals" like Jaggi for special treatment. It's often been said that we consent to what our leaders do through our silence and inaction. Mass action and a certain amount of noise can withdraw that consent. The simple, historical fact is that, from Sukarno to Marcos, and from Pol Pot to the Soviet Bloc, the biggest, toughest despots on earth have crumbled in the face of sustained, mass civil disobedience. Political analyst and columnist Gwynne Dyer notes that "the tactics that are required to protect the summits have become so large and politically embarrassing that they are simply not worth it any more."[16] They are politically embarrassing because they are public illustrations of a mass withdrawal of consent.

At first, anti-globalization protesters focused on defending the rights of the poor and dispossessed far away, in Third World countries. But these days, they've realized that by fighting for the rights of Chiapas farmers or Bolivian peasants they're also fighting for their own rights to education, health, protection at work and a clean environment. First Industrial Revolution values, which elevate the free movement of capital and the right of large corporations to make money above virtually anything else, can now, through the Bretton Woods Institutions, be enforced, with economic or even physical sanctions. This means that human values of almost any description have become so degraded that the line that previously kept poor, brown people separate from middle-class, white people is beginning to blur. It also means that for the first time, on the human level, those two groups are beginning to understand each other very deeply — and to unite.

## It Can't Happen Here

*As we rush to enter the race to the bottom in a globally competitive world, it is sobering to keep in mind just how deep the bottom is.*
— DAVID KORTEN[17]

The poor countries of the world, who complain vociferously about World Bank policies and IMF structural adjustment programs that gut their civil and social services and destabilize their governments, are a large part of the reason why world financial and trade organizations are under public scrutiny. Countries like Canada are supposedly the winners in the current value system, certainly in comparison to the Third World. But it's interesting to discover how much rich white people are beginning to have in common with poor brown ones. Canadians started to get the feel of their country's entry into the world of the globalized economic system in 1995. That was the year Liberal Paul Martin became finance minister, brought to office in a massive electoral swerve from the right to the moderate left. Canadians were disappointed and confused, however, to find that the policies of their new Liberal government were no different from those of the Conservatives, against whom they had voted so massively that their party had virtually collapsed. Partly to find out why, several Canadian NGOs fought for years to get IMF documents released into the public domain under the Access to Information Act. They succeeded in 2000. The documents make interesting reading.

Like Bolivia and many other developing countries, including Brazil, Mexico, Thailand and India, the Canadian government had been encouraged by economic experts in the late 1970s and early 1980s to borrow large amounts of money from international financiers for the same kinds of infrastructure and industrial development projects that looked so good to the poorer nations. When Canada discovered it couldn't pay the money back any more than Mexico or Thailand could, the IMF turned up to collect the money that had been created by the lenders. What happened next is an important illustration of how universal political, social and ethical values stand up against those of the First Industrial Revolution. Assets that are normally prized as good signs in a nation's population — large numbers of people attending post-secondary school, government-supported access to health care, reliable agencies for testing food and product safety, environmental protection, objective and local news sources, affordable national transport — have gradually, under the value system of the First Industrial Revolution, become evils to be purged from society.

There are many pages marked "secret" in Article IV of the IMF's "Consultation with Canada" of 1995. In one such section, entitled "Areas of Adjustment," the IMF stated, "While total Canadian outlays for health are well below those in the United States as a share of GDP, they exceed spending levels in other OECD countries. Cuts in EPF-Health transfers to the provinces could encourage greater efficiencies or cost recovery in the health sector." In terms of education, the IMF felt that "Canada's spending on post-secondary education as a share of GDP is the highest among OECD countries, and enrollment also appears to be among the highest. In this light, federal transfers could be reduced in order to encourage a more efficient use of education resources." The IMF even suggested an alternative way to encourage post-secondary education through interest-bearing student loans.

The IMF also recommended curtailing Canada's journalistic ability to maintain its cultural identity and to analyze government policy. "Subsidies to Crown corporations are large, and may be difficult to justify on efficiency or other grounds. Cuts could involve eliminating regional programming and other television services by the CBC; eliminating transfers to VIA Rail and the CMHC, the National Film Board, the Canadian Film Development Corporation." As for allocating funds to government bodies to do scientific research on the safety of food or the state of fisheries, the IMF declared, "In many areas, there may be a *limited need for an extensive federal regulatory or supervisory presence*. Such areas include agricultural policy . . . natural resource policy, Indian and Inuit affairs, social policies, fisheries and industry. In addition, federal funding for research is extensive; besides the research conducted within the natural resource-related government departments . . . there would seem to be scope for rationalizing these services, *with a view to increasing the private sector's responsibility for such activity*" (italics ours). The administration of the town water supply in Walkerton, Ontario, in the late 1990s, as we shall see ahead, is one example of an IMF-inspired private/public partnership for maintaining government safety standards.[18]

Despite the civil language that makes these points sound like suggestions, they came, after all, from the most powerful enforcer of the collective value system. Martin seems to have taken each one seriously. In absolutely no time, transfer payments for health and education dried up; federal and provincial scientific laboratories and regulatory agencies were downsized, many of them right out of existence; rail service became moribund; hospital emergency rooms overflowed; and gym, music and art instruction were phased out of schools. The very rich, especially the corporations, now pay much lower taxes. Martin was particularly good at getting rid of high enrollment in post-secondary education, instituting a crippling system of student loans; and Ontario, as well as other provinces, was compelled by staff and budget cuts to use private companies to keep track, rather badly as it turns out, of the quality of the human water and food supplies.

When we see documents like the IMF Consultation with Canada, the almost inescapable conclusion is that elected officials, even in prosperous First World countries like Canada, have become enforcers for the decisions of trade and business institutions like the World Bank and the IMF. This fact seems different from what happens in the Third World only because it is masked by greater general prosperity. International trade groups, as well as private business corporations, are now openly intervening in all our local and national political decisions. In a way, it's a kind of political coup, but we can't escape the fact that we have acquiesced to it, through our mass decision to elevate money and its constant increase to the rank of our highest social value.

Today, however, a more thorough analysis of that decision is beginning to emerge and there is a good deal of public controversy, asking trenchant questions such as: Just how badly did we need to pay that "national debt" back? Who should have taken responsibility for lending? And especially, are GDPs and balanced budgets the best ways to measure a country's well-being? As we'll see in chapter nine, there are still societies on earth that judge progress not by how much is bought and sold, but by levels of child mortality or literacy rates. Many groups are now trying to decide if perhaps we should be measuring the health of ecosystems and the state of our biological capital more carefully than we do the growth of bank-created, inedible cash. Such discussions are raging on the Internet, in the alternative media and at major conferences around the world. They are especially prevalent at the demonstrations and protests of the anti-globalization movement and in its spontaneous consensus-building outside the halls of the big trade and finance meetings.

## Changing the Inevitable

> *Even the smallest municipal councils aren't allowed to meet in a quorum without a public announcement and media access. This means that all those important IMF, World Bank and WTO meetings that you hear about would be illegal in your hometown, for fundamental democratic reasons.*
>
> — BOB NAIMAN, THE CENTER FOR ECONOMIC POLICY AND RESEARCH

The form that democracy has taken around the world, but especially in North America, was developed over 300 years ago by aristocratic, landed gentlemen who were profoundly suspicious of majority rule. They therefore adopted not direct democracy, the kind that is practiced in New England meeting houses and traditional aboriginal villages, but "representational democracy," where people vote for one leader who will, in theory, represent their interests at central meetings. Even direct types of democracy need to use representation in some form because of the practical difficulties of having too many people in the same room all trying to talk at once, or transporting them over distances. Representational democracy, however, not only exposes the lone representative to the many temptations and pressures at the centers of power, it encourages the electorate to think they've done their civic duty simply by going out and voting for someone every few years.

Like the idea of a "free market," we've started to forget that the word "democracy" means "self-governing by the people." Self-government means that crucial decisions are not just turned over to a representative, who is kept accountable only by the threat of withdrawal of power years later; it means that large numbers of people need to get involved in each decision. And now that we have workable forms of mass communication and don't all have to be transported to Paris, Washington or Bogota to be heard, maybe we can aspire to more direct involvement. For example, some people worry about global warming, while others buy SUVs. If both were to get involved in municipal, state and national decisions about what subsidies are currently supporting such vehicles and what their full costs actually are in terms of health and environmental degradation, methods such as carefully monitored plebiscites could be found to fairly license or tax such technologies. But if all we can do is send one representative off to a faraway capital to deal with the rich and powerful lobby wolves, we'll get exactly what we have now — a system that is very seriously corrupted by money and private interests.

The activists who not only show up on the streets but build the puppets and organize the teach-ins and soup kitchens at anti-globalization protests understand these issues extremely well. In many respects, the way they are conducting themselves in the context of chaos and tear gas is even more revolutionary than the goals they're pursuing. When we were in Washington D.C. for the IMF/World Bank protest in April 2000, we went to an all-night meeting of "affinity groups," the little corps of volunteers who do not direct, but rather set the tone of the protests. They are composed mostly of young people under thirty, with about 30 percent in their thirties and forties, and a noticeable number of gray-haired folks as well. Their meeting was held in a church hall in a poor and remote black neighborhood, the only shelter that hadn't either rejected them or been seized by police.

At least 400 people attended. Their affinity groups had been previously formed, but new groups were added that night. Because of the dangers of injury and arrest, people were urged to join with at least five or six others so they could keep track of one another. A number of people in each group volunteered for the possibility of arrest, to undertake activities like blocking highways or intersections, locking down and refusing to move. Others did not. They chose to participate in less confrontational activities and to remain at liberty not only for personal reasons, but so that help could be found for any jailed or injured group members. Each group sent up one member to speak for them in a central circle, right under their electorate's watchful eye. Interminable discussions took place. Everyone was granted equal time and consideration whether they had a strategy for keeping the delegates locked up in their hotels or whether they wanted to work out the details of a puppet fair at the other end of town.

As the hours went by, people became very tired; they'd been gassed and had been marching all day, with worse to come in the morning. But they didn't leave. They were trying to reach a consensus, one of the most painful processes ever invented by humans. Some of the suggestions were ridiculous; some were brilliant. Each suggestion was discussed at length, then a vote was taken on each point. It was excruciatingly time-consuming and often boring. It would have been much more efficient to organize the way the opposition does, hierarchically, with underlings executing the decisions of expert strategists. But it was clear that the activists knew that to conduct themselves in that way would negate the entire purpose of the protest. They were learning how to do things democratically; they know they can't condemn those who are not democratic if they aren't themselves willing to put that system to the test of constant use. A young woman who used to be in the Canadian Armed Forces said that at first she thought the inefficiency of this type of organization would drive her crazy. She also thought it was too open, making little attempt to keep secrets from the many infiltrators assumed to be in the audience. But secrets are the antithesis of democracy and are one of the major evils the protesters object to in the trade organizations; so activists avoid them if humanly possible.

By the time consensus was reached at about three in the morning, there was barely time for any sleep before putting the various blockade strategies into effect. But everyone had a clear idea of what they were going to do. So, despite the lack of leaders or formal plans, the next day the groups did a surprisingly effective job of blocking the meetings, frustrating the police and getting arrested in sufficient numbers to make their point. The protesters' confrontation and arrest strategy is not grandstanding; it's a Gandhian tactic, a frightening one that not everyone wants to try. But the activists know that confrontation forces the media to discuss the issue, or to at least take note of its existence. And getting the police to arrest or attack without attacking back enables the protesters to illustrate their non-cooperation, their act of withdrawing consent.

They use passive resistance, by and large. Even throwing back tear gas canisters, as protesters did in Quebec City, was a defensive act; the police were so padded, helmeted and armored it was difficult to imagine them getting hurt, whereas the protesters without masks were often injured and had to constantly withdraw to recover. But of course protesters can hurt police. In a recent race riot in England, violent protesters hit at least one armored policeman in the face with flaming Molotov cocktails, and several officers went to hospital. It's the general absence of such techniques that marks this movement as non-violent; its participants' willingness to be gassed, clubbed or arrested, together with the great rarity of any serious physical aggression against the police. Eight hundred people were arrested in Washington and 1,000 of the 7,000 protesters in Prague went to jail. In Quebec City, 50,000 people, not to mention thousands of innocent inhabitants, were gassed — and nowhere were any police hurt. Even the single death of an aggressive protester in Genoa, one out of nearly 200,000 people on the streets, could have been avoided if the police had used rubber bullets or not aimed at his head.

We don't want to give the impression that rallies and demonstrations are the only way to work for change, because in fact they are a means of last resort. Most people only use them when they feel that every other option for democratic input has been blocked. The reasons most countries tolerate them as much as they do is that, under regimes where the freedom to demonstrate is banned, people have absolutely no outlet, no way to express their desire to be heard or to have some say about how they will live their lives. And without the relatively peaceful outlet of the protest march, the desire to be heard can reach a boiling point. Even in the West, the people who take part in public protests spend most of their time working at regular jobs and would never be at a march, risking injury or arrest, if they thought that their elected representatives were responding appropriately to the issues they care about.

If we compare these relatively orderly and non-violent events to the terrorist attacks on Washington D.C. and New York City, it is clear that the anti-globalization protests do not intend to cause serious social disruption. They are not secret or sprung on anyone; they are held during financial organization meetings in order to illustrate a democratic withdrawal of consent. Even in the face of a militaristic response, the demonstrators on these occasions are making a democratic point, and the authorities know it — which is why they are tolerated at all. The good news is that by exercising their rights of freedom of speech, assembly and dissent, these hundreds of thousands of ordinary people are making sure that those rights aren't lost. Their sheer numbers make it clear that a mass refusal of global economic values is underway. Moreover, considering the size of the anti-globalization crowds and their passion about the issues, to say nothing of intimidation and repression from authorities, there has been very little real violence or social disruption at these events. Within a few days after a meeting, everything is back to normal, even in Genoa and Quebec.

But in fact, the mass withdrawal of consent does not have to be done on the streets in the context of protests and demonstrations. All around the world, people are finding ways to craft a new kind of value system, even from deep within the existing paradigm. People who live in the belly of the beast are also fighting back; they, too, are actively creating new kinds of financial institutions with new rules. They are quietly revolutionizing the economies of entire countries. The lessons they're learning are already out there, success stories in the real world, and they prove that our monolithic economic structure is beginning to develop some cracks. In fact, entire countries are figuring out how to withdraw consent.

## The Definition of Hope

*We have come to a point where the courage of exceptional individuals won't suffice; we now need humanity as a whole to become heroic.*
— ED AYRES[19]

In the late 1990s, when the country of Malaysia found itself in a similar but more desperate situation than Canada's, and it was its turn to have the IMF come in to impose structural adjustment policies, it shrank from the kind of crippling leverage that was destroying lives and the entire economic base of other Asian "Tigers" like Korea and Thailand. So it took a cue from Nancy Reagan, and just said "No." Rather than allow the World Bank and the IMF to sell off nationally owned institutions, impoverish the middle class overnight, cut back social services and destroy millions of jobs, Malaysia did something no other country has ever had the nerve to do. It defied the Bretton Woods Institutions and the world economic order, and withdrew from the international market.

Malaysia wanted to institute capital controls on its money, to prevent the kind of speculation that had caused the Asian crisis in the first place. With capital controls, a country can retain a hold on its own currency; India, China and Chile still have them. They limit the amount of money that can be taken out of the country or be converted to other currencies in order to control speculation, the kind of casino maneuvers that have led to the separation of our money exchanges from actual wealth and productivity. T. Rajamoorthy, a Malaysian lawyer and student of the IMF, points out that when it was founded, "the IMF actually fostered and encouraged capital controls," but that over the past few years, agreeing to allow free speculation on one's currency has become "one of the prerequisites for IMF membership."[20]

Capital controls and public deficit spending — the kind of policies FDR instituted in the United States following the Great Depression — were both primary tools of Keynesian economics. Malaysia applied them both. Rajamoorthy says that "There was veritable hysteria in the centers of economic orthodoxy . . . The idea that in a world in which neo-liberalism was triumphant, a country which had been a model of an open economy would resort to economic measures which were supposed to have been consigned to the Dark Ages of economic history, was simply unacceptable." But it wasn't long before even World Bank economists had to admit that this radical strategy seemed to be working. In the rest of Asia, people's savings evaporated as their currency was deserted by speculators. Huge sell-offs of nationally owned institutions drained even more wealth away into corporate coffers. In human terms, 34 million people descended from the struggling middle class to desperate poverty because of an economic crisis that most analysts now agree was both caused and bungled by the global financial institutions.

In Malaysia, none of this happened, and the country recovered from the crisis far ahead of anyone else, even in mainstream economic terms. They didn't even lose foreign investment; industry liked their capital controls, because they knew what to expect. Most importantly, Rajamoorthy says, unlike the other Asian Tigers and Canada, they were able to preserve their local sovereignty; they "did not have to open up important sectors of their economy to foreign capital, as Korea and Thailand did under the IMF bailout plans." Even the UN, in its latest Trade and Development report, supports the Malaysian action, and suggests that other countries should take note and make "capital controls . . . an essential part of their economic armory." In other words, even a small, developing country like Malaysia can change the nature of the world economic game.[21]

These huge economic entities may at first seem untouchable, but withdrawing consent works on other levels besides protests and governments. Merely by taxing all speculative investment by a tiny amount (about 0.05 percent), nation-states would have a powerful tool to control speculative currency attacks, curb tax evasion and money laundering, and provide funds for every pressing issue from hunger control to ecosystem restoration. The idea, called the Tobin Tax after its originator, Nobel Prize-winning economist James Tobin, has spread like wildfire across the world. Unable to fault it on moral or legal grounds, the world's governing international trade institutions declared it impracticable, and the IMF even hired one of their own economists, Rodney Schmidt, a former advisor to Paul Martin at the Canadian Treasury, to show how unwieldy it would be. Schmidt discovered that by using electronic names it would be very easy to impose a Tobin Tax on the currency market. When the IMF attempted to suppress Schmidt's report, he rather heroically quit his job and put his plan on the Internet; the address is at the back of this book.[22]

The Tobin Tax idea is so popular that hundreds of NGOs have sprung up in the past year or two to promote it; almost every country in the world now has grassroots organizations such as England's War on Want, Canada's Tobin Tax Initiative, the U.S. Center for Environmental Economic Development's (CEED's) Tobin Tax Initiative and France's ATTAC, pressuring for controls on speculation and cyber-investment. ATTAC, for instance, which stands for "Association for the Taxation of Financial Transactions in the Aid of Citizens," attracted over a half-million dues-paying members in less than a year of existence! Moreover, nearly a sixth of all European Union representatives have joined almost 400 other elected parliamentarians from twenty-one countries around the world in signing a statement that states baldly, "Freely circulating and unregulated capital destabilizes democracy. This is why regulatory mechanisms are necessary." And that's just the tip of the iceberg regarding what's happening on government and international levels.

## You Say You Want a Revolution?

*What if our economy were organized not around the lifeless abstractions of neoclassical economics and accountancy but around the biological realities of nature?*
— PAUL HAWKEN [23]

Paul Hawken, former mainstream entrepreneur, founder of the gardening company Smith & Hawken and author of *Natural Capitalism* and *The Ecology of Commerce*, says that what's most exciting about the great variety of groups involved in this Second Industrial Revolution is the fact that "they agree, to an unprecedented extent, on an extremely similar vision of the future." Hawken points out that that one of the most remarkable developments of the late twentieth century is the sudden appearance of "hundreds of thousands of non-government organizations (NGOs), which have spontaneously arisen in just the past few years. These organizations address everything from social justice and population to corporate and electoral reform, environmental sustainability and renewable energy." Hawken notes that "they also conform to both of Gandhi's imperatives: some resist, while others create new structures, patterns and means." Most of them are "marginal, poorly funded and overworked," he says, and "it's hard for them not to feel that they could perish in a twinkling. At the same time, there's a deeper pattern that is extraordinary": they are striving for consensus.[24]

The NGOs Hawken is talking about keep in touch on the Internet, by phone and at meetings all around the world. They work at the local, state and international levels, and they're all groping towards a vision of a truly sustainable world. They're writing down their ideas, says Hawken, "creating conventions, declarations, lists of principles and frameworks that are remarkably in accord." He mentions the CERES Principles, The Natural Step, Agenda 21, the United Nations Charter on Human Rights, the World Charter and scores more, several of which we'll talk about in greater detail. But most important, according to Hawken, is his realization that "never before in history have independent groups from all around the world derived frameworks of knowledge that are [so] utterly consonant and in agreement. It is not that they are the same; it is that they do not conflict. This has never happened in politics, in religion, in psychology; not ever."

Besides writing books that have changed the social and environmental focus of many large companies, Hawken brought The Natural Step to North America. This ingenious system sets up four simple conditions that have to be met if a society is to achieve environmental health and sustainability. The fourth condition, Hawken says, is the one that causes his mostly corporate audiences to balk, and underlines the difference between their attitudes and those of the activists working for a new industrial revolution: "Without social justice and fair and equitable distribution of resources, there can be no such thing as sustainability." Hawken says, "One of the most humorous aspects of teaching The Natural Step in corporations is that when you come to the Fourth System Condition . . . business people go ballistic. They think it's socialist, communist, the nose of the leftist camel slipping under the tent. Some are literally repulsed by it. We are in a country that was founded on 'liberty and justice for all' and if you raise that issue in the business community, some executives will fall off their chairs."

Hawken says he sometimes asks the people who reject the notion of social justice whether they believe in inequality and unfairness. He says they protest just as vehemently. So he tried to figure out how to find out what people really believe, or if human values and goals have really become twisted on a deep, personal level. One of his friends devised a workshop, the kind of event that's popular at management conventions and get-aways. His exercise was a one-day course in sustainability for the middle management of a powerful and unpopular multinational chemical company. Since they were operating firmly within the First Industrial Revolution paradigm, these people were not only making their livings manufacturing poisons that are proven carcinogens; they were working with all their might to convince other people their poisons are safe. Moreover, as Hawken says, they had "already rejected the Fourth System Condition about social justice and resource equity." Hawken's friend told them to break up into five groups; each one had to design a spaceship that would leave the Earth for a long voyage and bring its inhabitants back, "alive, happy and healthy," a hundred years later. At the end, they would vote on whose spaceship everyone would want to travel on, and that would be the winning group.

Hawken says, "Being engineers they loved the challenge, and the winning spaceship was brilliantly designed. Now bear in mind, this company makes pesticides and herbicides, things that kill life. On the winning spaceship, they decided that they needed insects, so they determined that they could have no pesticides [on board]. They also decided that weeds were important in a healthy ecosystem, and banned herbicides also. Their food system, in other words, was totally organic. This group of engineers and MBAs also decided that they needed lots of singers, dancers, artists and storytellers, because CDs and videos would get old and boring fast, and engineers alone did not a village make. There were many other things, but two were most interesting. One, they decided that not one of the products they made [their livings at manufacturing] on earth would be useful or welcome on this spaceship. And, at the end, they were asked if it would be okay if just 20 percent of the people on the spaceship controlled 80 percent of the resources on board. They immediately and vociferously rejected that notion as unworkable, unjust and unfair. And then they realized what they had said." In short, as Hawken concludes, "In small groups, with appropriate goals and challenges, we all know the right things to do. As a society within the world of corporate capitalism, we are not very bright."

Over the hundreds of thousands of years we've been on this planet, human beings have developed many values and many ways to live. The current paradigm of globalized capitalism directed by multinational corporations, which has grown naturally out of the precepts of the First Industrial Revolution, has spread like a proselytizing religion throughout the world. It has assumed that its concept of values (money) and lifestyle (ever-increasing security and luxury) is the best, and that people will all be better off and happier if they adopt them. But like many such dogmas, it has some fatal flaws. One is a misunderstanding of the planet's physical laws; the finite amount of air, water and soil on this planet means that it is able to supply only so much luxury and security to our growing numbers of humans, before these material comforts run out and people have to share or die off. Another flaw is its inability to step outside itself, like the chemical engineers on their pretend spaceship, and ask if this is how we really want to live — its failure to realize we do have many other choices.

The word "hope" does not necessarily mean feeling reassured that all is well. Hope is more like figuring out, from a very black pit, where the ladder to the far-away light at the top is. It's coming to a realistic understanding of how things really work, so that we finally know what we're dealing with, and therefore where to begin. In that sense, hope is here and then some;

the world is full of it, and so is this book. For possibly the first time in history, millions of people, all over the planet, are coming to the same conclusions, at the same time, about what constitutes long-term human happiness, widespread justice and equality, and real sustainability. They have come to a mass agreement that human activities cannot be separated from nature, and are trying to work out a system of living that is not destructive to the natural systems we depend on for survival. And they are even enjoying significant successes — inventing sustainable technologies, saving places like Laguna San Ignacio, rallying against the WTO and the IMF.

Energy is flowing out of every level of human organization, from government offices to neighborhood grocery stores. Even on the individual family level, parents are questioning the kind of economic structure that funnels their children into schematized, highly competitive schools, then spits them out to work in Dilbert-style cubicles for huge corporations that sap their spirits and don't even provide economic security. As we'll see in chapter nine, in some schools people are not just fiddling with curricula but are trying to make real systemic educational changes. They're not only creating new kinds of jobs, but also figuring out how to help young people aim for different kinds of life accomplishments. In the chapters ahead that deal with the practicalities of learning to manage our natural systems sustainably, we'll meet more people working on ways to resist what we don't want to have and build up what we do. We'll talk about the difficulties they face, as well as the triumphs; we'll analyze the complexities of the issues, as well as their fundamental simplicity. We'll even tell you how to get involved.

# CHAPTER 3

# USING COYOTES TO GROW GRASS
## Restoring Biodiversity

### Forever Wild

> *Alewives [are] in such multitudes as is almost incredible, pressing up such shallow waters as will scarce permit them to swim . . . If I should tell you how some have killed a hundred geese in a week, fifty ducks at a shot, forty teals at another, it may be counted impossible, though nothing more true!*
> — WILLIAM WOOD, NEW ENGLAND, 1630

> *We have hardly any wild animals remaining besides a few small species of no consequence except for their fur.*
> — TIMOTHY DWIGHT, NEW ENGLAND, 1801[1]

Two authors have collaborated on this book. As it happens, our homes are almost on opposite sides of the North American continent. The coast of British Columbia, where David lives, is envied all over the world for its wild diversity and untouched natural beauty. Its lush, temperate rain forests shelter eagles and bears; its glittering rivers are filled with salmon and trout; its coastal tidepools and clear waters support marine creatures from kelp and starfish to seals and whales. Many battles are being fought right now over the great wealth these resources represent, as timber companies, fishers, tourists and developers all claim the right to exploit its increasingly rare bounty. On the other hand, the opposite side of Canada, where Holly lives, is known for very different qualities. It has been thickly settled and exploited by humans for over 300 years. It is characterized by busy, industrialized cities, from Montreal and Albany down to the megalopolis of New York. Here, the battle between natural diversity and economic development has already been fought, and to a remarkable extent it has arguably been won by — of all things — the forces of conservation.

Holly Dressel's old dairy farm on the Quebec–New York border, only an hour out of downtown Montreal, is witness to this paradox. It includes more than the usual farm buildings, woodland, pasture and hay fields. It also supports two families of beavers, a pack of coyotes, a herd of deer, a flock of wild turkeys, dozens of nesting ducks and geese, hawks, owls, over-wintering herons, foxes, fishers and mink, as well as skunks, porcupines, raccoons, dormice and the occasional visiting bear or wolf. Even a cougar was seen basking by a road only four miles away. This twenty-first-century miracle of biological diversity has occurred largely because the farm benefits from an overflow of flora and fauna from the Adirondack Park and Forest Preserve: the world's first concerted governmental effort to preserve a natural ecosystem within the context of intense human activity.

The Adirondack Park is one of humanity's first attempts to legislate the protection of an entire ecosystem and everything in it to conserve bio-diversity. That word has many meanings. First of all, it refers to the entire biosphere, the thin skin of air, water and land stretched over the surface of the planet, where life as we know it exists in interlocking, interdependent sets of systems. These systems include all the billions of genes within species, all the millions of species within ecosystems and all the different ecosystems across the face of the planet. That bewildering diversity of life — from the varied geographic habitats covering the earth, to the gene inside a one-celled organism — is all termed biodiversity.

We now realize that biodiversity actually produces life. All these various interwoven life forms continuously replenish, clean, nurture and create conditions amenable to yet more life forms. We have been amazed to discover, only very recently, that it is life itself, living organisms, that create water, the atmosphere, soil and all forms of energy except the sun; even winds depend to a large extent upon vegetation patterns across the globe. So if we destroy microorganisms in the soil with chemicals or kill plankton through global warming, we are destroying our own source of life — our ability to grow food, find fish or deal with our wastes in the near future. That's why initiatives like parks and nature preserves that represent efforts to restore and conserve entire, living ecosystems are so important to our future, so important, in fact, to our very survival.

The Adirondack Park, one of our earliest experiments in the conservation of biodiversity, was founded by the extraordinary mechanism of a separate amendment to the New York State constitution. It is only a state park, not a national park; yet it includes 2.4 million hectares (6 million acres), which means it is still one of the largest preserves on earth. The Appalachian mountain chain encompasses 518,000 square kilometers (200,000 square miles), from the Alleghenies to the Catskills in the north all the way up to the Canadian border. Although the Adirondack Park comprises only one section of this vast, forested mountain range, it seems to be a big enough section to have made a difference. Even today, although it is second- and third-growth in many places, the Adirondack forest still shelters nearly all of the vast numbers of tree and plant species it started out with.[2]

Before the first Europeans arrived, this was a place of ecological plenty that was fully as stunning as the Pacific Northwest is now. The runs of smelt, alewives, sturgeon and salmon that swarmed up its rivers to spawn were prodigious. Letters to England as far back as 500 years ago fairly stutter with attempts to describe such bounty. Birds of every kind, including the now-extinct passenger pigeon, literally darkened the skies. Deer, bears, squirrels, rabbits and all the other animals we associate with the Eastern forest were so plentiful that the newcomers started up an economic system using animal pelts, primarily beaver skins, as currency. Yet reports from 1694, barely a generation after the first large waves of European settlers arrived, tell us the deer in the lower section of the Alleghenies, in Massachusetts, were so depleted that a closed hunting season was enacted. By the 1740s, deer wardens were losing the battle to protect the few that were left. And by the end of the eighteenth century, settler Timothy Dwight noted that deer were "scarcely known below the forty-fourth degree of north latitude"; that is, they had disappeared from every part of New England except for the northernmost reaches of Vermont, New Hampshire and Maine.[3]

The elk, bear and lynx were already gone; within another generation, by the 1840s, beavers were virtually extirpated and, even in far upstate New York, raccoons, rabbits, skunks and deer had also become rare creatures, only occasionally sighted. The reasons are now familiar: overhunting and habitat destruction. The new European immigrants converted forests to farms and towns, they hunted and fished wildly, they dammed rivers and diverted and polluted streams, and they started iron smelting works and timber mills. They also cut down trees as fast as they could. By the mid-nineteenth century, not only were nearly all the animals that we take completely for granted today gone, but their forest was largely gone as well.[4]

A lesson we apparently need to learn every single generation was being acted out back then in New York State. The early environmentalist George Perkins Marsh, in his 1864 book *Man and Nature*, publicized the fact that the destruction of forests causes major climatic changes and the steady depletion of watersheds. By the early 1870s, New York State employee Verplanck Colvin was writing, "The Adirondack Wilderness contains the springs which are the sources of our principal rivers, and the feeders of the canals. Each summer the water supply for these rivers and canals is lessened, and commerce has suffered."[5] The first "park or timber preserve," which Colvin went on to propose, was originally an entirely utilitarian idea, a means of conserving timber for later harvesting; the water supply was needed for drinking and canals, which were the commercial highways of the day, not for any conception of biodiversity. What ultimately made the vast experiment work were the thousands of park workers, trappers, farmers, residents and visitors who simply loved the forest enough to fight and make sacrifices for it in order to preserve real wilderness, as much as they possibly could. And that's what still makes it work today.

In 1883, all New York State lands were removed from the real estate market, but early attempts to preserve them were impeded by the usual bureaucratic delays. Government bills such as the infamous Cutting Law corrupted the process and undid conservation efforts by allowing timber interests into the forest. It took two long summers of drought and fires, in 1893 and 1894, to build the political will to erect a constitutional barrier to the timber industry's continual efforts to gain cutting rights in the park. The final amendment, composed in June 1894, reads: "The lands of the state now owned or hereafter acquired, constituting the forest preserve as now fixed by law, shall be *forever kept as wild forest* lands. They shall not be leased, sold or exchanged, or be taken by any corporation, public or private, nor shall the timber thereon be sold, removed, or destroyed." The amendment was approved by a large majority of the voting population, but what they approved was actually two entities: the Adirondack Forest Preserve of several hundred thousand acres, and the Adirondack Park, a much larger chunk of forest land that was still mostly privately owned.

The idea was probably that the state would eventually acquire all the land, but throughout the 1890s and early twentieth century, rich landowners like William Rockefeller and exclusive clubs, like the Adirondack League and the Tahawus Club, ended up controlling more than 303,000 hectares (750,000 acres) of the park. Since these wealthy and politically influential groups wanted to keep it pristine in any case for "huntin', shootin' and fishin'," the state gradually forgot about the original public dream. As Philip Terrie, author of the park history *Contested Terrain* says, it was "a park like no other the world had ever seen. It had people living and working in it. It had land owned by individuals, families, clubs and corporations. It had poor people dwelling in shanties, while down the road were millionaires who summered in mansions. It had land protected as 'forests forever,' and land where cut-and-run loggers savagely exploited the remaining resource in the name of a quick profit."[6] Like so many of the sustainability solutions described in this book, the continuing survival of the Adirondack forest is a protean, organic process, of which its founding was only the beginning. Mistakes were, and are, made. Triumphs, too. Its success as a system lies in its acceptance of extremely diverse methods of ownership and use — and it works in spite of what many would justly call its frustrating complexity.

The park's chaotic mélange of public and private ownership reached another significant boiling point nearly a hundred years later, in the 1970s, when the state again found the political will to enlarge the forest preserve itself from 1 million to 2.4 million hectares (2.4 million to a full 6 million acres). Together with environmental groups like the Nature Conservancy, the state bought up many of the old clubs and the family and corporate estates as they came on the market, and never lost an opportunity to nab a mountain top or complete a watershed. Scientific studies were instigated to determine just how much land was necessary to make the park "a viable and lasting entity." And with a view to future expansion, more regulations were enacted to control the activities of the remaining private landowners. The Private Land Plan and the State Land Master Plan of 1972 limited sprawl and development and made more efforts to curtail logging, protect riparian areas and reintroduce and strenuously protect wildlife. Terrie describes how Adirondack merchants and town officials were outraged, claiming that the new laws would "violate their property rights and stifle economic poten-tial." State efforts to enlarge the preserve area, these opponents felt, were also "a plot to destroy Adirondack logging and lock up productive lands for wealthy recreationists." Thirty years after the Master Plan was enacted, every move the Park Agency makes is still hotly contested. As Terrie says, "The region has become wilder and better protected, and it's simultaneously become more modern, developed, and rife with conflict." Meanwhile, the animal populations swell, the forests look better than ever, and the summer crowds pour in.[7]

A study of the history of the biodiversity protection effort exemplified by the Adirondack experiment reveals many surprising things. As in so many parts of the world — tropical rainforests for instance — where protection is so desperately needed today, people were living in the Adirondack park well before conservation was ever considered. There were towns, villages and settlements even in the first forest preserve, and the people weren't the usual aboriginal groups that are traditionally simply kicked off land the state or other powerful interests may want. They were deed-holding, tax-paying, voting landowners, some of them, like J.P. Morgan, the Rockefellers and William Seward Webb, very influential indeed. And of course there were the townies, guides, farmers and local woodsmen who supplied their needs. So from the very beginning, the Adirondack Park achieved a particular status, precisely because it could not be walled off from human habitation and development, as were other early conservation experiments like Yellowstone and Yosemite. Moreover, its forests had been shaved, its streams were often dry, and most of its fauna were gone, just as in much of the developing world today. Conscious rehabilitation work had to be done. For all these reasons, methods of use and ownership within the park became diversified. The many cabins, farms and towns inside the park boundaries were subject to a wide and creative variety of restrictions, regulations and types of ownership. Sometimes people with a homestead or hunting camp in the preserve were granted leases that ran for a hundred years or until their deaths; sometimes they were allowed to keep a place in the family, but not sell it. Expansion of towns was limited; landowners are still subject to many land-use regulations that keep them steaming and complaining to this day. Yet many landowners also supported the park and its conservation efforts so much that they have voluntarily willed their property to it upon their deaths.

Like any other effort to conserve prime land in a heavily populated area, the Adirondack park has been continuously under pressure to cut trees, make roads, build dams, make ski-trails and boat launches, as well as to provide housing and other accommodations for its many visitors. Sometimes it has succumbed to these pressures, and there are sections of the park, particularly near Lake George, that aren't very park-like. But those areas have also been steadfastly managed for flora and fauna. The Adirondack Park has been an unsung and extremely important pioneer in the whole concept of reintroducing species. This began back in the 1920s with the beaver; the efforts to restore this keystone species was a resounding success. Since then park managers have introduced everything from vultures to wild turkeys and moose. Generally, within a very few years of reintroduction, these animals begin to do so well that they start to appear on the outskirts of the park; only five years after turkey vultures were brought back, for instance, they were circling over the farm buildings of southwestern Quebec. Today, for the first time since the early nineteenth century, late summer afternoons not far from Montreal resound with the distant, comical gobble of wild turkey flocks. As for the rabbits, hares, skunks, fishers, mink, moose, deer, squirrels, black bears and all the other creatures that had vanished by 1850, they're back in such numbers that all over the Eastern forest region we now take them entirely for granted. We shouldn't. There are still a few wolves around, especially near the beaver; but by and large, the wolverines, wolves and wild cats, and also the cougars and elk have never really come back — the first two because there hasn't been enough political will to allow their reintroduction. The other big species have remained rare; perhaps the forest is in fact too different, too crowded, or too small to let them thrive.

It's not just the parks, of course. Farm and town land all around the Adirondacks, from Vermont and Pennsylvania to Quebec and Ontario, gradually adopted hunting and trapping legislation, which has gone a long way toward giving deer and game birds a breather. But without the huge, prime habitat available to the large animals along the entire spine of the mountains, the American northeast would probably be like Europe, with certain birds, some bunny rabbits and squirrels, but no big predators, large flocks of game birds or wild nuisances like beavers and coyotes. What this means is that the animals on the Dressel farm, most of whom have wandered to the edge of the St. Lawrence valley from that great forest to the south, have literally been rescued from extinction. They are voluntary fauna whose important and mysterious lives have been subsidized and saved by humans, and they're out there in great numbers. If you sit by an Adirondack beaver pond around sunset, the noise from all the animals — the red-winged blackbirds shrilling in the cattails, the swallows twittering excitedly as they scoop up blackflies, the owls hooting from the woods, the frogs in four-part concert, the ducks quacking, the little fish jumping, all soon to be joined by the unearthly yips of coyotes — simply drowns out any noise of lawn-mowers or highways, to say nothing of thoughts about such things. These creatures are mating and nesting and generally hooting and hollering because we humans decided their lives were valuable enough that we were prepared to give up some of our customary economic activities — not just for a little while, but for a century and a half and counting. They should be a very heartening example of the possibility of balancing the needs of a populated area with the preservation of wilderness and biodiversity. The Adirondack Park, for all its problems and shortcomings, is proof that we can save entire ecosystems, with all their waterways, wetlands, plants and animals, in the midst of large human populations and lots of human activity. If we really want to.

## Field of Dreams

> *"If you build it, they will come."*
> — FROM THE MOVIE *FIELD OF DREAMS*

The Adirondack Park was primarily an effort to save a watershed; it became an experiment in what we thought "wilderness" was in the nineteenth century; and eventually it developed into an effort to save an entire ecosystem. The fact that it happened at all had as much to do with changing aesthetics as with increased scientific knowledge. From the late Middle Ages up until the beginnings of the Romantic movement in the late eighteenth century, Europeans considered trees large weeds, and forests dark, gloomy and useless wastelands; the only truly beautiful landscapes were the fertile fields and pastures made by humans. The New Yorkers who wanted to save the Adirondacks were at the forefront of a movement that had begun to consider that other types of landscapes might be beautiful and useful in less obvious ways than a field or a byre. At first adherents to the growing wilderness movement were most enthusiastic about forests and craggy mountains, but by the middle of the nineteenth century, people were beginning to realize that without the boggy wetlands they had been filling in for centuries, clean water, and birds and other game would soon be in short supply.

Prairies were also considered to be boring places, blank canvases to fill in with crops, or at least European grazing animals. But by the turn of the twentieth century, pioneers like the famous American ecologist Aldo Leopold were engaged in trying to restore them. Leopold's experiments, chronicled in his famous *Sand County Almanac*, were among the first to trigger the recognition that natural forces like fire are as much the architects of landscapes as geology, seeds and rainfall. His work on the Curtis Place, an old farm owned by the University of Wisconsin, was frustrated when exotics, migrants, tree seedlings and agricultural weeds all grew merrily in the plowed fields he had carefully sown with native prairie grasses. The unwanted species took over so much that Leopold was forced to acknowledge that his efforts to help nature reclaim its former ecosystem must have been missing a basic component. Eventually, he realized that natural wildfires were the missing ingredient. It was the fires that made it possible for some seeds to sprout, got rid of non-natives and saplings and attracted crucial pollinators and seed dispersers to the rubble. With fire, his restored prairie finally flourished, and this flowering has continued from the mid-1930s to the present, although even at the Curtis Place the native meadow is still invaded by some exotics and weeds at its peripheries.

Since Leopold's day, many remarkable scientists have been working on bringing back the diversity of a perennial North American prairie. Foremost among them are Steve Packard in Illinois and Wes Jackson at in the Land Institute in Kansas. For the past 20 or 30 years, Packard, head of the Nature Conservancy in Illinois, has been trying to restore the prairies of northern Illinois and Indiana. He also has had mixed success. His fires did not always remove non-native shrubs; they still had to be hacked back every season, so that classic high-grass prairie grasses could be planted. Although he was getting poor returns on the grasses, he kept finding other plants he'd never seen before — thistles and flowers like cream gentians, yellow pimpernels, savannah blazing stars. It was years before he put the puzzle together and began to realize that the played-out farmers' fields he and other botanists had always assumed should be restored to high-grass prairies had never been prairies in the first place. They had been savannahs, "weedy thickets and tall grass growing under occasional clumps of trees." The nineteenth-century pioneers had called what they'd found south of Chicago a "barren." It was neither grassland for their cattle nor forest to be felled; therefore in their eyes, it was completely unproductive. Their "barren," the savannah, is a biome distinct from a prairie, and is remarkably dependent on annual natural wildfires. When the farmers suppressed fires, the land had quickly collapsed into thick brushy woods and was forgotten.

Fascinated, Packard bowed to nature and began collecting the "multicolored handfuls of lumpy, oozy glop," as he termed the fruits and seeds of the savanna volunteers, as well as other savannah survivors growing along abandoned railways, old cemeteries and horse-paths. He planted them, and within two years his fields were blazing with species like big-leafed aster, blue-stem goldenrod, starry campion and bottlebrush grass. A drought in

1988 dried up many of the non-native invaders, but was just what the reseeded savannah species needed; they took off. Today, Packard's fields are full of oval milkweed, which exists nowhere else in the state, and endangered flowers like the white-fringed orchid, which simply turned up on its own. Bluebirds, missing from the county for decades, arrived to nest, and the classic savannah butterfly, the Edwards hairstreak, now flutters gaily above the flowers. Packard doesn't know how half the plants got there, let alone the birds and butterflies. Most of the seeds were probably animal-dispersed; but why hadn't that worked before? Others must have lain dormant in the soil for decades, waiting for the right combinations of fire, drought and companion plants to venture out.[8]

This is a wondrous story, but it also illustrates the confusion we face when trying to restore things we haven't properly identified in the first place. Our difficulty comes partly from the way we've all been taught, like Newton, to look at parts instead of wholes, individual components instead of interactive relationships. In keeping with the way our society divides up professions into uncommunicative specialties, prairie researchers like Jackson and Packard are primarily botanists. They began by trying to restore prairies, which they saw initially as a community of plants. What if we all thought of prairies, and everything else, as something more? What if the restoration came in from the opposite direction, from trying to reconstruct a home for a more complex life form higher up on the food chain? Like a bird?

## Assembling Complexity

*On the road to extinction, traffic travels both ways.*
— KENNETH BROWER

Nonsuch Island is a mere 6 hectares (14.5 acres) of crescent-shaped land lying in the entrance to a Bermuda harbor. Its highest elevation is only fifty feet. It is one of the least likely places imaginable to stage a natural comeback, because it's been subjected to almost every indignity a piece of land could suffer. First, it was denuded of much natural vegetation and its native animals in the nineteenth century when a private owner grazed livestock on it, also introducing a tropical island's Four Horsemen of the Apocalypse: rats, cats, goats and pigs. Then the government used it for a quarantine station and hospital for the dreaded Yellow Fever, soon necessitating the construction of mortuaries and cemeteries. After the hospital was abandoned fifty years later, the island served as a marine research station and a school for delinquent boys. Many facilities, such as docks, tunnels and boat slips, were built on it. In 1947 its worst disaster struck — a cedar blight that destroyed 98.6 percent of all of Bermuda's forest cover.[9]

By 1951, Nonsuch was virtually naked rock — clad with only the skeletal remains of the cedars, and overrun by rats and goats. That same year, two naturalists, Robert Cushman Murphy of the American Museum of Natural History and Louis Mowbray, curator of the Bermuda aquarium, accompanied by a fifteen-year-old school boy named David Wingate, discovered a creature that had been thought to be extinct on a rocky islet near Nonsuch. The cahow, a black and white petrel with a pigeon-sized body and a huge, one-meter wingspan, had once numbered in the millions in the Bermuda archipelago. Remarkable flyers and predators that remained out at sea cruising above the Gulf Stream for months at a time, adult cahows had returned each year to their nests in burrows hollowed out under the roots of the cedar forests of Nonsuch and a few other Bermuda islands. Four hundred years before, passing Spanish sailors had called them "the devil's bird," because during the nesting season they filled the night coastline with "a strange, hollow howling." These birds hadn't been seen for centuries. Nonetheless, the bit of fluff the three enthusiasts dug out of a burrow was a cahow chick, and for David Wingate, it was love at first sight.

Settlers had come to the area around 1612. The cahow, like many extirpated species, were fearless, friendly and delicious, especially prized in time of famine — and they disappeared even faster than the deer of Massachusetts. The last recorded sighting was only eight years later, in 1620. Young Wingate, a descendant of the first setters, grew up and went on to study ornithology at Cornell, returning home to nurse the eighteen nesting pairs of cahows that had been collected by researchers in Bermuda while he was at school. He quickly realized that the cahow would never survive unless it had a real habitat, something as much like pre-contact Bermuda as could be devised. Louis Mowbray had managed to get Nonsuch Island declared a nature reserve, even though there wasn't much nature left on it. A few years later, Wingate began trying to restore cahow habitat. He began with cedars. He planted 8,000, but most of them died, succumbing to the old blight or blasted by the wind. As others who have tried to restore native forests have done, Wingate decided to plant a "scaffold species," a fast-growing non-native that would act as a windbreak until the cedars, the climax species, could become established. He chose casuarinas, an evergreen that worked perfectly, sheltering the native cedars until they were strong enough to crowd them out.

But Wingate was impatient. He used organic fertilizer to help them along; "I poured the stuff on," he says, "and man, how they grew." Soon he discovered he was feeding more than trees. Land crab numbers jumped so drastically that the island became spongy and hollow with their burrows, and at night the crustaceans swarmed over the ground like huge cockroaches. The local Bermuda herons, their natural enemy, which had evolved special short, stout bills just to deal with the crabs, were long gone. Wingate brought in their cousins from Florida. "The best thing we could do," he says, "was to introduce the nearest relative and hope to get evolution started again." Today, there are more than a hundred yellow-crowned night herons on Nonsuch, and the crab population is at a normal level. Importing herons and getting rid of the rats as well had another fascinating effect: it brought back much of the island's understorey flora, including a very rare Bermuda sedge. Wingate calls it the botanical equivalent of the cahow. "Could any biologists have predicted that the survival of this sedge depended on a crab-eating heron?" No, they couldn't; certainly not the way most biologists are trained today.

Wingate had moved his wife and young family onto the denuded island, and continued to live there on weekends and summers after the children had to leave to go to school. These were his busiest years: planting trees, nursing baby birds, and shooting the dwindling number of goats for supper. And for the first five years, he got no results whatsoever. "It was all very long term," he says, "not [as bad as] a cosmic . . . or even a geological time frame. But you have to think in a much longer time frame than, say, a politician does. The nature of exponential growth is that it seems agonizingly slow at first. But suddenly you begin to notice the acceleration."[10] Wingate later became Conservation Officer for all of Bermuda, working with the Bermuda Biological Station for Research and the Audubon Society, and continued with his seemingly impossible task of trying to resurrect the dead. He took orphan cahows from the original group of eighteen pairs and reared them by hand. He had to construct underground birdhouses to simulate the perfect crevices that appear in native forests where trees are tipped off their axis by the yearly hurricanes. It was a real labor of love.

Today, Nonsuch boasts a twenty-foot-high canopy of cedar and palmetto as well as olivewood bark, southern hackberry and other understorey plants. Two artificial ponds were excavated to recreate salt and fresh water marsh habitats. The nearly lost West Indian top shell whelk was reintroduced, but there are no mammals or amphibians on Nonsuch, and only one reptile, the endemic skink. Protection has been established for nestsites of green and hawksbill turtles. Today there are also fifty-three breeding pairs of cahows in the vicinity, but so far they haven't begun nesting on their newly created home on the island; they use the little islets nearby, and will probably spill over onto Nonsuch only when the old nesting territories become too crowded.

At the current rate of success, Wingate figures he knows when that will happen. He expects that by 2025 there will be 1,000 breeding pairs of cahows sweeping through the skies in figure-eights, filling the air with their haunting cries for half the year. He'll be dead by then of course, but he hopes to be buried in the old Nonsuch cemetery beside his wife, who died in a kerosene fire in their island cabin when their children were still in school. The remarkable story of this man's odyssey seems rather quirky and romantic, but there's nothing romantic about Wingate's assessment of what he's doing.[11]

The rest of Bermuda doesn't look much like its restored island, even though it's a picture-book tropical paradise, covered with hibiscus, bougainvillea, oleander hedges, royal poinciana trees and much more. That's because these are all imported exotics. Wingate admits that the native forest, in comparison, was "positively dreary"; it was a very simple ecosystem. "But primitive Bermuda," he says, "was stable for tens of thousands of years." Primitive Bermuda also gave birth to the cahow, a predator, the highest organism on the island food chain, the odd creature that has enchanted David Wingate. He admits it may not seem to serve any clear purpose to have another seabird around, even if it does live underground and howl on moonlit nights. The answer an old-fashioned biologist would give is that the cahow, and the ecosystem its presence has rejuvenated, teaches us something. Impatient people might ask whether that lesson is really worth all the trouble; whether the knowledge we've gained on Nonsuch will really add to our understanding of the web of biodiversity that provides us with the practical necessities of life. But in fact, the answer to those questions are coming in now, from far away in the American west, via the African veldt. And these answers have to do with very practical necessities, such as growing our food and keeping our grasslands from becoming deserts.

## Using Coyotes to Grow Grass

*Relatively high numbers of heavy, herding animals, concentrated and moving as they once naturally did in the presence of predators, support the health of the very lands that we thought they destroyed.*

— ALLAN SAVORY IN *HOLISTIC MANAGEMENT*

The successful restoration of an ecosystem seems to have a great deal to do with diversity, with having everything present — fires and butterflies, cahows and crabs, herons and sedges. In the Adirondacks, for example, a major element in that ecosystem's diversity, humans — nature's top predator — was never eliminated; they couldn't be. Perhaps because of its chaotic and undefined nature, the Adirondack Preserve simply aimed at including as many species as it could in its as-wild-as-possible mix of settlement, tourist facility and forest. But in many preserves and parks in Africa and the western U.S., for example, the first thing that managers and rangers did to restore forests and pastureland was to make value judgments about which species they would permit to live there. Ranchers across both continents did the same thing, as did the first settlers on the Illinois prairie. They eliminated the indigenous people, suppressed fires, and tried to keep out predators. They also made it a virtue to wipe out as many competing species as possible. They were trying to favor large herds of herbivores and healthy grasslands, and they thought their crops and herds would be more profitable if they didn't have to share them with any other species. And yet, all across the American West and on the African plains, in only two generations or so, the grazing animals, whether wild or domesticated, as well as the grass they fed on, began to decline. In fact, desertification is now proceeding across the western U.S.A. as fast as it is in southern Africa.[12]

Allan Savory began his long and varied career as a wildlife biologist in Northern Rhodesia. One of the most puzzling things he noticed as a young man was how dramatically grasslands deteriorated after game and livestock had been removed in an effort to eradicate tsetse fly. Eventually, he became a Game Department manager in Zimbabwe. In the 1960s, his team wanted to reintroduce elephants into grasslands they thought were declining because landowners had overgrazed them. But even with no grazing animals in an area, and even with no drought, the grass under their care continued to deteriorate and the land to desertify. After years of disappointment, Savory published a paper reflecting his despair; he concluded that once land was damaged to a certain level, nothing could enable it to recover. A decade later, faced with more catastrophic loss of grasslands in prime elephant country, he made what he calls "the agonizing decision" to cull large numbers of the herd, so the trees and grass could recover. It was a controversial decision that made international news, but it certainly wasn't done because the managers didn't love the elephants. He says now, "I thought there were too many elephants. I didn't know how wrong I was until a long time later."

It was only when Savory went to west Texas to study desertification there that he began to get a handle on the problem. Desertification actually means the decline of life forms in a landscape, that is, the progressive loss of biodiversity. It can occur in wet landscapes, like the Colombian llano, but it's usually associated with low rainfall. Like so many other scientists, Savory had been trained in modern, conventional wildlife and agricultural biology, a discipline that evolved in Europe and middle North America, where there are deep soils, good humidity and an even rainfall. Wildlife managers in Africa had been schooled in modern science by First World mentors, and these mentors all believed that the cause of the sub-Saharan Africa desertification was to be found in the traditional practices of the local people. Scientists and foreign advisors assumed the erosion, plant loss and soil degradation were being caused by what they observed: too many people with too much livestock, who were overcutting the trees, cultivating steep slopes and using shifting agriculture. These people also used common land tenure, which conventional managers felt worked against their interest in maintaining the land. They were poor and uneducated, and had little access to modern research, fertilizers, machinery or chemicals; furthermore, they were often victims of war and corrupt administrations, as well as prolonged droughts. So when Savory got to Texas, he was amazed to find exactly the same loss of diversity in the grasses, the insects and the animals that he'd been seeing in Africa. The impoverishment of the soil and the steady lack of ability to absorb and make use of the sparse rainfall were completely familiar to him from Zimbabwe. And yet, in terms of the tenets of modern land management, west Texas should have been in perfect condition.

In many ways west Texas was the exact opposite of South Africa. There were few people, and fewer cattle than even a century before, and actually too many trees, which were encroaching on the pastureland. The local people were practicing modern, stable agriculture on flat lands that were privately owned; in other words, they had plenty of self-interest in maintaining them. They were relatively rich, well educated, aided by plenty of research and government grants, with an abundance of fertilizer, machinery and chemicals. Furthermore, there had been only one year of drought in many, and they lived in peace with a basically uncorrupt government. Yet with all that, their grass looked as bad as the grass did in Zimbabwe, with more and more ranchers being forced to give up their livelihoods because of the desertification. Faced with this paradox, Savory was forced to conclude that something was wrong with the entire modern land management paradigm under which he and the Texas land managers had been operating.

Ecologically, west Texas and Africa do have a lot in common. Until recently they had both been rich natural pasturelands with an abundance of perennial grasses, as well as flowers, herbs and forbs, nourishing absolutely enormous herds of various hoofed animals. Both places got what is considered to be adequate rainfall, but in bursts, with long dry, dormant periods between the rains. As both sets of grasslands began to decline, they lost their ability to hold on to water when the rainy season did come, and so declined even further. Savory decided what was needed was a reclassification of land, not according to the old methods of what they produced (grasslands, wetlands, forests, etc.) or what their total rainfall was (arid, semi-arid, tropical, etc.), but according to how they needed to be managed.

Savory classifies land as "brittle" or "non-brittle," on a scale from 1 to 10, with 1 being a tropical rainforest, and 10 being a completely barren desert. Within this classification, however, the difference between rich and poor biodiversity and productivity is measured by types of vegetation and animals. Conventional management techniques had been developed for what he calls "perennially humid non-brittle environments," like Europe and the best agricultural land in North America, where some plant material is alive all year and some dying all year, some insects and microorganisms remain active at all times, and rainfall is even and fairly dependable. But Africa and West Texas are "seasonally humid, brittle environments" — most of their above-ground plant life dies back for much of the year because of lack of water, and insects and microorganisms also become dormant. In such a system, unless a big perennial grass plant that has shot up several feet high is either eaten by herbivores or burned off, it will have masses of dead material that chokes off new growth when the rains come. Intentional burning has been a widely practiced method of increasing food crops and animals on grasslands ever since Paleolithic times. But Savory discovered that many of the grasses preferred by herbivores will only regenerate normally if they are cropped by animals; when they are burned, many of these native perennials gradually disappear. In other words, the herbivores and the grasses they eat evolved together, and made a symbiotic whole; the grasses nourished the herds; the herds made sure the grasses could reproduce.

Savory realized that something else had evolved with the grasslands: predators. The lions, hyenas, cheetahs and dingoes in Africa, and the wolves, coyotes and eagles in the American West, had evolved to prey on the huge herds of delicious herbivores that roamed so plentifully on all these grass-lands. The activity of the predators chasing the herbivores around was as essential for the health of grasslands as the grazing activity of the herbivores. Savory found that in areas devoid of new growth and supposedly lost to regeneration, new seedlings could only take root in spots where cattle had been greatly disturbed by a predator. Where the panicked wildebeest or antelopes had bunched together and churned up the ground with their hooves, tearing up and trampling in the dead plant material and loosening the soil so it could receive seedlings and the new rains, regeneration was possible. Moreover, in their fear, the animals usually remained crowded together for some hours, urinating and defecating. As anyone who herds animals knows, herbivores will not graze in an area where they have defe-cated until the material is completely broken down, at least a year in temperate Canada. This fact led Savory to his next discovery: timing.

Conventional managers were right in assuming that grasslands needed a rest from grazing in order to recover. This method works quite well in temperate climates like England. What they didn't realize is that in more "brittle" environments, grasslands behave differently. They don't need an even rest over a wide area; they need a period of being torn up and trampled by intensive grazing in small areas, then a period of rest, then more intensive grazing — exactly what would be produced if the herbivores were being kept in tight herds and chased around the landscape by large predators. Today, cows will naturally select the species of plants that are the most nutri-tious to them and, if they are confined and forced to eat all species, their weight gain will suffer. Other African researchers, like botanist John Acocks,[13] realized that in nature, no single plant would be spared to take over the pasture from the others, as occurs now in cow pastures infested with burdock, duck weed or thistles. That's because, with their different diets, diverse species of herbivores would use all the plants equally —

another function of co-evolution. Obviously, if one type of herbivore, like cows, were kept on a pasture too long, both they and the grass would suffer. But if they were moved around, imitating the natural animal grouping that the grass evolved to withstand, things might be different.

Allan Savory's methods have made sense to a lot of people. In fact, almost two million acres of ranchlands, particularly in Oregon, Idaho and Washington State, are being run according to holistic methods and are prospering to a remarkable degree. What's even more significant is that ranchers aren't following his many management indications religiously. Instead, they're adapting his precepts to the special needs of the area's particular biodiversity, land tenure and size. The result is just what the word "holistic" implies: practices that are open to reality, constantly trying to perceive the whole that they are working within and, because the whole is alive and changing, being extraordinarily flexible and humble in response.

## Goal-Centered and Asset-Based

> *Once I was able to view myself as a part — and only a part — of larger wholes, all the tenets of conventional management began to fall, one after another: nature as a passive object; engineering as a godlike endeavor; species divided into 'good' and 'bad'; technology as the paramount solution; my family and my personal life as something apart from the way I make my living.*
> — ARGENTINE RANCHER

Doc and Connie Hatfield are part of a western ranching cooperative called Oregon Country Beef. Like many of their neighbors' families, their ancestors arrived in the area generations ago. Once the antelope and elk were hunted out, these settlers started to run cattle. The open range was still home to a lot of other animals: coyotes, wolves, mountain lions, eagles, prairie dogs and more. The ranchers saw calves and lambs being taken by eagles and coyotes, and even healthy adults attacked by wolves and cougars; cows' and horses' legs were sometimes broken by stepping in prairie dog holes. So they systematically removed every predator and burrowing animal they saw, by trapping, shooting and even poisoning them. For quite a while, at least two or three generations, western beef was king, and the ranches prospered. But by the late twentieth century, the current Hatfields saw their way of life beginning to die.

It's easy to see why if you drive through eastern Oregon. It looks like a pale yellow sea. The sparse grass that is the only noticeable plant life seems to be of one or two species only, and there's a lot of bare ground, Allan Savory's prime criterion for a "brittle" area. The Hatfields became very interested in Allan Savory's methods in the early 1980s. Doc Hatfield says he had long agonized over "whether it was possible to raise cattle in harmony with the land, and without a lot of expensive inputs like fossil fuel, chemical fertilizers, labor and machinery." But by 1986, the Hatfields were worried not just by the deteriorating condition of their grasslands, but by the image of the beef market as well. Beef was seen as unhealthy, fattening and full of cholesterol, pesticides, hormones and antibiotics. But even though the Hatfields were having lots of trouble with the health of their grasslands, they weren't using any of those chemicals on their animals. So, they decided to take over their own marketing campaign, and began sending about ten sides of beef a week to natural food stores in the area, guaranteeing its freedom from chemicals.

They had trouble getting funding from banks for this new venture, because they were using increasingly unorthodox procedures to raise their cattle. They also knew their main economic problem was wildly fluctuating market prices. So they took another big step: they established an organic beef marketing co-op to set prices based on the average cost of production, plus a decent return on investment, so that members would be assured of a reasonable and sustainable profit. Through the co-op they've been able to hold their prices steady despite declining ones elsewhere. That was more than twelve years ago, and the Hatfields are now in charge of marketing for the Oregon Country Beef brand. It's seen in grocery stores and restaurants throughout the Pacific Northwest, as far north as Seattle and as far south as San Francisco. Today, even the co-op is managed holistically, by keeping final goals in mind at all times, and by a careful effort to concentrate on group assets rather than defects. But the real hallmark of Oregon Country Beef is the Hatfields' grazing techniques. They keep cattle on grass for shorter, more intense periods and encourage the natural biodiversity of all the species native to their ecosystem, even the predators. They like coyotes, and they don't worry about cougars or eagles. They actually try to move their cattle around as if they were being chased by predators. And if they ever have a real problem with one, members of the co-op try to mitigate rather than destroy; they use dogs or llamas to guard the herds and keep predation within bearable limits. The Oregon Country Beef idea spread family by family, and after just a few years you can already see who is practicing these new "predator-friendly" management styles in eastern Oregon. Ranches on one side of a fence are brown or yellow; on the other side, the co-op farms are green and lush, with more trees and flowers as well as better grass. Co-op members have a modest but wonderfully secure income — and they enjoy the songs of the coyotes at night.[14]

Today, no fewer than 600,000 hectares (1.5 million acres) of eastern Oregon are holistically managed under the aegis of Oregon Country Beef. The cattle are breeds especially chosen for semi-arid lands. And they're managed according to the Co-op's "Grazing Well" principles, a set of mission statements not unlike the CERES principles or The Natural Step mentioned in the previous chapter. Chief among these principles is this statement: "Rodents, insects, birds, predators and other grazing animals all have their role in a healthy ecosystem. Grazings are planned in advance to coordinate livestock presence and forage removal with watershed, wildlife and human needs." In other words, grazing well is not all about maximizing beef flesh and paper profits. It's about living within the natural world of integrated, interdependent biodiversity, with the belief that cattle will flourish over the long term only if other life forms are around to help them.

Connie Hatfield told us that not only has the holistic method brought them better beef and a more stable market, but it's bringing back wildflowers, medicinal plants and other prairie grasses that hadn't been heard of since the days of the old pioneer diaries. "And," she says in wonder, "in some of our sinks, we're getting water now for most of the year, the first time in living memory!" Did they have to sacrifice their standard of living in order to bring back things like flowers and wolves? "Not at all!" Doc says. "What we've learned is that the economic and ecological are synonymous in the long time-frame."

One major precept of holistic management is to make a plan and then constantly monitor it to see if it works. The "Assume wrong" written under the word "plan" in Savory's management diagram is highly significant. No one is surprised if holistic management works out differently according to who's doing it, where they're doing it and when. This flexibility makes the whole concept difficult to define, but it makes sense when it's actually being practiced. The basic precepts of holistic management are to define the ultimate goal, to base actions on assets rather than liabilities, and to be humble and flexible if the first plans don't work out. Peter Donovan, a rancher who also writes for a quarterly published by Savory's Center for Holistic Management in New Mexico, points out that "This new type of management is something coming not only from the edges of power, but from the edges of economic security — by that I mean [from] people who are *not* funded by governments, universities or even NGOs, but farmers, ranchers, fishers, welfare recipients, protesters and so on. They're driven by necessity to figure out different ways to survive."

In that sense, it seems that calling the methods these people are discovering "holistic management" is no more accurate than saying they're practicing TNS or Natural Capitalism. The same patterns or paradigms, known by these or different names, are being picked up and adapted to situations in Kerala and Delhi, Germany and Brazil, Portland and Quebec City. "What they try to do," says Donovan, picking his words with difficulty, "is to look for peoples' or ecosystems' strengths and capacities, instead of managing the way we do now, fixating on that little problem — the 10 percent of unemployment or weeds, or whatever — that the old-fashioned management systems obsess about." He gives the example of "community development that doesn't look at Maria, the pregnant teen, but Maria who has such a beautiful voice and so much to give to her community." Holistic management is primarily a method of *process* rather than events. "This alone," he says, "leads to a different attitude towards time. You don't focus on cost, but on investment in the future. You don't panic about deadlines, but work towards moments of opportunity." In fact, it all works a bit like David Wingate's efforts on Nonsuch Island. The new management paradigm sets itself a really high goal, almost a vision, like the return of the cahow, or a completely whole and integrated ecosystem. And this vision keeps the whole process right on track.[15]

Judy Wicks, Ashok Khosla, David Wingate and Truman Collins evolved their own versions of holistic methodology without ever hearing of Allan Savory, as they felt their way toward business, manufacturing, bird habitat or timber-production sustainability. The holistic management that we've been talking about is really just one tendril of an unnamed growing organic management movement that is pushing up spontaneously all over the world. For example, it was evident in a non-violent anti-globalization protest group that we visited in chapter two. We saw that while such a group might not always be efficient about its immediate response to a crisis, it was very clear about not sacrificing its ultimate goal — a peaceful, egalitarian society — for a short-term reaction to a current crisis. An idea that didn't reach consensus or seemed to require a violent or aggressive response was simply not on the docket. A similar clarity of purpose can be seen in a town that has decided to protect its woodlands as part of a holistic vision of what its residents want for their collective future. A development proposal will be turned down with unusual serenity if it doesn't accord with their primary mandate. Yes, the new tax base would be nice; but if it doesn't lead to their agreed-upon ends, it will be a lot easier for everyone involved to see what kind of long-term gains and losses are at stake.

Perhaps what is most important about this methodology is that it uses biomimicry; that is, it takes its cues from natural, biologically diverse systems. Like them, it is self-regulating, non-hierarchical, cyclic, flexible, humble — and focused on the long term. Like David Wingate making mistakes on Nonsuch, or Allan Savory trying to restore grasslands, the holistic way is always ready to try something different, and if that doesn't work, to adjust, backtrack and, with care and more humility, try something else again. Some people might say this is just conservative procrastination, but the holistic process is slow because it is always striving for the ultimate goal of complete environmental and social sustainability — and it always keeps its eye on that prize.

### The Salmon Forest

> *Those salmon go all the way out into the ocean. And this is what the older people would think: these salmon, their bodies are sacred. They're gathering all these foods, just as we do. And they're bringing them back to nourish us. But the food also nourishes the bear. It nourishes the eagle, the cougar, the animals, the bugs, the nutrients, the microfauna; and that's what the next generation of salmon are going to live off.*
> — DON SAMPSON, COLUMBIA RIVER INTER-TRIBAL FISH COMMISSION

Conventional management systems in our modern world are very different from holistic ones. In British Columbia, for example, the trees are managed by the provincial Ministry of Forests; the grizzly bears are the responsibility of the Ministry of Water, Land and Air Protection; the salmon are managed by three federal departments and some provincial counterparts as well, notably Fisheries and Oceans, Indian and Northern Affairs and Tourism. Other departments and organizations that get involved with salmon management include Urban Affairs, Agriculture, Mining, Energy, Science and Technology and Environment.

How well does that compartmentalized approach work out in terms of salmon, forests and rivers — the "resources" themselves? We know that salmon need the forest. The trees that cool the streams make their lives possible. Tree roots prevent the soil from fouling the clear waters these fish require, and the forest stores water and balances an area's climate. That's one reason why so many departments are involved in salmon management. Development along rivers — dredging for shipping, dams for energy, new cities and factories and housing, mines — all that activity impinges on the quantity and clarity of the waters. Each department has a perspective defined by its mandate, its budget, its experts and the bureaucratic turf it defends. And because of this approach, the salmon, the forests, the rivers — and all the other life they support — are never dealt with as a biological entity, a whole, or as an end goal, like the return of the cahow. We've spent billions of dollars on government forest and fisheries research without ever coming close to understanding that the fish, the forests, the rivers, the insects, the birds and the fungi are not separate entities. They are all parts of the same whole, a single entity made up of interconnected and interdependent species, concentric wholes that intercept, overlap and depend on each other. But these facts have been known for a long time by people approaching reality from another perspective.

Don Sampson is a member of the Umatilla, a native group from the corner where southeastern Washington State meets northeastern Oregon. Umatilla tribal land centers around the confluence of two of the greatest rivers on the continent, the Snake and the Columbia. Currently, Sampson is the head of the Columbia River Inter-Tribal Fish Commission, a group of thirteen native tribes who make their own suggestions about ecosystem management to the many government and industry bodies involved. They've just recently gained an audience and a real presence at these river "stakeholder" meetings, but they've actually been involved in managing salmon for a pretty long time. "Because people always knew, even back in the old times, that we had a finite food base," Sampson says. "They had unwritten laws that laid out the use of our resources."

Sampson describes how certain native leaders had the knowledge and the authority to control where and when people could fish. He gives the example of Chief Tommy Thompson, born in the early 1900s. "He was able to recognize, just by the size and timing of the run and the physical characteristics of different salmon, where they were destined to spawn. So he would know at what specific locations to stop any fishery. They had a very sophisticated kind of science, therefore, but it also contained spiritual and religious beliefs. That's what governed how they would go about conducting and managing fisheries." Sampson understands science. He's a fish biologist himself, chosen by the Elders to be, as he puts it, "an interpreter — because I live in two worlds. I learned the white man's education and I understand their science. At the same time, ever since I was young, I was trained to understand the tribes' philosophy — our beliefs, the principles that we want to manage and live by. I interpret the science from the white man to our leaders, and then in turn I interpret our tribal beliefs to the scientists. But you know," he adds, smiling, "most of the knowledge I gained was not at the University of Idaho, in the Fishery Science Department. It was from the tribal fishers and elders who I worked and grew up with."

Sampson points out that back in 1977 his people were the only ones to realize the salmon were in serious trouble, and they sacrificed their commercial spring chinook fishery to try to help them. Even though only 5 percent of the fish mortality in the run was caused by their fishing, they thought that if they held back, the fish might recover. He says, "We figured, 'All right, we've cut our fishing and our harvest is down, but there also needs to be improvements in the way the dams are operated,' because it was the dams which were causing 80 percent of the salmon mortality. But the dams continued to kill thousands and thousands of salmon. You know, when you talk about sustainability, it's hard for the tribal people, who are at poverty level, to sustain 25 years of not going to work. But nobody else stepped up to the plate and did what they were committed to do."

By the 1990s the tribes decided to go to court against the state managers. "They started to listen to us then," Sampson says. Now the Commission puts together complex, science- and culture-based restoration plans that have gradually won more and more adherents. Their main challenge is to get the U.S. federal government, the National Fisheries Service in particular, to recognize their expertise and to regulate other non-Indian activities, so that the salmon can rebuild. And the biggest obstacle is the separation and isolation of all the regulatory bodies, as well as the short-term view that our conventional, politically based resource management systems encourage. "Of course the main trouble is that their political leaders are only thinking for the next couple of years, how they can get re-elected," Sampson says. "Our plans usually look ahead 200 years, in twenty-year increments of time. And political leaders from the state and federal governments look at, you know, only three or four years at a time, which is not even the full life-cycle of one fish."

The tribal vision is fairly easy to understand. They want to restore the rivers, which as well as being denuded by clearcutting, blocked by dams and polluted by industry and farming, in some cases don't have enough actual *water* left in them to support fish. These rivers have been so messed up, rerouted and plundered for agricultural, urban and industrial needs that it hardly bears imagining. And the tribal peoples have had so much trouble getting the various isolated segments of government to see the whole picture — which includes trying to raise salmon in rivers that have no water in them — that these days they're working mostly with other stakeholders: the local farmers, industrialists, fishers and timber barons.

"We have projects that we have put together with the local landowners," Sampson explains, "where we buy major tracts of spawning areas and preserve them for the salmon populations, so there won't be degradation of that habitat." In many cases, the Inter-Tribal Fish Commission actually buys back the rivers, by paying willing users to return or conserve irrigation water. The tribes are very clear about the fact that private citizens, the other stakeholders in the river basins, are their allies only if their own concerns are addressed. "We're prepared to sit down and work with the local folks, and we know there has to be a gradual transition in terms of their lifestyle, in terms of their needs, before we can all get more sustainable."

"Just a few years ago," Sampson continues, "we put together a vision for the Columbia River, which included all thirteen other tribes in the Inter-Tribal Commission. We asked, 'What do we think this river, this watershed, this home, ought to be like down the road?' And then we laid out specifically how to get there. We said, 'We have to quit looking at the river as a hydroelectric plant. We have to recognize it as a river, as a living entity, and we have to recognize its relationship to us and to everything around, the animals, the plants, the insects. We've got to think about water, which is our sacrament; which is our medicine.' And so we laid out our vision, a goal that's trying to protect, restore and rebuild the fish and wildlife in the basin: we recognized that health for us humans may come from that as well; not only physical, but economic health."

This vision led to what Sampson calls "the most recognized success story in the whole Columbia Basin, the Hematellah River Headwaters Plan. The tribes then worked with the local communities, the farmers, the ranchers, and the loggers up there, to put together a holistic plan. Under what we called the Hematellah Basin Project, we developed a system where irrigators are provided with a sustainable amount of water from the Columbia. In exchange, they put back into the Hematellah River, bucket for bucket, the same amount of water that they withdraw from the Columbia. That project has put a really significant amount of water back in the river. We also worked with the state, with the Fish and Game and Water Resource Departments, to rebuild the steelhead population that was the only native population that had survived. And finally we reintroduced the fall chinook, cohoe and spring chinook."

This reintroduction was extremely controversial, as some of the fish the Project used were from hatcheries and were being allowed to breed, which is considered by purists to be genetically dangerous. "But you know," says Sampson, "immediately the populations began to rebound. And the habitat work that we're moving forward with, augmenting the river by putting the water back in, that's working. The fish are spawning in that river again; the nutrients are rebuilding as they die. We're seeing a diversity of species we haven't seen for many years. Bald eagles are coming back to the river. We're seeing the blue heron coming back. We've got a lot of raptors. And we're seeing more bears and cougars coming back to the river." Virtually all these animals had been extinct in the area for at least a generation. Forty-five hundred spring chinook returned; less than a dozen had come back prior to the instigation of the Hematellah Plan.

This past year, the Umatilla had enough fish that their hatchery program can now use only native stock. Their tribal and sport fisheries have been revived. "And," rejoices Sampson, "we got an economy that is *not* going to hell. Our folks are saying, 'Great!'" He isn't just talking about the tribal economy. "The ranchers, they're up there fishing with us now. All of a sudden you've got the farmers up there too; they're even fishing in down-town Pendelton. The local folks are saying, 'We've got all these people coming in. They hear about the fishing, and they're staying in our motels. They're buying gas here. They're buying groceries.' These locals are asking, 'Geez, where are all these people coming from?' And I say, 'Hey, they're coming from the salmon!'"

Tribal, social, ecological, economic and personal benefits come from having a vision of where you want to be — an end and not just a means. The salmon has taken its place again in the Umatilla culture. Sampson says, "The greatest thing from the tribe's standpoint, and probably the biggest gift that I ever got, happened when we had our first spring chinook fishery. The young people, and even the generation my father's from, were never able to fish in this river, because the salmon were extinct. And now we see our sons and our grandkids catching them. One of my cousins, she came up to me and says, 'Oh, I'm so happy! My son caught his first fish.' He hooked a salmon; he couldn't believe it, he was so excited. So now he'll be having his first salmon ceremony, where he's recognized as a provider. They'll have a dinner; they'll honor him. He's twelve, and now he knows where his food comes from. He's proud to know that he's a provider, that he has his role in society. It's so great."

## Cores, Corridors and Carnivores

*If the biota, in the course of aeons, has built something we like but do not understand, then who but a fool would discard seemingly useless parts? To keep every cog and wheel is the first precaution of intelligent tinkering.*
— ALDO LEOPOLD, BIOLOGIST

Efforts to return to a more natural balance on the grasslands of the far west and bring back the salmon to the rivers of the Pacific coast are bringing great rewards in terms of rebounding wildlife and human prosperity. The ranchers in Oregon may be following the precepts of Allan Savory, and Don Sampson's people may be drawing on their traditions, but their methods are very similar and they are now being backed up by an entire school of scientific study and hard biological research. We're experiencing a growth spurt in the methods as well as the goals of conservation. When the Adirondack Park was created, the conservation movement was driven by pragmatic notions about watershed, timber and game animal preservation, but then moved rapidly into aesthetics and ethics. Yellowstone and Yosemite were founded on appeals to patriotism, deism, spiritual inspiration and aesthetics. This impulse rapidly evolved into the Wilderness Movement, founded by biologists like Olaus Murie and Aldo Leopold. Their feeling about the importance of maintaining nature intact was to gain popularity over the next decades. But it has really only been twenty or thirty years since scientists have become interested in understanding how the whole skin of biodiversity actually works across the planet.[16]

This widening of the scope of scientific inquiry to include the relationships between species in a healthy ecosystem is significant because it represents a shift of philosophical perspective. We are moving away from a belief in the superiority of human over natural management, toward an attitude of greater humility and respect for natural processes. By the 1980s, for example, biologists began to realize that measures they thought were "protecting" a landscape from natural disturbances like fires and floods were actually limiting its productivity, because it had evolved under these kinds of pressures. Consequently, western forests have become choked with fire-vulnerable species, to the detriment of the former fire-tolerant ones, and are therefore in much more serious danger of devastating wildfires than they were under natural conditions.

Today biologists have realized that confining wildlife within parks isn't always the best way to preserve it. A landmark study published by biologist William Newmark in 1985 proved that the rate of local extinctions in parks is inversely related to the parks' size, which means that "even regions as large as the Greater Yellowstone Ecosystem cannot provide sufficient demographic resilience and genetic-evolutionary fitness for key animals such as wolverines and grizzly bears."[17]

From this revelation came the concept of Cores, Corridors and Carnivores, a supposedly new idea of "rewilding" the landscape, that is in fact based on the old Adirondack Park model. It means that if we want to preserve biodiversity, we have to first establish core protected areas, like the Adirondack Preserve. Then we need less protected, shared areas where animals can also exist, the corridors of managed towns and farms like the Adirondack Park, that eventually spill over into other ecosystems, like the Catskills or the White Mountains of Vermont. And finally, we need to recognize that without the troublesome top-of-the-foodchain or "keystone" organisms, especially carnivores like bears, wolves, tigers, lions, otters, eagles and so forth, we will experience unexpected collapses in the whole ecosystem, like the loss of grasslands that occurred in Zimbabwe and eastern Oregon. Over the past fifteen years scientific data has been pouring in that vindicates the importance of the Three C's.

Take carnivores, for example. As Michael Soulé, founder of the Society for Conservation Biology, points out, the reason why deer are so fast, moose so powerful and bighorn sheep so agile is that they have evolved to withstand continuous pressure from the top predators in their ecosystem, primarily wolves and grizzlies. When wolves were removed from the Yellowstone ecosystem, for example, coyotes moved in to take their place. But coyotes hunt very differently from wolves, and certainly never go after elk or moose. The result was a decrease in foxes, as the coyotes took over their niche, and a damaging increase in elk herds, which, when unthreatened by predation, turned into pure grazing machines — what some biologists refer to as "meadow potatoes," eating everything in sight. Then Yellowstone Park reintroduced wolves. One of the first things they noticed is that after thirty years of steady decline, Yellowstone's trademark quivering aspens began to return to the edges of the park's beaver and moose meadows. That's because the wolves were reducing the elk and other grazers and were keeping them on the move, so they didn't have the leisure to spread out and methodically destroy plant growth. As an extra bonus, the willows and aspen, which are key food and shelter for birds, gave species like grouse a chance to regenerate.

Top carnivores like mountain lions, tigers, jaguars and bears are keystone species because they impose critical limitations on other populations. Other keystone animals create structures like beaver ponds or prairie dog towns which transform and enrich the landscape. Beavers are considered to have determined not just the hydrology but the botanical landscape for most of North America. They numbered in the millions when Europeans arrived, and when they were eliminated, everything from fishers, wolves and moose to herons, frogs, owls and butterflies suffered a violent collapse. Prairie dogs, elephants, gopher tortoises, rainforest bats and cavity-excavating birds have all been found to be key elements in the maintenance of the landscapes in which they're found. And researchers are discovering more amazing synchronicities every year.

## Living Together

*From New Brunswick to Alabama, there could be*
*cougars and Cerulean Warblers.*
— DAVE FOREMAN, ECOLOGIST AND ACTIVIST

In the triple-C concept of Cores, Corridors and Carnivores, the core areas have to be large enough to sustain reproduction; this is what national parks have long aspired to do. With new knowledge about just how large an area a big predator needs, biologists have moved into the concept of corridors — typically long, narrow, protected forested areas that link the core habitats of the big parks. Beavers first came back into the southern Adirondacks from natural forest corridors between New York and Pennsylvania. And the wild turkeys, bears and moose in the park have moved out to enrich southern

Quebec and Ontario the same way. Animals don't recognize our boundaries, and when hungry, looking for mates or impelled by instinct, they move across busy highways and golf courses, suburbs and farms in order to find what they need. Often, they never make it home. As Michael Soulé says, if we want to preserve the kinds of diverse, species-rich habitats that are good at purifying air and water, growing trees and generating soil, we have to learn how to live not only alongside, but *within* natural systems. "We must preserve or restore connections and corridors between [core habitat areas]. It's fundamental. We cannot entertain the idea of protected areas as islands any longer." And to date, the most ambitious wildlife corridor system in the world is right on track, beyond the planning phase and moving into reality. It's called the Y-2-Y Wildlands Project, and it stretches from Yellowstone Park in the south to connect Banff and Jasper Parks through the northern Rockies, all the way to the Canadian Yukon.

The Y-2-Y Wildlands Project is reminiscent of New York State's ancient and tricky mixture of protected areas, special management zones and private property. It will cover 43,000 square kilometers, (16,600 square miles,) and stretch through many politically distinct areas: Wyoming, Montana, Idaho, British Columbia, Alberta, the Northwest Territories and the Yukon. It will be difficult to manage, complicated and often controversial. And Y-2-Y is just one example. There's also the Sky Islands Wilderness Network, officially begun last fall. It encompasses 4 million hectares (10.5 million acres) of "megadiversity" in New Mexico, Arizona and northern Mexico. Corridors will link the famous "Sky Islands" of New Mexico, Arizona and Northern Mexico, where half of all North American breeding birds are represented. The Sky Islands are mountaintops that harbor temperate as well as desert species and ecosystems, and preserve an astonishing diversity of life at every different level of elevation.[18]

Y-2-Y and the Sky Islands Network are out west, in relatively underpopulated areas. But the east is getting in on the act too. By using the tried and true Adirondack mixed-use prototype, there is now an Algonquin-to-Adirondacks initiative underway between New York and Ontario's Algonquin Park. There is also a plan, called the Appalachian Wildlands Project, to stretch the same corridor south all the way to Florida. It started with an attempt in Maryland to protect the regions that feed the extremely productive and key coastal and marine ecosystem of Chesapeake Bay. As scientists took stock of the area, they realized that the entire eastern seaboard is suffering from a loss of songbirds that is reaching catastrophic proportions. It's not caused just by habitat loss. Because of the absence of big predators like wolves, lynx, bobcats and cougars, populations of medium-sized predators like skunks, raccoons and housecats, that depend almost exclusively on birds' eggs and nestlings, have exploded. Moreover, the roads that crisscross every inch of the east — including logging and illegal all-terrain vehicle tracks — destroy salamanders, toads and other amphibians. These creatures are like the invertebrates in the soil, the bottom of the food chain without which nothing will be able to live.

Wildlands preservation is attempting to address loss from the bottom as well as from the top by establishing cores, corridors and carnivores, even out east. The state of Maryland has already authorized $35 million to pursue this vision, but it will take the combined efforts of thousands of property owners, developers, citizens and politicians, as well as biologists, to make it a reality. But then, so did the Adirondack Preserve. "The key to the vision of the Wildlands Project — and its success," says Dave Foreman, the founder of EarthFirst! and a well-known defender of wildlife, "has been its good relationship with landowners. But we need to keep educating people about what opportunities are out there." For example, in the U.S. but not yet in Canada, the Fish and Wildlife Service has allocated funds to pay farmers to restore their wetlands — and then to leave them alone. As in most parts of the world with reintroduced predators, there will be compensation for farmers who lose stock; the extremely effective Defenders of Wildlife uses funds raised privately to reimburse ranchers for predator losses across the western United States. As Soulé points out, the most important development of all is the way the new goal of connections and corridors "is inspiring a much larger and longer-term view of what is possible for the future."

## Lions, Tigers and Bears

*What I saw in the destruction of wildlife reflects the condition of humanity and all other life on this planet. The wildlife problems that I first grappled with were little more than advance gusts of the violent storms that ultimately threaten the whole world.*
— ALLAN SAVORY

The question arises as to whether truly poor countries can afford a philosophy of saving animals and wildlife, because in any resource crunch, "human needs must come first." And since there are so many countries like India, China and large parts of Africa and South America where there are so very many needy humans, it doesn't seem likely that wild animals and plants stand much of a chance. By the time human needs are addressed, wildlife will all be gone. So we went to India, to visit TRAFFIC, the arm of the World Wildlife Fund for Nature that deals with the commerce in endangered animals, to try to find out if that's true. In a country with a staggering amount of tropical biodiversity and an even more staggering amount of human need, one would expect the news to be all bad. We spoke to TRAFFIC's director, Manoj Mishra, a wildlife biologist trained at the Wildlife Institute in Dehra Dun in the foothills of the Himalayas. He's a small, compact man in his early forties who exudes friendly energy and quiet self-confidence. He told us that India is in much better shape than we might expect.

"Nineteen-seventy-two was the watershed year for animal and habitat protection in India. That's when the first wildlife protection act was passed, comprehensive and country-wide. Before that, all we'd had were laws primarily made to regulate hunting on the state level. Prior to independence," Mishra says, "animals were mostly there for people's amusement; there seemed to be a lot of them, and no one thought of protection. One Maharaja in Madra Pradesh, for example, slaughtered 1,500 tigers all by himself. And then, for twenty years after independence, India opened itself up to big game hunters. There was organized butchery all through the 1950s and 1960s. The animals didn't have a chance." The wake-up call came when the World Conservation Union had its general meeting in Delhi in 1969. India prides itself on everything it possesses — people, religions, culture, history, forests, animals, food. "They told us we were losing this resource completely. Indira Gandhi then fought for the passage of our first Wildlife Protection Act. And what it does is totally ban hunting of any kind, country-wide. The only hunting allowed now is when rangers might have to cull animals that are spilling out of a park and destroying people's farms."

Although it is sometimes violated by poachers, the hunting ban is heavily enforced. Rangers shoot to kill, and in the last five years alone, more than 150 poachers have been killed in order to protect the animals. That sounds pretty inhumane to us, but as Mishra says, "There's a long tradition of trading products like musk (from deer), ivory, exotic timber, birds, bear bile, and otter skins, especially to feed the constant demand of the Far East." But in recent years, it's not just local or tribal people doing it. "Until the 1970s, the wildlife trade was very opportunistic. Now it's much more organized. A single tiger skin can be worth a hundred thousand dollars. These days, animal traffic is mixed up with drugs and arms. Much more money is at stake, and people are more willing to risk their lives." When we were in India, five elephants had been found slaughtered for their tusks in one of the country's show-piece parks in the north of India. What was uplifting about this terrible event was the outrage it inspired around the country. Villagers hundreds of miles away talked about it, and for weeks the papers featured it as a story with the same level of national interest as the Walkerton water contamination tragedy in Canada. There was television coverage, indignant editorials and bitter cartoons showing the government figures responsible for habitat protection sweeping the horizon with binoculars looking for poachers, while the bloody tusks piled up at their feet. In other words, in India, people care about such things — a lot.

The big-game poachers are seen as Mafia, as indeed they often are. Several people in the TRAFFIC office have to use assumed names and make sure to keep their addresses private. Otherwise, their seizures of contraband birds, pelts and snakes and their enthusiastic pursuit of convictions could get them or their families killed. This doesn't slow them down. It was a national holiday when we visited TRAFFIC's offices in Delhi, but more than half the staff were there, including the two heads, working in an atmosphere of controlled excitement. As we settled in at his desk to look at charts, maps and graphs, Mishra said, "Globalization is a big problem for us, with its removal of regulations, liberalization of markets, lowering of tariffs and downsizing of government bureaus. As a result, all kinds of things are relaxed and there are fewer inspectors and officials. And it's introduced things like your famous corporate courier services, which are being misused to transport this material. The killers are getting richer and smarter. The enforcement needs to do the same. We don't have enough good training in things like forensics, DNA, intelligence-gathering. We've been pressuring the government to make this a high priority."

Despite a frightening 2 percent annual increase in population that will make it the most populous country on earth in the twenty-first century, despite droughts and a long history of deforestation and degradation, India's wild animal habitat has increased over what it was a few decades ago. This seemingly impossible fact is due to the Forest Conservation Act of 1980, which was rightly seen as a necessary complement to the Wildlife Act. Under it, as Mishra says, "no state government can de-reserve forests without prior permission of the national government." In the Canadian context, that would mean that Saskatchewan wouldn't have been allowed to sell half its forest to Japan without Ottawa's consent. "This single provision put an abrupt end to one million acres of deforestation a year," adds Mishra. "Today, forest cover in India is actually on the rise. Satellite imagery shows it, and it's not sugar cane or bamboo; good forest really is slowly coming back. There's an immense political lobby out there that that wants to dilute this Act, of course; but the foresters fight them."

"The second important thing to happen in forest protection is that India banned all timber exports in 1995," Mishra says, "and logging is dying out in most of the country." When he says that India has forests, it's important to realize what he means. India's forests have packs of wild dogs, flocks of parrots and toucans, pheasants, mynas, munias and owls, pythons, rock snakes, cobras and monkeys. There is a bewildering array of plant and insect life, as well as small mammals. And plans are also in place to connect their largest parks with forest corridors, like the Y-2-Y Wildlands Project, especially practicable in the north where there are several big parks not too far apart. But perhaps the most spectacular of all, Mishra says with pride, is the single fact that "India is the only country in the world to have conserved and protected all of the Big Six remaining land mammals: the rhino, leopard, lion, buffalo, elephant and tiger. That gives us a lot of reason for hope; we still have the mega-vertebrates. Habitat is on the rise. We have good legislation in place. All we need is good implementation and motivated people. With better training and incentives, we could do it. We could save them all for the whole world. Nineteen percent of the land area in our country of a billion people is still forest, still wildlife habitat. And that's really something."

When Mishra says so proudly that the people of India have conserved these species, he means it. India is the Adirondack Park on a gigantic level. The animals it has are the animals its people decided they wanted, and then fought and made sacrifices to keep. Warming to his theme, Mishra told us two of the country's greatest success stories. "In the early part of the twentieth century, only fifteen or twenty one-horned rhinos were left in all of India. Kaziranga National Park was started because that's where this remnant lived. Now there are 1,500 of them!" There was a big fuss about expanding a population from such a tiny genetic base, but researchers haven't been able to find anything genetically wrong with the rhinos — no diseases or congenital infirmities. Even more remarkable is the story of the Asiatic lion. "By 1905, there were only sixteen or seventeen Asiatic lions left in India, and indeed in all of Asia. This remnant lived in only one place in the world: the Gir Forest in Gujarat." How they happened to survive there is really a fluke. Fifteen or twenty years previously, in the late nineteenth century, the local Maharaja had gone out to shoot lions, and realized there were very few left. So instead of taking trophies, he declared the area a reserve, under strict protection. At that point, there were still plenty in other parts of India, so what he did was for his own little ecosystem alone.

"As that remnant population built up in Gir," Mishra says, "it melted away elsewhere, until they existed nowhere else in India, or even on earth. By independence, we'd got them up to a hundred. Now there are 300 Asiatic lions in Gir Forest, and they are basically genetically sound! The government is currently setting up a second habitat for some of them at Kuno Sanctuary in Madha Pradesh. The first pride should be sent there and monitored next year." We asked about prey, and he said, "There's nilgai, bobul, black buck, chimcara, chital deer and wild boar already there. The habitat is very similar to their home in Gir, so we think they'll do fine." The survival of rhinos and lions in India is reminiscent of the situation we saw in the Adirondacks. It was neither nature, nor the "market," nor a comfortable condition of wealth for the entire population that saved these animals from exploitation and extinction. Their dwindling habitat was preserved with the support and sacrifice of local, often poor, human stakeholders. Their animal habitats were protected by legislation that is supported by the population. And with that breathing space, nature has managed to bring back the top predators — which means, by definition, that the rest of the ecosystem is still functioning.

Many people would say Indians can't afford to direct energy and money toward such goals. The resources that the country is spending on saving nature could in theory help some of the many sick and starving people who lack clean water, schools and roads. Why not take care of them first, elevate the middle class, and then, once they have the means and leisure, take time to save these relatively impractical luxuries, the rhinos and tigers? Mishra has heard this argument many times, and his attitude is clear: "Oh, right! The middle class all getting a car is what will save nature! Well, that's NOT how it works, and that's not what Indians want. Even if we're poor, we have to save our animals. That's the basis of life, that's our identity, that's morality, that's our heritage, and we know it. And that's why these efforts find so much popular support." He pauses and then says with feeling, "Nature is so good here — we have no excuse not to save it."

So we asked Mishra exactly how nature can be managed, even in such a poor country, so that it can support India's great populations for many years to come. His answer could serve as a template for almost any place in the world that wants to preserve biodiversity. He said, "What you need to do is empower the local public, but never give huge amounts of power to a decentralized body, like a state or a province. They're too vulnerable to corruption, and that bodes ill for the environment. In other words, whenever possible, give management powers to grassroots locals, villagers, tribes, farmers' groups, that kind of thing; but not to the state. And then use a larger, centralized body, the nation, the Supreme Court and so on, as watchdogs, to set country-wide standards and provide underlying legislation that helps the locals achieve a balanced environment."

## Bewildering Complexity

*Patients with a wide range of illnesses are often characterized by strikingly predictable, ordered dynamics. . . . [They] lose aspects of their individual variability, appearing remarkably alike with respect to their pathologic dynamics, appearance or behaviour. . . . Such stereotypy contrasts strikingly with the variability and unpredictability [of] healthy structure and function. Indeed, clinicians rely heavily on this pathologic loss of variability for diagnosis.*
— ARY GOLDBERGER, DEPARTMENT OF MEDICINE, HARVARD UNIVERSITY

All you have to do is look at an EEG and see it turn into a flat line to realize, as the eminent physician Ary Goldberger says, that disease is ordered, simple, uncomplicated and predictable. And although it's the opposite of what you might think, health is varied, unpredictable and disordered. Increasingly, scientists are finding that many of their assumptions about what is logical do not represent the way the world really works. For many years, for example, biologists and geneticists assumed that, as a species evolved over time, it would move towards simplicity, homogeneity and order. They theorized that it would gradually weed out less beneficial forms of extraneous genes as it became better and better adapted to its surroundings, as it became an alga, a tortoise or an ostrich that was truly specialized. So they assumed that the mark of a successful species — that is, one that had survived for millions of years — would be that its genes would be very homogeneous: simple, predictable and orderly. In the early 1960s, however, geneticists began to apply the tools of molecular biology to study specific genes in individual animals and plants. To their considerable surprise, they discovered that, rather than being genetically uniform and simple, there was a tremendous range in variation and complexity in gene forms from individual to individual, even within the same "successful" species. This phenomenon is now termed Genetic Polymorphism, and it is the very definition of a healthy, successful species.

Why is this true? The answer probably lies in the fact that conditions on this planet are constantly changing, usually very slowly, but radically all the same. Over geological time, for example, the sun has grown more than 20 percent hotter than it was when life first evolved. The atmosphere has shifted from having no oxygen to having a great deal of it. The magnetic poles have reversed, and then reversed again. Oceans have appeared and disappeared, as in the American midwest, with bewildering repetition. Climates have shifted between tropical paradises full of huge, cold-blooded reptiles to frozen ice ages populated by woolly, warm-blooded giants. And through it all, life has persisted. Its strategy for surviving these apocalyptic and continual changes has been diversity, complexity and unpredictability. That means that each level of life has its own diversity: a pool of many kinds of genes in each individual plant, animal and microbe; a pool of many kinds of individuals in each species; a pool of many kinds of species in every ecosystem; and many kinds of ecosystems the planet over. That way, someone or something could always survive, whatever happened. The totality of all these levels of life is what has come to be called "biodiversity." Scientists have finally realized that biodiversity is at the very heart of life's resilience and adaptability. Rigid sameness results in disease and death, as we see every day, without, perhaps, taking it suitably to heart. Monocultures, the cultivation of a single genetic strain or species in agriculture, forestry or fisheries is extremely dangerous, because it reduces an organism's resilience when a new parasite, disease or change in climate occurs.

So, if we lived in a world where all the humans ate one kind of plant, wore one kind of clothing and thought one kind of way, it's obvious they would be less likely to survive any new assault than in a world in which the humans had many options of plants and animals to eat, many kinds of fibers to wear, and many kinds of philosophies through which they understood reality. By reducing the variability of life forms around us through ignorance, greed or just mindless inattention, we simplify our own ecosystem and greatly reduce our chances for survival. As we've seen, when a high-level predator is introduced into a failing, simplified and brittle ecosystem, that introduction brings increased complexity to the interrelationship of all the species, which results in a sudden increase in the life and health of virtually everything in the ecosystem. If you bring back herons, you get sedges; if you bring back wolves, you get prairie flowers and more water; if you make sure soil is always full of organisms, you'll get crops to eat, virtually forever. It's something close to miraculous. All over the world, people are simultaneously recognizing these facts and are helping to change our shared view of the world. We are beginning to see this planet not as a machine made up of separate, independent parts, but as a complex whole made up of other, interconnected wholes, which link together into one vast circle of healthy, self-sustaining life, that it is our duty, our necessity and — best of all — a great source of our delight to maintain.

# CHAPTER 4

# A RIVER RUNS THROUGH IT
## Save the Water

### Life's Blood

> *There are widespread misunderstandings, especially in the wealthier parts of the world, about the quality and quantity of the world's water supply.*
> — MAUDE BARLOW

Without water, there is no life as we know it. It is so vital to plants, animals and even microorganisms, that all life forms that don't already live within the cradle of our planet's oceans, lakes and rivers have devised ways to carry water around with them as blood or bodily fluids. Humans, for example, are more than 60 percent water. Complex plants and animals need not just to hold it inside but to circulate it continuously, like rivers running through their bodies. If we visualize the thin skin of life stretched over the globe as a kind of super-organism, we can see that it, too, has water running through it — the rivers and lakes are arteries and veins; the oceans and the hydrologic cycle operate as its heart.

In fact, like the beating of our hearts, water is so much a part of our surroundings and our bodies that we tend to take it for granted. After all, water simply falls out of the sky; it's all over the ground as well, in streams, ponds, rivers and bogs, pouring out of millions of taps in every big city, all over the world. People who live in northern Africa, India or parts of China and South America may not feel so complacent, but even there it would come as a surprise just how little fresh water is actually available for use on this planet. Less than one half of one percent of all the water on the planet can be used by non-oceanic life; the rest is seawater or is frozen in polar ice caps. The only way we can get this usable fresh water is from rain. Rain is caught in reservoirs, lakes, rivers, aquifers and permeable soil, but to be any use to us, it has to fall on landmasses, not out on the oceans. Millions of gallons of water seep just below the surface where we can reach it with shallow wells. It also collects and is stored over time in aquifers, mysterious underground rivers and huge hollows in the bedrock deep within the earth that are accessible only by drilling.

For millennia, as we hauled the water out of shallow or "dug" wells in buckets, more rain water percolated down, constantly replenishing the supply. Traditional methods of obtaining water included collecting rain in small barrels and cisterns, building huge tanks and even artificial lakes to serve whole cities, and trapping it in catchment systems like check dams, artificial ponds, terraces, diversion channels and ingenious underground canals. These historic technologies were largely limited to catching rain from above, rather than pulling water up from below.

Our ability to obtain the water that's stored hundreds of feet below the surface is quite recent. Really deep wells that exploit huge underground aquifers like the Ogallala Aquifer, which stretches across nearly the entire American west, began to be made only at the turn of the twentieth century, when we had developed gasoline-powered drills that can pierce rock. This new technology was exciting; people could access water in places it had never been available before, "making the deserts bloom," as the fifties slogan used to say. Moreover, the old technologies had been very labor- and maintenance-intensive, so it was frequently a relief to abandon them for the new, deep-drilled wells. This meant that as the new technology spread, most of the old cisterns, check dams and so forth fell into disuse all around the world.

Of course, the other modern way to get access to water was to dam up and divert rivers. As we shall see, the dams that began to be built around the turn of the twentieth century were very different from the dams that had existed for millennia, mostly simple, earthen levees blocking up parts of a river to provide local irrigation water. With machines, water could now be pumped great distances, so huge amounts of it could be trapped behind ever-larger dams and re-allocated; in fact, entire river systems could be diverted. Areas that never before had enough water to be cultivated were opened up. The California desert, Israel, Jordan and many other arid lands suddenly turned green with lush crops. Big dams also provided hydro power for cities and for pumping yet more water, greatly increasing the ability of humans to control nearly all of the planet's life's blood.

But there is a problem. As anyone who understands the hydrological cycle already knows, of all the natural systems on the planet, water is probably the most obviously finite. It is exactly the same pool of water that goes around and around the globe, again and again. Drops that quenched a dinosaur's thirst and bathed Julius Caesar may well be present in your morning coffee. Most of the water raining down and being sucked back up again by evaporation, only to rain down once more, stays in the cycle. But some of it has been stored for very long periods in those deep underground aquifers. Because of our growing numbers, modern industrial and agricultural practices, and new damming and drilling technologies, this water too has entered the above-ground cycle; and much of it is being polluted or wasted. There has been so much drilling, damming, waste and contamination, in fact, that water experts from around the world agree that we're now facing a crisis.[1]

Allerd Stikker of the Amsterdam-based Ecological Management Foundation puts it starkly. "The issue today . . . is that while the only renewable source of fresh water is continental rainfall, the world population keeps increasing by roughly 85 million per year. Therefore the availability of fresh water per head is decreasing rapidly."[2] But this water is not being consumed just to slake the thirst of all the newly arrived humans. Agriculture uses close to 70 percent and industry 25 percent; less than 10 percent goes to households and municipalities. The amount the three categories use is doubling every twenty years; that's more than twice the increase in the population, so wastage and profligacy are obviously at work. The High Plains Ogallala Aquifer already mentioned, one of the world's largest natural underground storage tanks, is being depleted eight times faster than nature can replenish it. This water feeds the luxury crops of fruit and flowers being grown in California semi-deserts; it fills swimming pools all across the American Southwest; it runs lawn sprinklers so grass grows in the scorching desert; and it circulates in air conditioners, some of which cool outdoor patios so their owners never have to contend with the natural climate. The net result is that the water table under the San Joaquin Valley, the epicenter of California agriculture, has dropped nearly ten meters in many places over the last fifty years. That's nearly a foot of water a year that has been permanently lost.[3]

The deep-well drilling systems we greeted with such joy fifty or sixty years ago are now being called "water mining." Not only do they deplete the water that used to underlie whole ecosystems and keep them stable; they cause salts to invade freshwater aquifers. And when it comes to what are called "fossil aquifers," the really old, underground water storage areas, relentless "water mining" can cause the caverns and stone hollows holding the water to collapse, permanently reducing the earth's water storage capacity for the future. In California alone, the current rate of water use will, in only fifteen years or so, create a shortfall as great as the quantity of water currently being used by all the state's cities and towns combined. And as if that weren't enough, as most of us know, pollution caused by industrialization has already claimed nearly all the rivers and many of the lakes in the First World. Much of this water is so contaminated with poisons that it cannot even be used for industrial purposes. As developing countries joining the rush to globalization undergo rapid industrialization, heavy metals, acids and pesticides are leaching into their water supplies as well. According to a report issued by the UN and the Stockholm Environment Institute, by the year 2025, two-thirds of the world's population will be affected by water shortages.

But rather than amass more details of a situation that's likely to make everybody reach for a glass of something much stronger than water to drink, we'd like to visit one of the most disadvantaged places in the world, which has been faced with a growing, hungry population and an almost complete lack of water, and hear some good news about what its people have done — to get it all back.

## Drought-Proofing

*It doesn't matter how much rainfall is received, if it isn't captured, an area can still be short of water. It is unbelievable but true that Cherrapunji, which gets 11,000 mm of annual rainfall, still suffers from serious drinking water shortages.*
— CENTRE FOR SCIENCE AND ENVIRONMENT, NEW DELHI, INDIA

Uttar Pradresh in central India provides an example of what has happened in many other places over the past century. The area, which used to be called Bundelkhand, the "Place of the Bundel Kings," had reached the brink of disaster. It was traditionally a region of pastoralists, crisscrossed with grasslands, forests and rivers. From 1940 onwards the British railroad system started cutting the area's forests to fuel their national network of steam trains. After independence in 1947, there was a new onslaught of cutting for needed cash. Now the forests are all gone — and so is the water. Even today, however, Bundelkhand still has an annual rainfall of almost 1,200 cm (500 inches), which would be entirely adequate to support its population if it were spread out over the year. Unfortunately, it comes all at once, in the six or eight weeks of the monsoon.

Because of the deforestation and the area's naturally poor, rocky soils, there is no way for the land to hang on to that water. So it pours into brief, torrential rivers that tear past the thirsty plants and inhabitants, carrying all their rain off to the sea. After another month or two, every vestige of water vanishes, and the wide scars of the bleached, dry riverbeds are the only sign of its passing. Adding considerably to the problem is the quick fix of modern technology. From the 1960s to the 1980s, well-meaning government agencies and foreign NGOs ran all over India sinking deep wells into the groundwater table. The population quickly became utterly dependent on these wells as their sole source of water for drinking, animal needs and irrigation. Now, in some cases only a decade later, the groundwater levels have dropped precipitously; there are places on the Indo-Gangetic plain where people have to drill 274 meters (900 feet) to find any water. That's because without forests and rivers to absorb the rain, the underground aquifers are constantly being pumped out, but never replenished.

Even though shade, water, pasture and fodder are disappearing, cattle and goats haven't. In some parts of Bundelkhand, these animals outnumber the people. The state has 11 animals for every 10 people, almost three times the already high rate of 4 animals per 10 people that is the norm for the rest of India. So this large area of the central Gangetic plain that was once a productive forest is also extremely over-grazed and is rapidly becoming a completely unusable desert. As we drove along outside of the old town of Jhansi, looking at the acres of baked soil and stones, and gaunt cows sadly nuzzling denuded heaps of rock and drifts of garbage littering the edges of once-forested hills, it was hard to believe how quickly it had all happened.

Our guide to the area, retired Air Marshal Surrendra Sahni of the Indian Air Force, now in his seventies, pointed at several barren heaps of rock that looked as if they couldn't support a sick crow and said, "When I was young, these hills were still forests, and people came from all around to hunt tigers." Air Marshal Sahni is slender, upright and quick, with the energy of someone forty years younger. About a decade ago, he got involved with Ashok Khosla's Development Alternatives (DA), introduced in chapter one. A native of this area, he also spent a good part of his military career in the large army and air force complex in Jhansi. Charm, a commanding manner, impeccable integrity and what can only be described as a loving nature have enabled him to overcome the daunting challenges of class, caste and inertia that plague any effort to effect change in rural India — or rural anywhere. Instead of relaxing after his retirement, he has chosen to spend the past ten years working on issues of survival for the local people of this poor and very challenged region. And there is no issue in their lives more critical than water.

Even before the forests were cut down and the aquifer mined, the people of the region had needed to stabilize their water supply. The deepest forest can't hold on to 1,270 cm (500 inches) of rain if it hits all at once, and there were only a few natural lakes in the region that could store it, although many of the now dry riverbeds once flowed all year. Sahni and Development Alternatives decided to see if they could get at least a few months' more water out of these shadows of the past. They knew that before the magic of deeper and deeper drilled wells, the rural areas of India had depended on very complex systems of water harvesting and storage that varied according to topology, need and local governments. Typically, the local Maharaja was responsible for the largest structures, including big dams, water tanks (which could reach the size of natural lakes at times), step wells and other expensive installations. The local people helped with their labor, and also on their own kept up smaller systems of irrigation and water confinement, through a system called *goam*, voluntary labor, not unlike the *mit'a* system used by the Incas.

In this area, besides artificial tanks and cisterns, people had especially made use of what they call a *bund*, or in English a "check dam." These are larger versions of the kind of dams beavers make. A free-flowing stream is blocked with earth, sticks and rocks, creating a small lake above the obstruction, and the amount of water that flows below the dam can thus be controlled. Like beaver lakes, bund-impoundments not only store water for many months more than it would normally remain, but they also allow it to percolate down through the soil into the groundwater and deeper aquifers, thus replenishing wells for some distance in every direction. Development Alternatives has so far built thirty small, cement check dams in the area to impound the monsoon waters along several dry riverbeds. The dams are about 18 to 30 meters (50 to 100 feet) across, usually not more than 6 meters (20 feet) high, and are individually engineered for each specific river. They are now providing thirty villages with water, and are also putting about 1,000 hectares (2,250 acres) of cropland back into full, two-crop-a-year production. The villages have to pay 10 percent of the construction costs. Each dam costs about $5,000–$7,000 (U.S.) to build, so $500 to $700 has to be raised by the locals, always the trickiest part, since villagers are wary of outside projects that often come to nothing because of corrupt local systems. Moreover, for many years, the population had also become used to having such projects completely paid for by government or outside aid groups. It's a new experience for them, to be expected to invest their own very scarce time and money in a difficult and uncertain future. But DA has also resurrected the concept of *goam*. The villagers are required to help fund — and also to learn how to maintain — the entire technology.

The first check dam Development Alternatives built is next to TARA Kendra, or TARA Center, their experimental industrial village between Jhansi and Orchha mentioned in chapter one. The area was as desertified as any other, and the organization needed water to power their planned paper factory and other industries. Their workers built a very simple check dam behind the Center, hoping it would help serve their needs. The first year, they had water for four months instead of just two. The next year, they were delighted to get seven months of water. Now, only two years later, the river has become perennial again; it's a completely unexpected miracle, like the blooming of extinct wildflowers that followed the adoption of holistic management in eastern Oregon. The explanation seems to be that impounding the seasonal water for even a few months recharges the local aquifers so much that trees and shrubs grow prodigiously, as one might expect in such a climate. Their foliage and roots trap more water, more things grow in the revitalized soil, more rain percolates down into the groundwater, and the process mushrooms. The TARA Center workers have resurrected a dead river, and this former desert is now full of frogs, egrets and butterflies, all for $5,000 worth of concrete and engineering.

## Small Is Beautiful

*The answer to drought-proofing lies not in mega-water harvesting projects with medium and large dams. It lies in small water harvesting structures that are constructed at the farm and village level.*

— CENTRE FOR SCIENCE AND ENVIRONMENT, NEW DELHI, INDIA

While Israeli scientist Michael Evenari was studying ancient methods of rain-water storage in the Negev desert, he discovered something very significant, which fits in with all the sustainability criteria we've been talking about, particularly the one about natural systems working best in small, localized areas. His landmark studies showed that a small watershed will produce more water per hectare than a large one. A watershed of one hectare (2.5 acres) in the Negev provided as much as 95 cubic meters of water per hectare per year, whereas a 345-hectare (850-acre) watershed yielded only 24 cubic meters per hectare per year, about a quarter as much. There are other organizations and NGOs building check dams in India besides Development Alternatives, and they have all learned to work on this localized, village level, taking into account the fact that natural ecosystems change in small ways, and recognizing that massive efforts to manage a large area by a single means nearly always fail.[4]

Air Marshal Sahni also took us to one of DA's most impressive accomplishments, just beyond the ancient village of Rajpura, a two-hour bumpy ride in a jeep beyond Jhansi. Rajpura is at least 600 or 700 years old, with crumbling brick and stone houses painted in faded yellows and blues and gathered around a hand-dug, stone-lined well at least a hundred feet deep. The cows in Rajpura are particularly long of horn, the people shy and old-fashioned. A snake sadhu, one of the naked Indian holy men who have masses of dreadlocks and ash-covered skin, is in residence near the well; the women cover their faces and are seldom seen. The road is arduous, so few villagers go more than a few kilometers from home, and the river cuts them off from the big city. Rajpura is therefore remote, in both space and time.

Children take their water buffaloes past the old houses and out to a track that winds through lush fields of wheat and mustard. Black canvas piping leading to irrigation ditches runs alongside the track. At the river itself, there are no fewer than five diesel-powered pumps sucking water out of the several acres of pond built up behind the dam, sending it downhill to the crops. This procedure rather embarrasses Air Marshal Sahni; he says, "Development Alternatives would prefer that the villagers irrigated from their recharged wells, because the water is of far more benefit to the general ecosystem if it's allowed to seep down through the ground rather than being drained directly from the impoundment before it can be absorbed. Pumping directly from the stream is like spending your capital instead of your interest. But of course, we don't have that much control over what people do once the structure is in place. And if they really must pump, we wish they'd use something more efficient than these cheap, badly-running diesel things." Sahni says that the formerly barren lands can now be cropped not once, but twice a year. "But even though they're better off, the farmers spend their new earnings on better clothes and food or schools for their children, rather than a more fuel-efficient pump."

One of the reasons DA is so interested in studying historical technologies is that there were no polluting, expensive motorized pumps in the past. The technology was more cunning, made better use of gravity, and depended on simple methods like the bucket-swing affairs or water wheels that farmers still use along the Nile. These human- or animal-powered devices are now being more cleverly designed and adapted to modern use. In Africa, for example, many countries are using a children's merry-go-round that has been designed to pump village water while the children play! Sahni says, "There's a hill next to the dam where I could use just one pump to take water up to a tank, and then let gravity disperse it to all the local farmers; it would save both them and the environment so much diesel input! But we don't have the funds for that just now. As for solar pumps, that's a dream we keep looking into and hoping it will become cheaper. It's such a perfect energy source in this climate."

Like so many efforts to live within our means, DA's check dams are less than perfect; but the dam itself was a truly beautiful sight after our two hours of bouncing over rocks and watching half-starved goats trying to get the bare ground to yield some food. In an oasis that is green almost as far as the eye can see, six little boys were catching minnows to take home for a special curry dish; they were also splashing, swimming and hollering in the manner of all boys at swimming holes. Dozens of egrets were flying up and resettling on the surface of the water, as well as a few ducks and other water-fowl, butterflies and frogs; and the whole pond surface was carpeted with pink, flowering plants. Without Development Alternatives, Air Marshal Sahni, their backers, the villager workers and all the other people involved in this particular dream, this spot in March, four full months before the monsoon, would have been exactly like all the places we saw on the way in — just a baked bed of rocks in a near-desert of dry grass. There would have been no acres of ripening wheat, no happy little boys, no egrets, no beautiful water. In the short time we were there, we saw fish jumping in the water and a snake disappearing into the base of the dam. Somehow, they too have appeared in this recreated, perennial river.

Villages in other provinces have similar projects, aided by other NGOs.

In Raj-Samadiyala in Gujarat, for example, fourteen check dams on the Machchan River have provided villagers with enough water for indoor household use and a single crop, while women in neighboring villages with no catchment schemes have to walk eight kilometers each and every day for two pots of brown water. Ponds, earthen dams, concrete check dams and reforestation projects are showing up all over Gujurat. In another state, Rajasthan, drought had reduced the villagers of Neemi to poaching game in a nearby forest and working far away in the crowded city of Jaipur; the rest of the time, the men drank, in despair over not being able to sell their land or get it to produce. About five years ago, a local NGO, Tarun Bharat Sangh, helped them set up a holistic plan that began with a voluntary ban on drinking and poaching. With a start-up from the NGO, they raised money, built several check dams and renovated their old, silted-up water tanks; they planted trees and started an organic dairy. Today, wages have increased by 300 percent, land prices have shot up, they have a moisture-conserving forest, and the farmers are producing up to three crops a year, using completely organic methods. No one has to migrate out of the area or poach for a living any more.

Across India, hundreds of similar water entrapment structures are being built in the same small, self-financed way, each designed to accommodate specific local needs. Yet, on a wider scale, the central government tends to thwart these methods by constructing mega-dams and displacing millions of people and entire ecosystems. That's because India's government, like so many others, sees globalization and large-scale technical fixes as their main source of future prosperity, and has been slow to aid in the implementation of more humble schemes. Another factor is that no one, especially no one from outside the area, stands to make money on check dams and other old-fashioned water impoundment techniques. They're not even on the radar of the big funders like corporations and the World Bank, which have billions of dollars to allocate every year and naturally favor capital-intensive projects.

Nonetheless, the desperate state of many Indian provinces and the proven efficacy of the small-scale solutions are beginning to attract increasing attention. This past year, another New Delhi NGO, the Centre for Science and Environment, founded by Anil Agarwal, helped organize a National Water Conference in Rajasthan. More than 5,000 villagers from twenty-three of the country's most drought-stricken areas attended. And encouragingly, Federal Minister for Heavy Industry, Balabhbhai Kathuriya, was there as well. The participants all pledged to become Water Warriors, and to build, in his words, "not one, but thousands of check dams to ensure surplus water."[5]

## Not Wasting What You've Got

*In the Sind, one of Pakistan's two major provinces, 49 percent of agricultural land was moderately or severely waterlogged, 50 percent was highly saline and 27 percent was moderately saline. In the Punjab, the other main agricultural province, over 30 percent of all agricultural land is suffering from salinization.*
— UN DATA

Bringing water back from the dead, as they're trying to do in India, is one effective way to make sure there's enough to keep the ecosystems and people going. In many parts of the world that were dry and barren long before central India became desertified, it has also become critical to find ways to conserve what water still remains. Some time ago, Joyce Starr of Washington's Global Water Summit Initiative pointed out that "Nations like Israel . . . are swiftly sliding into that zone where they are using all the water resources available to them. They have only a decade or so left before their agriculture and ultimately their food security is threatened."[6]

Jordan is already there. Jordanians are allowing good agricultural land to lie fallow because they don't have the water resources to irrigate it. By 1995 all known sources of water across the country were already being tapped, and the demand for more is still growing, due to an influx of young refugees from Palestine and a general increase in the standard of living. Other countries in the Middle East have almost no water to live on, as statistics compiled over the last ten years illustrate. For example, they estimate that the United States has a freshwater potential of 10,000 cubic meters (2.6 million gallons) per citizen, per year. Iraq has half that, Turkey only 4,000 cubic meters; but even Egypt's potential of 1,100 seems luxurious next to Israel and Jordan's 460 and 260 cubic meters per person respectively. Because of that, both of these countries have become extremely innovative in their use of water.[7]

Ancestors of the Jordanian people include the ancient Nabateans, an Arabian tribe that built beautiful cities and temples in this region 1,600 years ago. Like the ancient Indians, the Nabateans had developed many cunning methods of conserving rain and river water. Archaeologists have discovered almost as many varieties of water entrapment methods as we observed in

India, including huge cisterns, stone water channels hewn directly into the cliffs, and even carved inscriptions alluding to the need to store and conserve water. One Nabatean irrigation method was to build low walls around small plots of land to trap runoff, and then to plant crops in the boggy soil, to grow up as the water seeped into the ground.

When the modern era introduced deep-well pumping that was able not only to suck up the groundwater but to tap into aquifers as well, the region's intricate system of cisterns, reservoirs and collection channels for catching rainwater collapsed, just as India's did. Now that aquifer and groundwater levels are dropping fast, several Nabatean methods are being revived. The low-wall method is again being used in Israel, at the instigation of the Ben-Gurion University of the Negev; Jordanians have also realized the folly of dependence upon tapping ground water and aquifers. Today, they're continuing to develop modern versions of rainwater entrapment and efficient use of irrigation that will help them recharge aquifers, and also not contaminate what little rain they get.[8]

Irrigation has been used for thousands of years to get water from lakes, rivers and wells out to the crops. As Marq de Villiers says in his book *Water*, "Where drainage is good and the soils not naturally alkaline, carefully managed irrigation can persist for centuries. In areas where [it] is used as a water supplement rather than the whole diet, little harm is likely to befall the land."[9] But irrigation has a real catch to it when people try to grow crops in a desert, where the soils are poor and where drainage is inadequate. Over-irrigation and poor drainage, common in places like Uttar Pradesh, the American West and the Middle East, where rain comes all at once or not at all, carry away runoff filled with agricultural chemicals and naturally occurring minerals and salts. The reason why oceans are salty is that all water leaches out the minerals in soil and carries them to the sea. Man-made chemicals in substances like asphalt, gas and oil spills, pesticides and herbicides are swept up and carried along as well.

The salts and chemicals end up precipitating on the surface of soils when the water used for irrigation evaporates in the desert sun. There they kill soil organisms and render the soil sterile. Moreover, when fields are poorly drained, the water table rises up and keeps the soil too waterlogged for plants to grow properly. Added to these problems is the relatively recent use of petrochemical fertilizers, which destroy all organic matter until the ground hardens like cement, and the use of pesticides, which also destroy organic life in the soil and threaten human health as well.

Together, irrigation and industrial farming are destroying fertile agricultural land at an incredibly alarming rate. Millions of acres of land across
the world have succumbed to salinization and contamination due to
irrigation, and millions more are in danger unless we figure out a better
way to move water around.

In the famous San Joaquin Valley in California, the source of almost
every North American supermarket's strawberries and lettuce, about
160,000 hectares (400,000 acres) of irrigated farmland are affected by
high, brackish water tables, the telltale symptom of advanced waterlogging
and salinization. More than a million of the state's 3.4 million irrigated
hectares (7.5 million acres) will go permanently out of production unless
they are drained by buried piping. But even in affluent California, farmers
are reluctant to make such an investment. It's only a short-term solution
anyway; the salt- and pesticide-laden water that's drained off just creates
problems downstream.[10]

Necessity is the mother of invention, and it's in the deserts of Israel that
an alternative irrigation technology has been developed. It's already been
forty years since engineers at the Technion-Israel Institute of Technology in
Haifa came up with a method called "drip-irrigation." It uses perforated
hoses to deliver much smaller amounts of water directly to the root-zones of
the plants. In this way, both runoff and waterlogging are avoided; 95 percent of the water goes to nourishing the crops, as compared to only 20
percent or less with conventional irrigation; as for spray irrigation, as much
as 92 percent of it can be lost to evaporation! Drip irrigation is being used
in more than 140 countries worldwide, even on the subsistence level. Poor
villagers in Egypt, China, Peru, Mali, Niger and Senegal are all benefiting
from it, and thousands of businesses have been supplying such equipment
to the First World for many years.

But drip technology still has a long way to expand; even though it also
increases crop yields by between 20 and 50 percent, only about 2 percent of
the world's irrigated fields are using it. These days, the Israelis are even
developing something called "minute irrigation," drip-emitters that will
create optimal air-water relationships at the root-zone, and could save more
soils and more watercourses.[11] Although buying the hoses requires some
capital investment, drip irrigation is still cheaper than underground pipe
drainage. The kinds of subsidies that today fund ecologically dangerous
big dams, poisonous agrichemicals and dubious genetic technologies could
instead help farmers to purchase or lease long-term equipment for drip

irrigation. As we'll see in chapter five, "Eating Humble Pie," some countries are already moving in that highly intelligent direction.

## Green Roofs and Earth Toilets

*If you're short of water, the choices are conservation, technological invention, or the politics of violence.*
— MARQ DE VILLIERS

There is much talk about how wars will be fought in the future over water, and yet so far, places like Israel, Palestine and Jordan manage their water in a relatively civilized manner, even in times of war. And countries like Iraq, Syria, Saudi Arabia and Turkey, who may not be on speaking terms about much else, have managed so far to share the same rivers and watersheds, although sometimes even within countries things get pretty tense.[12] What most water-pressed people are trying to do these days, besides making sure they have some jurisdiction over the rivers or aquifers flowing through their territories, is to hold on to whatever water they've got.

In Jordan, for example, water rationing has already become a way of life, and legislation has reflected that ecological reality by harkening back to Nabatean technologies. Newly constructed homes and apartment buildings must now have rooftop water storage tanks fed by runoff rainwater— that is, cisterns — in addition to whatever may be piped in. Jordanian women in particular have always been charged with the job of obtaining household water, and it is not unusual for modern homes to have three separate sources.[13] Tap water, which may be rather nasty, is used for washing laundry and watering the garden; spring water, purchased in times of shortage, is used for cooking and drinking; and rainwater is collected as the preferred source for cooking and drinking. So Jordanians are being encouraged to introduce everyday conservation measures: to put bricks in toilet tanks to reduce the amount needed to flush, to water plants in the morning or evening to reduce evaporation, to watch water meters and reduce water use accordingly, to reuse wash water, known as "gray" water, and to be very careful to keep pipes and tanks in good repair to reduce loss from leakage. These initiatives, which began in schools, have now been successfully implemented in Palestine, the West Bank and Egypt, and are the subject of much television prime-time urging.

It seems only normal for desert countries to implement such measures, but it's instructive to know that even in Germany, where the rainfall is high, the vegetation lush, and the rivers, streams and groundwater plentiful, people take the same kinds of precautions. In fact, in much of Europe, toilets are routinely manufactured with a choice of two flushes — a small amount for urine, and a larger for, as the Germans put it, "the bigger business." Low-flow shower heads are the norm, and water and electric meters are placed prominently in homes and apartments so that people can keep track of what they're using. "Gray" water is often recycled automatically by village or city systems, and there are regular inspections of urban water delivery systems for leaking pipes, which can cause waste, contamination and illness.

Even in places like the Pacific Northwest of the United States, where water would seem to be problematic not for its scarcity but for its over-abundance, cities have begun to implement strategies to make sure it's not wasted or polluted. The problem in a city like Portland, Oregon, is that the copious rainwater picks up contaminants from tar roofs, car parks, side-walks and industries, and then sweeps the polluted water into overloaded municipal sewage systems that overflow and contaminate the rivers. Too much water, in other words, can also cause waste because our parking lots and buildings don't allow it to soak into the soil and replenish the groundwater, any more than hardpan or denuded deserts do.

Eric Sten and Dan Salzman, the Sustainability Commissioners in the City of Portland, have instituted a stick-and-carrot approach to rainwater conservation. Salzman explains, "Property owners who want to build green roofs to absorb and purify the rain are given subsidies and tax breaks. Homes are being offered important grants to make sure that roof runoff is channeled into the lawn or shrubbery before it hits the sewers. Or we do the whole thing ourselves, and places that do nothing can be subject to fines." The green roof concept is becoming widespread. In both Europe and North America, gardens, lawns, shrubs and even small trees are spring-ing up on the flat roofs of big apartment or office blocks. The greenery looks great and sometimes serves as a little park for the tenants. More importantly, it soaks up rainwater that otherwise would flood into the sewage system, and allows it to follow the cycle nature intended, storing a lot in the soil and the plants themselves, and releasing the excess as water vapor and oxygen.

As for sewage, schemes to spread municipally treated sludge on farmers' fields as fertilizer, which have become common in the United States, might be attractive if the sludge did not also contain massive quantities of indus-trial pollutants, including pesticides, PCBs and heavy metals. Soil can be contaminated by toxic chemicals, and diseases like meningitis can be spread when this sludge is passed off as organic when it's not. In fact this pretense is the theme of the blackly comedic and much recommended book, *Toxic Sludge Is Good for You*, by Sheldon Rampton and John Stauber. Organizations such as the Citizen's Clearing House on Hazardous Waste and Lois Marie Gibbs's highly effective toxics watchdog (see chapter eight), are also monitoring the problems incurred by this practice. The long-lasting damage to our soils, and especially to our water, that is caused by spreading toxic sludge is so serious that the only conclusion we can come to is that either we have to learn to keep these toxic compounds out of our sewers — and that includes soaps and household cleansers — or we have to treat human waste differently.

The composting toilets invented in the sixties, which reintroduced an entire generation to what all bathrooms used to smell like, were a very limited success. These days, new technology in the form of better fans and containment tanks has made "earth toilets" a viable concept again, even for public buildings with a lot of traffic. This sludge really can be made safe for use on farmland; it's the perfect answer to both our toxic- and water-waste woes. One of the best systems serves 560 students every day in a new classroom building on the campus of the Vermont Law School in southern Vermont. Another method of treating sewage is to put it through a simulation of natural purification; that is, to let it be cleansed by a carefully constructed wetland. This method of recuperating water and dealing with wastes is gaining popularity all over the world. An example from the new sustainable housing village on the Khanawake Mohawk Reserve outside Montreal is described in chapter eight.

If we continue to avoid dealing with the wastes that accompany both sewage and runoff, we will eventually have critical shortages, if not of water itself, then certainly of good drinking water, even in places like Oregon and Germany. The regulations both places have put into practice seem to reflect the simple common sense of taking care of what you have. But one thing conservationists have learned over the years is that for legislative changes to actually change habits on a day-to-day level at least some of the stimulus for the legislation has to come from within the community. Both Oregon and Germany have regional and municipal governments that were elected partly *because* of their interest in environmental sustainability. Not only do these bodies have the support of their citizens when they instigate programs to install environmentally friendly roofs and toilets, but the demand for such things has often come from the citizenry in the first place. This means that when people who care about water, soil or air quality get involved in local politics, it can have very important, long-term effects in every part of the world.

## Five Million Children a Year

*Even high-end cost estimates for providing universal access to water and sanitation amount to only 7 percent of global military expenditures. A relatively minor reordering of social priorities and investments — and a more comprehensive definition of security — could enable everyone to share the benefits of clean water and adequate sanitation.*
— SANDRA POSTEL, GLOBAL WATER POLICY PROJECT[14]

The village of Lalliput in central India serves as a perfect example of how quickly and easily positive changes can grow in a community if a project has staunch support from the local people. Here, Development Alternatives found an unlikely ally — a teenaged girl named Pinkie, the daughter of the local headman. As Air Marshal Sahni, the liaison for this project, candidly admits, "She's the whole reason we've done so well there." Pinkie is a rebel, the only girl Sahni says he's ever seen in rural India who wears pants and a baseball cap instead of a sari and earrings. She and her two more conventionally clad sisters run the village's new Internet service out of their own home. It's a big, white house on the only hill, commanding a view of the whole town, with the usual goats nosing about, polished earthen floors in the simple interior, and drying millet and bougainvillea sharing the rooftop with DA's satellite dish. Here, in a room decorated with bright posters of the Hindu gods Hanuman and Ganesh and kids' drawings done on Microsoft's Paintbox, Pinkie and her sisters train the local children in the mysteries of WordPerfect and the World Wide Web. But even more of Pinkie's efforts have gone into getting community support for Lalliput's own water and sewage system.

Pinkie helped DA set up another check dam to provide water for a system that was built and is run by the villagers. She also worked on the much more socially delicate project of introducing a system of carefully engineered pit toilets, located where they will not pollute any food or water sources. These unobtrusive little huts now provide the women of Lalliput with the privacy most villages lack. Currently, most women in rural India have to wait until nightfall, for modesty's sake; only then can they creep out of the village to use the fields as a toilet. This ancient social custom is not only extremely bad for their health, but it exposes them to further threats from the scorpions and cobras that come out to hunt at night. And of course, the habit of using fields of food crops as a bathroom can spread diseases like cholera and the ubiquitous dysentery, caused by E.coli, cryptosporidium, campylobacter and other parasites or bacteria, which can often be fatal, especially to children. In fact, UN figures show that every year, five million children die from drinking unclean water.

Outsiders had been stopping by to deliver this message for forty years, but social customs are much stronger than belief in a stranger's opinion on how people should deal with such personal concerns. It took a local woman to convince her peers to make a change that is extremely simple and obvious in terms of hygiene, but earthshaking and profound on a social level. Pit toilets are ideal in this hot, dry climate because they allow wastes to break down harmlessly, away from the water supply. And although Pinkie says Lalliput villagers have already noticed a big decline in illnesses since they set up this system, even she may never realize how many people will owe her their lives in the years to come. Of course, India's casual attitude towards basic hygiene is legendary and is one of the main reasons its rivers are in such bad shape today. But it's not only in Third World countries that illness can be caused by poor management of a community's fresh water. And the solutions to First World water contamination can often be just as simple.

Very recently, in prosperous, middle-class rural Ontario, seven people died and more than 2,000 others became horribly ill because of bad drinking water. What affected half the population of Walkerton wasn't a freak industrial chemical spill or an agricultural pesticide in their wells. It was an organic contamination from feces. Cows live in the town's water drainage basin. After an excessively rainy spring, one of the older wells the town used for drinking water was invaded by runoff from a big cattle feedlot. That is indeed normal life on this planet. Except that for many years now, in developed countries, we've known how dangerous bad water can be, and we've instituted expensive chains of regulations and inspections as well as chemical purifiers to make sure we can all use town and city water with confidence. A set of cultural beliefs banishes the women of India to dark, snake-infested fields at night. The excellent safeguards on Canadian water were altered, not by confusion about the science or by poverty in the Canadian community, but by a social belief just as dangerous as the one that puts the water at risk in Lalliput.

An integral part of neo-liberal economic theory and globalization, discussed in chapter two, is the idea that public agencies should be economically self-sustaining; services like health care, education or food- and water-testing are considered too expensive when run as non-profit public services by state or municipal governments. Private, profit-making companies, who are credited with being leaner and more efficient, are assumed under this set of values to do a better job at delivering almost any service. As we also saw in chapter two, recent cutbacks on the delivery of such services by government and the initiation of public/private partnerships have been driven not only by the ideology of neo-liberal economics; they were instigated in response to a clear request in the IMF's 1995 Consultation with Canada. In order to comply and to maximize efficiency, the Ontario government began taking itself out of the non-profit testing business. Around 1997, the government began to contract out the work of making sure Walkerton's water was safe to a for-profit private company in far-away Arkansas. The Ontario government distanced itself from water safety even further by *not* requiring the company, A&L Laboratories, to notify health or environment officials of any irregularities; they only had to notify the municipal waterworks manager, who in this case was also largely untrained.[15]

Under the public system in place just a few years previously, all Ontario water was tested locally and at regular intervals by a fleet of trained government inspectors who had to report any contamination to both local managers and the provincial health ministry as soon as they detected it. That system worked well. As recently as 1994, over 75 percent of the province's plants were undergoing yearly inspections. By 1999, that was down to under 30 percent. Maude Barlow, author of "Blue Gold," a special paper on the global water crisis, and the new book of the same name (with Tony Clarke), points out that "We really did have a good system in Ontario. We had watershed management, we had strong testing in the regions. There probably were areas that could have been improved, but instead of getting stronger, what we used to have has been steadily deregulated, piece by piece. Testing was cut back and regulations on corporate farms and industries have been smashed, so as not to 'interfere with their economic growth.' But there's absolutely no reason why a government system that is adequately funded and politically supported would not have continued to give us pure water."[16]

Infection from the organisms that invaded Walkerton's water involved more than simply getting diarrhea and then getting over it. Two of the small children affected have developed a severe platelet disorder similar to hemophilia and may never lead normal lives. Many other residents were traumatized by the painful, invasive treatments required; and of course, seven people died.[17] But like the deaths in rural India that continue to occur because of a social belief, Walkerton's deaths could have been easily prevented. In both instances, the solutions are almost ludicrously simple.

Many public interest groups, notably the Canadian Environmental Law Association, are currently demanding provincial or even national safe-water laws. Their request was recently dismissed by the Ontario Minister of the Environment, but the writing is on the wall. The United States has had a safe drinking water act since 1974, and British Columbia passed special legislation to protect drinking water in 2001. Here in the First World, there is no practical reason why we shouldn't always have clean water. We know how to do it right — and most communities still *are* doing it right.

Of course, organic contaminants like E.coli are only part of the problem. The petrochemicals we burn, the heavy metals we mine, the plastics and other non-biodegradables we throw into landfills, have all contaminated our water to even more frightening degrees. But as we'll see in chapter eight, "Wrestling with Pluto," there are ways to avoid — and even clean up — these persistent toxins. For now, we need to be asking ourselves how much we really need certain commodities, and we need to find ways to make them differently. Keeping water pure is one reason why Nike, as we mentioned in our first chapter, has banned PVCs, and why The Natural Step conditions concentrate on the elimination of toxins in the environment. That's because wherever we may dump or store our industrial poisons, they nearly always end up in our water.

Basically, water purity in the First World, which has the information and the technology to deal with all aspects of the problem, is largely a question of values. Rural India is beginning to harmonize its social values regarding feminine modesty with its desire to maintain a healthy population. But in places like Ontario, people have to measure a different set of abstract ideas, in this case the values of private versus public efficiency and the sanctity of a balanced budget against the dangers and expenses of a compromised water system. Above all, wherever we live, each of us has to make sure our own municipality is operating under values we feel we can live with. We have to keep demanding the simple, commonsense methodologies — like keeping all kinds of animal or chemical waste out of our water — methodologies that we already know from long experience will keep our water safe.

## Damn Dams

*Big dams did not start out as a cynical enterprise; they began as a dream. They have ended up as a nightmare. It's time to wake up.*
— ARUNDHATI ROY, AUTHOR[18]

Ever since the early twentieth century, dams have been hailed as a major answer to problems of water scarcity in all countries, especially poor ones. Dams reroute water from one area of a watershed to another, control flooding so that people can settle on flood plains, open up more rivers to commerce and expand agriculture into arid areas. There's a double dividend in that the controlled water can be directed through turbines to produce electricity, thus solving energy scarcity problems as well. But there's a big difference between a simple catchment dam to preserve rainwater in a dry riverbed and a huge dam affecting an entire watershed. Small dams don't interfere with the normal flow of a river; as at TARA Kendra and Rajpura, they are often able to restore and preserve a river so that water can percolate down to replenish the water table and gradually restore the entire system. Big dams, on the other hand, can be designed to gain complete control over the natural flow of rivers and to power huge turbines for electricity generation. But they wreak massive changes on the landscape. One of the world's largest reservoirs, Ghana's Akasombo Dam, for example, has flooded 4 percent of the country's entire land area. It is no longer unusual for whole river basins to be altered and for river systems to be completely diverted from their normal outlets, dried up or vastly increased; they may even change direction and end up draining another watershed.

In our desire to control our water supply and move it here and there, we never thought very much about the effects of redesigning the flow of the earth's circulatory system. We forgot about the fact that rivers are the veins and arteries of our planetary life's blood. Today, we're just beginning to recognize the negative effects of such enormous interference in natural hydrology. Silt that used to fertilize floodplains and estuaries, providing nourishment for crops, is held back; whole species that depended on the seasonal arrival of water for their reproduction, hatching or migration now suffer when it no longer comes. The Aswan High Dam on the Nile is a clear example. It now holds back 98 percent of the 124 million tons of sediment that used to fertilize Egyptian fields every year after the floods had receded; the result has been a precipitous drop in soil productivity and depth on the Nile Delta, and disastrous changes to the estuary and the fish in the

Mediterranean. We're beginning to realize that harnessing rivers for our immediate use can have incredibly serious effects on the entire web of life. Today about 20 percent of the world's 8,000 recognized freshwater animal species are threatened with extinction, and biologists agree that large dams are the biggest factor in their decline.

As often happens with human developments, we mastered the technological skills to make these massive changes before we understood the reverberations. But the engineering skills involved in reordering the arteries and veins of the earth are pretty spectacular, and the exciting sight of lights going on in valleys and water rushing into dry fields seemed worth any cost. As Indian author and activist Arundhati Roy says, in most countries the ability to do such things also became associated with the entire concept of modernity and progress, and dams were "a kind of concrete flag of patriotism." They have marched across the valleys of almost every country in the world as proof of industrialization and national technological expertise, which is why they're still going up in places like Africa, South America and China.

The United States led the way into this exciting new world of planetary water control over a century ago. By the 1930s, two agencies and a work force had been created in the U.S. just to build big dams: the Bureau of Reclamation, the Tennessee Valley Authority (TVA) and the Army Corps of Engineers. During the Great Depression, big dams were considered to be the remedy for poverty among rural Americans, just as they're touted today as the technological answer to poverty in the Third World. Even today the early dams are impressive. But the big embankment dams, the ones that close off the end of a broad valley, have become the most massive structures humanity has ever erected. The current monster, the Tarbela Dam in Pakistan, contains 106 million cubic meters of earth and rock, more than forty times the volume of the Great Pyramid.

In the United States, where these huge structures were first built, however, great numbers of large and medium-sized dams are now reaching the end of their life span. They did what they were supposed to do; they irrigated whole valleys, made desert and floodplain housing possible, and brought electricity to a lot of people. But we discovered that they also left an undying legacy of salinization, waterlogging, silted-up reservoirs, water-deprived estuaries, destroyed forests and diminished agricultural yields because of disrupted seasonal floods. They also caused the extirpation of millions of plants and animals dependent upon natural riparian habitat, and in the tropics, many human deaths from diseases like schistosomiasis and malaria. Even the Tennessee Valley Authority, which has inspired numerous river basin developments all over the world, didn't do so well at home. As Patrick McCully puts it in his book *Silenced Rivers: The Energy and Politics of Large Dams*, "Despite the tens of billions of dollars spent by the TVA, the population of the Tennessee Basin is in many ways poorer than those living in nearby areas who did not 'benefit' from TVA development."[19] Moreover, today we have developed alternative ways to generate electricity that make many of these dams simply unneeded. [20]

In short, in the First World, we have learned that dams don't create water; they just move it from one spot to another. Even though we may have more water upstream for the fifty-year average life of the dam, we'll have less downstream, and a lot of other problems we never thought about before, any more than we thought about our hearts beating before we started blocking our arteries with saturated fats. That is why today virtually all First World countries have an actual moratorium on building more big dams, and around the globe an increasingly successful movement has sprung up to stop their construction anywhere. Many groups are even urging that we bring down old dams to restore rivers to their natural flow, before we lose any more of the benefits of the planet's natural hydrology to this short-term technology.

The International Rivers Network, the major NGO concerned with dam resistance, says, "Opponents of big dams do not believe that no dam should ever be built. They do believe that dams and other development projects should be built only: after all relevant project information has been made public; after the claims of the project promoters of the economic, environmental and social benefits and costs of projects have been verified by independent experts; and when the affected and benefiting groups agree the project should be built."[21] Criteria such as these are eminently reasonable, and once they became established in North America, exposed the true economic failure of nearly all big dams. They could do the same thing for China, India and everywhere that the planet's circulatory system extends.

## The Ultimate Habitat Restoration

*In the United States, whose 5,500 large dams make it the second most dammed country in the world, we have stopped building large dams, and are now spending great amounts of money trying to fix the problems created by the existing ones.*
— INTERNATIONAL RIVERS NETWORK[22]

Dams have a finite life span. Since North American dams were the first to be built, they're the first to start falling apart. Dams crack and break and their reservoirs silt up so that the water no longer goes through the turbines or flows downstream as intended. In the U.S. and Canada alone, 2,200 dams are currently considered to have outlived their usefulness, or are actually considered unsafe. And within the next 20 years, 85 percent of all U.S. government dams will be beyond their intended life span. Moreover, 500 private hydropower dam owners will also have to renew agreements with the Federal Energy Regulatory Commission within the coming decade. And today, all the people who have learned about the issues of biodiversity, water safety, forests, estuaries, fisheries and floods associated with dams are demanding that the costs and benefits of each and every dam be reevaluated in the light of knowledge we have acquired since they were first built.

Dam decommissioning is already underway in the First World. We're learning some pretty exciting things about how to do this, as well as what kind of benefits it brings. In 1999, only one short year after the old Edwards Dam was removed from Maine's Kennebec River, literally millions of alewives, an edible migratory fish species that depends on upstream spawning grounds, returned to a stretch of the river that hadn't seen a single alewife in 160 years. Besides helping the increasingly endangered Atlantic salmon, the destruction of the dam is also expected to benefit striped bass and the rare shortnosed sturgeon. In Wisconsin's Baraboo River, the number of different fish species more than doubled, going from 11 all the way up to 24 when dams were removed and the river began to flow freely for the first time since 1850. Two more dams will come out of this river by 2002, returning nearly 200 kilometers (124 miles) of water to free flow. Other countries are following suit. In France, the removal of two dams on Loire River tributaries in 1998 was the centerpiece of attempts to restore the only river that supports native salmon in the entire country. One 12-meter-high (39-foot) dam operated by the state-owned electricity utility was blown up in 2000, and its removal has restored the entire tributary to its wild state. And most remarkably, one huge mega-dam is also toppling.

The Rasi Salai Dam, the first of a massive scheme to build thirteen dams on the Chi and Mun rivers in Thailand, was so ineptly designed that its reservoir was built on top of a geological salt dome, so it cannot serve its primary purpose of irrigation. Thousands of people occupied the dam site for many months, demanding that it be taken down and their river returned to them. In July 2000, Science Minister Arthit Urirat ordered the gates of the dam to be opened for two years, to restore the land and undertake proper environmental impact assessments. This is a remarkable precedent, and hopes are high that true decommissioning will follow.

Back in Canada, a salmon fishery is being revitalized by another dam dismantling. The Theodosia River in British Columbia historically supported runs of 100,000 pink, 50,000 chum and 10,000 coho salmon, which, after the dam was built, had sunk to 2,000 chum and only a few dozen coho. "Dams were never meant to last forever," says Mark Angelo, a driving force behind the Theodosia deconstruction who also heads the Fish and Wildlife Department of B.C.'s Institute of Technology (BCIT). He adds, "Dismantling an old dam is the ultimate in habitat restoration." The Theodosia dam was originally built to power a pulp mill, but it diverts 80 percent of the river even when the mill doesn't need the water. Angelo says that when his group, the River Recovery Project, first looked into the possibility of decommissioning, the pulp company balked. "There was an adversarial relationship at first; but after we all took a good look at how the water was used, everyone could see it was only a marginally beneficial dam, even the mill. They realized they could do without the water if they used what they had more efficiently; and now we have a wonderful working relationship with them."

BCIT is using the Theodosia as a case study as well as a precedent. Angelo says, "In the Theodosia, it's a water flow issue, because so much water was being diverted to the mill that the salmon had nothing to live in. So as we gradually increase the flow over a few years, we have a golden opportunity to do lots of baseline studies: how gravel and organic debris move through the system, what kind of invertebrate populations and fish stocks are still there, what the salinity levels at the outlet are now, and how increasing the flow will change that. We want to do this properly, so that the Theodosia can set a precedent for how rivers can be restored and dams can be reconditioned. It will provide data that can be extrapolated; for example, we're in a great position to chart how fish stocks respond to increased water flow, and what other kinds of animals will then move into the system."[23]

Near the Theodosia, in northwestern Washington State, the huge 82-meter-high (269-foot) Glines Canyon Dam and the 32-meter-high (105-foot) Elwha Dam are still standing only because the government is amassing the final funding to effect their removal. They were built in the early 1900s to power timber mills in what is now the Olympic Peninsula National Park; they single-handedly destroyed magnificent local runs of salmon. The Elwha

River sockeye is extinct, and the river's ten other fish species suffered drastic declines, as did all the creatures that depended on them. After twenty-five years of steady campaigns by the Lower Elwha Klallam Nation and conservation groups, the U.S. Congress purchased the dams in 1999, and will bring them down very soon, at a cost of over $100 million.

Talking about the costs of dam removal is misleading; in almost every case, removal is far less costly than refurbishing or repairing an old dam, even without the double dividend of restored fish and wildlife habitat. On the Baraboo in Wisconsin, for example, the cost of removing the small Oak Street Dam was $30,000, while repairing it would have been ten times as much. In Maine, removal costs of the 8-meter-high (26-foot) Edwards Dam were roughly one-third the estimated $9 million price tag of upgrading its fish ladders to meet new mandatory relicensing conditions. Paying reparations to the Elwha people in Washington State for the way the dam has been proven to violate their treaty fishing rights would cost far more than removing the old dams. This is what you call getting a big bang for your buck.

Former Quebec premier Robert Bourassa, who initiated the James Bay Project, believed that letting rivers take their waters to the sea was a terrible waste of freshwater and that huge reservoirs are just as good as natural lakes. Well-known water expert Sandra Postel points out that many people are now realizing this attitude reflects "a pretty minimal understanding of what the primary function of a river or a lake is," as well as the fact that reservoirs have been found to be significant emitters of greenhouse gases, thus adding to our climate change problems.[24] Postel says that even a decade ago, setting minimum flows to maintain the health of each river system "might have seemed a radical notion. But thanks to a flurry of court decisions, legislative actions, administrative rulings and citizens campaigns, the process is underway."[25]

In the early 1990s the U.S. Congress ruled that 987 cubic kilometers of the water that annually irrigates central California be kept in the river system to maintain fish and wildlife habitat. It even set a goal to restore the natural production of salmon and other ocean-migrating fish to twice their average levels. Farmers who used to divert water from the highly productive San Francisco Bay estuary, home to 120 species of fish, must reserve 400,000 acre-feet for the ecosystem. The city may have to cut back in dry years to meet this goal, but as Postel says, "All Californians will gain in the long run, as economic activity comes into better balance with the water environment that supports it."[26]

## Liquid Wealth

*What happens when you "privatize" something as essential to
human survival as water? What happens when you commodify
water and say that only those who can come up with the cash to
pay the "market price" can have it?*
— ARUNDHATI ROY

There are answers to all the major problems we're facing regarding the
planet's water supply. As we have seen, active movements and proven technologies are already engaged all around the world in dealing with scarcity,
misuse and waste, dams and other alterations of natural drainage patterns,
and contamination from infectious organic agents and chemical poisons.
But the final problem we have with water is perhaps the thorniest: ownership. Even though water is an absolute necessity for all life and we've
developed many ways to move it around and conserve it, we haven't really
decided who it belongs to. Water tenure is handled differently in different
parts of the world, and only recently are we paying serious attention to
which forms of ownership actually work out.

In India, for example, all watercourses are legally owned by all the people, so Development Alternatives doesn't need to get special permission
from a landowner to put up its lifesaving dams on any river course, any more
than any Indian needs special permission to walk or fish along the country's
long coastline. The same is true in Mexico. But many studies have shown
that where water is considered a common good so it can be provided as
cheaply as possible, as it is in most of North America, it's wasted. And where
it's subsidized for agricultural use, as in the American West, it's wasted on a
scale that beggars description — sprayed into the air so that 90 percent of it
evaporates, slopped so generously over the crops that it ends up destroying
the soils that it was supposed to fertilize. On the other hand, as Arundhati
Roy asks, what if water were owned privately and priced according to
its true worth? How could non-profit organizations, a village or poor
individuals ever get access to it?

Back in 1999, in Bolivia, we found out what would happen if water
were made too expensive for poor people to buy. All that country's
water rights were awarded to a profit-making American corporation,
and the price immediately skyrocketed — although service did not. In the
subsequent demonstrations demanding that the government tear up
the privatization contract, thirty-six Bolivians were killed by police,

175 were injured, and two children were blinded. The wars people imagine will be fought over water between, say, Israel and Jordan, could, in cases like Bolivia's, end up being played out between everyday citizens and a government protecting the interests of private corporations — and no one wants to see such a thing. There is an argument for privatization, of course. In countries like the former Soviet Union and other cash-strapped Eastern European countries, many cities' present water-delivery systems have been so neglected that they need massive replacement; but these countries have no tax base to achieve it. Recently, Bucharest, Romania, signed a contract with the French water giant Générale des Eaux, part of the Vivendi Group, to rehabilitate their network. Perhaps it will work out. But deals between municipal and state governments and big business for enormous projects often go hand in hand with political corruption.[27]

About twelve years ago, the mayor of Grenoble, one of France's loveliest and most prosperous cities, made a decision not unlike that made by the Conservative government in Ontario prior to the Walkerton tragedy, a decision that seems to have been based on the same basic philosophy. He decided to privatize the city's water services, in order to provide better and more efficient services. Under the aegis of a private corporation, the water works in Grenoble would make money for shareholders; it would also avoid the bungling, overstaffing and inefficiency of which publicly administered water services are so often accused. COGESE, a subsidiary of Lyonnaise des Eaux, another French water giant, got the contract. As in Walkerton, a lot of people, especially in local government, opposed the privatization scheme, but it did find enough political support to proceed.

Again, water rates immediately soared; services did not. It was later discovered that between 1990 and 1995, tariff increases brought Lyonnaise des Eaux over $10 million U.S. in excess profits for providing the citizens with water, and almost $4 million extra for treating their sewage. Even after forced contract renegotiations in 1995, the company still managed to make an excess of $2 million on the city's water and more than $300,000 on the sewage. How did they make so much money delivering a service that was formerly non-profit, paid for by citizens' taxes? The subsequent trial revealed that during the first six years the company had invoiced people for 51 percent more water than was actually consumed, which gave them a tidy $3 million extra. Then they indexed rates to inflation in such a way that that they were able to make unnecessary price increases of 4 and 5 percent on every cubic meter of water consumed or sewage treated. As for the idea that pricing water high will inspire conservation, the system set up by Lyonnaise des Eaux would have granted lower rates to those consuming the largest amounts of water, and those saving water would have paid premium rates. That was moot, however, as these quotas somehow nearly always produced a rate increase.

As the Grenoblais saw their water services deteriorating, two NGOs, ADES (Association for Democracy, Ecology and Solidarity) and Eau Secours (Save Water!) were formed. They led the fight that ended in the 1996 court conviction of Grenoble's mayor and an executive of Lyonnaise des Eaux, for accepting and paying bribes. Not only had the company paid the mayor's campaign expenses, but it was proven that they actually recovered the cost of their bribes to the mayor and others, including members of the city council — almost $6.5 million in all — by billing that amount to the water users! Emanuele Lobina, writing in the February 2000 issue of *Focus on the Public Services*, says, "Corruption is one of the practices adopted by French water multinationals to secure enormous profits. With an increasing body of evidence exposing the irregularities and the costs of the French system of delegated management, this should not be promoted as a global model."[28] Today, Grenoble has returned to its tried-and-true system of municipal water management, and water rates are back to normal. The citizens, however, are paying a lot more attention to the issue.

## If It Ain't Broke, Don't Fix It

> *Today, companies like France's Suez are rushing to privatize water, already a $400 billion global business. They are betting that $H_2O$ will be to the 21st century what oil was to the 20th.*
> — *FORTUNE MAGAZINE*, MAY 15, 2000[29]

The situation described in this epigraph from Shawn Tully's article in *Fortune Magazine* is exactly what Maude Barlow, Chair of the Council of Canadians, has been warning us about for years. It's the reason why she wrote "Blue Gold" and organized Canada's first Conference on Water, held in August of 2001. Other aggressive steps to protect Canadian water from privatization and export include the Council of Canadians' local Water Watch Committees, now set up across the country. Volunteer activists are keeping track of sudden corporate grabs on the water supply. Someone probably should be watching. As the *Wall Street Journal* declared in 1998, "After telephones, power and gas, water is the next utility to be shaken up by international competition."[30] Besides allegations of corruption and increased fees, Barlow mentions Walkerton and points out that, "When water is privatized, the public often loses its right to be informed about water quality and standards." For example, when Ontario Hydro was broken up into three new private companies in 1999, the government of Ontario made public its intention to eliminate access to information laws. Lack of access to information can be dangerous. In Sydney, Australia, the water supply is controlled by Suez-Lyonnaise des Eaux, and in 1998 people discovered that it contained high levels of the dangerous parasites Giardia and Cryptosporidium and that the public had not been informed, even though the company had known about the contamination for some time.

A recent paper entitled "Public Sector Alternatives to Water Supply and Sewerage Privatization: Case Studies,"[31] shows that it is also very rare for private water companies anywhere in the world to engage in environmentally sound practices like river restoration or separation of organic sewage from chemical waste. The reason for this is, of course, cost, and is illustrated by 1998 tables comparing costs and capital returns in Sweden, where the water is municipally owned, with Britain, where water is managed for profit. In Sweden, under municipal ownership, the average cost to the customer was only $.29 (U.S.) per cubic meter of water, whereas under private ownership, consumers in Wrexam, England, paid an average of $1.25. In general, then, especially in terms of "return on capital," public systems were found to be much cheaper for the consumer; but of course, cheaper rates are not necessarily a good thing in prosperous countries. They may mean that Swedes are wasting more water than the English, so there needs to be some kind of price juggling to make sure that doesn't happen.

What is more significant is that costs of operation were also much lower for the municipally owned water companies than for private corporations, which seems to contradict almost everything we're told about privately versus publicly owned utilities. In other words, the more expensive rates don't even guarantee efficiency. Such comparative studies have repeatedly shown that "Privatisation carries significant risks in water and sanitation, given the nature of the service as a natural monopoly, the de facto lack of competition on an international scale, the difficulty of regulating multinational companies, and especially in developing countries, the potentially very high economic and social costs of monopolistic behaviour by commercial operators."[32]

So where did the idea that public utilities were no good come from? Well, as in Walkerton, most utilities used to function pretty satisfactorily, but since the late 1980s and early 1990s they have suffered from government downsizing and new demands for profits in every sector of life. And of course, some have been deprived of funding for so long or have been so badly administered from the beginning that they really are no good. An interesting example is the Servicio Nacional de Aguas y Alcantarillados (SANAA) of Honduras, created in 1961 as the state's water supply and sewer service. It was badly set up, too centralized, top-heavy with staff, and, as with many large bureaucracies, it also suffered from poor communication between departments, as well as no clear strategy for development. Wages were low, unions were angry, morale was down and customers were dissatisfied. In 1994, the now-familiar Washington Consensus recipe for salvation came down from the InterAmerican Development Bank: privatize all your water.

This ultimatum galvanized the Honduran state bureaucracy; with union support, they opted instead for complete reorganization. Fascinatingly, they applied the holistic principles we outlined in chapter three, "Using Coyotes to Grow Grass"; not only would they fix themselves, they would aim for a very lofty vision of their collective future. SANAA encouraged its employees to praise each other with buzzwords like "dedication, integrity, pride and unity," and fostered self-management and self-organization on every possible level. They decentralized, reduced the overstaffing by 35 percent, made billing local (a huge improvement), and while increasing the price of water, made sure that there was a subsidy that delivered the first 20 liters (4 gallons) for free, which was enough to keep people without a cent from misery. They then increased pipeline networks threefold and enabled the population to receive piped water twenty-four hours a day for the first time in their country's history. By making infrastructure repairs that reduced leaks, they were able, in the capital city of Tegucigalpa alone, to save an incredible 100 liters a second. The upshot of their efforts was not only the salvation of publicly owned water and sewage in their country but the recognition of SANAA, in 1999, as a United Nations Model Project.

Obviously, not every private water service behaves as badly as Lyonnaise des Eaux did in Grenoble, and not every public one is as inspiring as SANAA. The point is that there is no empirical evidence that public sector water utilities are less efficient than privatized water companies. And since they do not have to come up with profits to investors, figures show that they deliver the water at a better price. Public utilities can also exist in many different forms. They can raise investment finance like a business, and from all the same sources private companies do — banks, government funds, international institutions like the World Bank or the Asian Development Bank, bond markets and so forth. As non-profits, they can also qualify for grants and aid; the city of Lodz, Poland, for example, found that grants from the Polish National Environment Fund would finance their new sewage plant much more cheaply than the deal offered them by Vivendi. Water utilities can also be cooperatives, the biggest being SAGUAPAC, in the city of Santa Cruz in Bolivia. And, while developing countries are said to need private expertise because of their lack of infrastructure, there is now a very large, vibrant system called PUPs (public-public partnerships), which arranges for a publicly owned water company in a First World country to provide expertise and help finance a new company in a developing country. There are few if any such agreements or initiatives in the private sector. Why would there be? They don't increase profits.[33]

## The Work Agenda

*For the poorest and weakest, water is for drinking,*
*not fighting over.*
— KADER ASMAL, WINNER OF THE STOCKHOLM WATER PRIZE

Global threats to water from uncontrolled corporate tenure and trade are alarming, but it's important to remember that they are not yet widespread. If people react now, they can withhold consent from the philosophy that underlies the commodification of water. As Maude Barlow says, "To date . . . the harm done to water has been largely unintentional and reactive — a combination of benign neglect, ignorance, greed, too many demands on a limited resource, careless pollution and reckless diversion." She suggests ten common principles to govern our approach to water in her report "Blue Gold." Key among them is the assertion that water should be left where it is whenever possible. Barlow says, "One of my key principles is that nature puts water where it belongs. The more we tamper with it, the more the whole system collapses. Commodifying it so you can, say, take water from northern Canada and send it down to Nevada, which honestly is one of the grandiose plans that's afoot, is not only going to feed a culture of water waste in the U.S., it's going to despoil the whole northern ecosystem. It's playing god. And nature will bite."

Sandra Postel points out that it's essential to get a handle on agricultural use. Because agriculture accounts for between 70 and 90 percent of global water use, "reducing irrigation needs by a mere 5 to 10 percent can free up substantial quantities of water. Switching from a water-intensive [crop] like sugar cane or rice [or flowers for export] to something less intensive [like wheat or corn], investing in drip irrigation lines or low-pressure sprinklers, scheduling irrigations to more closely match a crop's water needs, are just a few of the ways farmers can save." As for the thorny issue of ownership, like many other analysts, Postel believes water should be free only for survival uses. "If farmers were required to pay prices for water that reflect its true cost, many would make these efficiency improvements. By heavily subsidizing water, governments give out the false message that this resource is abundant and can be affordably wasted — even as rivers are drying up, fisheries are collapsing, and species are going extinct. Yet virtually all governments do subsidize water use — typically by building these large water projects like dams, and then charging farmers only a fraction of the water's true cost."[34]

On the surface, it seems that Barlow has a slightly different view. Although she also believes that water is a basic human right and must remain a common, public good, not a private commodity, beyond that, she says, there is a role for marketing. "We can have a price conversation if we agree on one thing: no profit. We need to guarantee a certain amount of water per person, and there actually is such a clause in the South African constitution! So you might prioritize it this way: water is first for people, second for nature, third for business. Beyond that you can price it, but not for profit; for infrastructure expenses, for pollution clean-up, system refurbishment, reclamation of rivers or wastewater; to distribute to the poor, help nature, whatever. If we can agree on those basics, then we can have the pricing discussion."[35] If ecosystems and real human needs are protected by laws, water marketing can have positive effects, as we saw in chapter three when Don Sampson's tribe bought out irrigation rights to save salmon; and city people will be more careful if the prices they pay for water have some bearing on its true value. The SANAA option — of providing a basic amount for free, and then charging for use above that — seems to be a really good one.

If we look carefully at the examples we've seen, from Bundelkhand and Walkerton to the Elwha Dam and SANAA, it appears that the most effective measures for the day-to-day management of our water supply can be summed up in Barlow's advice: "The best advocates for water are local communities and citizens, who need to participate as equal partners with government."[36] Members of the World Water Contract, an organization working out of Europe, are seeking ways to make these principles a reality, with the creation of a Network of Water Parliaments and a World Water Treaty. They have active chapters in Montreal, in Toronto, and probably not far from where you live. They've written a manifesto that they're doing their best to get adopted by the UN and other international bodies. They're demanding a network of Parliaments for Water and a World Observatory for Water Rights.

World Water Contract activists also want a World Water Treaty, which would exclude water from international commercial conventions, preventing it from being commodified on the WTO model; they single out agriculture as the primary waster of the world's water, and call for implementation of solutions like drip irrigation and water catchment systems; they want a fifteen-year moratorium on the construction of *any* large dam. The movement was begun in Portugal by ex-President Mario Soares, and now has members in countries from Sweden and Italy to Morocco and Bangladesh. Contacts for the World Water Contract, the Council of Canadians and all kinds of other organizations are listed at the back of this book. All they need is some good, local help.

CHAPTER 5
# EATING HUMBLE PIE
## Growing Good Food

### A Little Paradise

*Rice terraces are the most ecologically stable and productive agricultural system ever invented, capable of supporting a large population indefinitely.*
— STEPHEN LANSING, ANTHROPOLOGIST AND AUTHOR[1]

The island of Bali, in the Indonesian archipelago, a rich kingdom of mountains and golden beaches lapped by tropical seas, meets all our criteria for a heaven on earth, and more. The Balinese long ago transformed their forested land into tiers of terraces ascending the volcanic slopes in order to grow rice, vegetables and fruit — enough to nourish a large population. In the last thousand years they have had to change their gentle and prosperous lifestyle very little. Bali's people are well-nourished and beautifully dressed, and they have enough wealth and leisure time to be able to pursue traditional arts like weaving flower garlands for their temples, creating their famous shadow puppets, dancing and enjoying festivals and music. Their island is perfect for wet rice cultivation, and rice is the fountainhead not only of Balinese prosperity, but of its culture and religion as well.

Most forms of agriculture on this planet exploit previously forested soils; farmers remove trees so that the stored-up nutrients deposited by centuries of rotting forest vegetation will nourish their crops. But typically, if they are not carefully managed, such ex-forest soils become depleted fairly rapidly. Irrigated agricultural land is even less viable. Irrigation usually brings a gradual decline in fertility, as well as the waterlogging and salinization we discussed in chapter four, in as little as two generations — and at most in only a century or two after the trees are cleared. Yet Bali does use irrigation; the irrigation systems that have kept Bali a rich garden for a thousand years also forced it to develop an advanced form of social planning. In fact, it is arguable that its centralized civilization developed in order to manage both water and rice.

One of the world's experts on Bali, American anthropologist J. Stephen Lansing, has spent many years in Indonesia studying the country's culture; he soon learned that to understand the Balinese religion, he had to understand its farming techniques as well. Lansing began by focusing on Bali's traditional religion, which is centered around the water goddess, Dewi Danu. Served by a large community of priests, priestesses and worshippers and a system of temples that line the island's watercourses, she is said to live in a large, deep lake at the very top of the island, the single source of all its rivers and streams. Lansing began to wonder if the complicated ceremonies performed by water priests in the goddess's temples — located at the upstream edge of each paddy and terrace, and at the lake itself — might have a practical as well as a cultural purpose. Balinese irrigation systems, he says, "can be extraordinarily complex." About half the rivers and streams on the island run only half the year, during the monsoon season, and these watercourses have cut deep channels along the flanks of the country's volcanoes, which make it very difficult to get at the water. To overcome this problem, Lansing explains, "The Balinese build weirs or diversionary dams across a river, diverting all or part of the flow into a tunnel. The tunnel emerges as much as a kilometer downstream, at a lower elevation, where the water is routed through a system of canals and aqueducts to the summit of the next hillside."[2]

The cosmology of their religion is equally complex. It has a great deal to do with the sacredness of all water, both up and downstream, and especially with the timing of its release. Worshippers at each temple, from the single farmer at his shrine up to the united temple at the lake, have yearly meetings in which the high priest, the *Jero Gde*, assigns dates and times of irrigation water release to each water-sharing village, or *subak*, and therefore to each and every farmer. The timing of the release of the sacred waters naturally influences dates of planting, the variety of rice that is planted, the timing of the harvest and the scheduling of fallow fields or alternative crops. In other words, Lansing realized, the high priest controls the entire agricultural cycle, and also arbitrates any conflicts over water or land use.

Lansing first arrived in the country in the early 1970s, when the power of the water temples and priests was still in full force and the paddies were in their traditional condition. Throughout the late 1970s and the 1980s, he watched as the old ways were overcome by a mandated central government policy that favored modern Western methods of growing hybrid rice and using fertilizers and pesticides. He even ended up personally influencing the outcome of this national experiment with industrial agriculture. What happened with the water temples in Bali is an important lesson that illustrates how natural systems work and how people can work in concert with them — or destroy them — according to their approach.

## A Little Respect

*These people don't need a high priest, they need a hydrologist!*
— AMERICAN IRRIGATION ENGINEER IN BALI[3]

Even during his first visits to Bali, Lansing had begun to suspect that the colorful festivals, dances and ceremonies going on at every temple and the noisy public activities surrounding what outsiders called "the water cult" or "the rice cult," obscured the priest's role as ecological manager. He realized that the flow of water — the planned alternation of wet and dry phases organized by the temples — governs not just when water is available for planting, but "the basic biochemical processes of the [entire] terrace eco-system." He knew about a major ecological theory that systems characterized by steady, unchanging supplies of nutrients are less productive than systems in which nutrient cycles vary. The controlled influxes of water in the paddy system, as well as the planned dry periods, create what are called "pulses" in the biochemical cycles. The cycles of water pouring in and then drying out alter pH levels and circulate mineral nutrients such as potassium and nitrogen. The alternation between aerobic and anaerobic conditions in the soil also changes the types of microorganisms, discourages weeds, stabilizes the soil temperature and even fosters the growth of nitrogen-fixing algae. Finally, and probably most importantly for the longevity of the terrace ecosystem, it establishes a kind of sub-pan or foundation under the soil that *prevents* the usual drainage that occurs in volcanic soils, which is what usually causes nutrients to leach down into the subsoil where they become unavailable to plants.

These biochemical cycles also affect the presence of life in the soil, leading to perhaps the most important practical result of the temples' complicated system of water supply. Pests are controlled by the availability of food and other life support systems. If there is a very large supply of the same food, pests will multiply to take advantage of it. If not, their numbers remain relatively small. Both flooding and rice stalk burning are methods of pest control, but as Lansing says, the whole process depends upon cooperation among the farmers, because pest control areas that are too small are not helpful, either. "It would be useless for a single farmer to try to reduce the pests on his own field without coordinating with his neighbors, since the pests would simply migrate from field to field." Both methods, the burning and flooding of large and small areas, are very tricky. The farmers are trying to outwit not only the scores of bacterial and viral diseases that attack rice, but also the many insects and rodents. So, as Lansing says, "How many hectares must be left fallow and for how long depends on the species characteristics of [each] rice pest." In short, a very high order of knowledge about the paddy ecosystem on the micro and the macro level is demanded in order to keep the terraces going.[4]

There is yet another factor to consider. If everyone plants and harvests at roughly the same time, the widespread fallow period will defeat many pests by depriving them of habitat and food. But if the same variety of rice or crop is used, everyone will need water at the same time, and there won't be enough. "Striking an optimal balance between these two constraints is not a simple matter," says Lansing, "since choices made by upstream farmers have implications for downstream neighbors and constraints such as the amount of water available for irrigation vary by location and by season."[5] There are still other management considerations on top of all that; although the main crop is rice, the temple-managed paddies also produced protein for the population by providing habitat for eels, frogs and fish during the flooding cycles. Even the dragonflies hovering over the ponds were eaten, and the systems' large flocks of ducks had to be carefully managed so that they ate insects like the brown planthoppers waiting in the gleaned fields for the next crop, but didn't damage young rice stalks.

Of course, no sooner does an anthropologist discover something these days than it vanishes, and the water temple management system was no exception. The fall of the Indonesian dictator Sukarno in 1965 coincided with what was being hailed as an exciting scientific breakthrough in the field of agriculture. Agronomists and plant geneticists in the United States at first, and then at the International Rice Research Institute (IRRI) in the Philippines (still making the news today with its work on genetically engineered "golden rice"), were breeding new hybrid strains of rice that everyone was told would guarantee food self-sufficiency for the poor. Populations were growing, and countries had economic as well as political reasons to pursue self-sufficiency; they wanted more rice so that they could sell it for foreign exchange and convert their subsistence farming economies to industrialized ones.

By the mid-1960s, the IRRI had developed something they thought was perfect: a rice called IR-8, which matured in only 125 days and produced an amazing 6,500 kg of grain per hectare (5,800 pounds per acre) on its test plots. Indonesia was sold on this new variety and through regional and local bureaucracies began an aggressive program to convert its agricultural system. Since the new rice was heavily dependent upon chemical inputs for its yield, the government instituted a system of subsidies for fertilizers and pesticides. They even set up a People's Bank to provide credit to small farmers, so they could purchase the chemicals and machinery that were the prerequisites of the new "miracle rice." Results were rapid. By 1974, 48 percent of the terraces of south-central Bali were planted with IR-8 rice; by 1977, that had climbed to 70 percent.[6]

The practitioners of the Green Revolution worked then (and still do now) under the reductionist assumption that agriculture is a purely technical process, and that production can be optimized if everyone simply plants high-yielding varieties as often as possible. Like the financial system of continuous growth on which this Revolution is philosophically based, they also externalize such factors as the health of the soil, the general abundance of water, the ability of natural systems to deal with the chemical wastes these practices create, and the social systems of the farmers themselves, to say nothing of effects on other species and the wild ecosystem. In their view, if a project works in a Philippine lab or a test plot in Iowa, it will work equally well on a volcanic terrace in Bali. Problems with soil fertility and pests can be handled with petrochemical inputs, and problems with water will be solved by deep-drilled wells or more dams and diversions.

But water wasn't the first problem. Within only three years of its first plantings in Bali, IR-8 had proven itself susceptible to the brown planthopper, which attacked the new rice, destroying two million tons in Indonesia in 1977 alone. Scientists at IRRI quickly came up with IR-36, which was resistant to planthoppers and matured even more quickly. The government was so excited about this breakthrough that it forbade Balinese farmers to plant their native varieties any more. The experts said then, and would say again, that native varieties take much longer to mature, are less responsive to fertilizers and produce less grain per head. Visions of repaying all their debts and having coffers full of foreign exchange with which to modernize and become rich inspired the government to legally mandate double- and even triple-cropping of IR-36 and other high-yielding hybrids. Even more significantly, Lansing says, "Farmers were instructed to abandon the traditional cropping patterns and to plant high-yielding varieties as often as possible"; in other words, to help themselves to water and plant their terraces regardless of the irrigation cycle or their neighbors' needs. Foreign consultants, mostly American, had been brought in to help modernize Bali's irrigation systems, and formed the Bali Irrigation Project (BIP), funded in 1979 by the Asian Development Bank, an arm of the World Bank. The country had borrowed about $40 million (U.S.) to build thirty-six new weirs and canals. Although this project wouldn't bring more land into cultivation, it was supposed to give the farmers enough water to plant crops continuously, which in turn would provide enough foreign exchange for Indonesia to pay back the loan.

By the late 1970s, the water priests were losing control over both irrigation and cropping patterns. Religious observances in the temples continued, but field rituals no longer corresponded to the stages of cropping. In order to meet the projected yields, as soon as one crop was harvested another was put in, with no fallow period or vegetable planting in between. Soon, Lansing says, "district agricultural offices began to report 'chaos in the water scheduling' and 'explosions of pest populations.'" IR-36, although resistant to planthopper, had turned out to be easy prey for a viral disease called tungro. The district office of Gianyar reported in 1980 that "a temporary remedy was found in the new rice variety PB-50. In one cropping season, tungro was reduced, but immediately afterward the new rice was afflicted by *Helminthosporium oryzae.*" PB-50 then turned out to be just as vulnerable to rice blast, a terrible disease spread throughout Asia by the IRRI itself, which had imported the blast fungus as part of its research. Moreover, the chemicals that were used to control noxious insects and fertilize the soil were also destroying the fish and eels the villagers had depended upon for protein; even their birds were disappearing. To top it all off, the rates of testicular cancer in paddy farmers began to rise alarmingly; the disease is linked to pesticide exposure.

"By the mid-1980s," says Lansing, "Balinese farmers had become locked into a struggle to stay one step ahead of the next rice pest by planting the latest resistant variety." They also had a poorer diet and more health problems. So, "despite the cash profits from the new rice, many farmers were pressing for a return to irrigation scheduling by the water temples to bring down the pest populations." But there was a cultural disconnect, the same one we have seen many times before. The experts advising the central government, as well as the Western-educated Indonesian elite, were locked into the assumption that culture and religion have nothing to do with agriculture, that they are externalities to science. Lansing says, "The proposal to return control of irrigation to water temples was interpreted as religious conservatism and resistance to change. The answer to pests was pesticide, not the prayers of priests. Or as one frustrated American irrigation engineer said to me, 'These people don't need a high priest, they need a hydrologist!'"

## And a Little Humility

*The kind of thinking that has gotten us into this situation*
*is not the kind of thinking that will get us out of it.*
— ALBERT EINSTEIN

Officials at both BIP and the Asian Development Bank saw the decline of the water temples simply as a typical cultural loss, the "almost inevitable result of technical progress." But by the mid-1980s, the irrigation situation had become so chaotic and disorganized and the rice so rife with bugs and diseases that a team of agronomists from Udayana University was commissioned by Bali's Department of Public Works to investigate. They reported that the government needed to take note of "the connections between the hierarchy of *subak* temples and cropping patterns." At this point, Lansing got directly involved. He found Dr. James Kremer, a systems ecologist, and together they decided that creating computer imaging of the various water management methods might take temple functions out of the realm of faith and superstition and put them into a language that modern experts could understand. They constructed a simple model based on two actual Balinese river sheds. They ran it through the computer using different basic planting/irrigation systems: every *subak* was randomly assigned its own cropping patterns; every *subak* followed the same cropping pattern (the Green Revolution method); and finally, the *subaks* were planted in clusters that imitated the patterns created by the water temples.

When plantings were done randomly, the models showed a harvest average of 4.9 tons per hectare. When the model was run according to the water temple patterns, the harvest jumped to 8.57 tons per hectare. When the models were run to also allow for pest infestations and modern hybrids, most yields were higher for Green Revolution varieties (up to almost 10 tons per hectare) for *one year*, but were then followed by catastrophic pest losses of up to 100 percent of the crop the following season — exactly what had happened on the ground. The temple-controlled method, on the other hand, kept rice yields and pests in a productive balance, averaging about 17 tons over *two* years, in contrast to the Green Revolution's 9 tons. Lansing ran many experiments that convinced him that the temple method must have evolved over many, many years from initial random planting. The models showed, he says, that, "the temple networks are intrinsically capable of doing a better job of management than either uncoordinated planting (the Green Revolution system of 'every man for himself,') or centralized government control." And they place a premium on cooperation: "All farmers who share water from the same source must cooperate in construction, maintenance, water allocation and the management of disputes."

Like most large-scale methods for obtaining human cooperation, Bali's traditional paddy agriculture works through a visible system of social networks. The little shrines at the upstream points link the physical irrigation tunnels and ditches to the social world of the big temples and therefore to the villagers who attend their services. The rituals inside the temples, which feature offerings not just to local gods but to the gods of other streams and rivers in the system, help the congregation remember and acknowledge their relationship to the other farmers up and down the line. The computer model helped transform the temple rituals — the flowers and incense, the dancing maidens and the clanging bells and sounding horns — into the kind of mathematical graph modern planners can relate to. Eventually, everyone from the BIP to the Ford Foundation and the Asian Development Bank began to understand. A late 1980s report from the formerly hostile BIP reads, "The substitution of the 'high technology and bureaucratic' solution in the event proved counter-productive, and was the major factor behind the yield and cropped area declines experienced . . . The cost of the lack of appreciation of the merits of the traditional regime has been high. Project experience highlights the fact that the irrigated rice terraces of Bali form a complex artificial ecosystem which has been recognized locally over centuries."[7]

Bali is enjoying the proverbial happy ending. The good news is that it's still a paradise. After nearly a decade of disastrous harvests, the water temple system has received recognition by state bureaucracies and has resumed informal *de facto* control of Bali's agricultural system. Farmers today have been able to find and again use many of their once-banned native seeds; but even more importantly, they are now respected and are even being consulted by modern Westernized bureaucracies. An official document from one state's recent Project Evaluation Mission expresses gratitude for the *subaks'* "technical advice" on spring development, water allocation issues,and canal and tunnel building. And it says, in what for a bureaucracy is very strong language, "In light of the minimal success of the Project Office to develop new irrigation areas, [we] suggest that there would be benefit from seeking advice from the [*subaks*]. At the least, this exercise would be of assistance in bringing the two parallel water development and management institutions into closer contact, and could have far-reaching impacts." It certainly could.[8]

## Getting More with Less

*Hunger is not caused by a scarcity of food,*
*but by a scarcity of democracy.*
— FRANCES MOORE LAPPÉ, AUTHOR

Miguel Altieri, a respected agricultural expert who teaches at the University of California at Berkeley, points out that we already have about half again as much food available, worldwide, than the human population can eat. "The world today produces more food per inhabitant than ever before . . . 4.3 pounds [2 kilos] for every person, every day; 2.5 pounds [1 kilo] of grain, beans and nuts, about a pound [450 grams] of meat, milk, eggs and another pound of fruits and vegetables. The real causes of hunger are poverty, inequality and lack of access."[9] Altieri's facts are echoed by almost any specialist on food and hunger in existence. Frances Moore Lappé, who wrote the famous book *Diet for a Small Planet* thirty years ago, singles out the main reason for inequality of access to food. "Increasingly, public discussion about food and hunger is framed by advertising by multinational corporations that control not only food processing and distribution, but farm inputs and seed patents." In other words, agri-business and chemical corporations have something to gain by influencing our conception of how best to grow food. She points out that hunger "can never be solved by new technologies, even if they were to be proved 'safe.' It can only be solved as citizens build democracies in which government is accountable to them, not to private corporate entities."[10]

For example, Lappé is critical of modern livestock feeding practices. We feed ruminants grain, she says, not because it is a food they would eat in nature, but because we want to fatten them faster. They used to convert grasses that were inedible for us into high-grade protein; but today one half of the world's grain goes, not to feed people, but to fatten animals, and it doesn't all turn into flesh. More than half of that food is excreted by the livestock or used for energy. Lappé calls livestock animals "protein disposals" rather than "protein factories." "And now," she says, "we're performing the same disappearing trick with the world's fish supply, in fish farms, feeding fish to fish." Why have we adopted such inefficient agricultural practices? Lappé says it's because we produce for the market, not to feed the hungry: "The hundreds of millions of people who go hungry cannot create a sufficient 'market demand' for the fruits of the earth. So more and more of it flows into the mouths of livestock, which convert it into what the better-off can afford. Corn becomes filet mignon. Sardines become salmon."[11]

Indian physicist Vandana Shiva, another agriculture and food activist, is a recipient of the Right Livelihood Award, "the alternative Nobel Prize," for her many publications on food production. She points to reams of studies by universities, the UN and FAO (the UN's Food and Agriculture Organization) showing that the most productive form of agriculture is not our modern, tractor-serviced, big field monocultures, but multiple-crop (termed "polyculture"), manual-labor-intensive smallholdings. As we've seen with water and livestock and now with agriculture, the natural physics of this planet favors variety and small, localized production. FAO charts of countries from countries like the Sudan, Nigeria and Uganda, Burma, India and Nepal all show maximum productivity on tiny farms ranging in size from between one and two hectares — the typical peasant smallholding.[12]

When a farm gets larger, productivity drops. In Brazil, for example, Shiva points out, "the productivity of a farm of up to 10 hectares [25 acres] was $85 per hectare, while the productivity of 500-hectare farms [1235 acres] was only $2 per hectare. In India, farms of up to 5 acres [2 hectares] had a productivity of 735 rupees per acre, while 35-acre farms [14 hectares] productivity levels were about half of that."[13] Green Revolution methods, which need machinery, expensive chemicals and monocultures, are not suitable for smallholdings, and the heavy subsidies and government incentives that have accompanied them demand big fields. This has meant that over the past thirty or forty years, government subsidies have gone to larger, less efficient farms and agribusinesses rather than to the small, more productive farmers.

In India, Shiva says, "the displacement of varied crops, which were mix-tures of cereals, legumes and oilseeds, by monocultures of High Yielding Variety (HYV) crops for export, has undermined food self-sufficiency in a drastic way." The small peasant, who concentrates on food for her family and does not fit into the cash crop package, is displaced by the subsidized, richer farmer and loses access to the food she used to grow for herself. Ironically, this loss has ended up being expressed as a food "surplus" in many national statistics. Both Indian economist V.K.R. Rao and nutritionist C. Gopalan agree with Shiva's analysis that the "surplus" food stocks that have built up in India since the Green Revolution — up from 63 million tons in 1966 to 128 million tons in 1985 — have been created not by better yields, but by people losing access to their land and not having any money. In other words, this grain goes into warehouses because an increasing number of Indians cannot afford to buy it. Statistics also show that during this same period, "food consumption dropped from 480 grams per capita per day, in 1965, to 463 grams per capita in 1985."[14] That doesn't sound as if more poor people are getting fed by industrial farming.

The good news about what at first seems to be a desperate situation for the poor is that, despite the continuous efforts and global pressures of indus-tries and government, much of the Third World's arable land is still in the hands of peasants, in those efficient smallholdings. Against all odds and with no outside support, they are still producing their own food, using the only methods we know of that stand up to the criteria of sustainability. Shiva says, "it would be no exaggeration to say that small, family-run farms are the answer to our terrible problems of declining agricultural productivity and vanishing biodiversity."[15] When countries have pulled back from large-scale, industrial farming for a variety of political and economic reasons, and espe-cially when they've also paid attention to indigenous knowledge, they have experienced benefits in terms of food production that are nothing short of astounding.

In Indonesia, subsidies for the use of pesticides were eliminated in 1987, and restrictions were introduced on the use of 57 pesticides in rice-growing. By 1990, not only had pesticide use decreased by 50 percent, but rice yields had *increased* by 15 percent. Farmers' net incomes increased by $18 per farmer, per season, and the government was saving $120 million a year. What's more, this $120 million of Third World money was no longer going out to enrich large chemical corporations; it became available for much-needed internal social programs.[16] In Bangladesh, a "No Pest" program led to another reduction in pesticide use of a full 76 percent. This did not cost the country any of their rice harvest, as they'd feared, but instead gave them yield increases of 11 percent!

A United Nations Development Program project on sustainable agriculture introduced an indigenous system of raised fields that had evolved in the Altiplano of the Andes to nearby South American countries. These methods tripled and quadrupled yields in Honduras, for example, raising them from 400 kilograms per hectare to between 1,200 and 1,600 kilograms per hectare. Finally, the World Resources Institute, a Washington-based think-tank, reviewed sustainable agriculture projects affecting almost two million households in the Third World, and found that farmers' yields of wheat, corn and sorghum *doubled* when they switched from industrial, high external-input agriculture to "biodiversity-based, low-input," organic polycultures.[17]

So, even with an extremely inefficient system — industrial agriculture set up to benefit export markets — we have half again as much food as we need to feed the planet. If we implemented more small polycultures, we could feed a lot more people — and they'd have the land security they need to take care of themselves without expensive and politically and socially difficult redistribution programs. To say that small polycultures meet the sustainability requirement of double dividends is putting it mildly. Not only have the countries which have maintained or introduced such programs saved their land and water systems from more contamination by dangerous poisons, but they have simultaneously achieved what the poisons were supposed to be doing all along: they have increased their food supply. This is so contrary to what we've been told about chemical farming for the past fifty years that we were hardly able to believe it, and we spent a great deal of research time on this question. But again and again, all around the world, in every kind of agricultural production, we found that growing more food does not work the way agribusiness and the multinational chemical companies have been telling us.

## The Old Job Is Done

*There is growing evidence that the Industrial era has already ended in many sectors of the economy outside of agriculture, and that agriculture will soon follow.*

— JOHN IKERD, AGRICULTURAL ECONOMIST

Thousands of examples coming in from around the world in scientific research done by governments, NGOs and universities support the conclusion that the benefits of industrialization to farmers, both Third and First World, were not only greatly exaggerated but hid a tragic contradiction. One of the reasons that so many farmers all over the world have been forced off an increasingly degraded and poisoned landscape since agricultural industrialization first began is that, for what seemed to be very good reasons, we collectively decided to value the kind of wealth that is created through industrialization over that created by nature.

The tragedy for people struggling to grow food, whether they are peasants in Bangladesh or wheat farmers in South Dakota, lies clearly in the underlying goal of "industrialized" agriculture. It was created not to help farmers, but to provide cheap food for a growing urban population, the labor force for expanding industries. In other words, as agricultural economist John Ikerd says, "Sustainable farm profits are inherently inconsistent with industrial agriculture." Its goal is *not* to make farmers prosperous and keep them on the land, but to get them off. And this might help explain why the industrialization of agriculture in the Third World is causing chaos and misery, and also why its architects seem to be unmoved by that distress. They have another vision of human well-being.[18]

In the early 1900s, Ikerd points out, before we began to industrialize agriculture, more than half the people even in the United States were farmers, and it took about half the country's total resources — money, time and effort — just to produce food and clothing for the population. Government planners realized that, in order to have more goods and services and take advantage of the products and comforts that were emerging out of the new technologies being developed by the Industrial Revolution, they needed to free people up from the task of providing food so they could go to work in the factories and offices of the emerging new economy. They also had to make sure the cost of food and clothing was low enough that very large numbers of people would have the disposable income to buy the goods their new industries were going to produce. In short, he says, "We had to make it possible for fewer farmers to feed more people at a lower cost . . . Through specialization, mechanization, simplification and routinization, we bent nature to serve our needs . . . Fields and feed lots became biological assembly lines, with inputs coming in one side and commodities coming out the other."[19]

The result was extremely efficient agriculture, in terms of how many people were needed to produce it and how little its products were valued at the marketplace (although that value did not, as usual, reflect ecological inputs and losses). In any event, the people "freed" from farm work labored in the cities to make a much more diversified economy boom, and, as we like to say, "got us where we are today." But today, Ikerd explains, we're using agricultural methods that are so efficient in terms of low costs and low employment that there is very little more left to be achieved. Less than 2 percent of the population in the United States produces all the food, and people have to spend only about 10 cents out of every dollar to buy that food. Even more remarkably, the producer gets only one penny of those ten cents, while the other nine cents go to the marketing and chemical companies. We now pay much more for packaging and advertising than we do for actual food.

So, as Ikerd says, "Future gains from further industrialization of agriculture must be squeezed from the farmer's penny. [That means] it simply doesn't make much difference to society any more whether there are more or fewer farmers, or whether farmers are more or less efficient." We also don't need to get more people off the land, because "there are no good paying factory jobs left for displaced farmers, or for anyone else." If farmers were slave labor getting absolutely nothing for producing food, the average consumer would only save one more cent out of each dollar spent just on food. So we can't make food much cheaper by intensifying, verticalizing or mechanizing and putting more farmers out of business.[20]

The second problem with industrialized agriculture, in Ikerd's analysis, is that, "At the same time that the benefits to society of an industrial agriculture have declined, the perceived threats of that agriculture — to the [global] environment, the natural resource base, and to the quality of life of farmers, rural residents and society as a whole — have risen." These concerns, which the Bali story typifies, are very well documented and have led to the growth of what's called "niche markets" for a variety of more sustainably produced products. Because industrial agriculture has succeeded in making food so cheap, even if farmers were to increase their share of the pie by 50 percent — another 5 cents on the food dollar — retail food prices would only climb by 2 percent, and average consumers would only have to spend 2 percent more of their total income on food. Clearly, especially in the First World, such a choice would be more than feasible for most of us, and this is in fact is what is happening. A whole variety of new food choices have been appearing, first in health food stores and farmers' markets and now even in supermarket chains. Ikerd calls this new movement "post-industrial agriculture," and lists the many names it goes under — organic farming, alternative agriculture, humane agriculture, biodynamic farming, Community Supported Agriculture, local food systems, permaculture, Integrated Pest Management, the predator-friendly meats we saw in chapter three, and a host of other movements, "which, by one means or another, address the broad question of sustainability."[21]

It isn't necessary to go into long definitions of each one; they differ from each other in many ways, but they have similar goals. Organic farming basically eschews the use of chemicals, but it doesn't promise that the animals it raises are humanely treated; organic beef cows or pigs might be cooped up all their lives in a feed lot or crowded pen eating grain that doesn't have pesticides on it. Although the "certified organic" label still remains the best way in most of the world for consumers to guard their health from exposure to carcinogens and food-borne diseases like Mad Cow disease and E.coli contamination, it generally, but not always, addresses the issues of sustainable practices, like conserving water, working with nature, protecting biodiversity and so on. That's what movements like "bio-intensive" and "bio-dynamic" do. And like all the management systems we've seen so far, they're still groping their way towards the definition of that word "sustainable," by being flexible, learning from mistakes, talking to others and keeping their eyes on the prize — producing really good food that doesn't harm the resource base. None of them claims to be perfect. But all of them are learning how to grow food in the post-industrial age.

## Happy as a Pig in . . .

*We can talk all day about the environment and about clean food, but if our farms are not fun, not profitable, or too much work — our children won't want them, and we're spitting in the wind. Romancing the next generation is the ultimate test of sustainability.*

— JOEL SALATIN, VIRGINIA HOG FARMER

Joel Salatin is a good example of a post-industrial farmer. He's an organic pig farmer in the heart of one of the most intensive hog-producing areas in the world — the North Carolina/Virginia Corridor. One county in North Carolina is home to 2.3 million pigs; they actually outnumber the people.

These industrially reared pigs are crammed together, usually in metal quonset huts and barns, 20,000 to 100,000 at a time, chained so they can't lie down, fed by a few workers who have to wear medical masks and special clothes to cut down on the spread of disease. These animals consume an industrial brew of fattening proteins, hormones, wastes and medicines, and are rushed off to slaughter at the earliest opportunity. The staggering amount of manure such a place produces is kept in huge lagoons of urine and feces outside the buildings. Problems with this quantity of pig effluent have led to big pollution worries. During recent flooding following a hurricane, North Carolina officials just held their breaths as the flood waters rushing through the pig manure containment basins threatened to destroy the region's entire drinking water table. Today, the state is trying to gradually withdraw licenses from its over-supply of hog farmers and cope with the results of the excessive industrial exploitation of this animal, which has also led to horrific fish kills and mysterious human diseases around Chesapeake Bay.[22]

The unpleasant side effects of cheap pork reflect the purely physical fact that natural systems can process toxins only so fast. Even a natural creature like a pig, whose excrement in its evolutionary habitat is actually beneficial to the soil, can become as dangerous as a toxic waste dump if not raised in accordance with the simple planetary laws of hydrology and decay. People will argue that we need cheap food, but there's a limit to how cheaply it can be safely produced. Costs need to reflect reality, and by trying to make the natural wealth of the pig conform to the artificial wealth of the profit dollar, we're creating terrible problems.

People like Joel Salatin can show us how to get out. He has published four books, including his latest, *Family-Friendly Farming*, and has been featured in many magazines, like *The Smithsonian*. He raises farm stock — pigs, cattle and poultry — on a 220-hectare (550-acre) spread in Swoope, Virginia. Salatin produces about 600 pigs and sixty beef from his herd of Brahma/Shorthorn/Angus cattle for slaughter every year. The farm also raises 10,000 broiler chickens a year and produces 50,000 dozen eggs from 3,000 layers. He currently sells to about 400 local families and thirty area restaurants. Salatin embodies almost every quality we've been discussing in this book: holistic management, in which he doesn't crisis manage, but makes his goals consistent with his highest aspirations; biomimicry, in which he experiments with production systems that significantly mimic nature's; and values, in which he pays attention to the real bottom line of happy animals, satisfied customers and a healthy community and land base. And, of course, he sees a profit. The farm grosses $250,000 a year, and supports four adults at salaries commensurate with what each person would make in a $35,000-a-year city job.

The farm has to be viable economically or Salatin couldn't keep it going. "I'm an unabashed capitalist," he says, "But capitalism without ethics is just greed." He sees the animals on his farm not as economic units to be exploited, but as partners helping keep the land and his family healthy. "The starting point for animal husbandry," he says, "is to let the animal express its uniqueness."[23] What he means is that he looks at how a pig actually would like to live, and then sets up his operation to maximize that potential to his own benefit. "For example," he says, "we entice the pig to work for us, replacing machinery and petroleum inputs in the process. In the winter, we bed cows in the hayshed every couple of days with straw, wood chips or leaves to lock nutrients with carbon, to minimize leaching and vaporization. In between the layers of bedding pack, we add whole corn. In the spring, when the cows go out to graze, we turn pigs into that anaerobic bedding pack, which has fermented the corn." The glorious smells and tastes of partly fermented corn and other nutrients are heaven to the pigs, who root through the bedding enthusiastically, going after the edible bits, aerating the pack and initiating aerobic composting. Salatin says, "This saves the step of windrowing compost [with a gas-powered machine]. It creates a perfect and passionate living environment for a pig, and it replaces tractors that rust and depreciate with 'pigerators' that grow and appreciate!"

Salatin knows about Allan Savory's methods of mimicking the patterns of grazing animals being chased around by predators in order to increase pasture fertility (see chapter three). He's figured out ingenious ways to pasture all his animals this way, in crowded Virginia. He says, "On our farm we run thirty pigs on one quarter-acre at a time; we move them every ten days. We've got these areas that are all brambles, briars, shrubs and bushes. We don't use bulldozers to deal with them, we use pigs to convert that forested scrub to healthy pasture. What they do at first looks awful; you'd think we'd wrecked the land. But we're providing the pigs the kind of habitat that they would have in nature. They express their physiological distinctiveness by rooting in it and just ripping it up. A couple of weeks later, the way they've torn things up has stimulated the succession of more valuable species than were there in the first place. It's a process that pushes natural regeneration succession, and it comes naturally to both to the pigs and to the land; the land evolved with this kind of disruption in the first place. So in just one season, our pigs have converted the overgrown scrub to the kinds of perennial grasses and clovers we can put the cows on."

Salatin says he's read the management classics and he understands that the great plains and pastures of the world that support agriculture became endlessly fertile "not by plowing and fertilizer, but because of co-evolution with large populations of herbivores. The antelope and wildebeest on the African plains, the huge herds on the Steppes, the buffalo here — you name it — there's always been a symbiotic relationship between herbivores and foragers." So Salatin follows Savory's basic grazing principles, bunching up the grazers so they disturb the soil, then moving them off so it can rest. Calculating the amount of land needed per cow demands real skill. "It's an art, not a science," he says. "It depends on whether the cows are dry or not, the time of year, the type of pasture. It's not rocket science, though; if you know your land and animals, you can figure it out. It mostly depends on the paradigm you start from. You'll never get the right balance if you're starting from the industrial paradigm — treating living, individual creatures as if they were dead things, numbers in your profit margin." Salatin feels that everyone has to live in a paradigm of respect if they want good food and happy, healthy lives. "You can't disdain these creatures' distinctiveness and then have a society that accords the right kind of respect to individual people. As soon as life is adulterated to nothing more than profit units, if we look at plants and animals as inert collections of electrons, neutrons or genes, then pretty soon we ourselves are no different than any other collection of salable neutrons, like a plastic doll or a copper fitting."

## Chickens Got Rights, Too

*It blew my mind, I got real kind; and I set my chickens free.*
— GILBERT SHELTON, CARTOONIST

Salatin's interest in each individual's right to a decent life even extends to his chickens. His brand-name broilers are called Pastured Poultry, and they get to move from place to place just like the cows and pigs. He uses several trailers, which he calls "eggmobiles," and hooks them together like a train to move his birds around safely. They follow the cows by a few days, in order to eat fly larvae and other insect life hatching in the cow pies. This not only creates bright, glossy yolks in their eggs, it spreads the manure and takes care of any pests attacking the pasture — grasshoppers, caterpillars and the like. He says 100 birds will eat up seven pounds of insects a day, and he uses them to "sanitize behind the herbivores and improve the pasture, while making good chicken meat." The other model he uses he calls the "feathernet"; it consists of two 150-meter (450-foot) ovals of electrified netting, enclosing 1,000 birds in about a quarter-acre.

Most chicken farmers confine birds so that, throughout their entire lives, they never see the light of day. That's because losses to predators — cats, dogs, owls, hawks, weasels, rats — can be very heavy. But Salatin figured out a way to get his chickens outside without providing a feast for the hawks. The webbed fence is made of plastic with embedded electric wires; there are two hoop houses on skids within each net, providing weather protection, shade and nest boxes for the birds. The whole thing is hooked together with feed sleds and moved to fresh pasture every three days or so. This sounds expensive and high-tech, but in fact, Salatin says, "The initial capital investment is about $2,000 per 1,000 birds, and that's a one-time investment, with an amortization rate of ten years." He refined this system from one being used in Australia. He says they get "fantastically delicious eggs," 125 dozen a day, that they can sell for the premium price of $1.75 (U.S.) a dozen. In Canada, such eggs can go for as much as $6 a dozen. Salatin claims that one person can gather the eggs and run the operation with only about seven hours of labor a week and net a $10,000 (U.S.) a year profit. But best of all, the chickens get to live outdoors, flap around, have social lives and eat what they evolved to eat.

So why isn't everybody doing this, instead of the ghastly business of burning beaks off and nailing chickens to their perches, feeding them their own manure and dead comrades, creating what Salatin calls "fecal factory" eggs, for less money per worker? He says the answer is to be found in comparing the employment goals of sustainable and industrial agriculture. The industrial model has set a goal of using as little human labor as possible. "It's supposed to be nasty to work on a farm, so they try to use very few people." As with student-to-teacher or nurse-to-patient ratios, however, domesticated animals need human care, and the fewer the humans, the worse that care will be, which explains the need for all the antibiotics and other drugs in the feed. Worst of all, Salatin says, we look upon farm work as hard labor. "We think it's much better to be in some city apartment working a salary job. The USDA is very proud of the idea that one single farmer can feed so many thousand people. But that's one of the big differences between what we're doing now and sustainable methods. Organic growers shouldn't be apologizing for needing more people to work our sustainable farms; but

the industrial paradigm thinks that if you have warm bodies on a farm —
lots of work that you're providing for your family — that's a liability."

## This Is Your Supper on Drugs

*In his most recent report, Auditor General Denis Desautels
concluded that the Canadian Food Inspection Agency
is so understaffed that it can not guarantee the safety of
Canadian meat.*
— QUOTED BY BRAD DUPLISEA OF THE SIERRA CLUB[24]

When David Suzuki and Holly Dressel were small children, it was an
educational treat to take the little ones off to a farm to see the pigs in their
sties and the cows in the pasture, to pet the family pony or feed the chickens
that were always scratching around the back porch. Today, no parent in
his or her right mind would want a small child to see how our food animals
live, or even to run through a cornfield pretending it's a jungle as Holly
used to, or dabble all day in an agricultural runoff ditch as David did, for
fear they'd be exposed to herbicides and pesticides in the soil and the water.
To a very uncomfortable extent, modern industrial farms have become a
pig, chicken or cow's version of a concentration camp, and even our most
nutritious and delicious food plants, like spinach and strawberries, are now
coated with poisons.[25]

Joel Salatin thinks that modern attitudes have classified old-fashioned
farm work as dirty and degrading, but that the further farming gets from
traditional methods, the more truly dirty it becomes. He had his chicken
manure analyzed recently, and there isn't any salmonella even in it, much
less in his birds or their eggs. "E.coli, Campylobacter, all these contaminants
that people have to worry about in their chicken or their hamburger, are not
intrinsic problems with healthy animals; they're a symptom of what's wrong
with industrial agriculture." They are the result of animals developing
infections and other health problems because they're overcrowded and
being fed unnatural feed that they weren't evolved to digest.

Carbodox is a drug used to accelerate weight gain in pigs and cut down
on the swine dysentery that is common in overcrowded conditions. It is
so carcinogenic that it presents a serious health risk to farm workers if
they even touch it. Health Canada scientists have called for an immediate
"emergency" moratorium on its use, but senior managers are dragging
their feet. Since the Reagan and Mulroney years, North American food

regulatory agencies like the FDA and the Canadian FIA have shifted from the "precautionary principle" approach to a "risk management" policy. Rather than requiring that any substance suspected of being harmful be controlled until further research is done, risk management gives an agency the right to determine how many people it will allow to get ill or die before it decides that the substance is sufficiently dangerous to be controlled.[26]

In the summer of 2000, pork was given a Class 1 recall from Quebec supermarkets, the most urgent recall that exists, because a veterinarian had happened to stumble on some pig farmers who were illegally injecting their animals with Carbodox only days before slaughter. The residues from this drug are so powerful that researchers also fear contamination of the environment at large from the animals' feces. Recently, the Canadian Health Coalition called for this drug to be banned, but no ban is yet in effect.[27] Why would we take risks with such a substance? It's used because it masks the illnesses pigs get from living unsuitable lives and being fed unnatural diets. Industrial farmers will say they just have to, to get the weight gain that translates to profits. But farmers like Salatin are their competitors. He says, "I haven't suffered by not using hormones. I don't care if they do gain weight that fast. I want an unadulterated, healthy product. And if the pig takes 30 percent longer to grow, it takes 30 percent longer to grow."

None of the really terrible risks we hear about in our food supply are inherent in organically grown meats and other food. So if there are such easy options, why aren't we taking them? It's back to value systems. Industrial farming saves money, or at least it's supposed to, and it certainly makes life better for the large chemical companies that manufacture the inputs. We've had to talk a lot about markets in this book, because they are key to realizing how natural systems and the creatures in them are valued. But sometimes the fancy, complicated modern method doesn't even make the money. Salatin notes that the cost/benefit ratio on the average industrial stock farm is $4 worth of petrochemical, hybrid seed, hormones, medicines and other inputs for every dollar of profits — a quick explanation for why so many farmers go out of business. He claims his ratio is only $.50 of inputs to each dollar of profits, an 800 percent improvement on industrial farming. He says, "Instead of paying for machinery to run the farm, we let the animals do the work . . . we have no vet bills and we get a premium price for everything we sell; it really is more tasty and nutritious."

Organic growers like Salatin have to get the price support they need to keep in business by sidestepping not only the industrial/chemical model but the global economy as well. He does what he calls "relationship marketing." "Agriculture spends a lot of time and money cultivating markets in Sri Lanka and Japan. How about knocking on a neighbor's door and offering some good, healthy food? We need marketing models that encourage consumers to rebuild the link to 'grandpa's farm' and develop relationships that let us learn from each other." So he finds his customers locally and supplies the families and restaurants nearby. To those who would argue that it's selfish to produce fancy, organic food for rich, local North Americans who can afford it, and that the starving poor need cheap, mass-produced sources of protein, we have to state the simple truth of the matter: even cheap meat is not going to the starving poor. It goes to feed people who are sufficiently well-off to buy local products wherever they are, but whose local producers are being forced off the land because their market has been destabilized by undervalued imports.

It's not easy for organic farmers to buck this global trend. Everything, from slaughterhouses to regulations, from taxes and subsidy systems to market openings, works against them. Salatin says, "the single most limiting factor preventing the wider use of sustainable, organic methods is the government regulations that favor big industry. They're not set up to accommodate clean food, but food that's coming from the industrial system." A small dairy that wants to go organic or avoid the growth hormone rBGH will not be able to get its milk to market; the bulk tankers will either mix it all up with the contaminated stuff, or they will refuse to pick up such a small amount. There are similar constraints in slaughter-houses and meat-packing plants. However, these problems are beginning to be addressed through legislation and consumer demand. We need to make good food a priority, as people have in Europe; they're getting what they want, and we can too.

If we want clean food in our future, Salatin says, we have to open our minds to a different way of valuing life and the way natural systems evolved in the first place. After all, because of his belief in holistic management, he found a way to move his pigs and chickens around a small Virginia farm as if they were being pursued by lions across the African veldt. "Our paradigm so influences what we're willing to see," he says. "It limits the questions we ask, and the questions limit our answers. [Even if we're] asking, 'How can we produce beef with organic grain in a feedlot?' We should really be asking, 'Why have a feedlot? Why feed ruminants grain?' Imagine what it would do to the Chicago Board of Trade and the multinational corporations if the

70 percent of all U.S. acreage currently devoted to grains for livestock were returned to perennial polycultures, managed for high-density, short-duration grazing by livestock!"

## Survival Factors

*All endangered breeds need to be conserved as an insurance against unknown circumstances.*
— LAWRENCE ALDERSON, *RARE BREEDS*

If the countries of Europe share one cultural characteristic, it's a deep, traditional interest in food — how to grow it, when to harvest it, how to cook it, what should be aged, what should be fresh, what should be served warm or chilled — in short, how to ensure the finest taste and quality at every meal. Lately, Europeans have been undergoing a series of traumas regarding their food supply. First it was animal feed. When industrial agriculture introduced the practice of feeding protein from the waste carcasses of animals to vegetarian ruminants like cows, the European population was assured again and again by their scientists that the animal ingredients in the feed had been reduced to their basic components; they were now no more than neutral atoms and molecules, generic proteins whose animal origin had become scientifically indistinguishable from a protein derived from a vegetable source.

Then Mad Cow disease hit Britain. Many political analysts believe that the sense of betrayal felt by the electorate cost the Conservative government their jobs. Most of the rest of Europe went into denial, refusing to import English beef but continuing to eat their own. The French did rise up to some extent when they realized the degree to which they had lost control over their food supply, and they demanded political action. There is a great deal more support now for France's already strong organic movement, worth over $2.5 billion (U.S.) and growing at almost 25 percent a year. But the European organic movement as a whole got another boost over the winter of 2000–2001, when Germany and Holland began testing their beef herds for Mad Cow disease. They found it. In fact, they quickly realized that the only reason they hadn't found it before was that they hadn't been testing for it (which is still the North American method).[28] Thousands of cattle were slaughtered, with all the emotional and economic loss that entails. When we were in Europe in January of 2001, almost no one was eating beef. Pork and chicken had become the main entrées, but if consumers had known about Carbodox and fecal factories, they probably wouldn't have wanted them, either. Of course, many people did make that leap, and an enormous amount of pressure to favor organic farming has spread across Europe, even penetrating the former Iron Curtain countries.

In England, an Organic Targets bill before Parliament has a mandate is to make one-third of all farmland in the UK organic over the next nine years, and one-fifth of all food sold would also have to be organic. In Germany, they've gone further; they already have such a law in place, and 20 percent of German land will be organic by 2010. The former Ministry of Farming has become the Ministry for Customer Safety, Food and Agriculture, thus removing the division between bureaucracies presiding over food purity and agricultural matters, a division that was partly responsible for the contamination problems. The former minister was ousted in disgrace, and a popular Green Party member has been put in charge. What's most important of all is that the government has put its money, literally, where its mouth is. It is providing subsidies to organic growers and withdrawing support from industrial farms. Not all at once, of course; farmers will be given time to adjust and convert.

There is another reason for organic and sustainable farming. It was found that the heaps of cattle and sheep mercilessly slaughtered across England, Germany and France during the Foot and Mouth epidemic — the tragic waste of the deaths of every kind of animal, from painstakingly bred prize bulls to pet lambs — was made necessary not by the horrors of the disease itself, but by our attachment to the global economy. Foot and Mouth is a relatively minor disease of cloven-hooved animals like cows, pigs and sheep. It very seldom kills them; in the case of cows, it can reduce milk output, and it doesn't affect the humans who eat their flesh. In many countries, like India, for example, it is endemic; the populace just lives with it, the way we live with childhood diseases. But it does interfere with trade in cattle across national borders. A country that doesn't have the disease doesn't want stock from countries that do. So the reason for all those piles of burning corpses was not that the animals were going to die anyway or were going to infect all their fellows with a terrible disease, or even because their illness affected their real value, their ability to produce milk or their meat. It was that their illness affected the business of global agricultural trade. And the reason it swept through Europe's herds like rice blast through IR-8 rice is that animals, like crops, have been monocultured by industry.[29]

Cattle, pigs and other domestic animals used to be bred to suit the weather conditions, the food supplies and the markets of separate localities, which in one place might favor lean meat and fatty milk, but elsewhere pay a premium for the opposite. In Europe alone there used to be thousands of variations on the theme of the cloven hoof; many of them are described by Lawrence Alderson in his book *Rare Breeds*. There were the lean, long-legged Grey Steppes cattle, bred to travel over the difficult terrain of eastern Hungary, and the small, hardy Auroise of the Pyrenees, which could draw loads as well as produce milk. There were the ancient, docile White Park cattle of Wales, strikingly feminine in their snowy coats, black noses, ears and stockings, and the comically short, all-black Kerry of Ireland, which can produce milk on pasture that wouldn't keep any other cow alive. The Wiltshire Horn sheep has, instead of wool, a matted covering of hair that can be peeled off. The dark-brown, goat-like Soay sheep from the Outer Hebrides dates back to the Bronze Age and is said to produce the world's most delectable mutton. The pale-eyed, black-fleeced Hebridean may be crowned with as many as six horns and is able to graze and browse brambles and other tough plants, making it "of considerable value in ecological projects controlling invasive scrub."[30]

Old swine breeds include the gargoyle-like, curly-fleeced Blonde Magalitza of Hungary, rich in lard and tusks, and the British Tamworth, which originated in Barbados and now does extremely well in other tropical climates. Several pigs have habits in keeping with the coevolution theories of holistic management. Germany's Bentheimer has a grazing pattern that clears an entire area of grasses, leaving only dock-weed; the Rotbunte's eating habit favors rushes. Many of these breeds are being kept alive only by hobbyists or government programs trying to conserve genetic diversity, and those mentioned here don't include the many other varieties developed in South America, Africa or Asia, or the hundreds that are now extinct. And yet in an era that prides itself on market choice, only a few European breeds — Holsteins, Jerseys, Herefords, Black Angus, and an even more limited number of swine and sheep varieties — are readily available. This is because under optimum industrial conditions these breeds are able to produce more meat or milk per pound, in less time, than the old, local varieties. But like IR-8 rice, that doesn't mean they're resistant to local diseases or can thrive in particular climates on local food. In other words, the breeds that are currently popular have squeezed thousands of local varieties out of the market and even out of existence, not because they are superior in meat taste, wool quality, disease resistance or hardiness, but because they produce fast money in an industrial setting.

Many of these old varieties of animals were prized for their disease and climate-hardiness. Knowing what we now know about plant diversity, it should come as no surprise that Jerseys and Holsteins would need heavy doses of antibiotics and hormones just to stay alive in some parts of the world, or that monocultures of them would succumb to the most devastating epidemic of Foot and Mouth disease in history. The now rare breeds may have developed resistance to this disease, although no one knows; what has doomed them is that they simply will not thrive under industrial conditions, which means that they cannot be crowded and fed so unnaturally. It's time to consider the possibility that having animals that demand better care might be good for us as well as them. Unless we want to preserve and learn more about local varieties of animals, as well as of plants, there will be continuing waves of tragedies like the smoking piles of corpses that spread across Europe in 2000. There is a kernel of really good news in all this. Diseases like Mad Cow and Foot and Mouth can be *eliminated* from our list of worries if we simply adapt the organic agricultural methods that also eliminate toxins and enrich our soils. Reintroducing local breeds will help vary our food and fiber supply, at the same time insuring us against diseases by forcing us to be more humane to our domestic animals.[31]

## The Poor Got Taste, Too

*A fertilized plant jumps up fast and falls right over.*
*Our plants are strong and healthy.*
— BENGALI ORGANIC FARMER

Back in the 1970s and 1980s, when Vandana Shiva first began to realize what full agricultural industrialization might do to India, she got involved in founding a new organization called Navdanya. The idea behind it was simply to advise and help peasant farmers in Indian villages who wanted to maintain their traditional methods but were being discouraged by experts or forced out of their former markets. Today the movement is active in several hundred villages in many Indian states, helping over 20,000 farmers conserve 2,000 local varieties of rice and at least a thousand other crops. We visited Navdanya's headquarters, an 8-acre parcel about 10 miles out of the northern Indian city of Dehra Dun. It's on flat, fertile land surrounded by the Shivalik mountains, the brittle, pointed foothills of the Himalayas.

Butterflies and a black and white hawk fluttered and swooped over us as we toured the farm's plantings of 245 rice varieties, twenty kinds of wheat and ten kinds of barley, plus local varieties of mustards and other greens. Two mud-brick buildings decorated with tribal motifs house seed samples from all across India. Another building dries and stores the organic seeds that Navdanya supplies to its clients. On a terrace surrounded by the farm's puppy, cats and burro, Bija, the friendly woman who manages the farm, served us an organic lunch. It featured a choice of millet, amaranth, wheat or corn chapatis, yoghurt, homemade wild mint chutney, betthua (lamb's-quarters) saag curry, a kidney bean dish, a millet and curd dessert and many other delights. It was delicious — and easy on foreign stomachs. Everything, of course, came from the farm. Then we walked back through the mustard and wheat fields to meet the farmers. About half the local group of eighty showed up, all women, most young, and without exception attired in their nicest saris for the event. We had been billed as a group of foreign experts come to speak to them about food issues, and the meeting began with Jorg Haas, from the Ecology and Sustainable Development Desk of the Heinrich Böll Foundation in Berlin.

Jorg was very eloquent about the crisis that had been raging in Germany when he left. Mad Cow disease had just been detected in German herds, and the recognition that the disease is apparently spread by feeding rendered meat to cows had inspired serious government regulations and encouragement for organic farming. While he was speaking, the women started whispering among themselves. We thought at first they might be getting bored by hearing about events that were so far away, but it turned out to be something quite different. Vandana Shiva had already explained to us that we were in the shadow of the World Bank Watershed Program for this part of the Himalayan foothills. She told us that they had introduced all the accoutrements of industrial farming to the area, distributing tractors, hybrid seed, and especially free pesticides and fertilizers, with a lavish hand. Then, as often happens in Third World countries, after a few seasons of free chemicals, the samples suddenly dried up. Many local farmers had already depleted their soils and become dependent on hybrid seeds; now they had to find the money to buy the chemical inputs.

The women we were talking to had gone through this experience. They'd always used the traditional organic, polyculture methods of the region; then the Watershed Program started giving them free urea and other chemicals, which they had used. The results were disastrous. Like nearly all Indian farmers, the local people work small holdings without tractors and equipment. The women farmers applied the urea, a form of nitrogen fertilizer derived from petrochemicals, by hand. They worked in soils that were saturated with it. They can't do it any other way, and of course they go barefoot. The women said their hands and feet, "just started to melt." The way they described it was that the skin would go "soggy," and they'd have pain and eczema, even fevers. We asked, "Why, with such a direct experience of its poisonous qualities, did people keep using the urea?" An older woman replied, "In theory, everyone knows what's wrong, but they're so in debt to the chemical traders, who keep telling them everything will be all right if they just use more, that they can't get out."

Navdanya was already active in the region, distributing pamphlets, holding meetings and offering its profitable farm as proof of its methods. So these women, at least, were able to find the information and market support they needed to enable them to reject the chemicals. Their hands and feet healed, and they say that their food once again tastes good and is keeping them healthy. It would be difficult to find a group more committed to an organization or more satisfied with the way it has improved their lives. And yet, the majority of farmers in the area are still buying chemical inputs.

As Jorg Haas continued to talk about Mad Cow and the 400,000 cattle in Germany that were being killed and burned at the time, the audience grew increasingly agitated. We wondered if they were reacting to the needless slaughter of cattle; after all, they are Hindus, and believe cows should never be killed, even for meat. But it turned out that they had recently been offered free packets of grayish "cattle feed," for their milk cows, again from the World Bank's Watershed Program. There was no list of ingredients on the packets, and their immediate thought was that Europe was dumping their unsalable and poisonous cattle feed on them. None of us had jumped to this conclusion so rapidly, but there are few people more aware of how the world works than Third World peasants, and few people with more reason to be suspicious.

When it came time for questions and answers through interpreters, the atmosphere was electric; the women were very angry. A confident farmer of about forty in a lilac shawl stood up and said, "I was one of the first members of Navdanya. I stopped using urea. Now I see we must have more members; we have to spread this realization of what is happening to our farms and our food!" Shiva had been taking the surplus produce from these members and selling it at a food co-op hundreds of miles away, in Delhi. Another woman suggested they start up their own local, organic market in nearby Dehra Dun, attracting enough new members to keep it well stocked.

She pointed out, "There's no way the purity of the food we grow can be matched in other markets!" This challenge was received with great enthusiasm, and the women immediately split into smaller groups, chattering like birds, setting up their new market. Shiva told us later this was typical of the swiftness with which Navdanya farmers grasp the implications of the international influences that are affecting their lives; she was very satisfied that we were there to watch it happen.

Before we left, someone asked the women what their dream was for their future, to describe their holistic vision of a sustainable life. A woman named Maya said, "My first dream is that the strength of my body stays with me, and with our children too, and obviously we need our farms to be strong and healthy." A beautiful young woman with a little boy of about five at her feet said, "My children walk one kilometer each way to school by themselves. Food is the center of their lives, so it's the center of mine." She talked about how her little boy was much happier if she had millet chapatis ready for him after school, which she can only raise organically because they're not hybrid seeds. Someone else asked if, as industrial farmers claim, organic yields are lower, won't there be a shortage of food? A woman named Lila Wati gave the answer we had heard everywhere from Bali and Oregon to Germany and Quebec. She said, "If we do good compost once every three years, we have wonderful yields. High doses of urea make it look like more for that first year, but you don't get as nourished by the food it makes, and anyway, that yield doesn't last."

## Having Your Cake and Eating It, Too

*Is transgenic technology really essential . . . or is it, as nuclear power proved to be, just a distraction from available, superior, but systematically suppressed and overlooked alternatives?*
— AMORY LOVINS, CO-FOUNDER OF THE ROCKY MOUNTAIN INSTITUTE

In our first chapters, we discussed how to determine whether a technology or practice is ecologically and socially sustainable over the long term. We looked at the precepts of holistic management, the four systems conditions of The Natural Step, and the definitions of the First and Second Industrial Revolution described by architect Bill McDonough. When it comes to agricultural technology, the most recent and controversial technique is biotechnology, the process of taking genes out of one organism, like a spider, and splicing them into another, like a potato. We are told this technology is safe, modern and holds enormous potential for the future. But given the state of the natural world and our utter dependence upon agriculture as the source of all our food, the real question becomes: is biotechnology sustainable?

We have been told that genetically engineered (GE) material just disperses in nature, but in fact, it is remarkably permanent. Biologically engineered genes and DNA have been found to persist in soil organisms, in insects, pollen and especially in water, and have been found in agricultural ditches as much as a kilometer from an original site. The antibiotic-resistant marker genes used in the process have survived digestion by cattle and even bees, and therefore pose a threat of increased antibiotic resistance up and down the food chain. This is one reason why the technology is under a *de facto* ban all across Europe.[32] The genes themselves are not confined to the original, patented plant, but can be spread by wind and pollen to other varieties of the same crop, and even to wild relatives. Canada is already having tremendous problems with genetically engineered canola, which has not only spread its herbicide-resistant trait to other canola, but is now affecting its many wild relatives, creating what are being termed "super weeds." The situation is so serious that one reason the Canadian Wheat Board is actively fighting the introduction of herbicide-resistant GE wheat, apart from market considerations, is that the species has many wild relatives that could become forever contaminated with herbicide resistance.[33]

*Bacillus thuringiensis*, or Bt, is a natural insecticide. A gene encoding the lethal characteristic of this bacillus has been injected into many varieties of crops, including corn, potatoes and cotton, even though it affects not just pests, but a broad spectrum of benign organisms such as Monarch butterflies and lacewings, and beneficial micro-organisms in the soil. There are concerns that it could hold dangers for human consumption over the long term.[34] Biotech firms also admit that crops engineered to contain the Bt gene will accelerate the natural process of insect resistance that has made so many other pesticides obsolete. For that reason, they suggest a complicated system of planting "refugia," or non-Bt crop species at specified distances from the main crop, to make sure there are still insects in the area who haven't been able to create a genetic tolerance to the Bt gene. The refugia are not only complex and difficult to maintain; studies have shown that few farmers, even in the First World, abide by such regulations for Bt crop use, which only marginally slow down the resistance process in any case. Once insects are all resistant to Bt, critics say, the biotech companies will then produce increasingly dangerous and poisonous pesticides for use on our food crops.

And of course, like all the products of the Green Revolution, genetically engineered seeds tend to replace local crop diversity with one, patented variety; in fact, from the developing company's point of view, that's their main purpose. So, like IR-8 rice or Holstein cows, Bt corn and Round-up Ready Soy are already displacing scores of existing, non-GE, non-hybrid varieties, which could, with all their genetic potential and local suitability, become extinct like so many others before them. Finally, like all Green Revolution varieties, GE crops demand large amounts of water and very strict regimes of chemical inputs, fertilizers, herbicides and, in the case of all but the Bt varieties, pesticides. Not only are these regimes difficult for the small farmers most capable of producing large amounts of food to maintain; they place a still greater burden of industrial chemicals and water pollution on the earth.

It's obvious even from this thumbnail analysis that biotechnology conforms to four out of the six criteria that Bill McDonough listed as characterizing the First Industrial Revolution: "pollutes soil, air and water, requires thousands of complex regulations, destroys biodiversity and cultural diversity, and produces things that are so highly toxic they require thousands of generations of people to maintain a constant vigil." Indeed, while biotechnology's potential benefits are very high, its potential for negative impacts borders on the cataclysmic. Certain products of biotech, like the recently revived "terminator" gene, could, if spread by pollen to other plants, destroy the ability of large numbers of plant species to ever reproduce themselves again. What that would do to agricultural productivity doesn't bear thinking about.

Biotechnology also violates all four systems conditions of The Natural Step. This is why it isn't accepted by any of the companies trying to abide by TNS guidelines, from Nike and the White Dog Café to Collins Pine and the German consumer-rating group Stiftung Warentest. It depends on materials extracted from beneath the earth's crust; it "systematically subjects nature to increasing concentrations of substances produced by society," that is, the chemical inputs and the artificial seeds themselves. It subjects nature to "over-harvesting or other forms of ecosystem manipulation"; that is, it pushes soils, water and seeds to extremes that do not allow for natural recovery and which, over time, will destroy the ecosystem. Finally, it does not allow resources to be used "fairly and efficiently in order to meet basic human needs globally." It in fact sequesters crop seed, which farmers have saved for themselves or traded freely for hundreds of thousands of years, into the hands of a few, extremely wealthy companies. Over time, they will be able to charge as much as they want for the diminishing number of crop seeds available and for the chemical inputs that enable them to work. This is not democratic or fair. And possibly worst of all, as we have seen throughout this chapter, since small, organic plots planted to a variety of crops are the proven method of producing the most food per hectare over the long term, biotech will also diminish the supply of food.

But we live in an age of advanced technology, and people do want to develop drought- or pest-resistant crops, and foods with increased nutrition, shelf-life and disease resistance, or less fat. If we believe such improvements cannot be foregone, the fact is that they are already available through non-GE methods that are cheaper and not at all dangerous. For example, the International Crops Research Institute for the Semi-Arid Tropics (ICRISAT), based in the Indian state of Andhra Pradesh, has pioneered two conventionally bred, drought-tolerant chickpea varieties "that have reversed the fortunes of poor farmers . . . suffering from acute water shortage." These chickpeas mature quickly, in only 85 to 100 days, and therefore escape the severe end-of-season drought. Even though conditions were unusually harsh in 1999, farmers growing the new varieties harvested as much as 1.7 tons per hectare, saving them from crop failures that have, in the past, resulted in mass out-migration, malnutrition and farmer suicides.[35]

Since the introduction of corn, or maize, to Africa in the 1930s, it has become one of the continent's staple foods and a mainstay of the economy. Because corn constitutes more than 40 percent of the total grain crop in sub-Saharan Africa, "higher maize yields mean more food and income for poor farmers," according to Ian Johnson, Chair of the Consultative Group on International Agricultural Research (CGIAR). Another NGO, the International Maize and Wheat Improvement Center (CIMMYT), worked directly with farmers to produce characteristics that would be valued, not by a foreign market, but by the growers themselves, such as corn that can be eaten in its "green" or sweet stage, and corn that yields well despite drought and poor soil conditions. Less than 5 percent of the farmers in the region have the land base necessary for Green Revolution technologies, so the average farm size for which this variety was intended is one-half to three hectares (1–5 acres). The new seeds aren't even hybrids; poor farmers can't afford to buy seeds every year, which is one of the reasons it's almost impossible to imagine that expensive biotech crops could feed them. For thousands of years, they've saved what they needed for their next crop, but even hybrid seeds that aren't patented and don't require royalty fees like GE seeds will lose their vigor or fail to germinate. The traditional, open-pollinated varieties like CIMMYT's new Zm 521 will allow poor farmers to completely bypass the cash economy — and still feed their children.

Even the home of the Green Revolution, the Philippines' International Rice Research Institute, is starting to see some of the contradictions in its own industrial methodology, and their web site admits candidly, "The Green Revolution's impact on diet appears to be huge. Although some diseases, such as pellagra and neurolathyrism in India, have been eliminated through the increased availability of rice and wheat, eating more of these grains may have actually increased micronutrient malnutrition. In the all-out effort to avert widespread famine and simply feed the ever-increasing number of mouths, scientists for the most part ignored nutrition in the new rice and wheat varieties. Farmers also commonly abandoned planting nutrient-balancing crops . . . in favor of the high-yielding new cereal varieties."[36]

IRRI scientists have announced their "discovery" of a traditional variety of rice that was accidentally found to be high in iron and zinc, two micronutrients, which, like Vitamin A, are seriously lacking in the Third World diet. It looks as if this rice could help address problems with anemia that are rife in poor countries; between 40 and 60 percent of the women and children in Asia, for example, are iron-deficient. IRRI's Director, Ronald Cantrell, admits that, "One of the most exciting aspects about this research is that the results have been achieved using traditional science; no biotechnology was involved." IRRI has collected the local seeds that they and other large agricultural and economic institutions had convinced peasants to stop using. The rediscovered rice has a wonderful flavor and aroma, is high-yielding and tolerates low temperatures. But although its virtues are news to the scientists in the labs, the very names of the old rices that the Green Revolution has often forced out of existence give clues that their local developers always understood their properties, although probably not in the same language terms. The Laotian variety that translates as "Neglected Fields," means that the rice grows under poor conditions; "Fat Duck" means it tastes good; Leum Phua, "Forgot Husband," means the rice produces so much grain that the woman farmer has to neglect her family to deal with it.

In Third World fields, there are at the moment no drought-resistant, extra-nutritious or higher-yielding crop varieties for the poor that are genetically engineered. Several have been in the pipeline for many years, but they haven't worked out as the bio-engineers had hoped because of the systemic, scientific limitations of the technology, which we discussed at length in our last book, *From Naked Ape to Superspecies*.[37] Virtually every conventionally bred solution we're discussing was publicly funded, which means the researchers were looking for solutions to social and environmental problems. But the private money supporting genetic engineering has something else in mind.

## Nobody Asked Us

*Nobody from the government, nor from these companies, ever asked us what our problems are. I'm sure they don't even care. All they want is to make a profit.*
— ORLY MARCELLANA, PHILIPPINO FARMER

When the biotech industry talks about its breakthroughs for the poor, like blight-resistant yams or papayas, they're really talking about things like one papaya variety that has been engineered to be resistant to papaya ringspot virus. This disease is not a problem for poor farmers, but only strikes the recently established export-oriented papaya monocultures.[38] There has also been a big fuss about a GE technology called Golden Rice, which has been engineered to express beta-carotene in order to alleviate childhood blindness among the poor in the Third World. The biotech industry hit *Time* magazine and the PBS airwaves with claims that half a million children a year will avoid blindness because of their new product; former U.S. President Clinton declared, "It could save 4000 lives a day!" However, even the Rockefeller Foundation, the major funder of GM-rice development, has said that such claims greatly exaggerate the possible benefits. There is as yet no proof that the beta-carotene in this rice can even be taken up by the human body, and in any case, Vitamin A-deficient children would have to eat 9 kilograms (19 pounds) of this rice every day in order to get their minimum daily requirement.

Greenpeace campaigner Charlie Kronick says, "Our view is that the billions of dollars that have been spent developing this rice, and the false hopes it has raised, [have] diverted valuable resources away from more sensible ways of tackling Vitamin A deficiency. Far from saving children's sight, Golden Rice is preventing other, more certain methods from being developed."[39] These "more certain" methods are, once again, almost embarrassingly simple; but they don't stand to make anyone much money or glory. They include plain old vitamin-fortification of the rice, already proven to work fine; training mothers to add some puréed carrots or greens to their children's rice; and Vandana Shiva's passionate suggestion to stop using chemicals and go back to letting the women and children weed out the native greens that they used to add to their food supply before herbicides were used on the fields.

Genetically engineered crops have been uneven performers even in terms of profitability, exhibiting such significant losses in yield that the term "GE yield-drag" has been coined to describe the phenomenon. Weird and costly deformations have appeared in Bt cotton, as well as a more than occasional necessity for spraying with stronger pesticides, even though the special seeds were supposed to rule out any added inputs. These problems are labeled "anomalies" by the industry, which attributes them to isolated local weather and soil conditions. That's a good point. The GE seeds come out of a kind of central chemical kitchen that has nothing to do with the specific social and environmental systems in which they're placed. When the intent is to pay attention to local assets and diversity, very different forms of insect and weed control are developed. For example, the International Centre of Insect Physiology and Ecology (ICIPE) in Nairobi recently had a breakthrough; they have come up with new methods for controlling two scourges of food crops in eastern and southern Africa, an insect called the stemborer and the parasitic weed called *Striga hermotnthica*, all without chemicals or any other fancy, expensive inputs.[40]

## Integrated Pest Management

*All of this is being accomplished right now, using the conventional hybrid seeds presently available, and without the need for expensive inputs such as synthetic pesticides and fertilizers or GM seeds.*
— INTERNATIONAL CENTRE OF INSECT PHYSIOLOGY AND ECOLOGY, NAIROBI

As we said, corn is the most important single crop in southern and eastern Africa, but losses from stemborers run from 15 to 40 percent, and from the striga weed, another 10 to 20 percent. "When these two pests occur together," reports the International Centre of Insect Physiology and Ecology in Kenya, "farmers can lose their entire crop. By preventing such

losses, an additional six to eight million people in the region can have food."
For many years, farmers have known that planting certain crops together,
termed "inter- or companion-cropping," can increase fertility and discourage pests. This knowledge has been refined, and today, a methodology
called Integrated Pest Management (IPM), first developed in the 1970s,
is becoming more and more widespread.

IPM pioneered, or rather revived, an old method called "push-pull." It
means that food crops are planted together with two other types of plants,
one that will repel the pests (the "push"), and another that will attract them
(the "pull"). In this case, the Kenyan researcher planted molasses grass
(*Melinis minutifolia*) and the leguminous silverleaf (*Desmodium uncina-
tum*) between the rows of corn. The grass also repels ticks, and the silverleaf
fixes nitrogen. The combination suppresses the striga weed by a factor of
40 when compared to a corn monocrop, and is nutritious fodder for
animals. Like the Indian polyculture systems, Kenyan farmers used to
intercrop in the past. Reviving their methods with additional scientific input
and understanding "helps restore the balance of nature that humankind
has disturbed by . . . practices such as over-intensive monocultures, misuse
of pesticides, and soil depletion," says ICIPE.[41]

The project has also identified over thirty wild grasses that can serve as
hosts for stemborers and might also be used to attract the pests away from
the fields. This technique has been tested on over 450 farms in two districts
of Kenya and has now been released for general use. "Participating farmers in
[the area] are reporting a 15 to 20 percent increase in grain yield." There are
more double dividends: the improved fodder is increasing milk yields. When
farmers use this multi-crop system, they get a return of $2.30 (U.S.) for every
dollar invested, compared to a $1.40 when they simply grow corn alone.

The people using industrial farming and biotech are crisis managers,
honing in on the "problem" of a particular disease or pest, but never getting
a holistic vision of an entire ecosystem that has other valuable components
to cherish and encourage. The industrial perspective sees pests as enemies
that must be defeated in an all-out war. In its view of an ideal future,
the ecosystem will produce the crops, plant and animal, that humans
have decided to insert into it — and nothing more. IPM is not an organic
technology, and will employ pesticides as a last resort; for that reason, it has
been somewhat compromised by its industrial agriculture clients. But it is
still premised on the acknowledgment of a "pest's" fundamental right

to exist, and relies on three principles: first, although we may not know why a particular pest is present, it's part of the ecosystem and must contribute to the general health and wholeness of that system in some way; second, its invasive behavior is often the result of introducing crops into the area, is probably not natural and indicates an imbalance; and third, nature will provide antidotes in nearly all of these situations.

Of the two approaches to pests, the more gentle methods have been developed over thousands of years, with mixed results, but to the benefit of humans, who have grown in numbers and prospered. As for the industrial methods, it's only been a generation since we declared war on insects, and so far, we're not doing all that well. In forty years of escalating pesticide use, not only have we failed to eradicate a single pest, but their numbers are rising. We've poisoned our soil, air and water worldwide in order to get rid of them, but today we have far greater problems with pests than we ever had when we used milder methods and accepted some losses.[42]

## Taking the Ball and Going Home

*We would be better off if everyone trying to "help" us just went home. If they did, then the people in the country would be able to come up with their own ideas.*

— FARHAD MAZHAR, CO-FOUNDER OF NAYAKRISHI, THE NEW
AGRICULTURE, BANGLADESH

One of the most worrisome aspects of modern industrial farming methods like genetic engineering is the fact that once a company isolates a gene and puts it into a new organism, however banal or minor the result, they are allowed to patent it and charge a royalty any time it is ever used. As we've seen with so much plant and animal research, these "products" were actually developed over hundreds of years through the attention and hard work of local farmers. The new system not only ignores that contribution; it takes the farmers' knowledge, turns it into a commodity and makes them pay money to get it back. The farmers of the Third World are much more aware of this aspect of biotechnology than the farmers of the First; that is why their protests have tended to be more vocal and even violent. But in the north of India, there are movements afoot to cut the ground right out from under this system of industrializing both food and knowledge.

In seventy villages north of Dehra Dun, farmers have banded together to refuse all use of chemical inputs and become what they call *beej rakshaks*, or "seed-keepers." Together with the peasants, Navdanya and Vandana Shiva's Research Foundation for Science, Technology and Ecology have worked out a strategy for self-protection: "pre-emptive patenting." They take the many local varieties that they have been growing, storing and sharing, and patent them for the village or the local collective. The patent stipulates that these seeds can never be sold for money or otherwise taken away from general use of all the farmers in the region. So when the biotech prospectors turn up, the material has already been legally sequestered, kept out of their hands.

Most Navdanya farmers live on marginal land, where crop diversity has not yet been destroyed by hybrid varieties, because of the unsuitability of the soil or climate. Since these farmers cannot really participate in the cash economy, they depend on saving seed every year. Other, more prosperous neighbors have tried the new hybrids and realized over time that they were losing both food security and land tenure because of the high cost of seeds, fertilizers and pesticides; so they have also gone back to the locally developed crops. Both kinds of farmers conserve local crop varieties *in situ*. This has been proven to be a far better method than the gene banks of governments and institutions like CGIAR, IRRI and ICRISAT mentioned above.

Over the past ten or fifteen years, researchers have been shocked to discover that the majority of the world's seeds conserved in gene banks have lost their fertility. Local seeds are alive; they did not evolve under the conditions of urban cold storage, and when farmers reuse them every year, that keeps them in the normal evolutionary cycle. But land is scarce, and it's difficult for a farmer to grow a traditional variety if its immediate economic value is not apparent; for this reason, the seed-keepers are helped by the collective to maintain all the varieties.

So far, these movements have saved 3,000 varieties of seed and have also served as the foundation for several lawsuits against the patenters. Shiva and her organizations and allies have managed to overturn two notorious patents: one on all the products of the neem tree, a source of natural pesticides and antiseptics for thousands of years, and another on the famous Basmati rice, which was patented in all its forms by a Texas conglomerate. Both foreign-owned patents were finally overturned in court, but the battle was long, costly and exhausting. "Countries need to protect their biological heritage with laws," says Shiva, "not turn them over to multinational corporations to be sequestered from the people who developed them."

## Just Saying No

*Monsanto is the first major corporation to have been [nearly] destroyed by civil society.*
— PAUL GILDING, BUSINESS CONSULTANT, ECOS GROUP[43]

It's impressive, the way so many communities affected by biotechnology are resisting a technology supported by so many huge economic institutions. In fact, the massive and well-organized resistance to this technology by such large numbers of people worldwide has never been equaled in human history. Europeans especially, following their experiences with Mad Cow disease, have not allowed themselves to be persuaded of the safety of yet another industrial addition to the food supply. Europeans have moved very quickly to get full labeling of genetically engineered ingredients in all food across the entire continent, and they've also stopped all commercial growing of genetically engineered material and the use of GE materials to feed their animals. They achieved this classically through demonstrations, sit-ins, boycotts, petitions, blockades and thousands of letters to food companies and to the government. Especially in England, Ireland and Germany, many people risked arrest by ripping up the crops; in France, hundreds of farmers broke into warehouses and spoiled the GE grain.

Europe has been joined by many other countries like Thailand, Sri Lanka, Brazil, and recently, Colombia, all of which have placed moratoriums on the growing of these crops on their national soil. Many other countries, including Japan and Thailand, have demanded — and are getting — full labeling, which has seriously affected the international market for crops like American corn and soy and Canadian canola. Still more countries, such as India and most of Africa, are taking in biotech little by little, trying to stall for time, trying to balance the fierce economic pressures with fears for their real wealth of biodiversity. All in all, apart from China, only the centers of the industry — the U.S., Canada and Australia — have adopted this technology with almost no controls. But even in the U.S., many lawsuits are pending that may overturn this trend. Right now, there are American campaigns against McDonald's and Nestlé, protesting their policies of removing all GE material from their products in Europe even as they continue to feed it to North Americans, simply because the North Americans haven't yet made enough fuss. There are also lawsuits pending against the Environmental Protection Agency for granting licenses without proper tests and evaluations. Even Canada has managed to ban one

GE product, the hormone rBGH, which doubles milk production in cows, but at proven costs to their health.

Amory Lovins of the Rocky Mountain Institute thinks the mass alarm over this new technology is reminiscent of the fight against nuclear power, fought and mostly won twenty-five years ago. "With transgenic crops as with nuclear fission, the key choices are not between unwelcome alternatives — nuclear warheads or subjugation, nuclear power or freezing in the dark, transgenic crops or starvation, transgenic crops or runaway disease." The only sustainable future technology, he believes, rejects "those all-bad choices, and chooses attractive ones, outside the orthodoxy." As we've seen, the good news is that there are lots of choices outside the orthodoxy, and they're certainly not expensive. They do require changing our First Industrial Revolution mind-set about conquering pests and being a lot more clever than nature. They require realizing that we really are in a post-industrial world, and that it isn't necessary or even safe to drag everyone else through the same mistakes. In short, along with the toad genes already slipped into our food, it may be time to eat a little humble pie.

## Yum

*A significant part of the pleasure of eating is in one's accurate consciousness of the lives and the world from which the food comes.*
— WENDELL BERRY, "THE PLEASURES OF EATING"[44]

It's time to eat better, in every sense of the word. The best news of all is that in almost any city in the world, it is still possible to find relatively pure, unadulterated and uncontaminated food. In big supermarkets in Paris and Chicago, Seattle and Frankfurt, people are able to find organic or bio-dynamic or sustainably grown food. Navdanya is even bringing it to poor people in the northern Indian city of Dehra Dun, and so is the Nayakrishi or New Agriculture movement in Dhaka, Bangladesh. Of course, it's not easily available everywhere; consumers have to do a little research, by getting on the Internet or asking their neighbors, and they probably won't be able to find an organic peach in the middle of winter. The price is generally higher as well, although that factor varies wildly according to location. Not every molecule will be perfect, but all of us certainly can reduce the odds that every mouthful we take is exposing us to a cocktail of carcinogens, parasites, E.coli and salmonella bacteria, Mad Cow disease and endocrine disrupters.

Interestingly enough, when people make this effort, they discover a strangely unexpected dividend. They all say that the food tastes better, and that their bodies feel more energized after they eat food that is organic, biodynamic, family-farm raised and so on. Is this just some kind of delusion? The nameless heritage yellow potato that comes out of Holly's organic garden, for instance, is the same species as a sprayed Idaho that traveled the national average of 1,300 miles to get to her plate, but ask anyone who's eaten both if the experience is the same. Her heritage tomatoes all taste completely different: some are dark purple, green with stripes, yellow and fuzzy; each one tastes completely different. They don't produce the same volume of fruit, but they are incredibly delicious, and they are remarkably resistant to diseases and pests. The apples in her neglected orchard have a dozen shapes and colors, and every old variety is shockingly different in taste. Some have flesh that is mealy and golden, others taste icy and look translucent; their skin comes in every shade from white with pink stripes to scarlet, from bright yellow to bronze. And they ripen, resist insects and produce fruit all at different rates — biodiversity in action. We've talked about the social, political, ecological and health reasons that underlie the traditional, whole, and organic food movements. But we haven't talked about the most appealing reason: how this food tastes, and how it makes the human body feel.

Of course, some people will say that it's all very well for rich yuppies in Oregon or subsistence farmers in India to stick to traditional foods raised in traditional ways. They claim we can't possibly feed large urban masses using these principles, without inducing suffering and starvation. These efforts at sustainability will never be sufficiently widespread to make any difference; in short, they say, we have no choice but to put up with the "acceptable risks" of chemicals and the continuing degradation of soil and water. The arguments that we have reviewed, which demonstrate that smaller-scale, diversified organic farming is not only sustainable over the long term, but more productive, so far haven't gotten most governments or institutions like the World Bank to even listen, much less be convinced. So what would it take?

How about if a whole country went organic, cold turkey, overnight? Would there be mass starvation and misery, without the heavy machinery, the petrochemical inputs and the big global marketers like Cargill and ADM? Would the country's food system, their citizens' health, and their culture collapse? Well, as it happens, this experiment has been playing itself out over the past ten years very close by, with some surprising results.

## Chemicals Collapse; Food Flourishes

*We are reaching biological equilibrium. The pest populations are now kept under control by the constant presence of predators in the ecosystem. I have little need for application of any control substance.*
— PRESIDENT OF A HAVANA INTENSIVE GARDEN

When the Soviet Union collapsed, Cuba, long cut off from any Western markets, lost its only source of foreign exchange; it had for many years supplied the Soviets with almost all their sugar, but the former Soviet countries could no longer buy it. By losing Russian oil and gas, Cuba also lost all its sources of petrochemicals for agriculture. Cuba had followed the typical pattern of former colonies: it produced luxury crops for export — sugar, bananas, coconuts, coffee — and imported the food needed to feed its own people; as recently as 1990, 30 percent of Cuba's food was imported. Sugar especially had been prioritized as the source of the foreign exchange that would enable the island to prosper, accounting for 80 percent of Cuba's export earnings. So all aspects of the usual Third World Green Revolution scenario were present: soil decline, extensive water and land contamination, and an exodus from rural communities to cities as mechanized mono-crops took over the landscape. People were facing a dangerous dependence on outside sources of food and non-renewable energy. Despite claims by the Cuban revolutionaries that they would correct this dependence, it continued until Soviet aid was withdrawn in 1989. But then, millions of tons of fertilizers, pesticides and herbicides vanished from the market; Cuba had no choice but to revolutionize its agriculture in order to feed its 11 million people.[45]

Over the next ten years, there were plenty of shortages and rationing, but virtually no starvation, malnutrition or serious crises. Cuba retains one of the highest literacy rates on earth, at 98 percent; its infant mortality rate of 9 per 1000 compares favorably with that of most industrialized countries, and is considerably better than the survival rate for American black children; moreover, it has *improved* since the food crisis. But Cuba had to jump, cold turkey, from a very high level of dependence on agricultural chemicals to virtually no chemical inputs at all. They made major changes in the big collective farms that constituted the bulk of their agricultural input, partly by allowing farm workers to produce their own food in small, organic polycultures to make up for stagnant wages. Cuba also invented urban agriculture, a new form of food production that is growing at the astonishing rate of 250 to 350 percent a year.

Cities in Cuba now grow nearly all their own food, freeing up the country farms for export items, and even export items have few chemical inputs. In cities like Havana, the use of chemical pesticides is forbidden. The goal of the National Urban Agriculture program is to produce enough fresh fruits and vegetables for everyone, and several cities have already surpassed these goals. Farmers are now some of the best-paid workers in Cuba, and organic food is available for everyone, at regular prices.

"Self-provisioning gardens" attached to schools and businesses produce food for that institution's cafeterias; raised container beds grow vegetables, herbs and spices for public sale. "Intensive gardens," city plots planted for maximum yield, use the latest organic and bio-intensive methods; and other programs produce everything from eggs, flowers and rabbits to medicinal plants and honey. The San Francisco-based NGO Food First, which is particularly interested in how sustainable food issues relate to human rights and justice, sent their program director for sustainable agriculture, Martin Bourque, down to Cuba to check out the situation in person.

Bourque says that going organic was originally a crisis plan, the only way the authorities could think of to "suffer through" the frightening withdrawal of the necessities of modern food production. "When they first began this effort," he says, "most policy-makers could not imagine any significant amount of rice [for example] being grown in Cuba without the full Green Revolution technical package. But by 1997, small-scale rice production had reached 140,000 tons, 65 percent of the country's needs." Today, says Bourque, "Everyone agrees that sustainable agriculture has played the major role in feeding the country and is saving Cuba millions of dollars." By 1999, the urban growers of the new organic agriculture alone were producing, besides the rice, 46 percent of Cuba's fresh vegetables, 38 percent of the non-citrus fruits and 13 percent of the roots, tubers and plantains. Food is still expensive by Western standards, says Bourque, but rationing programs make sure everyone has access to the basics, and, "Cuba has clearly grown itself out of the food crisis of the mid-1990s." Today, teaching sustainable farming to other farmers, researchers, academics and activists from around the world has also become a growth industry in Cuba.[46]

Cuban authorities still consider their situation a crisis response, and they still tend to run the country's large communal farms on the bigger-is-better, heavily mechanized Soviet prototype. Generally speaking, they are committed to organic agriculture not for reasons of sustainability but out of necessity. The socialist model of global development has always been almost indistinguishable from the capitalist one, in its externalization of natural inputs and its lack of understanding of the finite nature of air, soil and water. The fact that a new paradigm of post-industrialized agriculture has not penetrated the old socialist model is especially noticeable in Cuba's embrace of biotechnology. Some fairly disastrous experiments with GE rats and fish have brought unwelcome censure from the international community. At the moment, Brazil is fighting the introduction of the genetically engineered Cuban Tilapia, which it fears will contaminate wild genetics in the ocean. Cuba's response has been surprise and confusion; the government is proud of its feats in organic agriculture, as well as its growing ability to insert foreign genes into living things, apparently without seeing that one technology undermines the other. In that sense, nobody in the sustainable agriculture movement sees the Cuban system as a role model; but the Cuban experience proves that food can be grown in completely adequate quantities for large populations without chemical inputs. It can even be done suddenly. But it doesn't need to be.

Critics of organic farming worry that if everyone were to switch to organic methods tomorrow, there wouldn't be enough food to go around. That might be true; organic vegetables and fruits and meats are already in high demand, and it's difficult for existing producers to satisfy the growing market. But every year there are more organic producers, and as we said, there could be much better government programs to reward sustainable practices, instead of programs that encourage agribusinesses to grow high-input genetically engineered soybeans that have to be dumped as food aid because no one wants to eat them.[47] These changes are coming about slowly; they will take time. We could use a little more speed, but there's very little chance we'll be overwhelmed by them overnight. And if we were, well, it's a good idea to remember what happened in Cuba.

CHAPTER 6

# LISTEN FOR THE JAGUAR
## Who Owns the Forests?

### Community Living

*We should place less emphasis on competition between
[forest] plants, and more on [how they] distribute resources
within the community.*
— DAVID READ, UNIVERSITY OF SHEFFIELD, UK[1]

Ever since humans first stood upright and walked out of the forests to the
savannahs, we have been going back to the forests for most of what we've
needed to survive: water from springs and streams, fish, game animals, edible leaves, roots, fruits, fungi and nuts, building materials for our shelters,
medicinal plants, and even feathers and dyes for dressing up. But that list
doesn't even begin to measure the real value of forests to us. Forests not
only create but also retain a great percentage of the fertile soils on earth, the
material that provides us with our food base. They absorb water into the
ground and protect and purify it in lakes and streams. We have learned the
hard way, only after forests have gone, that transpiration from tree leaves as
well as their ability to trap cloud and fog actually creates an area's rainfall.
And of course, forests manufacture our atmosphere, absorbing the carbon
dioxide that is poisonous to us in their tissues and exhaling the life-giving
oxygen we need to survive. We have also recently learned that the presence
of forests greatly softens climates — warming cold ones, cooling hot ones,
mitigating wind and frost — to an extent never before realized until we
began to lose them. All the elements necessary to the survival of the

complex "higher" life forms — soil, water, atmosphere and a moderated climate — come from the collective life that makes up our planet's forests.

The strange modern idea that forests are just trees and that a mono-cultured stand of Eucalyptus genetically engineered to express pesticides is the same thing as an ancient community of beech, brambles, vines, ferns, fungi, flowers, animals, birds and all the other living things and products a complete forest would provide, is certainly one of the most striking symptoms of how disconnected our modern culture has become from the reality of nature. We have also only recently learned something else: trees not only shelter and provide food for other organisms, like fungi and birds, but they shelter and feed each other. Recent research has shown that some species, like stands of aspen, are united by a shared root system, and thus are outgrowths of one larger organism, and that different species even aid each other in difficult times. Due perhaps to our own social paradigms, we have tended to see forest growth in terms of competition for light and space, a kind of Darwinian contest that resulted in one tree "winning" and shading out the others. This does happen, but we're now discovering that trees cooperate and nourish each other fully as much as they compete.

Some trees give their more heavily shaded neighbors carbon dioxide, this is, food, via the underground fungi that help all their root systems draw up water and minerals. Plants need access to the sun's energy to capture $CO_2$, which means that when they're heavily shaded they can't feed as well. In experiments performed by the Ministry of Forests in Kamloops, British Columbia, scientists found not only that birches in the sun subsidize neighboring firs but that they do so even more generously when the firs are in heavy shade. The study helps us understand how all the young trees sprouting in a forest can survive with so little light; their neighbors, even their neighbors of different species, feed them. No one has yet understood what's in it for the fungi that do the transporting, except that it's starting to look as if forests are much more than trees. They're a kind of composite organism of interwoven life forms that are both competing *and* cooperating. David A. Perry of Oregon State University says, "When we look above ground, we see a bunch of individuals. When we look below and see all the connections, that individualism becomes much less clear."[2] Suzanne Simard, the B.C. researcher who discovered the underground connection by feeding trees different carbon isotopes, points to the fact that in modern forestry, managers weed out species like birch because they think they are competing with preferred trees, like Douglas fir. She says, "These species we think of as 'weeds' or 'trash trees' are serving as critical links, and once we sever those links, we affect the stability of the ecosystem."[3]

These findings also strongly imply that the berries, mushrooms, wildflowers, mosses and herbs in a forest, to say nothing of the microorganisms, soil biota, insects, birds, bats and other mammals, are serving their own interwoven purposes in keeping the entire system going. As we have seen with so many other natural systems, a given forest's productivity depends on the diversity of life forms within it. In fact, in a healthy forest, the diversity of the plant and animal life is also vital to its survival. It has a strong economic value for surrounding human communities as well, and forest clearings and edges in particular provide, as anthropologist Scott Atran says, "the highest-yielding, least labor-demanding source of products that humans have ever known." When forests are appreciated as interrelated, self-sustaining organisms, and their rich diversity is allowed to thrive, they will continue to provide thousands of products and benefits almost indefinitely.

The question of who should manage forests and who should be able to claim these products and benefits, including the forests' production of basic life support systems like soil, water and air, has always been important. Today, as forests melt off the earth, victims of high human population density and global economic pressures, these questions of forest management and tenure have become even more urgent. Fortunately, a lot of people around the world are finding answers.

## Who Owns the Forest?

*The highest-yielding, least labor-demanding production strategy known to Man.*
— SCOTT ATRAN, ANTHROPOLOGIST

For most of the human past, people used the products of their nearby forests in much the same way they used their gardens and agricultural patches; they used and managed both, making their living off the ecosystem at large. Today we're realizing once again that forests can support us without being cut down. Even in remote areas such as the Amazon or the Congo, the forests are seldom primeval, or even natural. They have been carefully managed by humans for thousands of years through burning, planting and selective cutting to favor certain species and certain kinds of animal habitat. This use, termed "traditional agro-forestry," is often so gentle that modern scientists can walk through a forest that has been profitably managed by local users for hundreds of years and believe they are alone with elemental nature, or even that the forest has been terribly neglected and needs their own firm management hand.

Francis Hallé, the famous French tropical botanist, describes traditional agro-forestry best. "Picture a circle," he says. "Within it is primary forest — real jungle or rainforest inhabited by the myriads of creatures that have evolved in such places, from insects and molds through to birds and large mammals. Picture another circle outside it, forming a ring." This is what Hallé calls "the secondary forest," and is the location for what are variously termed forest gardens, swiddens or community gardens. On the periphery of that second circle is the village. From the village at the edge, people go in to their family plots — generally no more than a day's walk away, within the second ring. They usually have several plots in the same area, but sometimes they're scattered in different directions. These plots are cleared from the secondary forest by slash and burn, but they are very small, usually under a third of a hectare (less than an acre). They are closely planted with a very large variety of plant species; in other words, they are the typical small-holding polyculture upheld by Vandana Shiva and by UN and FAO studies as the prototype of sustainability.

In Guatemala, for example, there will be corn, beans, squash and root crops such as yam, cassava, manioc and macal. Banana, coconut palms and other fruit-bearing trees will provide more variety and shade for the crops that need it, like sweet potato. Other plots are similarly heavily planted with many species, at different times and according to soil type and drainage, to allow for different harvests and to avoid disasters like animal or pest predation, or poor weather. The plots are tended more or less constantly throughout the season; one of the most difficult chores is guarding them from animals when harvest approaches. However, even if one or two plots are destroyed, there are others. To supplement these gardens, the people also plant and care for individual useful trees, shrubs and other plants. They may have planted them deliberately, gathering seeds or cuttings from the primary forest; or they may have simply fertilized, weeded and protected the seedlings they found in the area. These plants — palms, banana, nut and fruit trees, rare medicinal herbs, for example — are scattered willy-nilly. They are considered to be the "property" of whoever first planted or started taking care of them, and if, for example, a neighbor should take the nuts from someone else's tree, he would be in as much trouble as a cattle rustler would be from a rancher. The harvest will be physically defended, and the "thief" can be forced to make restitution, or suffer humiliation before the elders; he or she may even be fined or beaten.

What is shared as common property in these systems is not the garden plots or the valuable trees; it's the primary forest. Taking care of particular trees, and harvesting them within that forest, creates "tenure," a convenient, loose term for ownership, in the sense of "holding" in trust, while getting use and profit from something. The idea of tenure can, but does not necessarily, include written deeds or contracts. Whole groves of certain trees that will be good for construction, for example, may be planted or protected in the primary forest and left for 50 years or more, so that succeeding generations will have building supplies. They are culled in small numbers, usually carefully limited by tradition and even religious proscription. You can't drag home many sixty-foot logs in a small village without all the neighbors knowing you're taking more than your "share," so there is no reason and no opportunity to over-exploit. Under this system, everyone has a right to useful material from the primary forest, but only within certain limits.

Most countries in the world retain some sense of the common value of forested land, and it is very often owned and managed collectively by government. Even in the United States, the champion of free enterprise, millions of hectares of forest lands are in government hands, and nearly all of Canada's vast boreal and temperate rainforests are held as Crown Land. In Germany there are federal, provincial and even municipal forests, where everyone can gather dead wood for their fireplaces or hunt rabbits and wild boars, but no one is allowed to take away all the trees and turn the forest into something else. The forests in Third World countries are basically held by their governments as well, and are left to the devices of the original aboriginal inhabitants until something of value is perceived in them. Then, like forests in Canada and the United States, they can be logged or cleared, when the government grants tenure in the form of paper leases and contracts to agricultural or recreational developers and large logging corporations. But the underlying assumption remains: the forests that we still retain are understood to be held in common by governments for the benefit of the people at large. This principle sounds pretty equitable, but it hasn't worked out that well in practice, largely because of First Industrial Revolution problems we have already analyzed: over-exploitation for industrial goals, a fragmented understanding of a forest's true values, and confusion about the basic philosophy underlying the idea of common ownership.

The core of modern forest tenure is that the purpose of forest owner-ship by a large entity such as the government, forestry corporations, or private corporation is largely to make money. The theory of "the tragedy of the commons," developed by professor Garrett Hardin in 1968, is a major foundation for our current belief that this is the best way for forests to be managed. It assumes that, "When resources such as trees are 'free' or open to everyone, costs arising from their use and abuse can be passed on to others. The rational individual has the incentive to take as much as possible before someone else does. No one is motivated to take responsibility for the resources. Because they belong to everyone, no one protects them. The causes of overpopulation, environmental degradation, and resource deple-tion may be found in [this] freedom and equality."[4]

Traditional users of a resource, typically indigenous but sometimes agricultural people who had been in the area for a long time, used to be considered to "own" it, but by the 1960s, it was decided that common tenure was bad for a resource. The destruction of commons ownership has been enthusiastically upheld by governments and forest products industries all over the world. Ironically, their idea of what they were replacing was based on how the concept of a "commons" was perceived by another mod-ern Western ideology, communism. It turns out that neither the Western governments and industrialists nor the socialists understood how traditional users were really managing their forests.

As we pointed out above, true forest peoples have developed very clear concepts of forest tenure, as well as methods for limiting the use of the resource and protecting it over the long term. Unfortunately, these limits are destroyed when a timber or mining company licensed by the govern-ment moves in and starts to take trees that local families have been waiting forty years to harvest. This panics people. They see immediate gain if they do the same — what we might call "pre-emptive logging" — and they often join in or acquiesce to changes because the new management methods strike too deeply at the roots of their cultural systems to be assimilated and under-stood. Forest management systems are so ingrained in the culture and life view of traditional peoples that they often have difficulty describing them to outsiders. There may be very little concerted resistance to extremely invasive change, although that has been growing in places like Borneo, northern Quebec and the Amazon over the past decade or so. And the latest genera-tion of linguistically fluent, unusually sensitive researchers, like Stephen Lansing in Bali, has also been able to help people articulate what seem to them to be the givens of life.

Some accounts supporting the theory of the "tragedy of the commons" were written by modern scientists observing forests or other user-managed ecosystems that had already been disturbed — that is, the Westerners came in after the traditional rules of the indigenous people had been violated and the locals were adopting outside practices in self-defense (practicing "pre-emptive" hunting or harvesting, as the Cree of northern Quebec did when their territory was first opened up to sports hunters). We have often interpreted practices that people are using in a partially destroyed social system as the normal way "common land" was always treated, because that's how it was operating by the time an industrial or colonial observer happened upon it. In fact, the rules that govern common land use, when undisturbed, are, if anything, more stringent than the rules that apply to "private property." In our society, property "rights" often permit owners to despoil their land completely of trees and animals, and even to dump toxins in shared water courses. When their behavior seriously threatens the future of the larger system, the worst thing they have to fear is a fine. Traditional violators are fined as well, but they can also be publicly humiliated, lose their tenure rights, be ostracized or worse. In West Africa, for example, local people who take more than strictly prescribed amounts of live and dead wood from common mangrove swamps are threatened with death, disease and general family ruin by the priests, on behalf of the angered tree spirits. This may seem a bit harsh, but in fact the only healthy swamps left in Benin are in areas where people still practice the indigenous religion of Voudoun; people in Christian and Muslim areas have destroyed their mangroves.

Often, federal governments, especially in the First World, are far from the forests in question, and are susceptible to the advice of the many cadres of experts trained in modern science. Once they become the managers of their country's forest commons, they generally subject their holdings to a series of conflicting management styles according to the reigning theory of proper forestry at the time. That's how Germany turned all its beautiful, dark forests into tidy and ecologically delicate pine monocultures that have been shockingly ravaged by windstorms, pests and pollution. Today, German foresters are touring the world, trying to relearn natural forest polyculture from indigenous peoples and private owners. In the United States and Canada, the horror of fire damage, coupled with growing numbers of people living near forests, led to such enthusiastic suppression of natural fires in the 1950s that Western forests in particular began to lose many of their normal climax species, and much of their diversity. Today these forests are clogged with small "trash wood" species, ironically much more prone to truly devastating fires; still another management style is necessitated — the controlled burn. But when the human users of the forest live within it, forests usually retain more of their natural resilience.

## The Edible Forest

*We in the past are not felling very much forest. They only plant corn; for this reason, they fell much forest — cedar, mahogany . . . They are not planting much of anything. For this reason, if it doesn't come out good, this year, the next, they fell more big forest . . . so now, there is no possibility to have more forest.*
— ITZA MAYAN FARMER[5]

In Guatemala about eight years ago, the young anthropologist Scott Atran taught himself a dying Mayan dialect so that he could interpret the forest science of the people of the Petan Peninsula to the rest of us. Atran asserts that the mode of cultivation practiced by the Itza Maya sustained both the ancient and modern Indian cultures of this region by regenerating their forest's biodiversity — indefinitely. In other words, to an unusual extent, they didn't simply catch or gather the resources of the forest; they actually learned to cultivate it as a huge, complex crop. If we want to hold onto the soil, water and air-creating capacities of our forests, this is a skill it might be useful for more people to learn. Atran lived with the Itza and interviewed them in their language. As he made comparisons with ancient Mayan crop names, he discovered that plants that are considered wild today are in fact the Itza Mayan crops, which they cultivated inside the forest.

Atran points out that outsiders, from the Spanish *conquistadores* right up to the waves of recent settlers from the cities, have been so fixated on the European staples of beef cattle and a few cereals supplemented only by beans, squash, chilis and other field species, that they didn't even notice all the food being hauled out of the forest every day by their Mayan neighbors. It is not by chance that the ramon, or breadnut tree, for example, is Petan's most abundant tree species. It was carefully nurtured for generations for its leaves, fruit and bark — all edible — and is nutritionally comparable to corn except in amino acids, where it is superior. Contemporary Itza confirm that their ancestors used to eat this tree "before corn." They also still call it the "animal milpa (garden)," and list thirty species, including howler and spider monkeys, catamundis, tapirs, squirrels, parrots of many kinds, toucans and macaws, that depend on it for survival. The brush around established ramon trees is controlled with machetes to help seedlings and fruit production, but sparingly, because the Itza believe that "too much thinning allows in too much sunlight and wind, which causes the protective vines and mosses on the tree to dry, the bark to split, and the trees to die."

Far from understanding the use of a mature forest, the Spaniards would complain in their frequent periods of cereal crop failure that they were being "forced" to eat ramon, sweet potato, manioc, yams, plantains, mamey and spote fruit. The fact that these foods were always available during supposed famines only shows that unlike the Spanish exotics, they were suited to the soil and climate, and that the locals were nurturing them for their own use. Like all agro-forestry practitioners, the Itza Maya had small plots scattered around the secondary forest, several per family, with varying soil type, crop mix and planting times, so they didn't ever experience the Spaniards' full crop failures. The species mix made for a delightfully diverse diet: at least forty trees and thirty other plants provided everything from fruit and starch to flavorings, resins and building materials. A sampler includes allspice, wild pineapple, monkey apple, mamey, chicle, cedar, mahogany, logwood, locust, coyol palm, cabbage palms and uncounted medicinals. This is the tropics, of course, which can produce food species far more luxuriantly than a temperate forest. But it's in the tropics that people are now having the most trouble getting food, making us despair at the loss of the carbon sinks and atmospheric stabilizers that logging the huge forests brings about. It's worth knowing that forests can provide crops and can fill human physical and economic needs — all without being cut down.

Atran calls the local garden plots "artificial rain forests" because they are incredibly high-yielding and require little labor. He says they imitate a mature forest's diversity and preserve its nutrient cycle, while giving predominance to species deemed most useful to people. Trees are not fully cleared, but are thinned to provide shade where needed. Weeds are suppressed by root and vine crops like manioc and squash, rather than being pulled. Crop rotation restrains the effects of species-specific pests, drought or too much rain. These gardens have supported hundreds of thousands of people without being changed or expanded. Even allowing for fallow periods, occasional crop failures and more forest than currently remains, they can produce a remarkable 320 kilograms per hectare (800 pounds per acre) of food per year, a cropping rate that is comparable with the yields of many modern food crops. Most importantly, linguistic and archeological evidence reveals that these practices have been fully sustainable for at least 400 years, since lists of Mayan food sources and the remains in middens perfectly match the composition of surviving Itza Mayan gardens.

Atran and several of his colleagues at the Center for Cognitive Studies of the Environment at the Bio-Itzaj Reserve, San Jose-Petan, Guatemala, analyzed the difference between the Itza care of the forest and that of the more recent immigrant ladinos from the cities. As the quote at the head of this section describes, the newcomers use modern methods of large, monocultured fields that are all corn, all beans or all tomatoes. In this lush, tropical ecosystem, there are a great many pests, and a mono-culture does not survive long. The use of chemicals to keep a foreign farming style going degrades the land so quickly that the new farmers must continuously cut more forest to get at fertile soils. But their practices dry the soils out and degrade them, so that trees can't come back very easily. The Itza Maya, like the water priests in Bali, conserve their agro-forestry practices as part of a social, cultural and spiritual whole that views the environment and all its species, including people, as mutually dependent, in a very profound sense.

The remaining Itza have seen much of their fertile, edible home disap-pear. Today they say about their forest, "Listen for the sound of the jaguar. When there are no more jaguars, there will be no more forest. And then there will be no more Maya." This image accords with what contemporary science now knows about a forest being far more than merely a collection of trees. Considering what we have learned in the past few years about the holistic nature of forest ecosystems, the interdependence of trees, bats, birds, fungi, microorganisms, ferns, flowers, insects and reptiles, right up to the largest keystone predators like jaguars and man, it is obvious that the Itza are not just being poetic. The Maya are forest people; they know that with-out its top carnivore, the forest will not survive. With the help of remaining forest-users like the Itza and outside-the-box researchers like Scott Atran, we are finally starting to learn what a forest is, and how to both use it and preserve it. What is encouraging is that we found that such lessons are being learned simultaneously all over the world — even back in the U.S.A.

## Giants of the Forest

*Ensure local knowledge and control are central to*
*decision-making and planning.*
— PRINCIPLE 4 OF ECOLOGICAL PRINCIPLES FOR SUSTAINABLE
   FORESTRY

Our very recent discovery of how the traditional agro-forestry of indigenous peoples works and why it needs to be more widely practiced may seem
to be nothing more than an interesting story about an exotic place. It feels
distant in both space and time from the controversies involving industrial
forestry that we're facing in the First World. But in fact, it is more applicable
to modern, industrially exploited forests than one might think. For instance,
there is a huge forest in the heart of North American logging and timber
country, at the juncture of the borders of central Washington State and
Oregon. It has been owned and managed by some well-established residents and users, the Yakama Indian tribe, whose tenure goes as far back as
anyone can imagine.

A comparatively generous late-nineteenth-century treaty gave the
Yakama complete control of the more than 267,000 hectares (660,000
acres) of forest on their 566,000 hectare (1.4 million-acre) reserve, as well
as considerable harvesting and managing rights to more forest and range
land off the reserve. In all, it amounts to about 5.5 million hectares (12 million acres) covering nine counties and over forty watersheds — nearly a
quarter of the state. The 9,000 Yakama tribal members not only harvest
over $40 million worth of timber every year; they are a mainstay of the town
of Yakima, Washington, local employers on a significant scale, and a considerable source of timber-managing knowledge that has attracted researchers
from around the world. As an indigenous people, they are also in the rare
position of being able to have an effect over a big chunk of an important
natural ecosystem, right in the heart of the industrialized First World.

The only significant period in which management of their forest got
away from the Yakama was between about 1930 and 1970. The U.S.
Federal government, through the Bureau of Indian Affairs (BIA), took
over the forest during this period and managed it in accordance with
the forestry style prevalent at the time. Fortunately, they didn't clearcut or
plant large monocultures of fast-growing species; the Yakama had retained
control over the amount of timber sold, and clearcutting and monocultures
weren't allowed. But the BIA did initiate serious fire suppression, which left

the forest with its primary ecological problem, as we shall see. By the 1970s, the Yakama were so dissatisfied with BIA forestry that they decided to manage their holdings themselves. The forests in other parts of the state, including nearby reserves, were largely ruined by the BIA policies of fire suppression, overharvesting of the biggest trees and clearcuts; the Yakama are the only ones who still retain the prototype, an ancient forest exhibiting the high stability of a climax state.

They retain, for example, 14,500 hectares (36,000 acres) of huge ponderosa pine cathedral groves, which shade open, grassy floors and are filled with game, flowers, berries and birds. It's a vision of what the primeval natural forest in this part of the world looked like for centuries. The most pristine section of Yakama Forest is high in the foothills of the Cascade range, in close proximity to the glitteringly white, unreal presence of both Mount Adams and Mount Baker, which dwarf even its huge trees. But that section is less than 20 percent of the total Yakama holdings. The rest of their forest is the tribe's sole support, and is commercially managed in a remarkable way. Forest earnings take care of the entire tribal budget, including their buildings, Band Council expenses, recreation and cultural facilities, all the children's educations and even small income supplements for each tribal member. The forest also supports 300 full-time natural resources employees. The tribe has its own wildlife and fisheries biologists, and seldom has to look beyond its own borders for scientific experts.

Carroll Palmer is a quiet, handsome man in his forties, a traditional Indian who is also a forester and the director of the entire Yakama Department of Natural Resources. He says, "Until we took back control in the 1970s, the forest was managed for economic benefits only. So the big, beautiful four and five-foot diameter trees were routinely cut, and skids tracked over the open meadows where people were used to getting their medicinal plants and huckleberries. But at least since the 1940s or even before, there were no clearcuts. That means when we took over, we had more options to implement a more holistic management style." Today, the tribe has intensive ten-year plans with constant input from the population. This set-up keeps their goals diverse and democratic, and prevents the usual dictatorship of "experts" that afflicts modern Western culture. "People are monitoring Council decisions on a daily basis," says Palmer. "We hear right away if we do something someone doesn't like."

The Yakama's stated goal is simple: they have a vision of a forest with the highest possible diversity of species, ages, ecosystems and uses. For instance, they have re-established several hundred acres of huckleberries, which, under the no-fire policy, had been encroached upon by brush and tree seedlings. "Nowadays, people go up there and camp for months, picking and camping," says Palmer, with a wistful sigh, as if he'd rather be there than in his office. When we made the two-hour trip from the Band Council headquarters up to the berry meadows by jeep, we found out why. Acres and acres of high-bush huckleberries, with the occasional rough camp half-hidden in the brush, backed by trackless and beautiful forests on every side, look out as if from a stage at the shimmering mirage of Mount Adams, which fills half the sky up from the horizon.

Palmer says that a large proportion of his people still gather berries and hunt, with as many as one out of every ten depending exclusively on the land. They gather more than seventy other species of food and medicinal plants as well, "so we have to be really sensitive to what hunters say about habitat problems or the decline of any plant species or bird, and to the protection of all the salmon streams." Just in terms of fauna, there's a lot to keep track of. Every kind of animal indigenous to the great Western forests is present, from deer, marmots and chipmunks right up to spectacular creatures like alpine goats on the crags and glaciers of the mountain. There are hawks, eagles and the famous spotted owls, as well as a large number of big carnivores like black bears and cougars — numerous enough to be a bit of a worry to the foresters as they go about their daily work. The Yakama forest also includes many rushing mountain streams and small rivers, with one salmon run returning thanks to the reintroduction of some short-term hatchery fish. People are excited at the prospect of getting the fish back because to the Yakama, the forests are primarily the home of salmon, which are the center of community life, just as corn is for the Hopi or cows for central-Indian villagers.

Maintaining the forest so that all species, including the salmon, will thrive, is accomplished by democratic means, fully in keeping with traditional forms of agro-forestry management evolved by forest users all over the world. Every year, a General Tribal Council is held, at which every single person over eighteen years of age votes. They elect and monitor a smaller council of fourteen members, who are then divided into eight four-member committees that oversee the daily activities of management. One committee, Tribal Administration, is also divided into Human Resources, Law and Order, and Natural Resources. It's all set up to be highly democratic, simple, direct and easy to influence, and as Palmer says, there's not much of a time-lag between any change and input from the members. The Yakama aren't selfish, either. There are places for outsiders to camp, hike and swim, so they can come and enjoy this amazing wealth.

## Evolutionary Fire

*Restore degraded landscapes, forests and sites.*
— PRINCIPLE 8 OF ECOLOGICAL PRINCIPLES FOR SUSTAINABLE FORESTRY

In the fall of 2000, the Yakama Council was trying to cope with a serious infestation of spruce budworm. Mike Johnson, an entomologist on contract to the tribe, is working with the tribal forest managers to deal with the problem by using Integrated Pest Management techniques (see chapter five). Johnson, a thin, boyishly enthusiastic scientist who is very focused on the insects that are his specialty, led a tour into the forest so we could see what was happening for ourselves. "The western spruce budworm is indigenous in this area," he explains, "and historically it really isn't that bad a pest. The problem is fire suppression over the last 80 to 100 years. Grand and Douglas fir are the host plants; when these species are small, they're perfect vectors for the pest. The thing is, this is a ponderosa pine forest that now has too much Douglas and grand fir in it." Historically, the firs would have been thinned by natural and Indian-set fires — in fact, this forest evolved to accommodate the assaults of periodic fires, the same way the prairie evolved to accommodate the perturbations of grazers' hooves. Ponderosa pine are very fire-resistant, and they were the dominant species here. Under evolutionary pressures they become not only amazingly tall; their branches are extremely wide spread. There is very little understorey like shrubs or brambles; just fine grasses. Within the groves, the fires also used to remove undergrowth and competing species like firs, and the pines themselves shaded out most of the competition.

The Yakama are trying to implement the basic principle of holistic management — to mimic biological systems that have been so productive in the past. Johnson says, "In order to work with nature as much as possible, the Yakama base a lot of what they do on old settlers' diaries and other records, which repeatedly mention things like, 'four men can ride abreast through the forest without impediment.' They also gather tribal memories of things like how many teepees could go up in the forest at any one time." The ponderosa loses its ground branches as it grows, so there aren't any for at least twelve feet up. Fifty- and sixty-year-old people can still remember much more of this type of forest, idyllically open like a child's vision, inviting people to walk through it. Such forests are nearly all gone even in the Far West. Today the woods are usually dense and impenetrable, full of many more small trees and much more brush and undergrowth, reminiscent of the scrub forests of the East.

Because the entire forest organism was regularly attacked by lightning and other natural fires, it evolved many ways in order to deal with them. Many seeds, notably the ponderosa's, propagate only after a fire, while others can be sterilized by it. The many other trees and shrubs now choking the forest evolved as short-term residents, fixing nitrogen and otherwise enriching the soil between fires, and leaving only a few individuals to struggle to adulthood under the ponderosa canopy. So today, the species balance has changed, and the forest has become less vigorous and less resilient when subjected to assaults like pests.

Mike Johnson says that one of the things the advocates of fire suppression didn't know "is that the budworm propagates by overwintering in a silken hybernaculum or cocoon. In the spring it crawls out, up the bole of the tree, and then makes a kind of silk balloon and sails out to hit its next host. If the trees are widely spaced and there aren't too many of the preferred fir hosts, most of these worms will fall to the ground, where they die." Under normal conditions, the budworm population remains small. But if there is an unnatural lack of fire, the ballooning worms will hit hosts wherever they go — and most of them will survive and turn into a plague that eventually infests even unpreferred hosts like the ponderosa. Today, the only thing the tribe can do is thin out the stands of Douglas and grand fir manually; "We can't do it fast enough," Johnson says. "We're eighty years behind."

Using IPM techniques, the forest managers have been spraying with *Bacillus thuringiensis* (Bt) to protect a stand of trees until they can get to it. The Bt commercial insecticide is produced naturally by bacteria under the control of a single gene; that gene has been isolated by genetic engineers and inserted into crops, to which many pests are now developing resistance. But so far, spraying it the old-fashioned way still slows down the budworm. Ironically, the small trash trees and brush that have flourished because of fire suppression invite fires that are much more dangerous than the natural, historic ones. When there is so much fuel to feed on, fires can become incredibly hot, managing to destroy even the ponderosa and other species that have evolved to survive smaller fires. This is why forest fires these days are so dangerous and so likely to burn out of control, and why they can truly devastate an area for generations to come.

The Yakama forest workers are fortunate in that they retain a living template to base their ideas on, the most beautiful forest most of us will ever see. Their prize 14,500-hectare (36,000-acre) remnant is the model the Yakama keep in mind when managing all their holdings. Its huge trees were saved from the BIA's saws back in the 1940s because they were just too remote. In the past, Mike Johnson had only overflown this forest, and he was delighted when we all went together to see it on the ground. "It's perfect!" he cried, running from one huge ponderosa to another. "Look at the Doug fir; there are just a few! And look how far the budworm silk would have to swing to find a host. It would never make it!" Indeed, there were no pest problems here, even in the few firs. With the glaciers of Mount Adams as a backdrop, the towering ponderosas looked like huge columns of the most glorious cathedral; the ground was carpeted with soft, pale yellow grass, and the scent of warm needles and the cool breezes wafting off the mountain made the place seem more like a dream than a forest. In only a half hour or so, we saw three eagles and ten hawks; our driver pointed to where he'd seen a wild sheep a few days before. There was bear scat in the grass, and the tracks of a timber wolf, who had lain down only a short time before we arrived, at the center of a circle formed by four soaring trees, each 2 meters (five to six feet) in diameter. And the space between each of these unimaginably tall giants was as wide as four men on horseback.

## Drums Among the Trees

*Conserve all native plants and animals.*
— PRINCIPLE 5 OF ECOLOGICAL PRINCIPLES FOR SUSTAINABLE FORESTRY

We've been seeing why indigenous or aboriginal peoples — traditional users, in short — are usually the best people to trust with the health of an ecosystem. But of course, like any generalization, this isn't dogmatically true. The only reason the Yakama ever chopped down their trees traditionally was for teepee poles and canoes. They've had to learn how to do forestry, and they've made mistakes that they not only admit to, but take visitors to see and learn from. They can no longer use traditional methods like controlled burns as much as they'd like, because of the present state of the forest and the many towns in the area. So they're feeling their way along to sustainable forestry as best they can. In other parts of the world, traditional approaches may have been forgotten, outlawed, or outmoded because of many changes in the area. And of course, traditional people are . . . people. They make mistakes; and they are prone, like all of us, to do things not because they've reasoned them out, but just because they've always done them that way.

Charles Abugre is a Ghanian social and political analyst who works with several non-profit groups, including the Ghana Integrated Social Development Centre and the Third World Network, in his home country along the West African coast. About ten years ago, he adopted a child, and later traced her family origin to one of the many distinct tribal groups in the country, the Gurune of the northeast. Taking on extra children is, incidentally, common among more affluent Africans; urban households often include ten or fifteen children, only three or four of whom were actually born to the parents. Charles Abugre's child inspired his curiosity about a part of Ghana that is remote and seldom visited by people from the more populous south. He also found some obscure writings by a Catholic social worker named David Miller, who had chronicled an unusual movement in the area.

This part of Ghana bisects a section of the Sahara shared with Burkina Faso, and although it used to be forested, it is now one of the driest, poorest and most ecologically degraded areas in the country. Abugre says about six years ago, two decades into their own experiment with modern Green Revolution agriculture, the Gurune — who number about 3,000 people spread over several thousand arid kilometers — started holding talks with each other. They were beginning to realize that under the Green Revolution methods they were worse off than ever before. Abugre says, "They said, 'We can't continue this level of degradation of our lands. We are losing traditional medicinal plants. The things we used to use to treat eye infection, to treat the healing of bones, all of these are disappearing. Sacred groves are going; wetlands are going. We have to get them back.'" The degradation resulted partly from population pressure, but also from the fact that, as crop lands deteriorated, people had to extend farming into any kind of terrain they could to survive. Once they realized what was happening, the most immediate barrier to reforestation was, ironically, not so much the pressure on the land as the tribal beliefs about the trees that composed the sacred groves. Many of the ancient groves that still conserved what little rain fell were dying of old age. No new trees had been planted because of a community belief that if a person plants a tree, when it begins to flower, he or she will die.

The Gurune wanted their medicinal plants back and secondarily their sacred groves. And once they decided that, like the holistic managers we've been discussing, they didn't concentrate on the problems and liabilities of their degraded, treeless farmland, but on their vision of restored vegetation. Because their fundamental beliefs still blocked the way to the realization of this vision, they actually stepped back and questioned their core cultural paradigm. They held meetings with their elders and holy people, the priests, priestesses and soothsayers. They began, as Abugre puts it, "to question the gods and ask: 'If people are proscribed from planting trees, how is it that we have been preserving sacred groves for the gods in the first place? How could we have been preserving these clusters of wetlands? And aren't we supposed to have our traditional medicines?'" They decided to sacrifice to the gods, and beg leave to regenerate the sacred groves. Abugre says, "So they started to plant the trees that no longer existed — to regenerate seeds. They even traveled very far away. They walked miles to bring back the old medicinal shrubs. They also renamed and redesignated areas where groves used to stand but no longer existed, and they asked people to give up their farmland for tree and wetland regeneration. So they started growing and seeding and regenerating all over the place. And once a year they began to meet to sacrifice and to celebrate what they were doing."

These people had lost a lot. They too had used small, polyculture plantings, in which grains like sorghum or corn were interspersed with green peas, beans, black-eyed peas and banbara beans. The creeping beans and bush beans, yams and so forth filled up the understorey, providing nitrogen fixing and weed and pest control, while the larger plants and fruit trees provided shade and wind shelter in the searingly dry summers. "When [petrochemical] fertilizer showed up," says Abugre, "they broadcast it and had a lot of growth when the rains fell. But they just had corn or millet, none of the beans and things shading the ground, and that ruined the polyculture. These new varieties, these hybrids, have to be planted alone, with herbicides and pesticides. After a while, the whole system of mixed cropping disappeared. It took them thousands of years to work it out, but it took two decades, at the maximum, to destroy it." The new crops take more water and use up more land. The fertilizers and chemicals degraded Ghana's delicate tropical soils. So gradually groves of trees, sacred or otherwise, as well as old water holes, sinks and wetlands, either disappeared because of greater water demand, or were put into crop production because of the new system's greater requirement for land.

Exactly as in Bali, the social and religious systems, even the art forms that used to be an integral part of Gurune traditional life, waned along with its more mundane farming practices. An interesting indication of the intertwining of spiritual beliefs and material practices is the fact that, as the groves began to grow back, so did people's attraction to their local culture. "In the past," Abugre says, "every time there was moonlight, people of that community would gather in the house of the *Timbhana*, who is the fetish priest. In that area we don't have the kinds of political chiefs that Southern Ghana had. The leadership was around traditional priests, who didn't have political power; they had spiritual power, basically. So now they've started meeting again at the *Timbhana*'s house, singing during the moonlit nights, regenerating an interest in their community."

"Out of this process," Abugre continues, "there has emerged a number of social groups that were also disappearing fast. Their poetry and drama groups started to meet again, and they began to make their music and to revive their drumming systems, which were rapidly being lost. Then women's groups, which more recently had focused on protection and issues of household violence, began expanding to include collective trading, communal cultivation, even the recording of music." In short, the people are regenerating along with the land. The Gurune had at first been primarily concerned with restoring sacred groves for their gods and being able to grow the shrubs whose seeds are used to treat endemic eye infections. But the results were more far-reaching. "It's the most miraculous thing," Abugre says, "They took us to see some of the growth sprouting, and you can see how the water holes are protected, and they are actually staying for most of the year, for the first time in decades, even as late as November, December, which is the *Hamatan* season, the dry Sahara wind!"

Abugre thinks the religious prohibition warning of death when new trees flower may originally have been put out by the elders to limit the planting of certain species, especially exotics. He agrees that when any group of people, Westerners certainly as much as anyone else, begin to take their culture's ideas as dogma instead of understanding their larger context, they can become dangerous and destructive. "They're not afraid now of the trees flowering," he says. "They're planting oaks and many other varieties that had vanished. They're collecting all the seeds of their trees and medicinals again. They are trying to trace back the seeds of plants they remember that they haven't yet found. They're starting up their polycultures again, their mixed plantings of crops, and cutting back on the chemicals as well. They're bringing all that back to the community. This place that had been so degraded — you can really see the change."

## Attaining Mervana

*Our foresters have studied economics, but they haven't studied the forest ecosystem, which is the basis of this whole thing.*
— MERV WILKINSON, FORESTER AND LANDOWNER

Fortunately, the good news in forestry doesn't come exclusively from indigenous, village or tribal sources. A growing number of private land-owners in First World countries, who bought up forests with cash and are trying to make a regular living from them, are also doing what they can to make sure their holdings will be passed on to their children and grand-children. All over the world there are examples of how small and large woodlot owners are learning to be real stewards of the forest. Naturally, most of these examples are concentrated in areas where there are still forests in good enough condition to *be* managed, like the large forested area stretching from northern California between the Pacific and the Rockies, extending all the way up to Alaska. One still heavily forested but also heavily logged section of that ecosystem lies halfway up its length. Vancouver Island is a place where a lot of mistakes have been made, but also where, shining through the huge clearcuts, is one of the most convincing examples of how well even a small forest can provide for quite a few people, indefinitely.

The particular small forest we're talking about was named Wildwood by its owner back in the 1940s. At 88, Mervyn Wilkinson has maintained a small 55-hectare (137-acre) forest for nearly sixty years, and has become something of a legend among people who care about forests. He's also done many cuts on his property, using selective logging and a philosophy based on one of the primary principles of sustainable forestry: "Establish a rate of cut that sustains the integrity of the forest." Back in 1945, Wilkinson estimated that his forest grew at the rate of 1.9 percent, meaning that as long as his cut never exceeded that, the trees would constantly replenish themselves. In subsequent years, the many American, European, private and public foresters who came knocking at his door showed he wasn't far off; determined by computer, his forest's growth rate was between 2 and 2.1 percent. "Which means," he says, "I've been undercutting for all these years, yet still making a good living." He's taken almost two-and-a-half times of his forest's original volume in his long life — and his land still has 10 percent *more* wood on it than when he started. He has provided full and partial employment to 26 people, all on less than 55 hectares (140 acres). And he could keep doing it forever.[6]

Like many far-seeing private owners, Wilkinson did this by selecting trees for their value, not their volume. He selects good furniture wood from suitable species when they are at just the right age, and sends other "trash trees" to the pulp mill, instead of pulping all the species together or selling them for fuel like most owners do. Like the Yakama, he favors as much variety as possible, which gives him a choice of large, middle-sized and small timber at any given cut, as well as many other products, like mushrooms, berries and medicinal plants. Like other user-managers we have been discussing, he knows that the numerous non-marketable species sharing his forest are not competitors for its products, but indicators of its health and resilience. He exults in the fact that, as he puts it, "The trunks on the giant old Douglas firs here are veritable apartment houses. This one nearest the road has a brown creeper nesting in it. We have four active families of pileated woodpeckers — an indicator of a healthy old forest — a pine marten who moves through and cleans out the squirrels, and occasionally species of owls, barred, barn and great horned. There are also otters, deer, beaver and a cougar stalking our lambs in the spring."

Merv Wilkinson knows all about the animals in the woods. He's famous for working so continuously in the forest with them that even wise old buck deer don't bother to hide when he's around. He says, "So much lives in symbiosis here that the more I study it, the more I am in wonder at the carefully balanced intricacy of all life in this forest — including humans!" He's on the board of Jon Young's Wilderness Awareness School in nearby Washington State, which we will visit in the last chapter of this book. The people at the school have a joke about Merv's name that pokes a little fun at some of the serious feelings of wonder and awe that his empathy with the forest inspires. They say that having a symbiotic relationship with the forest as wonderful as Merv Wilkinson's is the goal they're all striving for. They call it "Attaining Mervana."

The main source of Wilkinson's livelihood and the life of his forest is the soil, which has been built up over thousands of years on this rocky, glaciated island. There's not much soil, he says, but what there is has been pronounced by Dutch scientists to be among the richest they have ever seen. Besides the sub-soils that provide the trees with anchorage and minerals, forest soils contain organic matter and plant nutrients being broken down by bacteria, microorganisms, fungi, "all the bugs and critters that churn it," as the forest veteran says. "[It's] a balanced, complex entity. When you clearcut your forest and burn, it destroys the soil, and that's a crime against nature." Clearcutting means taking out many hectares of forest at a time, leaving huge areas stripped and barren, exposed to sun and rain. British Columbia has seen the error of its ways and in 1994 finally restricted all clearcuts to less than 40 hectares (99 acres) — which is still too large for most environmentalists. Massive areas have already been destroyed. As Wilkinson says, "Once they're through, there's no more forest, period. The . . . soil is so devastated it won't grow trees. We have 3.7 million hectares (9.2 million acres) of insufficiently reforested land because of malpractice in the logging industry." And thousands of people out of work. "Given the average growth rate of B.C. forests, that same land [that they've ruined], under my system, would have 3,400 people employed in the logging end, to say nothing of processing. Three thousand four hundred of our loggers wouldn't be out of work."

Even when clearcuts have successful growth in replanted seedlings, they are ecological disasters in the making. Plantation trees are not only the same species, they're the same age (and these days, because of the very latest cloning methods, they have the same genes as well.) Wilkinson tells the story of the massive European blow-down of trees in a 1986 hurricane, in which England lost 14 million trees, Holland two million and Germany six million. Wilkinson says, "It hit England first. The Germans knew it was coming, so they sent their foresters out to be where they could observe when the winds came. They were stationed, ready with their notebooks. They had people at the multi-species, multi-aged forests, and people in the monocultures. Observers at the mixed-height forests noticed that the trees worked against each other as the wind hit. The primaries, the younger trees, would bend first and the secondaries would bend next, and then run into each other coming back. Results: they diffused the wind, so the loss in those forests was very minimal." Klaus Gros, a senior forester with the German government Forest Service, told Wilkinson on a visit that in such a storm, "You wouldn't lose nearly the trees that a monoculture will. Our . . . solid mono-height forests, like a field of wheat, they got rocking, and on the fourth or fifth rock, the whole thing went down, like a domino! We have learned a lesson. No more mono-aged forests." And that means no more clearcuts.

As we've seen with the spruce budworm, departing from the evolutionary plan for a forest can degrade it more subtly than the sudden crash of a
storm or fire, but the losses are just as tragic. The herbicides laid down to
protect sickly industrial clones from the competition of trees like willow,
alder and maple also destroy the soil's chance to be rebuilt by their inputs of
humus and nitrogen. Alder, frequently considered a trash tree to be killed
with herbicides, actually innoculates the soils against disease and pests; that's
why nature puts it out first. And insects, diseases and pests treat monocultures of trees the same way they treat monocultured food crops.
Wilkinson points out: "I've seen disease [and insects] my whole life in the
forest, little pockets here and there of all one species. But never, till we got
to clearcutting, did I see epidemics." Even the reassurances we're given
about new seedlings restoring logged areas through tree-planting programs
are a joke to anyone who checks such areas a few years later. Wilkinson says,
"They plant from plugs, a way of growing a lot of seeds in a minimal space.
The roots are deformed . . . there's no proper taproot. The young tree
is completely vulnerable to wind." And it can't feed properly. "The root system isn't teased out, the soil isn't carefully placed around it. If they survive
at all, they bush, developing multiple tips. And then," Wilkinson says, "the
industry rushes in with the fertilizer. It's like giving a dose of drugs to a drug
addict . . . [It just] kills off all the understorey and all the systems in the soil."
More fundamentally, as Barry Ford at the environmentally sustainable
private company Collins Pine says, "Why do they [the big industrial compa-
nies] have to plant trees in the first place? What's wrong with their soils and
their regeneration? They should be asking themselves if their cuts are too
big for the forest to naturally regenerate, the way ours does."

Logging rates that respect the forest's capacity to renew itself are the
key to sustainability. But even when forests have been clearcut, replanted
with the wrong things or soaked in chemicals, there's sometimes still hope.
Six hundred miles away from Wilkinson's forest, along the California-
Oregon border, Orville Camp bought 65 hectares (160 acres) back in 1967,
intending to subdivide it for housing. It didn't seem to be worth much else,
stripped of anything marketable by clearcutting, with nothing but brush
and fuel trees growing on it. Camp began to restore it, with an eye to selling
it as a housing development. Then he got hooked. After only twelve years,
he was producing 500 cords of sustainable firewood a year. Today, it's
called Camp's Forest Farm. He tends 140 hectares (350 acres) of trees,
mushrooms, huckleberries, hazelnuts and florals. "It's a management plan

for all the forest amenities," he says, "and most of the amenities are more valuable than timber." While it's true that his method doesn't produce as many jobs and income over the short term as razing and then replanting a clearcut, he knows his land will be far more productive over the long term. His *Forest Farmer's Handbook* is now in its fourth printing and he's a regular on the forestland training circuit. Camp points to the double dividends that come with holistic forest managements, and the double indemnities that attend treating forests as one-species, one-purpose commodities. He says, "We're converting our forests into tree plantations, and the taxpayers are subsidizing it. Even worse, it's not sustainable. The whole thing is absurd; there's no logic behind it except to grow a specific crop for a global industry, which is only a tiny fraction of what a forest can do."[7]

The methods of Orville Camp, Mervyn Wilkinson and similar private owners are economically successful, are socially and emotionally rewarding, and provide employment for a lot more people. "Costa Rica has put 15 percent more people in their forests through selective cutting than when they used to cut them clear," Wilkinson says, "and they still have their forests." Even Wilkinson employs more than twenty people on his tiny woodlot, and that irony reflects the fact that industrial forestry, like industrial farming, has a goal of providing as few jobs as possible. The number of logging and sawmill jobs under its auspices have shrunk steadily over the years.

Whenever campaigns are mounted to preserve forests for habitat or even to put some limits on cutting, the logging industry threatens massive job losses and economic downturns. In fact, all the statistics show the opposite. Over the past two decades, jobs have been lost largely because of mechanization in the industry itself. The average number of workers employed to cut and mill 9,400 cubic meters (330,000 cubic feet) of lumber per year declined from twenty in the 1980s to only nine in the modern mills and heavy equipment industry of the late 1990s.[8] Even in resource-rich Idaho, Oregon, Washington and British Columbia, only one worker in twenty-five made a living quarrying minerals, felling trees or milling lumber in 1993, down from one in twelve in 1969. Once towns free themselves from such extraction industries, they tend to do much better. In the Pacific Northwest, displaced wood-workers have been quickly absorbed into an expanding economy, real earnings have risen, and "once depressed timber towns [have] growing populations and mini-building booms."[9] Late in 1994, the mayor of Springfield, Oregon, considered one of the state's most timber-dependent towns, referred to the bitter controversy over protecting spotted owls in old-growth forests. He said, "Owls versus jobs was just plain false. What we've got here is quality of life. And as long as we don't screw that up, we'll always be able to attract people and businesses."[10]

## Taking Care of Business

*Collins Pine comes out [of the certification process] with flying colors . . . [but] I have to tell you that there's very few other industrial forests of that size and scale that would even come close.*
— ROY KEENE, FORESTRY CONSULTANT AND CERTIFIER

It's heartening to hear about aboriginal territories being preserved or reforested and private owners bringing in sustainable forestry methods, but much of the degradation of the planet's forest resource is happening on government- or industry-controlled tracts, where anybody remotely indigenous, traditional or with significant local roots is long gone. In Canada, Russia, the United States, South and Central America and Southeast Asia, forest lands are being leased to huge timber companies or are owned outright by them, and these companies are still largely dominated by First Industrial Revolution logic. Because of the global market, the timber companies say that industrial-style clearcutting and the replanting of mono-cultured tree plantations is the only forest management model that will maintain their competitiveness and their profits. Governments bow to the wisdom of the market place and their own need for foreign exchange. The trouble is, the companies haven't been in existence long enough to complete even one full crop rotation, so they really are just guessing about how well their sprayed, monoculture second-generation forest will produce over the long term.

Earlier we introduced Collins Pine, an Oregon timber company that has embraced a value system that goes beyond money, and at the same time is actually making more by spinning out its harvest over a much longer period of time. This rational practice requires a certain amount of self-restraint. For example, when Collins Pine forester Barry Ford noticed that an area they were cutting in their Almanor Forest in northern California wasn't regenerating naturally and they weren't getting new seedlings, he realized it had been stabilized for so long — 500 years or more — that the trees were no longer set up for reproduction. "That's when we started studying the microsystem. The rhyolite soil up there compacts, so we thought that was it; we tried to break it up and I've been analyzing all the nutrients. But until we figure out how to manage it, we've stopped cutting." It's still very useful to the company, Ford says. "Now it's become a study site to learn how this old forest managed to survive on such poor soils." In Quebec, a comparable situation — very poor regeneration on a site that has been stabilized to black spruce for centuries, in the boreal forest between Lac-St-Jean and Chibougamou — has only inspired the pulp industry to redouble their cutting.

The Collins Pine 43,600-hectare (96,000-acre) forest at Almanor is principally sugar pine, magnificent trees that grow up to 55 meters (180 feet) high, with enormous, two-foot long cones that smell bewitchingly like hot syrup. This species suffers from blister rust, so Collins Pine only takes seedlings resistant to the rust for replanting. Ford says proudly, "Our sugar pine has carried this rust-resistant gene for a whole century. That's why you need a big gene pool. Nursery stock from China brought the rust into British Columbia in the 1930s in the first place, and it spread. We plant local seed only, and we make sure we keep all the genes that have evolved in this forest around, just in case." While other companies are jumping onto the bandwagon of the latest forestry management styles — cloned super-trees and genetically engineered trees that express their own anti-spruce bud-worm Bt — Collins Pine vice president Wade Mosby says, "GMOs — oh my God! We're worried. Really worried about that. We'd never use those seedlings. We never even use clones. We use local seeds from the specific hillside or whatever we're planting on — only! And usually, we don't have to plant at all." Ford agrees. "We hate those fancy clones," he says. "They don't provide protection from new diseases. Fuserium just tore through the cloned Georgia pines that they spent all those years growing and raving about. More types of blister rust are just waiting out there."

"Living above the store," the sign of a personal commitment to a community and a business, which we talked about in chapter one, doesn't always have to be done literally. Wade Mosby tells the story of a young man named Walter Reid hired by Truman Collins Sr. fifty years ago to help him carry out a vision that had come to him after he had been trained as a forester at Harvard. Truman Collins wanted to turn his family's extensive land holdings into sustainable forests. Wade Mosby says no one was logging the way Walter Reid was at the time, and he was constantly attacked by other companies, foresters, academics and the industry. "He was completely alone, and he was only a young man in his early twenties! But he and Truman were so sure of what they were doing that they ignored all the experts, all the taunts and threats of bankruptcy. And Walter has lived to see his work honored as the best commercial forest in the whole country, one that has never been degraded by bad practices." Walter Reid, frail at 86 but radiant with pride, was present at the gala occasion of cutting the two billionth board foot at the company's Almanor Forest; because they listened to him, they still have as much wood in that forest as when he began managing it.

Today, following Collins and Reid's precepts, the foresters at Collins Pine walk their forest continuously, monitoring conditions like the temperature of streams, counting the number of osprey nests, noting how chipmunks are responding to the nurse logs they leave, and amassing other base-line scientific data that even governments seldom have the time to gather. They actually know every tree, perhaps not as intimately as a traditional user does, but certainly far better than other managers in the industry; they take pictures of every individual tree in the forest, a project that takes two full years, and they have done that every ten years since 1940. Except for "biomass correction," their term for getting out fire-attracting brush, they never cut trees smaller than a foot in diameter. Finally, like Merv Wilkinson, they've figured out their allowable cut, and they never cut more wood than they grow. Their painstakingly filed photographs and their own field experience tells them how much that should be. It's not surprising that there's a long line of foresters waiting for the chance to work at Collins Pine.

We've been talking all through this book about how consumers can tell whether a business or an organization walks its talk. When it comes to forest products, the certification movement has become very powerful. And the Forest Stewardship Council (FSC), based in Oxaca, Mexico, as the most trusted organization overseeing sustainable forestry, has its work cut out for it. They're an independent, non-profit NGO that includes environmental groups, timber and trade organizations, foresters, indigenous people's organizations, community forestry groups and other forest product certification organizations in twenty-five countries. They are extremely effective and reliable in northern countries like Europe, Canada and the United States. But certification can ironically create new markets in lawless areas like the Amazonian or Indonesian wilderness, inadvertently encouraging a separate black market for the very trees we need to protect. So until the new organizations can deal with such problems in developing countries, organizations like Friends of the Earth are still supporting a boycott of all tropical wood.[11]

There are also watchdog organizations, like Scientific Certification Systems, who go right into American forests to make sure that their management is really measuring up to the FSC goals and that product integrity is being maintained all the way to the consumer. Near the Almanor Forest is southwestern Oregon's Rogue Institute for Ecology and Economy, which certifies small operations and is affiliated with the SmartWood certification program. This program operates internationally to help private producers, especially small ones, get in on the expanding market in certified forest products. It has only been in existence for the past six or seven years, but has already led to fundamental and revolutionary changes such as the pledge of the U.S. hardware giant Home Depot and the Swedish furniture store IKEA to use only certified forest products in their stores. And it has translated into a market advantage for a few forestry companies with real integrity. Jim Quinn, the President of Collins Pine up until 2000, told the World Wildlife Fund in a 1998 interview that certification doesn't even increase costs in the long run. "That's because what we spend on certification, other companies spend on advertising and political contributions aimed at creating a favorable image. We get the favourable image by certifying, and we get a lot of good, free publicity as well. That publicity has greater credibility because it's not our own advertising."

Roy Keene, a logger turned environmentalist and longtime critic of government and industry practices, helped certify Collins Pine. He says he worries that more of the older, larger pines will be taken out of the stands at Almanor because of market pressure on the mills to produce products, and because of all the economic disadvantages under which a company like Collins Pine has to labor.[12] Their behavior is still the best in the business; but legislative and social changes are needed to help good companies like Collins Pine keep up their standards and become real forces in the industry. And as we'll see ahead, such changes are starting to turn up.

## Turning Point

*Make the well-being of the lands and waters the fundamental goal of management.*
— ECOLOGICAL PRINCIPLES FOR SUSTAINABLE FORESTRY

A couple of "good" companies here, and some well-managed private or community forests there, can be found scattered from the Rockies and the Pacific Northwest to Africa, Guatemala and Indonesia. But if we're going to save our water, air and soil, we need to manage a whole lot more forests sustainably — a whole lot faster. We have to get at those government holdings, the massive amounts of public lands that are currently leased to corporations. The moment for that has finally come as well. In April of 2001, a landmark agreement was signed in British Columbia that is unlike anything ever seen before, both in terms of those who joined together to sign it and in terms of what it is trying to achieve.

The area covered by the new agreement is the mid- to north coast and the islands of Haida Gwaii, a region that extends from the northern tip of Vancouver Island all the way up to the Alaskan panhandle. This is a narrow strip of forest pinched between the Pacific Ocean and the coastal mountain ranges, fed by high rainfall blown off the ocean. It supports the highest biomass — that is, weight of living things per hectare — of any ecosystem on the entire planet. It's home to a quarter of the world's remaining temperate rainforest, a truly magical place where Sitka spruce, hemlock, western red cedar and Douglas fir tower as much as a hundred meters (325 feet) into the sky. This ecosystem is also home to many of the world's last healthy salmon runs, as well as geoduck clams, pods of killer whales, murrelets, spotted owls, grizzlies, wolves, otters, sea anemones, beds of fat oysters, flocks of eagles, starfish in a bewildering array of colors and shapes, the magical, pure white "spirit bears" of the coastal islands — and much more.

Temperate rainforests are exceedingly rare ecosystems, occupying less than one fifth of 1 percent of all the land on earth — and most of them are already gone. Much of this one has already been razed, from northern California up to Cape Caution, British Columbia. These forests provide high quality lumber and paper products, but as the most valuable stands of fine-grained old-growth cedar and spruce are removed, pressure on the ecosystem has been causing collapses in its key components. As we noted in chapter three, "Using Coyotes to Grow Grass," certain species in each ecosystem are key to the survival of all the others. A water-living predator, the Pacific salmon, is so pivotal to the health of the temperate rainforest that the ecosystem is also called the "salmon forest."

For many years, environmental and First Nations groups have been warning that logging companies, abetted by government policy, were causing salmon populations to collapse by overcutting the forests. Company officials said overfishing and ocean warming were the problems; besides, the logging industry only wanted to cut 7 percent of the territory. As we saw with dams, however, the richest areas for industrial exploitation are also the engines of the ecosystem. The 7 percent of the forests that the industry considers "operable," or easy to cut, lies in the accessible valley bottoms, the same river valleys that produce salmon. And of course, they are also the preferred homes of the bears, eagles and biggest trees, and the village sites of the native people of the region as well.

For the past few years, the logging industry has been poised to develop the very last pristine forests of the entire temperate rainforest ecosystem — the north coast. Logging interests are considered, by the government at least, to be major stakeholders, because of the jobs they've provided and their heavy use of the area. But the people with the clearest claim to actual legal ownership of this coast are not the logging companies, but the tribal groups of traditional peoples of the north coast of British Columbia — the people of the salmon forests. The lack of signed treaties with the Canadian government has put these tribes in an interesting legal position today, because numerous court cases have determined that they still have rights not only to govern themselves, but to actual ownership of large areas of provincial land. Canada's Delgamuukw Supreme Court ruling of 1998, in particular, established that aboriginal title still exists in this area and cannot be ignored. But until the questions get answered about what the exact borders of their land are and what types of use the First Peoples are entitled to make of it, uncertainty reigns on the coast.

Besides native groups and the forest industry, British Columbia has been settled over the last century by many other people with their own claims to the area: the salmon fishermen up and down the coast, who have come to utterly depend on the fishery for their income; the truckers, loggers and sawmill workers who live off the forestry industry; all the town govern-ments that have sprung up to serve the people living along the coast; to say nothing of the tourism operators, and various nature and industry groups. All these people have demanded a seat at the government's negotiating table as "resource stakeholders."

Native land claims and stakeholders' battles brought frustration and insecurity into everyone's lives on the coast, but even as legal and adminis-trative battles were being fought about who owned what, the fisheries continued to be overharvested and the forests clearcut. Major environmen-tal organizations, notably Greenpeace, the Sierra Club of B.C., ForestEthics and the Rainforest Action Network, launched a national campaign in 1997, demanding that a chain of north coast watersheds be put aside as parks. As their symbol, they used a charismatic and affectionate white variant of the black bear that only lives on the islands of these forests, which they call the "spirit bear." They then declared an international boycott against wood extracted from B.C. forests. This campaign took fire. The companies and the government were forced to the table, and agreed on an eighteen-month moratorium on logging in a hundred watersheds until their final preservation status could be determined.

Of course, it wasn't just the boycott that brought down the logging industry. The companies involved had already realized that much of the forest that was economically accessible had already been liquidated. And the industry could see that, in both Europe and North America, consumers and mills were demanding more certified wood. Even wild animal protection was becoming a critical issue, as movements for initiatives like the Y-2-Y corridor gained momentum. In short, the industry was being forced to change its ways if it wanted to keep cutting at all, so it began to pay closer attention to the environmentalists' demands in order to regain lost markets and public credibility.

As we have already seen in the case studies in this book, one of the reasons the resource has vanished like a fire before the wind as the logging industry moved north is that this industry is a huge, multinational one with few local contacts. The universal characteristic of long-term, sustainable resource use is local control and local ownership. But without logging, the economic prospects for the major owner-user group, in this case the First Nations villages of the B.C. coast, are very limited. The native groups' clear statement that they need to have the right to exploit the economic potential of their lands, to log and fish on whatever land they end up getting, has stood in the way of their making alliances with most environmental groups. B.C. salmon fishermen were also concerned about their future. Government attempts to "save" the salmon resource by cutting back on the number of licenses were favoring large operators over small because the government claims it's easier to control a small group of big users than a large group of small ones. As a result of this policy, tenure rights have been taken away from more than 15,000 local residents and given to large, multinational companies who have little if any investment in any local ecology — with predictable effects on the fishery.

The increasing numbers of wilderness, fishing and wildlife tourism operations on the coast were also stymied. Would the area they were in be controlled by environmentalists or natives, or would it be shaved bare by the logging industry? If the former two got it, would they let the tourists stay? Despite heavy mechanization and the diminution of the resource, unions representing the many forest workers, especially the truckers, were also obdurate. They were insisting on maintaining existing cuts so that none of the jobs logging or transporting huge loads of logs out of the area would be lost, regardless of who eventually got tenure over the forest. And the towns, made up of a mixture of all of the above, wanted to be sure their own tenure, boundaries and rights to develop would be respected.

The David Suzuki Foundation (DSF) has been involved in salmon forest issues for the past six or seven years. This environmental foundation was founded by David in 1991. Its primary mandate is to examine and document the underlying causes of human ecological destructiveness, in order to seek solutions. The DSF's major focus is British Columbia forests and fisheries, and their research, like that of so many other environmental organizations, has also shown that the best managers of a resource are almost always the local users. So they began a long process of dialogue with the First Nations, in hopes that these original users and probable eventual legal owners would gain a better position in the discussion. The First Nations had been left out of the management process and ignored for so long that a level of trust had to be built up. The separate tribes and village leaders also had serious internal divergencies and many other issues to deal with, concerns that had mostly to do with pure survival: unemployment in some of the villages is as high as 85 percent. So their first request was that the DSF help them with job creation and economic development in their communities. This partnership proceeded so well that less than a year later, the First Nations asked the DSF to sponsor a conference so that the leaders and elders of all the mid- and north-coast villages could meet together to try to set up some mutual goals they could all work towards. The meeting was named Turning Point.

The Council of Haida nations came, as well as two Haida communities, Skidegate and Old Massett, the Haisla people of Kitamaat village, the Heiltsuk of Bella Bella, the Gitga'at of Hartley Bay, the peoples of Lax Kw'alaams, Metlakatla and Kitkatla, the Kitasoo and Xaixais of Klemtu, the Nuxalk of Bella Coola, the people of Oweekeno and the Xeni Gwet'in from the Nemiah valley inland of the mountains. The elected chiefs, treaty officers and elders of these groups arrived in Vancouver in May of 2000 to try to figure out what these scattered tribes and villages might possibly have in common in terms of managing the resource the entire province was fighting over. Suzuki and his wife, Tara Cullis, who had been flying in and out of the communities for years in order to try to establish a relationship, opened the meeting, setting the tone with their speeches. And then Tom Reimchen of the University of British Columbia came on to describe the intensive salmon studies he's been doing. Ann Rowan, the director of the Suzuki Foundation's Pacific Salmon Forests Project, says that Reimchen immediately launched into an extremely scientific discussion, with charts and graphs, about marine isotopes, fly larvae and South American song birds. She was afraid that such an academic beginning would lose the audience and destroy the feeling of hope and emotional expectation that had been built up.

Tom Reimchen is one of the rare new breed of ecologists who are trying to understand entire ecosystems, as opposed to focusing on the behavior of a few genes or molecules within one species. Certain isotopes of nitrogen (N15) become concentrated in salmon flesh during the marine stage of their life cycle. Ever since he learned that these isotopes can be detected in the flesh of any creature that ever subsequently eats salmon, Reimchen has been tracking how the forests of the B.C. coast actually work. N15 is a vital nutrient for all living organisms, including trees. Most species of salmon spend two to five years in the ocean, and when mature head back to their natal stream to spawn. As they run the gauntlet of predators waiting for them, their N15-filled flesh is consumed and then defecated by birds, mammals and insects throughout the forest. River otters, eagles, wolves, gulls, ravens and bears carry the salmon into the trees, and the tell-tale isotope is detectable in tree composition and forest vegetation long distances from any salmon stream. Even the fly maggots that feast on leftover carcasses load up on N15 before pupating. They hatch months later in the spring, just in time to transfer the salmon's nitrogen to the thousands of migrating birds arriving from Colombia and Brazil, on their way to the Arctic. The salmon bring the largest annual pulse of fertilizer into this forest, and therefore it's the salmon that are helping to create the giant cedars and firs. The largest trees, that 7 percent desired by the loggers, grow in the valley bottoms, not because of the availability of water, as previously thought, but because of the nitrogen carried to them in the bodies of the salmon.

Ann Rowan says the First Nations audience was rapt throughout Reimchen's story, and she didn't understand why until Roger Williams, chief of the inland Xenigwet'in, explained: "I know those stories. Those are the stories my grandmother told me, of Salmon-boy." There are indeed many intricate and beautiful stories about how Salmon-boy travels through the forest, meeting, feeding and benefiting each and every creature in turn. Rowan says, "The meeting took off from that point. We knew there's an intimate scientific link between the forest and the salmon, but these are the *salmon-people*. They are just as connected to those fish and trees as the otters and bears and everything else Tom was talking about. And what happened is, we all realized *that* was our commonality. Personal commitments to save the forest and the salmon started to flow out of every tribe, community and group. They drafted the Declaration of the First Nations of the North Pacific Coast, in which they committed themselves to the serious steward-ship of these lands for the future generations. This was really a powerful moment; when people recognized that they really *could* work together — and that there are very important things to work on. There are bigger things in life than our individual differences or our immediately perceived needs."

In short, the First Nations achieved a vision of what they all wanted, despite centuries of tribal differences and communities rife with social prob-lems. They visualized a prize, a real, long-term future. By supporting each other, they could put their separate and sometimes conflicting problems, their joblessness, social despair, the perceived need for immediate funds for this or for that, into perspective. They could protect the trees and salmon, and again have the forest that had been their birthright. After that, things happened fast. In December of 2000, the coastal peoples called a meeting of the CEOs of the biggest forest companies, unions representing loggers like the International Woodworkers Association, the environmentalists, the salmon fishers, the contractors on the coast, the truck loggers, the tourism operators, the mayors, and the government. They said: "Come meet with us; we need solutions."

"The First Nations were the only ones who could have done that and gotten everyone to come," Rowan says, "because everyone knows the fundamental instability in the region lies in the fact that the land claims aren't yet resolved, and probably won't be for years." The native leaders told the assembled stakeholders that what is needed is a truly comprehensive approach that will conserve the biological and cultural integrity of the coast. "Everyone had to admit that was what they wanted, too. Even the multina-tional timber companies want it now, because all the pressure on them means this is probably the only way they can stay in business." Management of this ecosystem is to be put in the hands of the users. In practice, this will mean that the B.C. government will meet with the usual ten or fifteen stake-holders, but that if the First Nations do not agree with their management plan, the government will meet directly with them, "government to govern-ment." This will enable the native groups to make sure that the only place

LISTEN FOR THE JAGUAR

they will ever want to live is being managed in a way they think is sustainable over the long term. They will have far more influence than any other group over what will happen, and all the other groups, including the unions, have agreed to this, if only to get out of the current impasse.

Perhaps most important of all is the fact that all the forest users have agreed to practice, without fail, the nine Ecological Principles for Sustainable Forestry used as epigraphs throughout this chapter. These principles, detailed in the report summary "A Cut Above,"[13] take into account all the aspects of forest management we have mentioned in this chapter: from the idea that the key goal is the sustainability and well-being of the land, to establishing a rate of cut that doesn't go beyond the forest's ability to regenerate; from ensuring local community participation in managing the resource, to conserving not some, but *all* native plants and animals. Forestry companies must get involved in restoring degraded forests and streams, and all the participants have agreed to "focus on what to retain rather than what to remove." Finally, as all holistic management demands, everyone has to "acknowledge uncertainty, act cautiously, and monitor the consequences of forest practices," to guard against becoming dogmatic or falling for the latest fashion or technology. In short, these guidelines will require all the north-coast stakeholders to be humble, to expect to make mistakes, and to pay attention to nature's responses to any intervention.

By signing on to this protocol, everyone from the industry to the fishers have committed themselves to an ecological perspective that will bring an end to industrial logging in the mid- to north coast and the islands of Haida Gwaii. This is a monumental achievement. The plan will commit 7.4 million hectares (18.5 million acres) of remaining temperate rainforest to truly sustainable, user-managed forestry. With any luck at all, there will be no more large, industrial clearcuts, no more clones and chemicals, no more destroyed stream beds, invaded Indian communities or hostile loggers threatened with unemployment. The remaining communities of wild animals will thrive. There are even plans to extend the protected forests to link up with the Y-2-Y coalition through its corridor programs.

As part of the agreement, an independent body of scientists will be available to provide First Nations and other stakeholders with detailed information on the effects of any proposed new cuts, roads, mitigation efforts or developments. They will also take on an auditing role. "You'll have somewhere to go if you don't like the cutting plans the government announces," Rowan says. "For example, a village can access the plans and send them to the scientific body for assessment; if they don't measure up, they can hold them up at the provincial level." Since the provincial government and the First Nations government both have to grant the licenses, this system also creates a balance to help counteract the political pressures felt by any provincial government. Making sure that regulatory systems are set up to provide these kinds of checks and balances is something that is increasingly being included in environmental management programs around the world.

"Everybody acknowledges this won't be cheap," Rowan continues. "We're moving from laissez-faire, break-neck extraction to an entire economy based on conservation. So there will have to be some mitigation funds for workers, for communities with no resources for different kinds of jobs." They're looking at carefully developed tourism and value-added wood products to replace the high volume pulp and lumber production of the past. They're all trying to work out a way to live and prosper without destroying the very basis of that prosperity. Greenpeace and the other groups have promised to withdraw their boycott campaign to see how the industry does; but they will still be watching carefully.

The Turning Point agreement is only one of several such solutions that are popping up independently all over the world. Even on the populous North American Eastern seaboard, the new Forest Conservation Initiative has resulted in the purchase of more than 120,000 hectares (300,000 acres) of the North Woods forest, a 10.5 million-hectare (26 million-acre) ecosystem spread through northern Maine, New Hampshire, Vermont and New York. Because of a sudden rush of buying and selling in the area — more than 2 million hectares (5 million acres) changed hands over just the past five years — authorities and environmentalists realized something had to be done or the entire ecosystem could be destabilized. They put together such a remarkably diverse group of foundations, funding bodies, government agencies, logging companies and individuals that there isn't space to list them all. Just a few include the Doris Duke Charitable Foundation, the Natural Resources Defense Council, the Nature Conservancy, The Conservation Fund, all the states involved, and many private industries and contractors. The area will be managed on the Cores, Corridors and Carnivores concept, with preservation habitat and wildlife cores, large areas that will be managed for sustainable logging, recreation and other carefully monitored activities, and an overall goal of stewardship of the entire forest entity. The complex tenure agreements include easements, leases and rentals, as well as outright public ownership. And of course there are plans to extend corridors out to existing parks — including the Adirondacks.[14]

Such initiatives are proliferating around the world. They're new, but they have the authority of 150 years of our experience in the Adirondacks behind them. They give people something very important — a stable natural environment, so they can plan their lives around and within it. In British Columbia, the First Nations finally see a real future for themselves, as do the tourism operators, the fishers, the towns, and the truckers; they're all in it together. Artist Art Sterritt of the Gitga'at of Hartley Bay emphasizes the most obvious advantage of such coalitions: "The power of the agreement is that it is consensus-based; it will live beyond governments." These unlikely groups of stakeholders are arriving at unified, holistic visions of the future, and a new era in forest management is about to begin. But it all takes an amazing amount of pressure: political, economic, environmental and moral. It also takes an unusual amount of human trust and cooperation. It's part of a real revolution, which is creating new kinds of businesses, saving animal habitat, altering the cars we drive, the houses we live in — and the ways we work out our problems. Like a baby, this revolution is fresh and new. And it will need a serious amount of energy and awareness, together with passionate support from everyone who cares about our incredible forest resources. If it gets that, it's not just the Haida and the loggers, the grizzlies and New England moose, who will have a more secure future.

CHAPTER 7

# SONG OF THE ALBATROSS
## Keeping Some Fish in the Sea

### Striped Glory

*In my opinion, this recovery was the greatest success story in
fisheries management in the world.*
— CARL SAFINA, AUDUBON SOCIETY LIVING OCEANS PROGRAM

Any avid fisherman who has grown up reading *Field and Stream* and
*Outdoor Life* magazines knows that one of the great experiences in angling
is standing in the spray of the cold surf of the Atlantic coast, casting plugs
into ravenous schools of striped bass, and finally, after a glorious battle,
hauling in a forty-pound beauty. For sports fishers, striped bass hold the
same exalted position on the east coast of North America as chinook salmon
do on the west. And like salmon, they are anadromous; they divide their life
cycle between fresh water and salt. They congregate in large schools,
feeding voraciously; and once hooked, they are ferocious, electrifying fight-
ers. Again like salmon, they are highly prized for the texture and flavor
of their flesh. Their two main breeding grounds are the Hudson and
Chesapeake rivers. In the increasingly populous and industrialized U.S.
coastal states like New Jersey, New York, Massachusetts, Rhode Island,
Maryland and North Carolina, all species of wild fish have had to contend
with human predation by sport and commercial fishers, with effluents
dumped into the rivers that have interfered with reproduction, with deforestation and more. Nevertheless, striped bass remained plentiful until the
1970s. After that, their numbers dropped precipitously year by year.

By the mid-1980s, as marine ornithologist Carl Safina, director of the

National Audubon Society's Living Oceans program and author of *Song for the Blue Ocean*, says, the situation had degraded so far that, "You could fish for bass at the best areas all night at the best time — the full moon in October — and not get a single bite."[1] Devastated sport fishers, environmentalists and governments, as well as all the industries that depended on this resource, began pointing fingers. Some demanded that striped bass be placed on the endangered species list to protect them from further exploitation. Commercial and recreational fishers blamed one another for being greedy. Water quality, pollution and urban development were all cited as culprits. These factors no doubt played a role, but the real problem was not hard to trace. It was the fact that the striped bass had been treated according to an industrial paradigm — as cogs in the well-oiled wheels of a state economy, not as part of an intricate natural system with its own rules and regulations that have nothing to do with human systems of supply and demand.

The various state resource experts and managers had assumed that the survival of young bass (as West coast managers have assumed for young salmon) is *not* dependent on the numbers of spawning adults. In their opinion the only factors considered crucial to the size of the bass population were the conditions surrounding the eggs and fry — water quality, temperature, turbidity and so on. Even though it would seem logical to most people to assume that if more mature fish were laying eggs, more juveniles would survive, the fry were monitored but the spawning adults were not. State resource agencies permitted so much overfishing that not enough adults were surviving long enough to breed. In other words, they assumed that the fish would somehow manage to reproduce at a rate commensurate with all the stakeholders' desires to exploit them. This assumption led government managers to overestimate the sustainable catch, just as they did with Atlantic cod in the 1980s, and are now doing with Pacific salmon. It's a management style that really doesn't consider the fish's reproductive needs — not even the very simple fact that fish need to be allowed to grow to sexual maturity in order to have offspring. The only kind of reproduction that interests most modern resource managers is the reproduction of money, with its more immediate and seemingly endless demands on their attention.

Eventually, all the stakeholders realized that while the decline in striped bass was a result of many complex factors, the only one that was immediately controllable was human predation. If anyone was to profit from this resource, the possibility of overfishing had to be addressed. Since the

Chesapeake River produces 90 percent of the striped bass on the coast, in 1982 the United States Congress passed a federal emergency plan to protect the juveniles surviving in it. Fishers, both sport and commercial, were only allowed to keep bass above a certain minimum size, in order to ensure that the new batch of juveniles would have a chance to mature and become spawning adults. Many state governments objected to this top-down interference in their jurisdiction, and fishing industries despaired about potential bankruptcy. But the federal officials persisted, and began shutting down state fisheries to force everyone to comply with the new rules. They also began a far-reaching publicity campaign to enlist the support of the fishers themselves, explaining the seriousness of the situation and offering the hope that, with everyone's cooperation, the striped bass might one day return to delight the hearts of surf fishers. Throughout the 1980s, it was impossible to go into any store along the entire length of the east coast that sold fishing tackle, licenses or even bait without seeing pictures of striped bass and reading the notices explaining the heroic sacrifices people needed to make to bring them back.

A new development affected reproduction and survival rates a few years later. Striped bass are predators, high on the food chain, so contaminants can become concentrated in their flesh via the process termed bio-magnification. High levels of PCBs were discovered in striped bass in the mid-1980s. Recreational and commercial fishing on the Hudson River were both closed. Although the states bordering the Chesapeake River still protested, closure of the Hudson River fishery quickly resulted in observable increases in the number of fish, an ironic result of the fact that their flesh was too contaminated for humans to eat. Acceptable size limits of striped bass along the whole coast were also gradually raised from 40 to 90 cm (16 to 38 inches) over the next six years, allowing more and more fish to reach sexual maturity. Commercial fishing was strictly controlled, while recreational fishers, whose catch had once been unlimited, were allowed only one fish per day.

On a Cape Cod beach one hot, sunny July day in the late 1980s, Holly was called from her sunbathing by two excited fishermen. They had had lines in the surf all day, and had just caught an enormous striped bass at least three feet long. None of the nearby sun-worshippers recognized the species. But the two fishers certainly did. They asked Holly to take a picture with her camera and mail it to them, so they could prove to their families that their fish story was true. When she asked them if they planned to eat it, they looked scandalized, and explained that, although they knew it was delicious, this was a striped bass; they had almost become extinct, and were just coming back. They were delighted to see such a big one, and all they wanted was the excitement of the occasional catch without destroying the fish for the future. After taking the snapshot, all three watched the big creature swim away. This bass was not the only one to be spared. Statistics show that many more sport fishers not only kept within the quota, but did even more, releasing all the striped bass they caught directly after the thrill of the tussle.

By the late 1980s, in less than a decade, the conservation measures were beginning to pay off. Larger numbers of spawning adult striped bass returned to the rivers, more eggs were laid, and the numbers of juvenile survivors rose steeply, disproving the old management assumptions. By the mid-1990s, the whole length of the east coast had bass again; they rebounded so strongly that, as Carl Safina says, "You could catch numbers of large striped bass in the middle of a summer day, which was previously unheard of. The whole idea that led to their return was protect the fish by size limits designed to allow each female to lay eggs at least twice, and leave enough fish in the water in general, by restricting catch limits." In other words, respect the needs of the fish. It worked.

It looks as if an enlightened government saved the day from on high; their strong measures certainly helped once things had reached the point of collapse. But it's important to remember that this species, as a resource, was collapsing in the first place because of expert, government management. In this case, the users of the resource were largely people who loved this fish not just for its taste and economic value, but for its beauty and its spirit. They were the first people to alert the authorities about its decline with complaints like Safina's: no fish during an October moon! The fact that they were ignored at first does not mean that the fishers themselves were not increasingly aware of resource distress. And when the controls came down, fishers responded by voluntarily limiting their catch even beyond the guidelines. Despite the various state governments' battle for the right to continue high rates of industrial extraction, the local users of the resource cooperated. They read those posters as they bought their bait. They wanted the bass to come back.

Today, there has been some backsliding. As soon as the fish rebounded, there was enormous pressure from industry and the state governments, especially New Jersey's, to open the fishery again; enough pressure to get government officials to reduce the size limit to 70 cm (28 inches) and double the sports bag limit to two fish per day. That pressure continues today. The result is that average sizes and numbers have noticeably declined, while fish over 13 kg (30 pounds) are rare again. There are no more posters about striped bass in the bait shops, and users, especially non-local sports fishers vacationing on the coast, can be forgiven for thinking that if there were a crisis they would be told. Their immediate and enthusiastic cooperation when the resource was perceived to be in trouble gives some insight into the way people are willing to limit their own activities if they are well informed about its real levels of resilience. We have done too little to keep users informed, and trusted too little in their self-control.

In this story, we see all the conservation elements mentioned by Manoj Mishra of TRAFFIC, a branch of the World Wildlife Fund in India mentioned in chapter three. He said that the way to sustain species on this planet is to allow local user-management of resources on a day-to-day basis, but never to give power to intermediate bodies such as provinces or states, because they are so susceptible to economic pressures. Larger bodies, like federal or international agencies, can establish ground rules and standards and, if necessary, enforce compliance. But that enforcement will never work without the understanding and approval of local users. When the users who depend upon a resource are truly local, the picture gets even better. They are the best source of knowledge, and make the best long-term managers we are likely to find.

## The Walrus and the Carpenter

*Self-regulation occurs more easily when it is part of other aspects of community life.*
— EVELYN PINKERTON AND MARTIN WEINSTEIN,
MARINE ANTHROPOLOGISTS[2]

One of the major difficulties in managing our ocean resources is a shocking lack of data. Only in the past twenty years or so have we realized what serious management problems we have, and specific studies that identify all the variables in ownership and use situations are still pretty rare. That's why the large amount of data that has been gathered on oyster fisheries along the coast of the Gulf of Mexico is so useful. The Louisiana communities working this resource have in some cases been established since the end of the nineteenth century, and although detailed information goes back only thirty years, we have some idea of what was going on as much as 150 years ago.

Interestingly, Louisiana oyster fisheries are dominated by Dalmatian fishermen from the Adriatic coast of Yugoslavia, who migrated to the area in the mid-nineteenth century. They brought with them a folk tradition of ownership in which each of their "oyster camps" worked on the pattern of what's called a "closed-access" fishing territory. Only the members of each camp could exploit their local oyster bed; outsiders were kept out, probably forcibly in the old days and by tradition and law later on; and social constraints worked to make sure oystermen within the group did not violate each other's separate camps. By the 1960s, as a result of their long tenure in the Gulf of Mexico area, these Dalmatian oystermen were granted legal status by the Louisiana Oyster Commission for leases. As Christopher Dyer, the researcher primarily responsible for gathering the data, puts it, "In essence, folk management practices were incorporated into the legal regulatory structure."[3]

The oystermen of Louisiana are described by Dyer and his co-author Richard Leard as a "homogeneous ethnic network of harvesters united through kinship, culture and local history." Young oystermen are regularly recruited into what has become the family business. They pay a fee to the state for working a geographically exclusive oyster ground, that is, a particular bounded area for each man or family. They reseed the area with larval oysters themselves to assure regeneration. They all use the same oyster dredges, a harvesting technology that keeps their costs down because it saves them from having to compete with harvesters who might escalate into more destructive and expensive equipment. Although researchers aren't sure exactly how it's done, Dyer and Leard say, "Presumably, some degree of stock and habitat assessment operates, given that the harvest has remained sustainable over decades of time."[4] In fact, they add, the high level of resource stability, quality of production and number of people employed over at least the last three decades, "could serve as a paragon for sustainable resource management and use."

Fisheries in the same ecosystem along the Gulf of Mexico that are almost identical but managed differently have proven to be far less stable and profitable for their users. In Mississippi, for example, the oyster business was dominated by processor-owned vessels staffed by hired crews until the 1960s, when it was opened up to all comers on a license basis. There had been political pressure to make oystering a kind of economic safety valve, like taxi-driving, to absorb new immigrants and provide some relief to unemployed locals. The processors had also been demanding harvests far exceeding the ability of oysters to reproduce. Predictably, the resource is neither healthy nor sustainable. A similar pattern was established in Alabama, leading again, as Dyer and Leard put it, to "a lack of commitment to the resource" and a high instability in the numbers of oysters still available. But in Florida, a closely knit Scots-Irish community established practices similar to those in Louisiana. There, a close relationship between the local processors and the community-based growers has led to a clear awareness of the limitations of the fishery, which operates on a closed-access model. The state has complied by legally mandating that only the most low-tech methods can be used in harvesting — oyster tongs, which are even better for the oyster beds than dredges.

In theory, resources like shellfish and lobster, which stay in place and don't swim long distances, should be the easiest of the ocean's resources to manage, even by absentee government authorities. They can't confuse the ownership issue by straying off into geographical areas belonging to other groups or even other countries. But in practice, it is almost only in traditional and community-controlled situations that even such localized species have flourished. Marine anthropologists Evelyn Pinkerton and Martin Weinstein, co-authors of "Fisheries That Work," a report documenting success stories of fisheries around the world, point out that the key to resource sustainability is management by a stable community with an economic dependence on that resource. When communities derive their primary income from a resource and have few, if any, other sources of livelihood to turn to, they are much more committed to the continuation of that resource. If community members are strongly identified with the area and their assets include well-established homes, and if the benefits of the resource are widely spread throughout their user-community, the resources can very often be managed almost indefinitely — barring, of course, intrusions by outsiders, the effects of global warming or catastrophes such as oil spills. It is only when people are allowed to just dip in and out of a resource, as opportunists, with no cultural or time commitment to it, or when they have no assurance that taking care of it will bring benefits to themselves or their children, that resources suffer. That's when the old theory of "the tragedy of the commons" plays out.

This tragedy is occurring in most of the oceans of the world because they are usually being exploited without specified tenure. The absence of clear tenure results in unaccountable and irresponsible exploitation, which is certainly reflected in the oyster fisheries of Mississippi and Alabama, whereas the clear tenure in Louisiana and Florida makes those fisheries work. It is significant that government agencies in all four states take their cue from the user-communities — *not* vice-versa. In Alabama and Mississippi, the governments have responded to citizen pressure to allow open access to oysterbeds, and have ignored their degradation. Louisiana and Florida governments, on the other hand, have responded to pressures to operate their oysterbeds under closed-access principles — the Louisiana oystermen even sit on the state Oyster Commission — and they have enthusiastically passed highly restrictive conservation laws, such as the tongs-only rule, safe in the knowledge that the industry and the community support them.

## David Meets Goliath

*To put it in a nutshell, the communities that are depending on the natural resources, that is, on forest and water and land for their livelihood, should own and manage those natural resources. That is going to be the major conflict in the twenty-first century; no doubt about that.*

— FATHER THOMAS KOCHERRY, NATIONAL FISHERPEOPLES' FORUM, KERALA

The Gulf of Mexico oyster fishery gives an example of a united, resource-based community influencing its government to protect their mutual source of wealth, while the striped bass story gives an example of an enlightened government enlisting an already concerned and cooperative user-public to help in the same process. But what happens when a community has no voice in its own government and no influence on industry? What happens when an unenlightened government actually colludes with forces outside the community, even outside the country, to overexploit a resource? What happens when a globalized industry, with the huge trawlers, long-lines and dredges that are quickly reducing the continental shelves to deserts, invades a local fishery? Can anything be done to save resources that are being converted from sustainable community use into instant cash machines by powerful international forces? The answer is yes.

One of the world's most viable fisheries still in existence lies off the west coast of southern India, in the Arabian Sea. The Indian state of Kerala is fringed with beautiful beaches and crowded by mountains lush with planta-tions of tea, spices and cashews. Its backwater streams and canals wind through vast coconut groves, past palm-leaf huts, luminous Hindu temples, mosques and Syrian Catholic churches. The few tourists in the area can sit on the beaches and watch local fishermen, using primitive wooden boats and hand-woven nets, hauling in their catch of tuna, swordfish, butterfish, barracuda, crabs, shrimp, lobster and a host of luscious species on which everyone will feast that evening. This part of Kerala is only a few miles away from Sri Lanka and Tamil Nadu, and the daily lives of its small and beautiful people are so centered around outdoor work, music and festivals that, especially with its waving palms, it's more reminiscent of a South Sea island than of mainland India. Currently, a million fisherpeople make their living on the Indian side of the Arabian Gulf. Even this large number of dependents would probably not put too much pressure on the resources of this hot, prolific sea — if a lot of other people, with no knowledge of the resource and no interest in its preservation, hadn't elbowed their way up to the table.

Like the communities in Louisiana and Florida, the fishermen who use this resource are a part of a fairly united ethnic community; they have lived on this coast for hundreds, perhaps even thousands of years. They all share the resource and their methods of working it are very similar; but like most Keralans, they are divided by the three prevalent religions — Hindu, Christian and Moslem — and are considered by their urban neighbors in the capitol of Tivandrum to be very low on the social scale, the poorest of the poor. They all use the same very simple fishing technology. They fish from two kinds of boats; one is a tiny catamaran, fashioned from three pale logs planed on one side and lashed together with coconut fiber rope at both ends. Taking such a craft out into the perilous surf of the Arabian Sea is not unlike fishing off a surfboard. They also use larger boats with high curved prows, which have room for several very long, bulky oars, and can hold up to thirty men.

Like the oystermen's methods in Louisiana and Florida, these techniques require very little capital investment. The small craft can be made by one man with free materials in a day and, with care, will last for a decade. The larger boats must be built by a boatmaker, but they last even longer. Recently, some fishermen have affixed small, diesel engines onto the larger boats, or on newer craft made of plywood. Either way, only the diesel-powered boats need any real capital outlay. The fishing is done with coconut fiber nets that the men make and repair themselves. Typically, a group of about thirty jump into the water out at sea to scare the fish into the nets, and then another group hauls the nets in from the shore. Depending upon the seasons and the religious holidays, even the smallest boats put out at night, their kerosene lamps making the fleet look like a scattering of fireflies a kilometer or so out into the treacherous swells and currents of the hot Arabian sea.

The traditional fishery technology in Kerala is not invasive; in fact, no one noticed any difference in the number, size or enormous variety of the species caught until about twenty years ago. Researchers have since traced the change back to the 1960s, when Norwegian trawlers, with the blessing of the Indian central government, first appeared on the Arabian Sea. Like all big trawlers and unlike the local users, they took fish out of the ocean day and night and in all seasons, including the monsoon, when most species spawn. Prawns were becoming popular in the United States and Japan, so the Norwegians started using huge nets to drag the bottom of the sea to get them. It is nets of this sort scraping along the bottom of the seas that are used to catch about half the fish in the world today. And they degrade the habitat every time they pass over. As Carl Safina puts it, "It's like harvesting a cornfield with a bulldozer that takes all the corn — and also takes the topsoil along with it." They pass over an area several times a year, until the bottom is scraped clean not only of the prey they seek but of anything else swimming around with it, including fry, spawn, larvae, coral and algae — the sources of future life. By 1975, 3,500 trawlers were scraping and trawling off the shores of Kerala all the year long. By 1997, the number of national and international trawlers and dredgers in Indian waters had reached 23,000.

Why was the Arabian Sea opened up this way? The explanation can once again be found in mainstream theories of global economics. The trawlers were intended to generate the foreign exchange that the Indian government desperately needed, because it had begun borrowing heavily from the World Bank. As we described in chapter two, back in the early 1980s developing countries were all incurring the debts that are still crushing them today, because Western economic experts were advising them to get capital from foreign banks in order to build up their industrial infrastructures. Borrowing revenue for new fishing methods was supposed to stimulate India's ability to build its infrastructure and modernize its own fleet, and so enable local fisherpeople to better exploit their own marine resources. India did not turn out to be the prime beneficiary, however; the big multinational corporations that were already mechanized came in and quickly took control of the new industry, and benefits went to very few Indians beyond the entrepreneurs who were already well-off. Mechanized fishing began to cash in the communal wealth that the fishery represented, and concentrate it in the hands of a few. It left nothing for the small, traditional fisherpeople to live on. Even a modest request to keep the intruders just 20 meters off shore, so that the local people could still survive somewhere, was ignored by the multinational boats.

The local catch continued to deteriorate in size, number and species. Trawlers would often tear up the fishermen's nets and damage their boats when they tried to fish. Throughout the 1980s, again succumbing to advice from institutions like the World Bank, the Indian government continued to accelerate the modernization process by withdrawing state support from the fisherpeople. Tax funds were directed instead into mechanizing India's own trawler fleet and into constructing the big fish-processing plants that began to open up along the coast. The new, modern Indian trawlers were, of course, not owned by traditional local fishers. They belonged to richer merchants and middlemen, the same ones who had always stood between the local community and its markets. As for the new fish-processing plants, they rapidly became infamous for their terrible working conditions. Charges that local girls are routinely entrapped with offers of good employment and then beaten, paid a pittance and prevented from leaving, have led to repeated Supreme Court cases and investigations that have shocked the whole country.

But since the government's policies resulted in an enormous increase in the export of Indian fish, experts at the World Bank felt their advice was validated. The large trawling firms, the multinational processing and exporting corporations and the rich Indians who had bought into them were in fact prospering. But over the same period, the average production of the traditional fishers declined by more than 50 percent; this has resulted in 98.5 percent of the entire population of these people descending from relatively sustainable incomes to well below India's poverty line. Moreover, although traditional fishers constitute 89 percent of the Indian workers in the industry, more than 92 percent of the catch was being taken by the mechanized trawlers, both foreign and Indian.[5] What's more, the fish being caught by these methods do not find their way into the stomachs of hungry Indians, as World Bank and IMF production statistics imply. They are processed and sold abroad, to seafood consumers in the First World who can pay the prices that make the whole thing profitable for the large companies that own the trawlers, the processing plants and the marketing infrastructures. Even though Kerala fishers already lived near cities, there were no programs to give them urban skills and no available jobs even if they acquired them. Above all, they had absolutely no wish to leave their beloved beaches and traditional way of life. Until the new methods came into practice, they had led decently healthy and happy lives.

## Fat Cats

*The role of subsidies to industrial fisheries is like [the role of] cats to cat food.*
— CARL SAFINA

Ironically, the proof that industrial extraction methods are not practicable on this planet, given the way resources actually function, lies in the fact that while local fisher communities have sustained themselves for hundreds of years, industrial fisheries have to be subsidized by society at large. A conservative estimate is that a full 28 percent of all revenues gained by fishing is subsidized by governments — about $20 billion (U.S.) a year.[6] Tremendous tax breaks, interest-free loans and outright cash awards go to keeping fleets of trawlers, draggers and long-lines on the oceans. Building boats, fueling them, processing the catch — all these jobs and the infrastructures for them are government-subsidized. These "perverse subsidies" account for the Indian government's going into debt to get its industrialized fishery started in the first place. As we have seen in chapters five and six and will see again in chapter eight, the same pattern applies to farming, forestry and many other kinds of natural resources extraction, such as mining and fossil fuels.

While sustainable practices lead to the "double dividends" we have often noted — providing more jobs, better food and more varied products, without jeopardizing future harvests — the "double indemnity" practices that require tax support at the same time that they destroy future resources are not even profitable once full accounting of the actual costs of inputs is done. We are actually paying to destroy our local and national resources for the future. This absurdity should give us a pretty good idea of how profitable it really would be to turn the situation around. Permit systems, which make not only individual fishers but whole national fleets pay a host country to fish, are in place in many countries, notably the United States, New Zealand and Russia. They not only enable the host to recoup some of its resource losses, but they act as a financial disincentive to overfishing. Such permits can assign tenure, as well; whoever is granted the fishing licenses effectively becomes the steward of the resource.

Carl Safina points out that until we institute more far-reaching controls on fishing, and especially until we stop paying people to overexploit, fishing subsidies will continue to be "probably the single worst thing that has happened to fisheries worldwide." They divert much-needed government funds from viable and sustainable programs — funds that could be used, for instance, to help Keralan fisherpeople educate some of their children with other skills, so that in future they wouldn't all have to live off the same resource. And "if the industry can't live off the resource, artificially propping it up allows it to have so much excess killing, or extraction power, that it suddenly goes from not being able to exist as a viable enterprise — to being able to destroy the resource."[7]

This "excess killing power" has serious military overtones. To find a school of tuna off Cape Cod, for instance, the fishing industry will deploy a small air force of fish-locater "scout" planes, as well as ten or more harpoon boats, rod-and-reel vessels and a net seiner. The boats will crackle with electronic devices like VHF radio reports, thermal sensors, sonar, video and other machinery to tell them exactly where the tuna are. Even at $80,000, which is what the Japanese market will pay for a perfect 200–250 kilo (400–500 pound) bluefin tuna, this kind of firepower is not economically profitable without all the subsidies the industry enjoys, and it's laughable overkill for any other species. In other situations where the preferred catch is prawns or scallops, the smaller tuna that might eventually have grown to be so valuable are routinely discarded as "bycatch." Safina says that each year the industry takes in marlins, sharks, tuna, sailfish and swordfish, as well as hundreds of other species, "an estimated 27 million metric tonnes of marine life that, dying or dead, are thrown overboard — a quarter of the whole global catch." In other words, tax breaks and subsidies not only encourage and reward overfishing; they subsidize complete waste. Safina says it's like trying to provide a bird sanctuary in your backyard but at the same time letting your cat out in the garden every day.[8]

The Arabian Sea, where the Keralan fishers were struggling with these developments, is a tropical ecosystem fringed with a latticework of mangroves and river estuaries that host an incredible variety of marine creatures. But even such a productive and resilient system as this can be destroyed when fishers deploy what oceanographer Sylvia Earle calls "weapons of war" against the creatures of the sea. Purse-seine nets, which allow nothing to escape, were introduced in the 1970s. Long-lines, sometimes 50 to 65 km (30 to 40 miles) long, were soon trailing out at sea, and the overall catch of fish in the Arabian Sea increased by a whopping 196 percent between 1969 and 1982. These lines have hundreds of baited hooks, and in addition to snagging their intended catch, they kill thousands of sharks, sea turtles and other endangered species, which again are simply discarded. These technological advances were being put into play precisely during the period in which the fisherpeople of Kerala were experiencing their descent into poverty. The subsidized cats were having a field day in the Keralan garden.

## Finding a Good Dog

*Do what you can do in your own country. Don't worry about us.*
*Stop all these kinds of foreign investments coming to our*
*countries. If you protect traditional fisheries in your own country,*
*that will protect them here as well.*
— FATHER THOMAS KOCHERRY

Something else was happening in Kerala as the fishery moved from local to international tenure; perhaps we should say someone was beginning to train and discipline an effective dog to chase off the cats. Since the days of a long string of socially enlightened maharajas, Kerala has been India's most progressive state, with a tradition of very high literacy levels, respect for women, very low child mortality and enthusiastic participation in political movements. New unions for fishworkers, which cut across the usual caste, race and religious barriers, were growing all through the 1980s as the fishery was being invaded: the All Goa Fishworkers' Union, the Kerala Federation (KSMTF), the Tamil Nadu Fishworkers' Union and the National Fisherpeoples' Forum (NFF). The NFF was led by Father Thomas Kocherry, an activist priest who still breathes fire into the movement twenty-five years later. The late seventies were the heady days of the rise of Liberation Theology, but when it died out due to a lack of support from Rome, Father Kocherry, together with locals, volunteers and other church workers like his NFF partners, Sister Cicely Plathottam and Sister Philomen Mary, just kept going. Today they operate out of a couple of cluttered rooms in a concrete compound just off the beach, surrounded by the palm-leaf huts of their union members. Throughout the 1980s, as conditions deteriorated for the fisherpeople and their resource, the NFF helped organize a long stream of hunger strikes, sit-ins and rallies, all bolstered by massive pickets of the national highways, railways, airports and government offices, even the blocking of harbors. And by the early 1990s the unions began to get some control over the trawlers.

The fishers used all the classic anti-globalization tactics such as marches, blockades, petitions and lawsuits — and more — for signaling the withdrawal of consent. Their case was desperate; they literally had nowhere else to go and no other kind of life they could live. So they had to adopt some pretty draconian measures to speed up the process. These very small men would take their tiny catamarans several kilometers out to where the trawlers were operating, surround the big boats, force their crews to get off, and then — set fire to the trawlers. They kept the larger, floating fish-processing plants from accessing the harbors by stringing their fragile vessels across the harbor-mouths. They were attacked and rammed, and quite a few fishermen died. Their resistance made the news, as these kinds of desperate tactics tend to do. And the hunger strikes involved more than Kocherry, Sister Cicely and Sister Philemon Mary; these leaders were joined by thousands of other people, and still are, as they continue to fight for sustainable fisheries in the states of Goa and Gujarat. But throughout the late 1980s and the 1990s, increasingly frequent blockades by fisherpeople and their growing numbers of sympathizers paralyzed the Indian rail service and embarrassed the government to the extent that committees and commissions were finally appointed. Their conclusions began to expose the serious flaws in India's fishery policies.

The upshot of that long period of agitation was that India declared its first national tenure of the resources around its own shores, creating a 32-kilometer (20-mile) fishing limit around the entire country. It also instituted a complete ban on fishing during the monsoon when the fish spawn, in effect throughout the Indian states of Kerala, Kamataka, Goa and Maharashtra. Additional restrictions are also in place: enforced zone regulations prohibit the big mechanized boats from coming near the shore. There is even a law against the infamous night-trawling in which the industrial boats used high-powered lights to lure all marine creatures in the vicinity to their deaths. Not anymore. These changes came about because a local, impoverished group of resource users, with no powerful allies and no modern technology, decided to fight to save their resource. And now, they themselves enforce the new regulations. Sister Cicely is a humorous, vital woman with wavy, graying hair who has done her share of fasting and agitating for the cause. When asked who makes sure the trawlers aren't out at night or in the monsoon, she says, "Oh, the fishermen; they watch the harbors; they have a large chain they can pull across the mouth. And they'll just stop them if they have to." She smiles mischievously when she adds, "They keep a sharp eye out."

Father Kocherry mentions that in the nearby Maldives, the island authorities have satellite technology that lets them know if anyone is violating their fishing space, so of course modern technology can cut both ways. But because his mission is with very poor people, these days he's working in the opposite direction, like the State of Florida when it mandated oyster tongs instead of dredges. He says, "Keeping the technology simple and non-capital-intensive is the only way to reduce overcapacity, because buying such things only increases the pressure to overfish in order to pay for your machinery and gas and so forth. So we're having a campaign, in which we're saying, 'You have to stop these profiteering groups. Don't fall for bigger boats and engines!' Because the fishers will not be able to pay for them with profits from a declining resource."

The people Father Kocherry works with are exceedingly independent and exceedingly poor. They have almost nothing in their grass huts, and if the bigger fish don't come, they can't buy oil, rice or school books for their children. The many outsiders who end up at Kocherry's door, people from Holland, England, the United States or Canada, tend to ask the same questions: How can the First World help the Third? If we shouldn't lend poor people money because they can so seldom pay it back and it cripples their future, if many of our technologies are unsuitable to their way of life, is there any way we can help them progress, get better jobs, better health and education? Certainly many First World people feel as much pressure to interfere by helping the poor of the Third World as the leaders of the Third World do to modernize and become like the First. Kocherry has worked with the poor all his life. He says apart from catastrophes like cyclones, earthquakes or floods, aid from foreign governments, in the form of cash, food, or technology, should come only during a time of crisis, and with no strings attached. Loans almost never help.

Kocherry agrees with David Korten's statement in his book *When Corporations Rule the World* that no developing country is developed through foreign capital. "This apparent gift of capital," says Kocherry, "only ends up in more exploitation. So I ask, why should we want it? Of course, our ruling classes go after it because they get commissions and kickbacks; they often divert the loans to themselves. We need to stop paying back into this scheme, and to do that, we need to stop taking out loans." India is very keen on computer technology, and has a large and well-educated English-speaking population well suited to benefit from it. If they don't borrow from the World Bank or private industry, how can they get the telephone and electrical infrastructure to get into this promising field? Kocherry says that we all need is to clear our heads and go back to basic economics; we know, deep down, that it's never a good idea to go through life on credit. "If you have a technology," he says, "we might ask you to teach it to us, but we must pay for that technology. If we can't afford it, we must sacrifice something else, buy your older, castoff versions or wait until we can. That is the only way a country can stand on its feet. There is no other way."

The fisherpeople of Kerala stood on their feet firmly enough to overcome incredible odds — international financiers, national and global economic policies, enormous market pressures and demands on their resource. They're still taking care of themselves the way they always have. But the long years of exploitation and the controlled but continuing presence of the trawlers have wounded Kerala's fishery. It's less than half of what it used to be, so damaged that still greater efforts will be required to limit fishing and make it truly sustainable again. But even wounded, it remains one of the most viable fisheries left on earth, as attested to by the tables in its markets groaning with spotted lobsters, huge butterfish, crabs, barracuda, bonita and swordfish — all caught with the simplest technology. In fact, technology is so simple here that it makes one realize that totting up the cash income of each country's resident to determine its GDP, our usual method of deciding how a country is doing, does not really give any true idea about what kind of life its citizens may actually be living — if the place has anything like an intact resource base.

In Kerala, cash is only one small element in a family's budget. There are coconuts, mangoes and bananas in every yard and along every roadside, there for the taking. Freshwater, too, is plentiful. Pigs and chickens, for those who eat them, don't require much outlay either. The fisherpeople pay no rent for the land their huts are on, and the materials they build them with are also free. One evening this past winter, as the sun was setting a couple of kilometers down the beach from Father Kocherry's headquarters, a group of fishermen were completing the long work of coiling their dried nets and covering their boats for the night. The water is dangerous on these shores, dropping off to a great depth directly from the beach and sucking anyone who gets in out to sea. But one man kept darting down to the water, hovering just at the edge, making grabbing motions in the receding waves with his hands, then running back before the next wave could seize him. Every time, he emerged with a fistful of fish. When he had a small plastic bag full, we asked the other fishermen if this was a common practice. "Oh yes," they said, beaming at us. "Those fish make a very good curry dish!"

## Ocean Cores

*It might not mean less fishing, but it does mean*
*you don't fish everywhere.*
— BILL HENWOOD, PARKS CANADA

The users of Kerala's ocean resources had to perform brave and concerted acts to protect their fisheries. But today, the planet's resources need more than just local action; they need protective legislation as well. And over just the past few years, the kinds of conservation policies that are helping protect forests and biodiversity are finally being applied underwater. There are increasing numbers of national and international preserves in the seas; there are methods of registering environmentally sound products and of punishing poachers; and there are even ocean equivalents of Cores, Corridors and Carnivores. This has happened because, although scientific studies on what's in the planet's oceans and the impact of human intervention on them are in their infancy, the science we do have all points in the same direction.

For example, research released by the National Center for Ecological Analysis and Synthesis in the United States found that the average population density of marine life is an incredible 91 percent higher within the world's relatively few protected marine areas than it is outside them. Moreover, the actual size of the marine creatures is 31 percent greater, and species diversity is 23 percent higher. A recent book by Callum Roberts and Julie Hawkins, *Fully Protected Marine Reserves: A Guide*,[9] notes that even a tiny reserve like the Hol Chan in Belize can have an amazing impact. It was established in 1987 as a no-take zone of only 2.6 square kilometers (1 square mile) intended to address some of the damage of overfishing and destruction of the shore mangroves. Four years later, this little haven from human predators had produced a six-fold — that's 600 percent — increase in biomass of commercially important reef fish. These restored populations not only spread throughout the fishery; they attracted so many tourists and divers, who began to damage the reef in their enthusiasm to actually see some fish, that legislators began to realize that it would be a very good idea to make such reserves much larger — something they're working on now.

The De Hoop Marine Protected Area (MPA) in South Africa, which covers 50 kilometers (32 miles) of shoreline and extends three nautical miles out to sea, protects sixty of the most heavily exploited species in the area, victims of recreational and commercial line fishing as well as beach seining and trawling. Their numbers have bounced up within the park ten-fold — a thousand percent — since the reserve was instituted in 1985, and of course since the fish swim around, the commercial and sports fishery outside the MPA is also benefiting enormously. In Kenya, in the thirteen years since the very modest Mombasa Marine National Park, covering only 10 square kilometers (4 square miles), was established, fish biomass within the park is more than five times greater than it is in the exterior, commercially fished areas. This park has had to institute night patrols to prevent poaching. Even so, fish catches immediately outside the park boundaries are 25 percent higher than catches further afield, and have led to a system of seniority being established among the local fishers, so the lucky ones can cozy up to the boundaries of the park. An added and not unexpected benefit is a balancing of the disturbed species mix. Sea urchins were destroying the reefs, but an increase of urchin predators like triggerfish and emperor fish within the park has resulted in healthier reefs.

There are many more examples all showing the same thing. Larry Pynn, author of a recent extensively researched, five-part *Vancouver Sun* series on Marine Protected Areas, points out that "No one is saying that marine reserves are the only answer to long-standing problems that plague fish stocks . . . But the overwhelming body of evidence is that marine reserves — not just one or two, but a network encompassing all ecosystems — are an integral part of fisheries management." In fact, a consensus statement signed early in 2001 by 161 leading marine scientists concluded that "Marine reserves are beneficial for conservation and biodiversity and . . . enough information exists to justify their immediate creation."

The key thing, of course, is to understand the oceans well enough to know which parts to protect. Besides the famous reefs, kelp forests and mangroves, there are muddy lagoons, seagrass beds, river estuaries, sand bars, islands, inter-reef gardens and the saline-to-brackish-to-freshwater marshes that line many coasts. They are all are part of the ocean's nurseries. Many marine species, like salmon and striped bass, require several places to live out their lifecycle; so preserving one area because adults live there may not ensure that the fry have their own habitat in which to grow. For example, red emperor fish larvae are laid along outer reefs; they drift in with the tides to inshore nurseries and only return to the outer reefs as adults. A prized sport fish, the barramundi, lives in inland waterways, only venturing out to the ocean to spawn and feed during the wet season. Jon Day, director of conservation, biodiversity and world heritage for the marine park authority of the Great Barrier Reef in northeastern Australia, says, "A lot of these bioregions are not sexy, but if we don't protect them, then we're just kidding ourselves that we're looking after the coral reefs."

## Ocean Corridors

*We were told we were interfering with peoples' right to fish. But what about the right of people to see marine life? Why do people who want to kill the fish have all the rights?*
— BILL BALLANTINE, LEIGH MARINE PRESERVE, NEW ZEALAND

More and more countries are concluding that we need the same kinds of zones on the seas that we are coming up with on land. And they are looking to the Adirondack Park model of core no-take, protected zones, surrounded by increasingly liberal circles where angling, tourism and even commercial trawling are permitted. Similar zones will ideally hook up with others to form corridors; after all, like bears and eagles, fish move around. Canada's most aggressive NGO in this field, the British Columbia chapter of the Canadian Parks and Wilderness Society (CPAWS) is pushing for a network of core, no-take reserves similar to those of the Great Barrier Reef Marine Park or the De Hoop MPA mentioned above, but with longer corridors. They are seeking to establish a Baja-to-Bering Straits initiative, that would create a network of marine reserves along the west coast of North America all the way from Mexico to Alaska, similar to the Y-2-Y initiative on land. Within the highly productive ecosystem of the Georgia Strait, the Georgia Strait Alliance, along with an international coalition, is pressing for the creation of the Orca Pass International Stewardship Area, which would include the San Juan and southern Gulf islands. The great predator for which the area is best known, the beautiful orca or killer whale, is now down to only 83 individuals. It's clearly time to do something for their habitat.

One of the most successful attempts to create this model is not surprisingly in the world's most spectacular surviving marine ecosystem: Australia's Great Barrier Reef. Its park stretches 2,000 kilometers (1,250 miles), more than the length of the entire west coast of the United States. It harbors

1,500 identified species of fish and 350 types of coral in more than seventy different habitats within its 347,800 square kilometers (134,000 square miles), which can be up to 60 meters (200 feet) deep, and as much as 200 meters (650 feet) out from the shore. Australia has been working on a plan to protect this whole system since 1975. At this point, only 4.5 percent of it is completely off-limits to fishing, but park scientists are trying to increase the no-take zone to about 20 percent. Anyone lucky enough to have snorkeled the Great Barrier Reef would support these initiatives and more. The reef is one of the treasures of the world, home to orange and white clown fish nestling within the protective tentacles of coral, giant clams, multitudes of darting angelfish, neon tetras and parrot fish. This otherworldly place also includes bat-like sting rays; gardens of jewel anemones in fluorescent pink, green and blue; black-tipped reef sharks; shimmering, blue-green chromis; groupers arranged like huge flagstones in vertical, gulping walls — all gliding over or popping in and out of fringed, undulating, red, blue, green and gold reef forests, every bit as wondrous as the animals living within them.

There are very generous sport fishing quotas in the Barrier Reef Park; people can take thirty fish in a two-day period, and only recently has there been talk of closing fisheries during the October and December spawning periods. So far it seems to work, because it's hard to get at these fish or even move around in this huge park; much of it is very far from shore. And the beauty of the place also has an economic component. As in the Adirondacks, tourism has always been an integral part of reef management, and countries that rely on marine-based tourism — and therefore have a pressing economic interest in an intact ecosystem — have moved faster and farther toward conservation than bigger countries like Canada and the United States. Nonetheless, as one looks out from Great Barrier Reef Park itself, legions of trawlers are visible on the horizon, just as they are in Kerala, "gnawing," as Larry Pynn puts it, "on the rich ocean bottom," and even on the reef itself. In a study by Australian federal authorities, it was found that a single pass of one of these trawl nets removed up to 25 percent of all the organisms on the ocean floor, and 13 passes destroyed 90 percent of all its life forms. These trawlers were after prawns, and so they tossed six to ten tonnes of bycatch overboard for every tonne of prawns they kept. Phil Cadwallader, Director of Fisheries at the Great Barrier Reef Marine Park asks, "Is that appropriate in a World Heritage area? Yet no politician will ban trawling in the Marine Park."

Today, trawlers are kept out of about half of the park, up from only about 20 percent at the beginning. But closure wasn't easy. Again, the industrial fleet had its hand out for subsidies, and it took $7.3 million (AUD) of federal money to restrict them even to that much. Cadwallader says that local environmentalists were outraged, wanting to know why taxpayers had to pay people to *not* damage a World Heritage area. But he points out that the government had encouraged the trawlers to get into business by subsidizing them in the first place, so they had to help them get out. It's tricky, because limiting the number of trawlers just inspires the remaining ones to upgrade their technology. That's why penalty provisions are now in place to counteract the attractiveness of more powerful radar and other technological improvements. Again, it's a question of the oyster-tongs type of legislation. People shouldn't be allowed to clearcut and slash and burn forests, dynamite fish, shoot deer with canons, steal birds' eggs and kill pregnant game animals, just because one person or group can cash in on the resource faster that way. There's now legislation in most of the world to stop such violent harvesting technologies, simply because they destroy the resource for everyone, for all time. Today, the managers of MPAs are pioneering far more stringent kinds of legislation within their parks, which will provide concrete data on how to slow down the catches outside them as well.

In the Great Barrier Reef Park, for example, fines set previously at $16,000 (AUD) for illegal trawling are going up to close to a million dollars, with the potential suspension of commercial fishing licenses. Bycatch limits are being set and inspectors are forcing prawn trawlers to install extrusion devices that allow untargeted species to escape, while trapping the prawns at the end of the net. There are even transponders with satellite linkups that tell enforcement officers on shore the exact location of each trawler. Cadwallader says with a small smile, "There are complaints about Big Brother . . . but it's not compulsory to do all this. Only if you want to fish in here, in a World Heritage area." And of course the industry does want to fish here; trawlers have a marked tendency to cluster at the edges of marine reserves, for the simple reason that reserves crank out the fish. But if such technological controls turn out to be effective, they can spread to other places — along national coasts, for example.

And yet, as we discussed in chapter two, like the turtle and dolphin extruder devices outlawed by the WTO, such legislation could be overruled by global trade rules as they now stand. Even World Heritage Sites have been threatened by massive industrial projects, as we saw at Laguna San Ignacio. So far, marine protected areas have not been targeted by the World Trade Organization, but they could be, unless the concept of tenure is resolved. The behind-closed-doors trade negotiations we know so little about need to grant such protected areas full exemption from trade rules, so that states can conserve their marine resources and make sure they aren't decimated by opportunists. "These resources belong to everyone — not just the fishermen," says Cadwallader, "and, at the end of the day, the area has to be ecologically sustainable, or it will collapse."

## User-Friendly Management

*The key is a core area of no-take reserves; these areas are just the beginning, the nucleus of [a wider] system.*
— BILL HENWOOD, PARKS CANADA

Australia is unusual in that it is a large country with a respectable proportion of protected marine area. In most of the world, the largest countries generally have the fewest protected areas. New Zealand's shoreline, for example, is only 6 percent of the length of Canada's shoreline, but its sixteen no-fishing reserves amount to 762,850 hectares (30,000 square miles), which is a staggering 2,500 times the protection Canada accords its own rich marine resources — and may explain why Canada has lost its cod and is losing its salmon. Many of the most successful reserves are found around Caribbean islands.

The Goat Island Marine Reserve near Leigh, New Zealand, is a fairly small preserve, protecting 5 kilometers of coast extending 800 meters out into the water. Although small, it welcomes as many as 200,000 visitors every year, everyone from locals and snorkelers to wading school kids; but its popularity came only after conservationists had waged a long battle against commercial fisheries and a small number of suspicious residents who feared losing their user privileges. The 250 people of Leigh are Maoris, New Zealand's only indigenous people. Journalist Larry Pynn met with two residents, Sarah and Perry Watts, who now enjoy the preserve and who confessed, "To be honest, we were all against it when it kicked off . . . We thought they were going to take our rights away." It did, in fact, affect their rights, but not their catch. They weren't always allowed to fish where they used to, but locals soon discovered the typical preserve spillover effect in the fishery beyond it.

In 1977 this reef was overrun with urchins, then making up 30 percent of all species; today, they're down to a normal, manageable 3 percent. Here too the species balance improved when overfished predators were restored. Watts says, "As a fisherman, I get the benefit of the fish that come out of the reserve. Most of the older people who fought against it are gone today. Their children realize the value of it. We love it; it's a good thing." And because of this local support, enforcement, always dicey in any understaffed game preserve, is now being done largely for free, through local peer pressure, to the extent that this national park is also seen as local community property that helps everyone make a living.

Real users, who wish to enjoy a resource for years to come, seem to welcome intelligent management. And yet, Pynn's fairly exhaustive look at Marine Protected Areas failed to find a perfect one. The United States has a particularly bad record, permitting fishing and trawling almost everywhere in its preserves, and often treating them more like Club Meds for humans than as nurseries for rare species of whales and fish. The supposed whale sanctuary in Maui, Hawaii, for example, does have educational and research value, and the line fishery permitted within its borders doesn't seem to affect the whales too much, but there is little protection for the whales from fleets of tourist-laden whale-watching vessels, or from fishermen and boating enthusiasts, all of whom crowd the creatures while they're trying to give birth and nurse. And Canada, which has the longest coastline on earth to protect, seems to be paralyzed. Besides its usual jurisdictional difficulties, it suffers from the malady of overstudying which places would be perfect, but putting practically nothing under actual protection. Critics like Bill Henwood, a senior planner for Parks Canada, say that governments spend far too much time planning preserves but precious little implementing and then patrolling them. Despite this, we're rapidly learning the encouraging fact that even flawed preserves like Maui's are much better than nothing; the numbers of humpback whales that winter there are gradually increasing.

And things are changing. In the summer of 2001, Florida governor Jeb Bush, the U.S. president's brother, announced an exciting addition to the chain of marine preserves around the world — 150 nautical square miles of "spectacular deepwater corals and critical fish spawning sites — the Tortugas Marine Reserve, the largest permanent marine preserve in U.S. history."[10] Not only does it contain many miles of seagrass meadows and mangroves as well as coral reefs, but the entire area will be "no-take," which means that nothing can be caught or removed. All marine life is to be protected, from krill, coral and larvae up to lobsters, sponges and barracuda. One part will be open to divers, another only to vessels holding permits that allow them to simply pass through. It even has a buffer zone to help it deal with water pollution from vessel discharges. The highest levels of government, Congress and the National Oceanic and Atmospheric Administration (NOAA) developed the management plan in order to address the previous "checkerboard" preservation strategies that had been deemed inadequate. Again, there is an economic, user rationale behind this wonderful development. As Cat Lazaroff of the Environment News Service puts it, "Because the economy of the Florida Keys is so closely linked to a healthy marine environment, [the former] piecemeal approach could have led to an economic collapse."[11] In other words, the holistic penny is starting to drop; Florida, as the largest user, sees in this new preserve not a restriction of its economic growth, but an assurance of future revenues, if it commits itself to stewardship of the resource.

## Marine Carnivores

*The albatross's message: consumer culture permeates every watery point on the compass. From sun-bleached coral reefs to icy polar waters, no place, no creature, remains apart.*

— CARL SAFINA[12]

Carl Safina, marine ornithologist and director of the Audubon Society's Living Oceans Project, tells about an exciting trip to Midway Atoll to indulge his heart's delight — watching rare ocean birds. Four hundred thousand Laysan Albatrosses live there, in the lonely center of the North Pacific, and Safina had come just after the breeding season, to watch the parents, who "glide in on seven-foot wings ... after flying perhaps 2,000 miles non-stop," to reach their chicks. They feed their babies for about ten minutes, then head off again, the ultimate in commuting families and latchkey children. He describes their "lovely, dark, pastel-shadowed eyes" and their calls of "Eh-eh-eh!" as they search for their babies. And he describes how he felt as he blissfully watched a mother feeding her baby by regurgitating her food load into its eager, gaping mouth, pumping out fish eggs and several squid — until she began to gag on a green plastic tooth-brush, which was lodged in her throat and which she couldn't expel. Safina says he could hardly bear to watch, and explains, "In the world in which albatrosses originated, they swallowed pieces of floating pumice [or wood] for the fish eggs attached to them. Albatrosses transferred this survival strategy to our toothbrushes, bottle caps, nylon netting, toys and other floating junk. Where chicks die, a pile of colorful plastic particles that used to be in their stomachs often marks their graves."

As carnivores, albatrosses are high on the food chain. So they not only ingest objects that look to them like eggs and fish but they concentrate chemicals in their tissues. As predators, their health is indicative of the survival of the entire ecosystem. At sea as on land, we are losing the "high trophic levels," the predators, first. The mega-fauna like killer whales, halibut, tuna, swordfish, barracuda, shark, albatrosses and ospreys are all in danger, just like the mega-fauna on land, not just from human predation, but also from contamination of their food. This is serious news, because, like the wolves, lions and coyotes, these predators play a key role in balancing ecosystems and making sure they remain productive. Probably the first scientifically accepted example of top-down ecological management was a marine predator — the sea otter. Hunted nearly out of existence on the Pacific coast of North America for their fur and also because fishermen viewed them as competitors for their catch, their decimation led to the near destruction of the entire fishery. That's because the spiny urchin, which was the preferred food of the otters, was left without natural enemies. It proliferated and began to destroy the entire kelp forest. Without the kelp forest, dozens of fish species lost their habitat and vanished from the area. But only a few years after otters had become protected by legislation, the urchins were back at normal levels, the kelp forests returned, and with them, the fishermen's catch.

So studying why a marine predator like the West coast sea scoter, a mussel-eating duck, seems to be declining, and learning how to protect it, becomes more significant than it might at first seem. Deborah Lacroix, a wildlife ecologist at Simon Fraser University in Vancouver, British Columbia, has found that while a single scoter can eat more than 4,000 bay mussels a day, like good sustainable fishers, they only take the medium-sized ones; they "farm" a spot, returning each year to harvest the one-to-two-year-old mussels, leaving the babies and the big ones that are too hard to swallow. And this act, quite enjoyable for the scoters, promotes biodiversity along the entire shoreline, allowing other life forms like limpets, barnacles and algae to flourish, as well as supporting other seabirds, who follow the scoters to clean up their leftovers.

Because their preferred food, mussels, are bivalves that store toxins and heavy metals, the health of the scoters reflects the contamination levels of the shoreline. And surveys show that levels of dangerous chemicals like tributyltin, which is used to prevent build-up of barnacles on ship hulls, as well as polyaromatic hydrocarbons (PAHS) and cadmium from fossil fuel burning, can be found at rates up to 200 times higher in scoters than levels of the same pollutants in other seabirds. There are still many scoters in the world; the North American breeding population is estimated at more than 500,000. But their state of health, like that of eagles, otters and wolves, reflects the condition of the entire ecosystem. "[Such a] species could have a big ripple effect," says Rob Butler, senior biologist with the Canadian Wildlife Service. "We have a responsibility to look after them. We have to protect a fair chunk of shoreline [to do that]." So now that we have understood that we need to protect the top-of-the-foodchain organisms like scoters, we will find ourselves protecting the mussels, the other birds and fish in the area — and ourselves. They are yet another indication of how marine protected areas can play a much larger role than just keeping marine life healthy and productive.[13]

## Land and Sea

*The Mississippi River, whose fine heartland silt once built fertile delta wetlands, now builds in the Gulf of Mexico a spreading Dead Zone — almost devoid of marine life — the size of New Jersey.*
— CARL SAFINA[14]

The reason why sea predators and other marine life suffer is gravity. Almost everything we throw out eventually washes down to the sea. We all know the stories of syringes and other biomedical waste washing up on beaches, and the toxic waste tankers circling from country to country being denied entry until they give up and dump their cargo at sea. These are all illustrations of why we absolutely must stop using certain kinds of chemicals and manufacturing certain kinds of items; and why garbage segregation and disposal have become a key environmental issue. A UN marine-pollution treaty makes dumping the kind of plastics that end up in baby albatross's stomachs illegal, but policing remains a problem. Still, ships can easily be required to carry modern equipment for segregating garbage and storing liquid wastes. Nevertheless, even though oil spills and discharges from ships, deliberate and accidental, have destructive effects on birds, mammals and fish, the greatest enemy of reefs, kelp forests, and all the other ecosystems that keep the oceans alive is on *land*. It's modern, industrial agriculture. Our knowledge of this fact should make the solution to our marine pollution problems very clear.

Larry Pynn calls industrial agriculture "the root problem" of coastland degradation. Agribusiness practices result in high concentrations of manure being drained into watercourses. It is these pollutants that have so poisoned Chesapeake Bay, for example, that formerly harmless microorganisms have become toxic, and now eat the flesh of the fish. The rivers transport the herbicides, pesticides and other deadly chemicals that are created to kill animals and plants down to the seas. Industrial farming practices such as over-plowing and cultivating huge monocultures are causing our topsoils to wash away, and they ultimately wash out to the sea as well. Finally, because of dams and dikes, our river deltas no longer trap silt and wash the water clean. Around the world, such run-off pours into the ocean unchecked; in the southern United States, it has created the famous Gulf of Mexico Dead Zone. Even the far less populous country of Australia dumps 23 million tonnes of sediment, containing 77,000 tonnes of poisonous nitrogen and 11,000 tonnes of phosphorus, out onto its famous reefs. These poisons have a direct effect on marine life, but in addition, the effluent itself smothers the living coral, generates an excess of algae and phytoplankton, and sets up a negative feedback of reduced light for the coral that is left. When we talked about double indemnities attending practices that aren't sustainable, we were being restrained. Here's an indication of multiple dividends for a sustainable practice — organic agriculture not only saves everything on land; it also protects estuaries and conserves marine life.

Organic agriculture does not use the poisons and fossil fuels that will kill everything from eagles and butterflies to our fish supply. It retains soil so that fertile sediments are not lost into the sea. It builds healthy, living cells in human and animal bodies which do not contain such high levels of carcinogens, all without destroying the necessities of life, like fresh water, air, soil and oceans. Again, its sustainability is evident in that it produces the multiple dividends that always appear when our method of producing what we need is in harmony with natural systems. It's cheaper; it's easier; it requires less fuel and no expensive chemical inputs, but it does require more human labor, all of which the world seems ready to see once more as desirable. And as we have shown, if practiced properly even over the short term, organic farming is fully as productive as industrial methods. Over the long term, it is incomparably more productive. The fact that it continues to grow at such strong rates — over 20 percent a year — gives us great hope, not only for our soils and freshwater, but for the seas; as we demand more and more organic methods of food production, legions of terrible contamination and conservation problems will simply melt away. We can hurry the process along by passing legislation against certain levels of chemicals or animal waste in any water course, concentrating especially on marine areas. Such legislation is already in place in states like Maryland, and is gaining wide acceptance by populations across Europe and North America.

Aquaculture is another kind of farming that has an industrial base and needs to be dealt with as a potential help or harm to the ecosystem. Since the 1950s, people have always thought that "farming the seas" for fish, lobster, shellfish and even kelp and algae, would be a necessary strategy for the future. And it's happening now. Shellfish can be pretty safely and sustainably raised, as we have seen with oyster fisheries; but there are serious problems with shrimp and fish farms. As Carl Safina explains, "Most farms use large numbers of cheap, wild-caught fish as feed to raise fewer shrimp and fish [than nature would produce with the same amount of food]."[15] And industrial-scale fish- and shrimp-aquaculture operations often permanently damage the coastlines where they're practiced. In Bangladesh, Thailand and India, where shrimp are grown for foreign exchange and exported to affluent consumers, diseases and pollution typically limit a farm's life to between five and ten years. Then the companies move down the line, destroying more productive mangroves and local fisheries with them, in exchange for the short-term, cash-producing shrimp lagoons. This problem has become so evident that the Indian Supreme Court has recently enacted a ban against the further expansion of the shrimp industry along its entire coast.[16]

Today, diseases that are increasingly decimating wild fisheries have been found to originate in fish farms, which shows that aquaculture is not fitting in with natural systems, and is already producing double indemnities. Species alien to a local habitat — like Atlantic salmon in Pacific pens — are very dangerous to native fish, and should not be raised outside their own territory. Most fish biologists agree that fish that are genetically engineered, typically with human growth hormones, to make them grow much faster than normal, don't even bear thinking about. They exhibit serious reproductive and health problems that could easily contaminate entire wild populations and destroy their viability forever.[17]

But with proper goals and standards, Safina says, some kinds of fish farming could work. He lists examples such as the well-run Maine salmon farms that use rivers to farm local fish, although the practice of caging the fish in rivers has to be done so as not to make the rivers unsightly, and the wastes must be carefully monitored. "In general," he says, "fish farming is best done indoors, onshore, with vegetarian species like the Tilapia," or with carp or catfish, since they don't have to be fed wild fish. Also, their wastewater can be purified before release, cutting down on disease and escape problems. Safina points out that the incredibly rich bounty of the seas — most of us only realized recently, for example, how delicious sharks and rays are — can never compete with the tiny subset that will be suitable for captive breeding. "Aquaculture," he says, "will not satisfy our needs and will likely cut down our choices if we concentrate on that one route, rather than taking care of what's already out there."[18]

Safina is by no means a vegan. He's an avid fisherman and consumer of seafood. He says, "I think it's okay to use what's in the ocean, to use what's in the environment around us. It's just not okay to use it up. The trick is simply to know what's enough, when we're getting excessive."[19] And there are ways now to do that. Audubon has published a "Guide to Seafood,"[20] which describes the multiplicity of fish available and indicates whether their populations are low, stable or good, whether management practices are good, fair or poor, and whether bycatch and habitat concerns create a high or low impact on other species and ecosystems. There are very few fully green lights; the report points out that fish are wild creatures, and that marine creatures are the very last of our planet's wildlife that are numerous enough to be hunted on a wide scale — which shows which way they're going. But of the ocean species, dolphinfish, red fish, flounder, mackerel, squid, crabs, and our old friend, the striped bass, will be fine even if some of them do end up on your dinner plate.

It is upsetting to see how many of the fish that were abundant just two or three decades ago are now in trouble: lingcod, rock fish, the once ubiquitous cod and tuna, the delectable red snapper, the no longer cheap bluefish and the briefly available orange roughy have all been overfished into near oblivion. But, as Safina points out, "In almost all cases, species do bounce back quickly, within about ten years, when we don't catch them faster than they can breed." That makes sense, and with a little self-restraint at the fish market and with the rod and reel, together with a good deal of pressure on our governments, we could make our own desires as users felt, and influence the market for fish and shrimp the same way we have for whales.

A major tool for exerting this influence has come into the picture just as we realized we needed it. The first global standards for fish labeling have been developed by the Marine Stewardship Council, in a joint effort with the World Wildlife Fund and the giant food conglomerate Unilever. Its Fish Forever eco-label will direct consumers to products such as Western Australian rock lobster and the UK's Thames herring. Over a hundred major seafood buyers in the United States, including Whole Foods Market, Legal Sea Foods and Shaw's, have pledged to buy from certified sources. There are also Turtle Safe labels to guarantee shrimp that have been harvested with turtle extruder devices. Although no longer required by law in the United States because of the infamous WTO ruling, these devices are still being used on a voluntary basis by a few wild-catch Georgia trawlers only. A similar campaign to publicize tuna caught by methods that exclude dolphins is credited with decreasing dolphin deaths in the eastern Pacific by an amazing 97 percent. There's even a new business, Ecofish, which will deliver to your door sustainably managed species, selected on the basis of population status, level of bycatch and the environmental impact of their harvesting. This New England–based company donates 25 percent of its pretax profits to support marine conservation efforts around the world.[21] We are getting to the point where the seafood consumer, by selecting only sustainably produced species caught in ecologically responsible ways, will be able to encourage the conservation and protection of this resource in the same way that consumers of certified wood products have helped activists save huge areas of forest around the world.

### Save the Whales, and the Air, and the Forests and Our Food

*The question is, when do we all become indigenous people?*
*When do we become native to this place? When do we decide*
*we are not leaving?*
— BILL MCDONOUGH, GREEN ARCHITECT AND DESIGNER[22]

Marine conservation initiatives are finally beginning to happen, but this is no time to relax. Larry Pynn's series on Marine Protected Reserves cites one example. "On paper," he says, "you'd be forgiven for thinking the West Coast [of Canada] is a leader in marine protection." British Columbia has designated ecological reserves, parks and wildlife management areas for marine life, and the Canadian federal government also has national parks, marine parks, migratory bird sanctuaries and wildlife areas. Ottawa can also, in theory, close fisheries to protect specific species for a variety of reasons, including excessive pressure on the resource and pollution emergencies. But these efforts look far better on paper than they do in reality. Colin Levings and Glen Jamieson, both federal fisheries scientists, agree that, "There are virtually no . . . actual no-take areas of sufficient number, size and scale to offer functionally significant marine ecosystem protection. [These are] almost nonexistent in Canada." Jamieson notes that the only truly effective no-take area is the shoreline off the William Head medium-security prison, where armed guards keep all boats away, and it isn't even an actual protected area. The rest are routinely invaded by fishers, recreational boats and jet-skis, and in any case, all put together, they only add up to about three-quarters of the size of Vancouver's downtown Stanley Park.[23] Surely our ocean diversity deserves better protection than that.

The problem, again, is tenure. When locals hear that one of their favorite fishing holes is closed to users, they don't believe it means them, especially if the closure isn't enforced. And if that closure increases the numbers of fish, then it becomes even more attractive to fishers. As we have seen, users will only obey such bans when they fully understand the gravity of the situation and have a vested interest in keeping the resource going; in other words, when they know that by controlling their own actions, they or their children, not some faceless stranger or multinational corporation, will benefit from the sacrifice. For too long, most countries have devoted their scientific expertise and their tax dollars not to conservation and real management, but to increasing extraction for the very interests who have no long-term investment in the resource. The result has been catastrophic, not just for the fish, but for all the local communities in places like Newfoundland, the Maritimes and the B.C. coast, which no longer have a livelihood or an identity.

It's becoming pretty clear that if we want to keep any of the things we need — pure food, timber, clean water, fish — we have to make changes in the way we value them, and in who manages them. We *need* to feel ownership responsibilities — as well as rights — over the necessities of life. We learned when we developed modern science and industry that if we isolated one fact or product from another we could manipulate it and eventually charge money for it. But we're learning now that if we don't notice the invisible relationships between all things — between a society that routinely tosses out unnecessary plastic disposables and the slow death of a beautiful, violet-eyed creature thousands of miles away — our own lives will also be at risk. It's time, in short, to stop isolating things from each other and start *relating* them to each other. We have to realize that what we do on land affects the seas; and what happens to the seas, happens to us.

A few years ago, a young friend named Ken Pizzolito accompanied Holly Dressel when she went to interview an expert at a lively and noisy rally against genetically engineered crops, where people had dressed up as mutant corn and tomato-fish. As they were leaving, Pizzolito said he used to feel paralyzed by all the separate problems of the world. He wanted to save the whales, but then he would hear about some other worrisome development, like global warming or genetic engineering. He couldn't decide which separate problem should receive his interest and energy. "I'd think," he said, "what if I worked to save the whales, but because all of us were working on so many different issues, there didn't end up being enough people fighting global warming? Then the whales would all die anyway because their habitat would be destroyed. The more I thought about all the separate environmental problems in the world, the more paralyzed I'd get. Finally, I'd just go out and drink a lot of beer. But now I finally realize that I just have to concentrate on what I care about the most. If I work on the whales, I *am* fighting global warming, and vice-versa. It's all the *same thing.*"

There is no real difference between the problems of land animals, ocean carnivores like whales and albatrosses, and humans. We now know that human babies are as much at risk from the PVCs in our plastics as are the young albatrosses. We are animals who live here too, who have no choice but to eat the food, drink the water and breathe the air, however contaminated they become. But we are the ones doing the contaminating. Now that we understand that it's our social and economic choices that have created industrial farming, fishing and logging, and that these choices were all based on cultural values, as humans we can change things. We can choose other values and other styles of management. Millions of people around the world are realizing this simultaneously; that's why organizations to certify wood, food and fish have sprung up so incredibly quickly, why new and old paradigms for business, farming, fishing and logging are growing at exponential rates around the world, and why there are thousands of people outside every major meeting that affects the world economy, demanding core value changes. As the famous "green" architect Bill McDonough, who we met in chapter one, puts it, people are starting to realize that we're all indigenous to this planet. Even in the most modern, developed parts of the world, more and more people are trying to manage their lives as if what they do will affect everything around them; as if they have tenure of this place, and will be passing it on to their children — as if it's home.

# CHAPTER 8

# WRESTLING WITH PLUTO
## Cutting Toxins, Cleansing Air

### Pluto's Curse

*In order for a society to be sustainable, Nature's functions and diversity are not systematically subject to increasing concentrations of substances extracted from the Earth's crust.*
— FIRST SYSTEMS CONDITION OF THE NATURAL STEP

Ever since we discovered the strength of metals like copper and iron in arrowheads and spears, we've been interested in the substances that we find below the ground. But all of them, from gold, zinc, copper, nickel and silver, to oil, gas, uranium and coal, are either directly or indirectly poisonous to us and to other life forms. It is an interesting fact that in nearly all known human mythologies, the underworld is a place of death and danger, not just to the body, but to the soul. Pluto, Odin and the dwarves of the underworld, or Mars and Vulcan, gods associated with the metals we bring up from below, all rule over dark realms that mortals enter at their peril. And while venturers to these realms may gain treasure, they are usually cursed by the underworld spirits whose purpose is to guard the treasure from such theft.

Pluto's revenge has never failed to find us, no matter how far away we have carried his treasures. Whether we pump oil from the oceans, extract gold from mountains, or scrape away our very farms and homes to get at nickel or coal, the fossil fuels and heavy metals we bring up from inside the earth poison our crops and our trees, destroy our children's immune and endocrine systems, give us wasting diseases, and kill our animals and fish — often many years after the money they made us is spent.

The similarity in myths associated with the underworld across so many cultures implies that somehow we've always known it was dangerous and unnatural to go underground and steal from Pluto. But now we know exactly why that's true, and having the coal mine cave in on us or the gas vein explode is the very least of our problems. We are gradually learning that the minerals, oils and gases that were sequestered beneath the surface of the earth by biology, geology and time actually have a reason for staying where they are. If they don't, they risk changing the make-up of everything on the planet's surface, including the atmosphere that protects the whole thing.

Unlike the planet Mars, which lacks an atmosphere, or Venus, which is constantly shrouded in water vapor, earth has maintained an average temperature within a comfortable range of 15°C (59°F) over millions of years. That's because our atmosphere is made up of a mixture of "greenhouse gases," water vapor, carbon dioxide, methane and nitrous oxide, which act like the windows of a greenhouse. The gases absorb some of the long wavelengths of received solar energy and radiate it *back* onto the planet instead of allowing this solar heat to pass back into space. If this atmospheric blanket were to vanish, the temperature on this planet would immediately plummet to about −18°C (0°F). The earth would become more like Mars, where the atmosphere is so diffuse that it is unable to hold any heat and its polar temperature is an unimaginably cold −120°C (−184°F). Venus, at the opposite extreme, is constantly shrouded in heat-trapping clouds of sulfuric acid and carbon dioxide, so its surface temperature is a hellish 450°C (842°F). Surprisingly, while greenhouse gases have such a potent effect on climate, they make up less than 1 percent of the volume of the atmosphere. That means that relatively small changes in their concentration can have disproportionate effects on the planet's temperature.

Our atmosphere was not always as it is today. Its composition evolved over the last four billion years as a result of the strategies of elemental life forms in trying to make use of solar and thermal energy. Before the first stirrings of life on this planet, the sun radiated 25 to 30 percent less heat than it does today, and the composition of the atmosphere was positively toxic to modern forms of life. The primeval atmosphere was devoid of oxygen, the life-giving energy source that fuels all animal life, but it was rich in carbon dioxide, the primary source of energy for all plants. And energy is in many ways inseparable from life; it allows organisms to move, grow and reproduce. From its beginnings in the hot minerals and cooling gases of the planet's oceans, unicellular life found ways to liberate energy from the chemical bonds of the substances surrounding it. These cells were able to extract energy from the heat pouring from the earth's interior, and eventually to capture energetic photons of light flooding the planet from the nuclear reactor that is our sun. By evolving a mechanism to collect solar energy and store it for later use in the chemical bonds of sugar molecules, living organisms were able to emerge into life forms that spread across the planet.

These were the elements of the process that became known as photosynthesis. When simple life forms first captured the energy of sunlight, they combined carbon dioxide with hydrogen from water to form rings of sugar, and released molecules of oxygen as a byproduct. The energy of the sun's photons was stabilized within the chemical bonds of the sugar, which were then stored, moved around and broken down to yield that energy back when it was needed. This is an incredible mechanism, because it allowed life forms to capture the endless energy flooding onto the earth from the sun. And it had a double dividend — the concentration of carbon dioxide in the planet's atmosphere was steadily decreased, because living organisms took it up from the atmosphere and incorporated it into their bodies. Since most of these organisms were plants, they also liberated oxygen as waste. Over millions of years, this process transformed the atmosphere into the oxygen-rich one we have and need today.

Great ecosystems of phytoplankton, kelp, mosses, grasses and trees gradually developed in the oceans and on land; they died, decayed and were covered up. Then these plant remains were crushed by geological forces and over millions more years formed deposits of coal, oil and gas, the so-called fossil fuels that would be discovered and exploited much later by descendants of the clever species that was to evolve on the plains of Africa. Because of this process of absorbing and thus sequestering carbon, both the production and uptake of carbon dioxide were stabilized. So the reason our atmosphere has remained conducive to life is that all the living things on the planet, the web of plants, animals and micro-organisms that make up the planet's biodiversity, kept on working to maintain the stable makeup of its atmosphere. What this means is that our atmosphere is not some kind of given, granted to us by our position in the heavens or the geological composition of the planet; it is the accumulated active exhalation of all the life forms living here. The air we breathe is continuously created by them, and by us as well. Living things both generate $CO_2$ and remove it, and this is what has kept its concentration in the atmosphere remarkably constant over long periods of time.

## Prometheus Unbound

*Respect the relationships between spirit and matter.*
— THE HANOVER DESIGN PRINCIPLES

Until humans learned to control fire, we were just another part of this breathing web of air and life. Fire allowed us to get at the energy in our food more efficiently and also made it possible for us to move into northern areas of the planet and open up whole new ecosystems for our use. But the discovery of fire was also our first step in releasing the carbon that had been stored in peat, wood, animal oils, coal and other fuels, and putting it back into the atmosphere. Even the simplest fuels found on the surface of the planet could darken the skies and affect our health, sometimes getting out of control to release yet more carbon in grass and forest fires; but by and large, the atmosphere was able to handle such sudden pulses of $CO_2$. However, when we discovered during the Industrial Revolution how to make machines that consumed fossil fuels, we began to reverse the entire process begun by plants so many millions of years before. Instead of sequestering carbon dioxide in living things or burying it safely below the earth's crust, our machines do exactly the opposite. By burning carbon-based fuels, they put the formerly sequestered $CO_2$ back up into the atmosphere. Unfortunately, we hadn't recognized the systemic difference between this type of energy and the energy we had derived from natural sources like the sun, animals and water when we enthusiastically made this atmosphere-destroying process the basis for modern industrial society.

Today, about twice as much $CO_2$ is generated by human activity as the biosphere can absorb, thereby elevating its concentration in the atmosphere above pre-industrial levels by almost a third.[1] It is continuing to rise at the rate of 4 percent per decade. According to climatologist Andrew Weaver, bubbles of air trapped in successive annual layers of Antarctic ice reveal that "Our level of atmospheric carbon dioxide is now substantially higher than at any time during the [previous] 400,000 year record."[2] All fossil fuels raise $CO_2$ levels, but some are worse than others. Coal generates the most carbon dioxide per unit of energy, making it the most "dirty" fuel. Petroleum pollutes the atmosphere 20 percent less than coal, and natural gas is the "cleanest" fossil fuel, putting out 40 percent fewer pollutants than coal.[3]

Currently, transportation alone accounts for some 40 percent of all our energy use; that's partly because the number of cars is growing faster the human population — world-wide, *ten times* faster. Every gallon (U.S.) of gasoline, when burned, creates more than 9 kilograms (20 pounds) of $CO_2$, an amount that would take a large tree about a year to absorb. It becomes mind-numbing to compute the amount of gas we burn in our cars, and the number of trees it would take to absorb that waste. But instead of saving our trees for this purpose, we are cutting them down to make into cardboard, commercial flyers and disposable packaging that we put into carbon-exhaling landfills and incinerators every day.

And carbon dioxide is not the only gas we need to be concerned about. Methane is an even more potent greenhouse gas, and we generate lots of it in our huge garbage dumps and landfill sites, in rice paddies and in the flatulence of our many ruminants, like camels and dairy cattle. The vast deposits of methane sequestered in permafrost in the Arctic will add to the proportion of methane in the air if the present global warming trend continues. Nitrogen oxides used as fertilizers in industrial farming have also become a significant source of greenhouse gases. And an entirely new group of greenhouse gases, chlorofluorocarbons (CFCs), created by the chemical industry for use in refrigeration and aerosol sprays, have a warming potential that is 20,000 times as powerful as carbon dioxide per unit of volume. CFCs are also the cause of the depletion of our planet's protective ozone layer, the main reason their manufacture has been limited, although not completely stopped, in the last few years. All these gases that trap heat add to our worries about the principal one, carbon dioxide, which is responsible for about 60 percent of global warming. When we analyze such statistics, the double-edged, double-indemnity nature of the climate change crisis becomes inescapably clear: we have been generating increasing quantities of greenhouse gases by burning fossil fuels, while at the same time diminishing our ability to remove them from the atmosphere as we cut down the planet's trees and destroy carbon sinks that could absorb that carbon dioxide.

## Smart Technology

*Anybody who says 'This is the answer' is an idiot. There are going to be a multitude of answers. That's the point. It's all about diversity.*

— BILL MCDONOUGH, GREEN ARCHITECT AND DESIGNER[4]

This situation sounds desperate, but it doesn't have to be. We have dozens of energy sources to choose from besides fossil fuels. It is only general inertia and pressures from vested interests in oil and gas that are preventing us from saving our atmosphere from potential catastrophe. Many people, entire countries in fact, are already reacting, and are changing their policies and practices to usher in new ways to power modern life. In the once-forested northern part of Germany, for instance, hills that had become torn and scarred during the communist era by huge, open-pit mines producing brown coal (a fossil fuel that burns dirty in the air and leaves dangerous carcinogenic toxic wastes around the mines) are today producing a new kind of power.

These hills are now covered with windmills, fueling Germany's new position as a world leader in this form of sustainable energy. In 1998, for example, Germany produced almost 3,000 megawatts of wind electricity, and in the state of Schleswig-Holstein, the natural breezes now deliver 15 percent of the state's electrical needs. Global sales of wind technology topped $1.5 billion in 1997 alone. Denmark, the world's second greatest user of wind-power, has been producing much of the know-how and technology for mills and turbines ever since the Danish Academy of Technical Sciences determined in 1975 that at least 10 percent of the country's power should come from wind. Today, wind is already generating almost that amount, 7 percent of the country's electricity — but the national goal has shifted. Denmark has now decided that within the next thirty years, it will derive *half* of all the energy it uses from wind.

Unlike the fossil fuels that propel most of our cars and heat most of our houses, wind is a free and unpolluting source of energy; and so is the sun, the real source of the energy that fuels all life. Although solar power is far from being as cheap and available as it could be if it enjoyed the government subsidies and incentives that gas and oil do, it is already growing at close to 20 percent annually, a rate to make the average stockbroker's mouth water. Many North Americans are probably unaware of how common those black solar panels are on the rooftops of Europe and many parts of the Third World. The dark metal plates visible on these panels are covered with glass, which absorbs the sun's heat in order to warm air or a fluid like water in tubes within the panel. The fluid can then be transferred directly to taps or to pipes to radiate heat throughout a building. The panels can also be used with photovoltaic (PV) technology. When sunlight strikes a semiconductor in a PV panel, electrons are liberated to flow as electricity; it's a rather miraculous way to power things, because there are no moving parts, no emissions, and the energy itself is free. These panels, termed "active solar" technology, are in wide use in the Far East, India, Africa and China, especially where economics, distance and terrain preclude running electrical wires on poles the old-fashioned way. In Japan, PV roof tiles have been specially designed to suit the aesthetics of local neighborhoods while providing the houses with their electricity. Similar thin panels called solar shingles can be adapted to any kind of roof, and could even cover parking lots to provide protection for vehicles, while generating a large amount of a city's energy needs. There are numerous sustainable energy plans available, for every country, as Guy Dauncey and Patrick Mazza describe in their book *Stormy Weather: 101 Solutions to Global Climate Change*.[5]

One of these plans, ironically, has been developed by the U.S. government. Despite the Bush administration's repudiation of the Kyoto Climate Change Treaty and its all-out effort to increase oil exploration, the U.S. government has funded what has been termed by the *Climate Change Gazette* "the world's most advanced solar [power] system."[6] Solar Two is a 10-megawatt project that uses molten salt to store solar energy, always the most difficult hurdle to overcome in solar technology. Its 2,000 sun-tracking heliostats focus the sun's rays onto a receiver mounted on a 90-meter (300-foot) tower, where the salt is heated to 574°C (1,065°F) before being transferred to a storage tank. It's doubly ironic that the U.S. Department of Energy, which helped pay for the $55 million project, cannot find an immediate market in the United States for this technology because of government subsidies that make oil and gas unnaturally cheap there. But many other countries, like Brazil, Egypt and Spain, are interested in a technology that can provide up to 200 megawatts of power per station, with no effluent, free fuel — and an unlimited future.

Passive solar buildings, very common in countries like Holland and Germany, are also becoming increasingly popular worldwide. Even in Canada, on the Khanawake Mohawk Indian Reserve in Quebec for example, a low-cost housing development of ecologically efficient strawbale houses finished its first prototype home early in 2001. Besides the active solar black roof panels for heating the houses' water supply and providing much of their heat, they have very large windows facing south and small ones to the north, as part of their passive solar design. A "heat sink," or wall of stone, tiles or cement, catches sunlight from the south windows in the center of the house and radiates it out in winter; excellent insulation ensures that no heat is wasted and air conditioning is not needed in the summer. Moreover, these buildings spare the earth by using paints that are free of polyvinyl chlorides (PVCs). Because the reserve is located along the ecologically sensitive shores of the St. Lawrence River, the builders have also constructed an artificial wetland with a system of plant-filled lagoons to gradually purify waste water until it's clean enough to be released back into the ecosystem.

Even in major cities, a great deal is happening in energy conservation. Although few people in Canada realize it, back in 1990 the city of Toronto pledged to achieve a 20 percent reduction in its $CO_2$ emissions by 2005, a commitment that was reaffirmed by the newly amalgamated city in 1999; they budgeted $23 million to make this pledge a reality. In 1996 the Better Buildings Partnership (BBP) was formed, and in conjunction with members like Ontario Hydro and Enbridge Consumers Gas, started certifying companies to retrofit existing buildings so they would become more energy efficient. One of the first buildings to take advantage of this program was a major national showpiece — First Canadian Place, Canada's largest office tower and the headquarters of the Bank of Montreal. Olympia and York, who own the building, commissioned the retrofit, investing $6.5 million in order to save 19.4 million kilowatt hours of electricity and reduce their $CO_2$ emissions by 27,000 tonnes annually. The investment will pay for itself in reduced energy costs in only about three years, and over the next ten will save First Canadian Place over $20 million.

The word got out pretty quickly that companies could save huge amounts of money by retrofitting, and in 1999 BBP partnered with Cadillac Fairview to renovate the Toronto Dominion Centre, another huge office complex, designed in the late 1960s by the famous architect Mies van der Rohe. They spent $40 million, half of which went to environmental improvements that reduced the building's $CO_2$ emissions by 35,000 tonnes a year, an amount that would have taken ten million trees to absorb. The changeover also saved as much electricity as it would take to run 6,000 homes. This was achieved by extremely simple means: by changing the 100,000 light fixtures to accommodate energy-efficient bulbs, and by improving the insulation, ventilation, heating and air conditioning systems. The energy savings translate into $5 million a year, meaning the entire remodeling investment, including the non-ecological, design improvements, will be paid off in less than eight years!

Even the Toronto Catholic District School Board is partnering with

BBP to retrofit 557,000 square meters (6 million square feet) of space in its schools. Although driven by the need to reduce expenses — the program will result in savings of $1.6 million a year — it will also mean that every year 7 million kilograms (15.4 million pounds) of $CO_2$ will not be released into the atmosphere. In its five years of existence, BBP has overseen 155 projects in Toronto, worth about $100 million in all. The dividends have been not just double, but quadruple: 3,000 jobs were created; $6 million in operating costs were saved; 72,000 tonnes (70.1 tons) per year of $CO_2$ have been eliminated — a fifth of Metro Toronto's original 20 percent target. An impressive return for a relatively small amount of money and effort.

### Car Bombs

*Automobiles' private benefits are enormous and well understood. Yet their abundance makes them the source of a disturbing share of social problems. They are the proximate cause of more environmental harm than any other artifact of everyday life.*
— ALAN THIEN DURNING, *THE CAR AND THE CITY*[7]

Despite the availability and undeniable advantages of sustainable energy sources like wind and solar power, the proliferation of polluting and inefficient SUVs and mini-vans that clog the roadways of the U.S. and Canada is tangible proof of government policies that subsidize and support all levels of the fossil fuel industry. In all forms of transportation, the rest of the industrialized world is moving in a very different direction. The Smart Car from MCC, the Lupo from VW and the A-Class from Chrysler, now ubiquitous in European cities, get a miraculous 75 miles to the gallon with a conventional gas engine, and nearly all European models are much smaller and more efficient than ours. But even in North America, Toyota's Prius and Honda's Insight, gas-electric hybrids powered by batteries recharged and supplemented by conventional gas engines, are showing up on the roads. They get double the mileage of a normal car, and even more in cities, where energy normally lost by hitting the brakes in traffic is directed to recharging their batteries. General Motors and Ford are hustling to get their own versions out within the next few years.

Amory Lovins of the Rocky Mountain Institute (profiled in chapters one and five) has spent much of his career designing what he calls "the hypercar," the most energy-efficient private vehicle possible. Because most of the energy burned by a gas engine goes to simply move tons of metal around, Lovins's hypercar uses the latest materials technology. Like the Smart Car and the Lupo, his invention is made of strong and extremely light carbon fibers and has a surface that is aerodynamically "slippery." But unlike the Smart Car and the Lupo, the hyper-car has a gas/electric hybrid engine, which also recovers energy lost in braking to recharge the batteries. The prototype already designed is therefore better than anything currently on the market; it gets a *hundred* kilometers to the liter (well over 200 mpg) and could cross the continent on a single tank of gasoline. What's even more interesting is that these days Lovins is working hand in glove not only with Shell Oil, but also with Ford Motors' new "green" executive, Bill Ford.[8]

Ultimately, Lovins is heading toward the world's most sustainable fuel source, one that, unlike oil, is not due to run out in the next fifty years. It's hydrogen, which, when used to power vehicles, expels only heat and water from a car's exhaust pipes. Instead of burning the hydrogen gas, hydrogen fuel cells pass it through a membrane that strips its electrons from the proton nuclei of its atoms. The protons pass through and combine with oxygen to form water molecules; the electrons are captured as the electricity that powers the vehicle. All of the major automobile manufacturers have invested hundreds of millions of dollars in hydrogen fuel-cell research, and they promise to have cars powered by hydrogen available between 2002 and 2004.

At the Expo 2000 World's Fair in Hanover, however, BMW already rolled out fifteen hydrogen-powered sedans; but, while sleek and efficient, so far they have done little more than sit around and look pretty. The problem is that the infrastructure of fueling stations, and especially the government subsidies that would make hydrogen competitive with gas and oil, are still missing. That's why the German Ministry for Transport, together with seven European oil and car conglomerates like BMW, DaimlerChrysler, Shell and Volkswagen, have collaborated on a strategy to force the market share of hydrogen vehicles up to 2.5 percent of Germany's cars by 2010, with a goal to reach a remarkable 30 percent as early as 2020. To achieve this, they will gradually remove oil subsidies and reapply them to hydrogen, so that there will be no overt effect on the consumer or taxpayer and the industry will have time to adapt. There is as yet nothing comparable in the works in North America, although Canada may have to think about such measures when it finally signs the Kyoto Climate Change Treaty.

Even if hypercar-like vehicles powered by hydrogen fuel cells gradually do replace today's inefficient and polluting monsters, the problems of street hazards, noise, resource depletion and lack of exercise will continue to plague the cities and towns that are built around cars. Urban design consultant and author J.H. Crawford proposes a radically different vision of cities that could greatly improve the quality of life for individuals and their communities. The solution he proposes in his book *Carfree Cities*[9] is to supplant cars by designing cities in which all basic needs are accessible on foot from every doorstep, where no commute takes longer than thirty-five minutes door-to-door, and transportation is provided by a fast, cheap and comfortable public system; in short, the European model. By emphasizing the need to rethink urban design priorities so they aim for a high quality of life for humans rather than for automobiles, Crawford envisions cities in which people take back the streets, and neighborhoods reemerge as vibrant social units. In his view, a desirable design for urban transport would allow people to go anywhere in the city in less than an hour, with no trip requiring more than one transfer. Bus stops, subway stations and green space would be available within a five-minute walk of any front door; and most buildings would be limited to four stories or less. He points to Venice, a city much loved by its inhabitants and its visitors, as an example of such a place.

But if there is only one Venice, plenty of other cities are already illustrating the benefits of Crawford's theories. For example, the main form of transportation in Gröningen, Holland's sixth largest city and home to 170,000 people, is the bicycle. In 1992, the city center was declared a carfree area, and today, an amazing 57 percent of all trips made in Gröningen are by bicycle. It wasn't always that way. In fact, what set Gröningen on a path to bicycles was a crisis in traffic congestion in the 1970s. It became so bad that, in 1977, city planners deliberately dug up a six-lane motor-way intersection in the center of the city and replaced it with greenery, pedestrian walkways, and bicycle and bus lanes. The planners continued narrowing some roads and closing others to car traffic, while at the same time building cycle paths and new houses that could only be accessed by bicycle. Suburban shopping centers were actually banned. The result was that driving became increasingly difficult but biking grew more and more attractive. Contrary to what some feared, business in the downtown area is booming. People are moving back into the city, rents are among the highest in Holland, and now business has reversed its usual knee-jerk stance against fossil-fuel conservation, and is encouraging even more restraints on cars.[10]

Portland, Oregon, has contrived to make itself car-unfriendly in the very heart of the car-worshipping world, the West Coast of the United

States. The attractions of an excellent and free system of light rail in the downtown core, strategically placed parking lots outside of town and narrow tree-lined city streets where electric buses, bicycles and pedestrians get priority in two lanes out of three, quickly inspire both residents and visitors to leave their cars and cycle, walk or use the public facilities. Not surprisingly, Portland has one of the most beguiling downtowns in North America, filled with friendly strollers enjoying the shops, restaurants and pretty sidestreets, and enjoying the fresh air. Moreover, as many European cities have already done, Portland has adopted a system of car-sharing whereby several businesses (or individuals) can share a car. The car is kept in a central parking lot where it can be checked out for use, rather like taking a book out of a library. People reserve ahead and return the car to the lot at a set time, and a registration card keeps track of gas and sends the bills. This means that instead of seven or eight separate cars with one person in each buzzing around town and taking up parking spaces, only one is needed. And people use public transport to get to work in the first place, without worrying about how they'll do their city errands or make it to meetings in inaccessible places. Of course, the cars provided are small and fuel-efficient.

The South American city of Bogota, Colombia, offers perhaps the greatest transportation surprise of all. Even though only 14 percent of the city's residents actually own a vehicle, with seven million people, that's still a lot of cars. Moreover, Bogota has an elevation of 2,600 meters (8,500 feet) and is surrounded by the Andes mountains, which trap the rising fumes. Cars clog the streets and park on sidewalks, and as in other cities, there are many car-related accidents and deaths. About fifty people are struck by vehicles each day. That's why the city began an experiment in the 1980s to close roads to car traffic. They began with Sunday afternoons. Then, on February 24, 2000, the streets of Bogota were closed from 6:30 a.m. to 7:30 p.m. for the city's first Carfree Day. Seven million people traveled by public transit and bicycle, and 800,000 cars were left at home. After the success of the Carfree Day, a referendum was held in which a startling 51 percent of the population supported having a carfree day every day of the week! The city has helped things along by doing what it can to discourage vehicle use. Gasoline taxes have been increased, odd and even numbered license plates are prohibited from driving in the city on alternate days, and parking fees have been doubled. Fast, articulated buses have been given two bus-only corridors, and the plan is to have twenty-two corridors by 2015 so that there will be a bus stop within a few hundred meters of every home.

The most remarkable thing about this revolution is probably its motivation. On a visit to Canada, Oscar Edmundo Diaz, then advisor to Bogota's mayor, Enrique Penalosa Londono, said, "We don't really care about the environment; we have other things to think about. We have social problems and lack of money. We have to stop building highways, because we need the money to build schools . . . A perfect city would be the one that would give us the opportunity to raise our kids without having cars attacking them, without having to commute several hours because of sprawl. Suburban sprawl is making North American cities crazy; so we are trying to create a new city, to give children the environment they need." There's another, even deeper agenda in Bogota: social equality. Diaz says that when they ride on public transportation, "the president of the company and the cleaning lady encounter one another as equals; there is no hierarchy there." In other words, the reign of the car, so enjoyable in many ways, so liberating, has also created huge problems in terms of unlivable urban areas, social inequality and pollution. Providing alternatives to cars has much broader implications than just fresher air and a protected climate.[11]

As we saw in India with Development Alternatives' methods of making house bricks and roof tiles, the amazing thing is that so many of the energy-saving principles that seem at first glance to be impossibly idealistic and utopian are finding practical expression, and are as fully understood in Delhi and Bogota as they are in New York. They are even becoming law in parts of Europe. This visceral and systemic change in how we look at the world and use its materials is inherent, for example, in the European Union's new law mandating that all automobiles become fully recyclable by 2002, and is the main reason why so many people are trundling around the Continent in little Lupos and Smart Cars. Their carbon bodies can be fully recycled, as can their engines.

In a way, the future is here; we have the technological answers to our most thorny modern problems. These exciting, double-dividend technologies fulfill all the criteria for real breakthrough modernity — they are clean and sustainable, and they can provide us with the energy, heat, light and materials to retain the modern lifestyles we all seem to want so much. But the reason we are developing them with such explosive rapidity is not so much that we're getting to be so smart, as that we're becoming very scared. We've realized that anything we bring up from beneath the earth's crust is dangerous, and can no longer be rooted up and used so lightly.

## Walking the Talk

*Real sustainability is about simultaneously being profitable and responding to the reality and the concerns of the world in which we operate. We're not separate from the world. It's our world as well [and] to be sustainable, companies need a sustainable world.*
— JOHN BROWNE, BRITISH PETROLEUM

If we know that the products from under the earth's crust destroy the atmosphere and poison us, and if we now have the technology to do without them, why are so many of us still driving dirty cars, using CFCs in our fridges, painting and inking with polyvinyl chlorides and phthalates and dumping heavy metals? Well, for one thing, sustainable technologies are fairly new and not yet well integrated into normal business processes. But the main reason is that there are a lot of powerful interests profiting from keeping business as usual, who choose not to believe that the products they make or the fuels they burn are really as dangerous as all the scientists say.[12]

Fortunately, cracks are appearing in the once united front of industrial denial. The insurance industry was among the earliest to break ranks, out of sheer self-interest. Payments for climate-related catastrophes such as hurricanes and tornadoes, fires and drought have been so high in recent years that they are threatening to bankrupt many insurance companies. In 1998, weather-related damage claims on insurance policies exceeded $89 billion (U.S.) and in that single year were greater than all weather-related damage claims in the entire decade of the 1980s. Not only are hurricanes, ice storms, heat waves and floods occurring with greater fury, but they are happening in places they have never been seen before.[13] In November 2000, Britain's largest property insurer estimated that "if left unchecked, climate change will bankrupt the global economy by 2065."[14] In March 2001, Munich Reinsurance, one of the largest firms in the world, estimated that climate change would cost the world some $300 billion a year in the coming decades.[15]

The oil industry has gone so far as to found its own support group to attempt to refute such charges, an extraordinarily well-funded lobby called the Global Climate Coalition, which initially included the American Petroleum Institute, the Automobile Manufacturers' Association, Western Fuels and virtually all the biggest oil, coal, and auto companies. The Coalition strenuously opposed all the mounting scientific evidence, and when that strategy began to fail, claimed that any action to reverse climate change would be ruinous to the economy, an argument they still employ today. The Global Climate Coalition has so far spent more than $60 million fighting attempts to reduce greenhouse gas emissions in the United States, including a $13 million ad campaign in 1997, which supported a resolution opposing ratification of the Kyoto Protocol. With the election of the oil-friendly Bush administration, this campaign has obviously borne fruit.

But despite such formidable opponents, the facts about global warming are gradually winning over more converts, and the Global Climate Coalition has begun to lose some of its most powerful members. British Petroleum and Shell withdrew from the organization in 1999 and announced new expansions into solar power and other renewable energy sources. They were followed by Ford, DaimlerChrysler, Texaco, the Southern Company and General Motors. These defections reflected a philosophical shift within the corporate hierarchy that was signaled by two landmark speeches. The first, by John Browne, group chief executive of British Petroleum, now advertising itself as "Beyond Petroleum," was delivered in 1997 at Stanford University. Browne said, "We must now focus on what can and what should be done, not because we can be certain climate change is happening, but because the possibility cannot be ignored." He then went on to commit BP to the voluntary monitoring and control of its own greenhouse gas emissions; he also announced that the company was committing $100 million to eliminating emissions of volatile organic compounds (VOCs).[16] In September of 1998, Browne went further, announcing a greenhouse target for 2010 of 10 percent below 1990 levels. Other companies have made changes as well, although they still have not abated their frenzied search for more oil and drilling sites: Shell has invested $500 million in renewable energy, Texaco is investing substantially in hydrogen fuel cells, and General Motors has come out in support of a 50 percent tax on gasoline.

The second speech marking a philosophical change in the oil industry was given by William Clay Ford, great grandson of Henry Ford and chairman of the Ford Company Board, at a Greenpeace business conference in London on October 5, 2000. "We're at a crucial point in the world's history," he said. "Our oceans and forests are suffering; species are disappearing; the climate is changing . . . Enlightened corporations are beginning to . . . realize that they can no longer separate themselves from what is going on around them. That, ultimately, they can only be as successful as the communities and the world that they exist in." While extolling the positive effect automobiles have had on society, he acknowledged that they "have also had a major negative impact on the environment . . . I personally believe that sustainability is the most important issue facing the automotive industry and industry in general in the 21st century." He announced that the company plans to have hybrid gas-electric SUVs for sale by 2003, and has entered into a $1-billion partnership with DaimlerChrysler and Canada's Ballard Fuels to develop hydrogen fuel-cell-propelled vehicles; and he promised to have a test fleet on the road in less than a year.

People who know the man are convinced that Bill Ford, on the personal level, truly believes all this. But we must remember the realities of corporate structure that we discussed in chapter one, "Making Money Like the Bee." Even the hands of the CEO of a publicly traded corporation are tied if new policies, however humanitarian or rational, conflict with the bottom line. For example, the Ford Excursion, one of the very worst vehicles on the road today in terms of air pollution, weighs almost 4 metric tonnes, is 6 meters long, literally the size of a boat, and averages a disgusting 12 miles to the gallon. Many cars like the Prius or the Lupo will have to take to the road to make up for even one Excursion. Bill Ford has admitted he has no plans to take it or any other such monster off the road, because they are still selling so well; and in 2002 the hybrid SUV was scrapped. So, even as we turn to the big corporations for research and development, and especially for signs that pressure and scientific evidence are bearing fruit, we need to keep in mind that, until they are controlled in ways that help them remain within certain social boundaries, large corporations are still much more likely to be despoiling the earth than to be helping it.

Talk is cheap, but it's usually a start. At all the world meetings of government and trade these days, as the protests mount and tear gas drifts in through the ventilation systems, both politicians and corporations are making encouraging noises. Although after recent events they would undoubtedly focus on international terrorism, at the annual World Economic Forum in Davos, Switzerland, in 2000, the CEOs of the world's one thousand largest corporations actually voted climate change the most urgent problem facing humanity. Echoing that recognition, in June 2001 James Wolfensohn, President of the World Bank, urged business leaders to expand their notion of responsibility beyond earnings, and to embrace obligations to society at large. He announced that the World Bank itself would become a more socially and environmentally responsible organization: "I believe that we must transform the Bank into a global leader on social and environmental responsibility — for other development organizations and the private sector to follow." This and other mom-and-apple-pie speeches have yet to be bolstered with real action, largely because of the way corporations are set up, and because of the internal, mainstream-economics mindset of organizations like the World Bank and the WTO. They are now also being sidetracked by concerns about military security. But the fact that they do address the issue of environmental and social responsibility is proof that our global society is beginning to come to a clearer agreement on shared values — and that the new shared values are sufficiently powerful that even those profiting the most from the status quo feel obliged to acknowledge them publicly.

## Better Living Through Chemistry

*When you look at the products inside a lot of office buildings and a lot of homes — the glues, chemicals, cleaning fluids, pesticides, herbicides — when you look at . . . the chemical soup that gets generated inside an office building with bad ventilation, [you realize] you're building gas chambers.*
— BILL MCDONOUGH

Pluto's curse affects more than just the atmosphere. The underground stores of ancient life that became oil and gas can poison water and earth, and our bodies as well, wherever we put them. As with global warming, the science is in on the effects of petrochemicals on living things. The only people who still deny the terrible damage petrochemicals do to living tissues are the companies that make them and the people who profit from the companies. To be more precise, they don't deny the harm, but they do try to dicker about how much of each of these poisons the human body can tolerate. Petrochemical companies always seek "acceptable levels" in terms of what a mature adult can absorb with no relatively immediate effects; but of course, those most vulnerable to these chemicals are children, babies and pregnant women, and the effects are delayed by months, years or even decades. The government standards for toxin tolerance we have come to accept also rarely take into account cumulative or synergistic effects; what happens to organisms that are being bombarded with tiny amounts of related or radically different toxins every day?

Most of us do know how dangerous these compounds are in an uncomfortable, abstract sense. But, as a leading oncologist constantly trying to cope with cancers and other modern diseases, Dr. Karl-Henrik Robèrt, developer of The Natural Step, can be more precise. If we are to have a healthy society that produces food, clothes and building materials we're not afraid to eat or touch, we need to apply concepts like Robèrt's First Condition requirement of The Natural Step. He naturally put this condition first because he felt it was the most important: the First Systems Condition for a sustainable planet is to stop bringing things that are buried under the earth's crust up to its surface. Every one of our efforts to find new energy sources and develop new products and industries must keep that aim firmly in mind. In the meantime, however, we also have to deal with the messes that are already here, and get some social control over the chemical and oil industries.

For forty years now, our politicians have been talking periodically about banning or controlling industrial chemicals, and if they're pressured long enough, their talk sometimes does lead to real progress. Just recently, for example, there was a major breakthrough in the regulation of toxic chemicals. Canada, which has clung to U.S. positions and lagged behind on issues like the Kyoto and the Biosafety Protocols, has rehabilitated its international reputation to some extent by taking the lead in lobbying for a new chemical control treaty. A UN convention announced in May 2001 sets out to ban the worst of our manmade chemical contaminants, dubbed "the dirty dozen," by 2004. Canadian Environment Minister David Anderson worked hard to get a hundred other nations to agree to ban or severely restrict these substances, which include furans, dioxins, PCBs and hexachlorobenzine. Most of them are pesticides, herbicides and fungicides, and cause horrifying malformations, diseases and deaths in fish, amphibians, mammals and birds, as well as in humans. The fact that these chemicals were created to kill life forms in the first place is a potent reminder of the interconnected wholeness of all life. We're finally having to acknowledge that if a substance can kill a creature as simple and resilient as a mosquito or a weed, it's probably poisonous enough to destroy more complex creatures like us, simply because all life forms are very much alike.

Of course, in negotiating this treaty, the United Nations was not prescient, nor was Canada ahead of its time. Neither body was acting entirely on its own volition; as usual, they were responding to pressure, and many groups of local grassroots activists deserve most of the credit. For the past ten years at least, worldwide movements have been trying to establish the dangers of these substances and get them banned. One such organization is the Center for Environment, Health and Justice (known as the CCHW), headed by Lois Marie Gibbs, who became famous for her fight to get compensation for the victims of Love Canal, one of the world's most infamous toxic waste dumps. Headquartered outside Washington D.C., her organization led the charge in the United States against many of these substances, especially dioxins and furans.

Back in the 1970s, homes for local chemical workers in Love Canal, a suburb of Niagara Falls in upstate New York, were built on a huge repository for PCBs, dioxins and other persistent organic pollutants (POPs). Gibbs's children had both become ill with terrible blood and immune-system disorders before she figured out what was making them sick. Years of fighting for her family's survival, then seeking acknowledgement that the chemicals were responsible, and finally getting compensation so that the Love Canal families could deal with their medical bills and move away, earned Gibbs a powerful nickname: Mother of the Superfund. The Superfund was established by the U.S. federal government after Love Canal to provide national funding for toxic waste clean-up. Thanks mostly to Gibbs and the activists in her first NGO, the Citizens' Clearing House on Hazardous Waste, not one single new toxic waste dump has been permitted to open in the United States in the past twenty years. And for more than a decade her organization has taken particular aim at dioxins and furans, both of them by-products of the incineration of municipal, hospital and hazardous wastes.

While some of the other dirty dozen — Chlordane, Mirex and Toxaphene in particular — are clearly implicated in certain kinds of cancers, dioxins and furans have been linked to more difficult to diagnose but even more deeply frightening immune and hormone disorders in humans and in many animals. Mainstream media reports about the new UN convention have tended to downplay its significance with such comments as, "Part of the reason for the relative ease with which the treaty has been accepted is that most industrial nations have phased out the chemicals on the list, so there are no powerful industrial lobbies to push for their continued use."[17] In fact, most of the North American chemical giants like Monsanto and Union Carbide are still manufacturing billions of dollars worth of these substances for the export market every year, and they have fought tooth and claw against every attempt at control. Moreover, dioxins are a byproduct of many chemical processes, including paper bleaching, which chemical companies definitely want to continue. And that, says Gibbs, is what makes the treaty "a real triumph for us. What the treaty means is that the dangers of these chemicals will finally be officially recognized. Then the compromises will start; we'll have debates and discussions about methodologies of control, and the industry will continue to fight every step. But once the treaty is ratified, it will make everyone, all the regulators, take such conversations seriously."

As we saw in the second chapter, "Withdrawing Consent," the best way for citizens to get politicians and special interests to do what they want is to apply relentless pressure. A recent PBS documentary series by Bill Moyers, *Trade Secrets*, made it clear that the chemical lobby in the United States is extremely well funded and invest their money in ways that ensure they have as little political interference with their business practises as possible.[18] Gibbs says the EPA's dioxin report, for example, "has been delayed, diluted and corrupted by industry so much it's unbelievable." So anti-chemical activists have shown up at meetings, conventions, boardrooms and government committee sessions, as well as out in the communities and on the streets. And they have applied every imaginable political, media and social pressure from the neighborhood level to the international arena.

Most government representatives at international meetings want to be seen as being on the side of the angels, and they especially need their colleagues from other countries to perceive them as having the backing of their own people. CCHW had groups of supporters chanting and protesting outside every chemical treaty meeting, regardless of the country, in order to show that regular Americans did not support the official position. "That bothered them so much," Gibbs says, "that they called our head office here to ask us to stop. Demonstrators also turned up with pregnant bellies made out of *papier maché* and signs saying, 'We Must Protect Future Generations.' The reps had to walk the gauntlet of that kind of thing whenever they went in or out." In short, the demonstrators simply displayed their withdrawal of consent in public, a method that, as we have seen again and again, is far more effective than most people realize.

With this kind of ammunition and a staggering amount of work on the national level, CCHW and its many allies around the world have been able to push ahead on the UN treaty. Gibbs says, "When we began, there was huge, huge opposition by all the manufacturers and the agencies themselves; we were alone . . . Of course, they're still fighting the treaty on dioxin and

POPs; but the real difference is they're not reacting to a small group any more. This is a huge, worldwide effort. Almost every country in the UN knows now that their very being is at risk; their food, water, fish, animals, are being contaminated; and that what we all really need is a radical change. It's not just about trees or fish or wildlife or even people; it's about survival. Rachel Carson said this to us so long ago. And now it's up on the international level." We're finally starting to get the social control over toxins that we need.

## Eco-Logical

*Eco Logic's business is to solve toxic chemical problems in a safe, cost-effective and permanent manner.*
— ECO LOGIC, FEBRUARY 2000

Canada has its own Love Canal; in fact, the country is living through a nightmare that never seems to end: the infamous tar ponds of Sydney, Nova Scotia — the largest toxic waste dump in North America. The effluent from the provincially owned steel mills and coke ovens that were the primary source of employment for the people of Sydney, Nova Scotia, for more than fifty years was simply dumped in the area without the slightest attempt at containment. It now contaminates the springs, streams, ditches, wells and the entire estuary of this harbor town. The "tar ponds" at the back of the estuary contain 700,000 tons of sludge containing every known polyaromatic hydrocarbon (PAH), including naphthalene, benzene, toluene and benzopyrene — all recognized carcinogens — plus PCBs. Besides that, more than 50 hectares (125 acres) of land where the coke ovens used to stand are saturated to depths of 25 meters (80 feet) with more PAHs, as well as arsenic, cyanide, lead and other heavy metals.

This is the carbon-sequestering material — safe underground but pure hell on the surface — that we need to keep out of our industrial stream. In Sydney, it was ripped out from under the earth's crust to feed industry, and has ended up in the air and especially in the water, contaminating a famous ditch that runs behind several streets. It even seeps into people's basements, where indoor arsenic levels have been found that are four times what the federal government considers safe to human health in outside air have been found. Elizabeth May, head of the Sierra Club of Canada, got involved in the tar ponds over fourteen years ago, when desperate and sick residents of Sydney called the Sierra Club for advice. She says, "That's more than *thirty-three* times the amount of toxins that were buried in Love Canal, the worst toxic dump in the U.S., whose clean-up spurred new laws and an entirely new method of dealing with toxic wastes, the Superfund. But here in Canada, we've still done nothing to really address this problem."

That's probably because the problems in Sydney have political as well as social and health dimensions. The government with the mandate and power to regulate and clean up the tar ponds, the province of Nova Scotia, is also responsible for the contamination in the first place. It was the Nova Scotia government itself that owned the Sydney Steel Corporation (SYSCO), the industry that caused this catastrophe and is responsible for the unusual lack of containment and care surrounding the coke yards. Moreover, for many years, the federal government ignored its own health and safety guidelines in order to encourage Nova Scotia in what was seen as a make-work project for a region of chronic underemployment. Just as at Love Canal, most of the people who live in this area are unemployed now that the mill is closed, and have only their contaminated homes to call their own; that's why they can't move. As resident Ann Ross says, "Without my house, I'd be a bag lady on the street."

The two most active environmental and social groups in Canada, the Sierra Club, headed by May, and the Council of Canadians, headed by Maude Barlow, took on the tar ponds. Together with the residents they did all the things that CCHW had done in their toxic dump and dioxin fights, and more. Governmental funds were allocated and committees were appointed. Millions were allocated in promised clean-ups, aborted sewage and incineration plans, public education coalitions and more studies. But they didn't help the people most affected. "It's always been an engineering project to clean up the estuary," says May. "Nothing for health or for residents." In April of 2001, the latest government data on tests made of people's houses the previous fall were finally released to residents. "And what they'd found," she explains, "was high levels of terrible things — arsenic, cyanide, lead, very high levels of benzenes, benzopyrine, PAHs, napthylene, large numbers of the toxins that are all created by baking coal. They usually find them right where the coke ovens used to sit, but these were in the neighborhood soils, in the water standing in people's basements!"

May herself even went on a hunger strike in April 2001. She sat on the steps of Parliament for seventeen days, supported in her ordeal by flowers from admirers and especially by pictures of the tar pond children sick with multiple birth defects, chronic migraines, nosebleeds, leukemia and other cancers of every kind. "Even when Maude and I wrote the book on the issue, *Frederick Street*, last year," she says, "we didn't know how the effects would keep multiplying, and how sick the children are. More and more children are getting sick all the time. There's a lot of leukemia, that's from all the benzene and PAHs. There are babies born with eye cancer, little boys with extra holes in their penises [are] not uncommon, all kinds of horrific things."

Despite wide support from the public and from politicians across the political spectrum to move residents out of the area, government promises to finally assess their health have resulted in an announcement, released late in 2001, that all the ill health in the area is not significantly higher than elsewhere in the province. The residents and their allies claim that this merely mirrors the "risk assessment" model under which our regulatory agencies now operate, and that the government does not consider their level of suffering drastic enough to be deemed actionable under current guidelines. It also means that no money will be allocated to move the residents. So the Sierra Club is calling for a full parliamentary inquiry; in Canadian parlance, this means getting out the big guns. It should get the issue the attention it deserves. Meanwhile, local groups in Sydney have formed a People's Health Commission to do their own door-to-door health assessments, by counting how many people in each home are ill, and with what symptoms.

But even if the people at greatest risk of the effects of the tar ponds are finally moved away, as they were at Love Canal, a deeper question will still remain. What about the birds, the other neighbors, the despoliation of the entire area? Is our only option to leave the tar ponds, and other places like it, to fester away for generations? And of course in nature, few things that we dump stay put. Tidal action is slowly moving the contaminated sludge in the river toward the mouth of the estuary, polluting a steadily wider area. May suggests a very simple technology. A coffer dam, which allows water over the top but traps sludge below until it can be removed and treated, would at least stop the spread of poison. But even if the government puts in a coffer dam, can we then remove and treat these persistent substances? The answer is a recent one: Yes, we can. A Canadian-invented technology that is now cleaning up toxic wastes sites all around the world could safely and permanently deal with the dreadful legacy of Canada's worst chemical catastrophe.

Thirteen years ago, a former Canadian-government scientist named Doug Hallett learned how to detoxify the hazardous wastes derived from coal and petrochemicals — all the terrible poisons like PCBs, PAHs, benzene, dioxins, furans, hexachlorobenzine, the whole range of agricultural pesticides and herbicides, and even the compounds that make up agents of chemical warfare. Compounds of hazardous waste made up of Persistent Organic Pollutants, or POPs, are termed "organic" because they are derived from petrochemicals, which are molecules of ancient organic life forms such as trees, marine life and grasses that have been fossilized. When recombined chemically and released on the surface of the planet, these buried, extinct life forms react in ways that are reminiscent of a horror movie: dead creatures, unnaturally brought back to earth, attack and cause gruesome deaths to living organisms. But the organic compounds we create by tinkering with petroleum are really just molecules held together by chemical bonds. DDT and dioxins, for example, are different arrangements of methane, hydrogen chloride and water, while PCBs are simply methane and hydrogen chloride.

Hallett discovered that by smothering these pollutants with hydrogen in their gas phase he could dissolve those chemical bonds and return them to their original state. He founded a company called Eco Logic, which has perfected a portable chemical reactor that can treat waste on site, thus eliminating the dangerous and often impracticable transport of hazardous materials that brought us so many PCB scares and spills in the 1980s. If they're dealing with a situation like the tar ponds or Love Canal, where the soil has become saturated with PCBs and other dangerous organic chemicals, the Eco Logic reactor can be brought to the site. The soil is scooped into it and heated, not with oxygen-burning fire as in an incinerator, but with hydrogen. Once the POPs in the soil have turned into gases, more hydrogen is pumped in, and it simply works away at the chemical bonds until they break. The new waste products are the basic constituents of the pollutants, like methane or hydrochloric acid.

The methane can be used as a fuel, or be further broken down in Eco Logic's "water shift reactor," where water chops up the bonds in methane or benzene to reduce them to carbon monoxide and hydrogen. Sodium hydroxide can then be added to the hydrochloric acid, resulting in a slightly salty water that can be used for cooling the reactor system and may be released into rivers with no adverse effects. Of the soil that's left, the other organic materials in the humus will have been broken down into their composite gases, leaving only inorganic materials like silica and metals. If the metals are dangerous ones, like mercury or lead, other technologies, usually employing acid leaching, can recover them to be recycled by industry. Any other stray contaminants, say the Eco Logic experts, can likely be taken care of by using living bacteria, in ways similar to the lagoon methods used to purify sewage.

It's all a perfect example of architect Bill McDonough's concept of the industrial nutrient stream discussed in chapter two. If the waste is organic, it should be returned to nature; if it's industrial, it should be returned to industry. And although far from cheap — costs range from $6,000 a tonne for solids like PCBs, to only $600 for soil — Hallett's solution is still cheaper than the only competing technology, incineration, which is much more problematic. Incinerators habitually release many equally dangerous compounds into the air, and they are saddled with toxic ash that they usually can only bury. In fact, the price-tag for getting PCBs right off the planet through dissolving their chemical bonds is actually quite low: it is identical to the cost of shipping them all the way across the country and burying them on a native reserve in Swan Hills, Alberta — a recently suggested and highly unappealing strategy.

Although it has yet to get rid of the wastes in the country of its birth, Eco Logic is far beyond the start-up stage. They have cleaned up all the PCBs in Australian toxic waste sites and are now working on that country's other organic pollutant dumps. They have contracts to clean up all the U.S. chemical weapon depositories by 2012, and they are currently destroying chemical wastes in Japan. The American military and Australian chemical industry love this process, because it's getting them out of a tight spot. Elizabeth Kummling, director of business development for Eco Logic, says that the new POPs treaty against the "dirty dozen" will probably increase their business, but only when each country puts legislation in place. "The reason we've been so successful in Australia," she says, "is that they have a law that requires them not to store PCBs, but to get rid of them." Because Eco-Logic can treat anything organic, no matter how frighteningly toxic, they've been the saviors of the U.S. military. They, too, are under legislative compulsion to get rid of stored chemical weapons. "It's all the same process for us," says Kummling. "I mean this stuff is really toxic; you get one drop on your skin and your whole immune system shuts down; but we can dissolve it out into its methane and hydrochloric acid constituents, no problem."

As for Sydney's infamous tar ponds, the Canadian and Nova Scotia governments have been tantalizing Eco Logic for years, sending samples off to be tested, hinting at the $62 million already set aside for remediation efforts. In March of 2001, Eco Logic was again asked to do some bench-scale testing; but the company hasn't yet heard anything else, and they don't want to speculate on the delays. It would be a huge job, estimated at as much as a billion dollars, to clean up the 700,000 tonnes of soil in the tar ponds. But the only other options — burying or burning it — will create more, not fewer, chemical bonds, and continued stalling will only dump the problem on our children and poison everything and everyone in the vicinity in the meantime. A simple, reasonably priced solution exists; all that's required is the political pressure to get it implemented.

## Tax Bads, Not Goods

*When the ill effects of leaded gasoline became clear, Malaysia simply taxed it, creating an immediate, nation-wide shift to unleaded gas.*
— EDITORIAL, *OTTAWA CITIZEN*[19]

National governments are now operating in a world where transnational corporations may be far wealthier and more powerful than they are. Politicians are still expected to serve the people who elect them, but these days they may feel their constituents are not so much the voters as the interest groups that have funded their increasingly expensive campaigns. And yet, governments and policy makers still wield a tremendous amount of power, especially in terms of legislation, subsidies and taxes that favor certain practices or certain industries, and they still play these cards to the hilt. And voters are powerful too; they may not always be able to control their politicians once they're in office, but they can still turf them out periodically and have a great deal of influence when they withdraw consent with public protests and lawsuits.

It's generally understood that when a government policy rewards an activity, it can encourage the populace to do more of it, while punishing an activity will discourage it. Governments net much of their revenue by taxing personal incomes, company payrolls and retail sales; and they also tax urban buildings on the basis of their size as well as their condition. But by doing so they send out very perverse signals. They are actually punishing socially beneficial actions such as economic activity, employing more people and keeping buildings in good repair. If they were to do the opposite, that is, tax practices that are socially or ecologically destructive, not only would they send messages to polluters and greedy corporations, but they would also be giving out rewards for altered behavior. Although business has always fought blindly against such taxes, in fact, if all businesses were subject to them, such new taxes would not have to affect their profits at all. Indeed, if a company were to eliminate destructive behavior altogether, it could avoid certain taxes and gain an advantage over more old-fashioned competitors who continue to pollute or downsize their workforce.

In a rather surprising editorial a couple of years ago, the *Ottawa Citizen*, a business-oriented newspaper, endorsed "green" tax reform. They pointed out that "a German tax on the creation of toxic waste resulted in a 15 percent drop in three years. A Dutch tax on the emissions of heavy metals like lead, mercury and cadmium produced a 90 percent cut in emissions within two decades . . . Sweden, Denmark and Holland have each shifted some of their income and payroll taxes onto carbon emissions, electricity sales, waste incineration and pesticide use. In 1996, the United Kingdom took a slice off payroll taxes and put it on landfilling. In 1995, Spain also cut payroll taxes, but raised gas taxes." Pollution taxes or green taxes have been called "corrective taxes" because they correct price distortions that result from a failure to include the full cost of resource depletion or environmental destruction in the end price of a product or an industry's activity. Europe has a somewhat lower ceiling on how much money corporations and businesses are allowed to contribute to the political process than we do in North America, so it is easier to get green laws passed there. Even so, they're not just a European tool. There are more than 450 environmental taxes already in place even in the United States.

Iowa's Groundwater Protection Act (1987) imposes a tax of 0.1 percent on gross retail sales of pesticides, 0.2 percent on gross sales of manufacturers and 75 cents per ton on nitrogen fertilizer; in 1993, these taxes raised $3.2 million, and of course, help protect the water supply. Minnesota extended the use of its 6.5 percent sales tax to cover garbage services, raising $24.3 million in its first year (1989–90); the state uses the money to finance recycling and waste reduction programs, as well as to close down polluting landfills. The state of Washington levies a surcharge on products that are considered to contribute to litter, and a dollar added to the sale of each new tire goes towards tire recycling programs. Massachusetts has a landfill tax of $1 per ton of solid waste; Oregon has a similar levy. Indiana taxes the storage of petroleum products, an excellent incentive to limit this practice, since most water contamination comes from leaky underground gas tanks. Former U.S. Federal Reserve chairman Paul Volcker and Martin Feldstein, past chair of the Council of Economics Advisors, have endorsed a carbon tax, that is, a tax on fuel consumption, which could replace part of California's retail sales tax. In short, governments don't have to reinvent the wheel in order to institute more green taxes; they just have to be sure the taxes are simple to administer and fair, and result in the desired behavior.

The Organization for Economic Cooperation and Development (OECD) represents thirty of the world's richest nations, which produce two-thirds of the world's goods and services; the organization is one of the most outspoken proponents of the benefits of economic globalization. But even they, on April 9, 2001, released a study[20] that strongly recommended a coordinated program to remove environmentally damaging subsidies and introduce green taxes, "to prevent irreversible damage to our environment over the next 20 years." Their own computer simulations demonstrate that removing subsidies in OECD nations, imposing an energy tax linked to the carbon content of fuels, and taxing all chemicals could result in a 15 percent reduction in anticipated carbon dioxide emissions by 2020. Sulfur dioxide emissions would also be 9 percent lower, methane 3 percent lower and nitrogen run-off 30 percent lower. Most importantly, in terms of countering the usual arguments against such measures, the economic costs would be almost negligible — less than one percent of the member countries' GDP in 2020.[21]

The usual excuse for not protecting our environment is that it will cost too much. But even the modest costs incurred in turning away from fossil fuels can be recouped simply by *gradually* removing all the incentives and subsidies currently enjoyed by gas and oil, and reapplying them as rewards to sustainable technologies. The citizen won't be paying higher taxes, and businesses will benefit — albeit in a different and, as it happens, much more profitable way. That's because, as it stands, taking things out from under the earth's crust not only poisons us; it's a losing proposition economically. The miners, the chemical and oil companies certainly know this, because they have begged for, and received, massive tax breaks and subsidies to enable them to "stay in business." In the United States alone (sometimes the subsidies are yet higher), the mining of minerals, even toxics like mercury and asbestos that are generally outlawed, receives a special income tax deduction called the "percentage depletion allowance." All investments in oil and gas enjoy a "passive loss" tax shelter that could be painlessly switched over to modern, energy-efficient technologies that do not currently enjoy any such advantages. Solid waste incinerators release tons of toxics into the air, but their construction can be financed with bonds that are exempt from federal income tax.[22]

When it comes to modifying fossil fuel use in transportation, the good news is that the automobile is probably the most massively subsidized technology in human history. That invisible tax support currently removes any incentive drivers may have for looking for greater efficiency, as the craze for Jeeps and SUVs proves, but if it were removed, it could easily finance the needed alternatives. In a World Resources Institute (WRI) publication, "The Going Rate: What it Really Costs to Drive,"[23] authors James MacKenzie, Roger Dower and Donald Chen point out that "Motorists today do not directly pay anything close to the full costs of their driving decisions. However steep the bills for cars, insurance, automobile maintenance and gasoline may seem to drivers, federal and state policies spare them many other costs. The net effect is to make driving seem cheaper than it really is, and to encourage the excessive use of automobiles and trucks." We all pay the costs of traffic congestion, lost time, lower worker productivity and increased maintenance. In 1989, gas taxes and user fees only covered 60 percent of the $33.3 billion spent that year on roads. The other 40 percent was paid by people who may not even have a car.

In the United States, the cost of highway patrols, traffic management, traffic accidents and police work adds another $68 billion to the subsidy total. Over 40,000 people are killed and more than 5 million injured annually, incurring unmeasured but very real costs that far exceed the measurable costs of medical expenses, funerals and lost work time. Parking is massively subsidized and is usually free in shopping malls; 90 percent of commuters drive to work and park for free. Half of the oil used by motorists is imported, and it costs the United States $50 billion annually to sustain a military presence in oil-rich countries to ensure the secure flow of foreign oil. After the war in Afghanistan, the military presence in the entire region, and especially in Saudi Arabia, has already become greater and more expensive. These costs say nothing of the loss of quality of life and democratic freedom to the people in countries like Nigeria, Colombia or Kuwait, whose national policies are manipulated for the benefit of oil companies. Further hidden costs of automobiles — loss of land to roads, acid rain, forest damage, reduced agricultural yields and health problems — are hard to calculate, but must be astronomical. In fact, for every $169 disbursed in direct costs per driver per year, it is estimated that between $2,356 and $3,116 are hidden. The authors of the WRI report conclude that in the United States taxpayers are subsidizing drivers to the tune of at least $300 billion a year! If that staggering public cost had to be borne by the actual users, there would be a massive shift in what, when and how much people drive, and in the perception of what really is the cheapest and easiest way to get around.

Of course, not every country is suited to bikes year round, and buses are not an ideal alternative environmentally. One thinks of Canada, for example, where a Winnipeg cyclist could die of wind-chill on the way to work in winter. Even in Germany, there is enough snow, sleet and nasty wind to make people think twice about bikes — and of course there are other considerations. The very old and the very young, people who are not in good health, people who have packages and luggage — how will they get around without cars? In Germany and many other European countries, trains provide the answer to most of these problems. From an environmental point of view, even if they burn fossil fuels, currently nothing moves people and freight around with less pollution and greater fuel efficiency than trains. Add modern, efficient, often electric engines, and we have the perfect answer to many of our transport needs.

Germany shows how it might work, everywhere. Light and heavy rail are seamlessly connected at shared stations, so that people can move from tram to bus to subway to inter-city trains with extreme ease — and all trains have racks for bicycles. Like car travel, train travel is taxpayer-subsidized in Germany, but not nearly so heavily. So with acceptable levels of tax support, a German citizen can get around a typical city on a rail pass costing about $55 (Canadian) a month. It enables the holder to use four systems, the U-trains or classic subways, their connecting buses, the S-Trains that run between cities, and in some cities, Berlin for one, charming electric trams as well. It's no sacrifice to use this system, which never seems to make one wait more than five minutes, nearly always has a comfortable seat or even a whole bench to lie on available, and not only connects every city but also reaches into the very heart of the countryside.

Perhaps most significant of all is the fact that trains are not used almost exclusively by the visibly poor, as buses are in North America, but are also the transportation choice for well-heeled middle- and upper-middle class people taking business trips, family vacations and so on. There is a luxurious first class with comfortable restaurants and individual TVs for those who can afford it. And there are great deals for those who can't. On the Good Evening ticket, if you travel at night, you can go the entire length of the country for less than $50 (Canadian). And on weekends regional trains offer old-fashioned train compartments for five people for a flat rate of less than $20 (Canadian) each, wherever the group wants to go in that state. Fast, efficient, reasonably priced train service is ubiquitous in Europe. Instead of tearing up our rail system, this is the time when North Americans should be expanding theirs as well. It's a national disgrace that neither the United States nor Canada has anything remotely like Europe's super-efficient, high-speed service. Trains can provide mass transportation that offers everyone options, and they all pay out double dividends: they're comfortable and fast, and intelligent taxes and subsidies can make them affordable. Most importantly, they can be adapted to be almost completely non-polluting.

## Double Dividends

*There is not much hope if we have only one difficulty; but when we have two, we can match them off against each other.*
— NIELS BOHR, PHYSICIST[24]

All through this book, we have noted that one way to tell if a practice is healthy for living things and can be sustained, given the physical laws of this planet, is to look at whether it produces double or even triple dividends. If what you're doing makes you a decent living, like Judy Wicks's restaurant, but also provides the whole community with valuable services that do not deplete natural wealth, then what you're doing is likely to be both profitable and sustainable over the long term. The same criteria apply to regulations and taxes.

Conversely, we should also be more aware of what produces double indemnities in our normal, everyday practices. For example, in the United States, the social security tax payments that a company had to make per worker increased by an incredible 1,325 percent in the twenty years between 1970 and 1992. Those were also the years in which "downsizing" became more and more attractive to businesses. It's hard to blame them; each and every employee was getting more expensive. Almost 13 percent of an employee's earnings have to be paid by the company in taxes, over and above other taxes and expenses they have. So proponents of green taxes have introduced double dividends into payroll taxes. For every percent that a factory is taxed for its carbon emissions, for example, that factory will have to pay 1 percent less tax for its employees. The workers will still get their full benefits because the government will still be collecting taxes. The factory will be motivated not to fire more people, but to cut down on emissions. Such double-dividend taxes are already in force in Germany, Spain and nine other European countries. Spain's new gasoline tax yields an extra $10 billion, which the country uses to offset the loss from cutting social insurance tax rates on employers and employees. It's another clear double dividend. In Germany, almost 1 percent of social insurance payments are now being offset by carbon taxes; and Germany is simply joining countries like Holland, Norway, Denmark, Belgium, Switzerland and Sweden, which already have similar taxes in effect. The UK is in the process of joining the green tax club.

Of course, taxes on gasoline, especially in North America, are very regressive. That means they penalize the poor more than the rich, because here private cars are often necessities. People have to get to work, however poor they are; they have to buy groceries or take the kids to school, and public transport is virtually nonexistent in much of North America, especially in rural and suburban areas. If people are really poor, giving them payroll or income tax breaks won't help much, since they make so little income. The way around that, says Kai Schlegelmilch, a specialist on green taxes who works for the German federal government, is to provide gas tax rebates to people under a certain income. Even better, they should be given rebates on more fuel-efficient vehicles as well. The money that is gained from the richer drivers should go into helping the poorer ones during this transition period and also into establishing long-term solutions like train, bus and trolley services. The uncomfortable but highly efficient jitney services that are found in the Third World — small trucks or buses that load up on passengers and ferry them from town to town — could also be adapted to North American use, to help bridge the gap. Ultimately, if towns, cities and suburbs are designed so that people can walk to buy their groceries, do their laundry and run their errands, they will. Such an inspiration might also result in the bonus dividend of getting the population's weight down and improving general health. As for picking up larger items, reinstating the old system of home delivery would put a few commercial trucks on the road instead of thousands of personal cars, and give people some welcome time away from the malls and the highways. So double dividend taxes can work for the poor, even in places that are inhospitable to anything but car travel.

The more subtle and less discernible dividends of other kinds of taxes can also help us determine whether they fit a model of sustainability. Over twelve years ago, for example, Italy introduced a tax on plastic bags. As in many southern countries with poor garbage collection facilities (good ones often just mean that municipalities are better at hiding the mess in one place), Italians found their beaches and beautiful monuments fouled by plastic bags, and were worried about sea life choking on them as well. They realized that there is a cost associated with plastic bags that is not reflected in their price. The cost of disposing of a non-disposable item had been imposed by the manufacturers onto society and nature. So now, anyone in Italy who wants a plastic bag has to pay an extra six cents for it, about five times its manufacturing cost. This means that canvas and woven fiber bags, which were common before plastic was introduced, have once again become competitive. This is another double-dividend tax, because it's simple, easy to collect (it brought the government an extra $150 million in its first three years), and existing businesses making permanent string and mesh bags are given a level playing field again, so they can make a living. Italy's tax removes an anti-environmental distortion from the economy. Had they chosen to offset it by removing some other burdensome, distortionary tax, like the payroll or building taxes discussed above, the advantages to society would have tripled or quadrupled.

Obviously, if we taxed corporations like Monsanto, Dow, Shell Oil and many others in proportion to what their chemical dumping practices alone have cost society, they would find it a lot harder to make a profit, and they would have a strong incentive to cut down their emissions.[25] And that's what the movement toward double dividends is all about: genuinely good economics, in which subsidies do not enable otherwise unprofitable, unsustainable industries to stay afloat. One way to judge the viability of any industry is to imagine if it could be profitable if governments were to remove all subsidies and favoritism of any kind. Could the largest number of people make a decent living over the long term in the logging industry, for example, by using selective cutting and sustainable forestry, or by putting in miles of roads and using huge machines to clearcut? With no tax help at all, would farmers still be spraying genetically altered corn with pesticides and raising hormone-laced pigs in crowded sheds, or would they pasture the pigs and keep away from pest-attracting monocultures? If economic activities can survive unaided, even just barely, then it's obvious their technology might be sustainable; and most of the sustainable businesses we have discussed in this book have been forced by the current industrial paradigm to do just that. At the moment, however, most of our society's perverse subsidies and taxes are still in place. Until double-dividend taxes are more widespread, the only way new technologies like solar or wind power can really get going is if they, too, get a level playing field; we gradually offer them their own subsidies as we remove support from their non-sustainable competitors. And then, when things are more or less equal, we see which methodology really produces jobs, security and social stability, over the long term.

## Sunny California

*The shenanigans of these companies have strengthened the hands of those who clamor for public power.*
— RACHEL BRAHINSKY, *SAN FRANCISCO BAY CHRONICLE*[26]

The rolling brownouts and skyrocketing energy prices that plagued California after the deregulation of their energy sector have left many people totally confused. In Europe, the deregulation of centralized utilities has given small environmental start-ups in wind and solar energy a chance to enter the grid. Why didn't that happen in California? Because California got a different kind of deregulation. As we saw in the chapter about water, when society permits large, for-profit, privately run corporations to take control of resources that are considered necessities, what nearly always ensues is a loss of services and a vast increase in prices. The energy revolution in California unfolded much like the private water-utility takeovers we looked at in Grenoble and England.[27]

Whereas much of the legislation in Europe protected small and medium-sized providers, in California a handful of very large corporations took control of both the delivery and the production of energy in much of the state. They split the business into two sectors: one group generated power; the other bought and delivered it. This consolidated the generation of power, pushing small and medium-sized utilities, especially green ones like solar and wind, out of business. And then, of course, the price of electricity went up. That meant that the companies that bought and delivered the power lost huge amounts of money. They began crying for state relief, as well as increasing charges. Two of the utilities, Southern California Edison and Pacific Gas and Electric (PG&E) — the same company made infamous by the film *Erin Brockovich* — claimed a combined debt of $12 billion. The twist, as Rachel Brahinsky, a reporter for the *San Francisco*

*Chronicle* puts it, is that both "have affiliate companies in both lines of work . . . so when the generators charged too much, they were essentially overcharging themselves. As a result, while one arm of each corporation suffered, another posted record profits. PG&E and Edison's parent companies have spent some $22 billion on new powerplants, stock buybacks and other purchases that far exceed their alleged $12 billion."[28]

It sounds rather like what happened with the water utility in Grenoble, and indeed, that's the way people are taking it. PG&E and Edison have been the object of protests across the state; consumers are demanding a return to public control of power production and supply with no bailouts for the big private utilities. What's interesting is that the models they want to emulate are still humming along, right there in California. Sacramento has a public utility; their monthly rates averaged $20 per subscriber less than those of PG&E did, and unlike the privates, they don't labor under a disincentive for conservation. Since public utilities don't show a profit anyway and don't have demanding shareholders, they don't mind if their customers use less electricity. In fact, utilities like Sacramento's promote conservation by, for example, giving away free shade trees to reduce air-conditioner use. When the citizens of Sacramento voted to shut down their nuclear power plant, the municipal utility turned to renewables, installing active solar generators on the top of city carport roofs to help make up the deficit. While the rest of the state was reeling from blackouts and price hikes, the Los Angeles Department of Water and Power, California's largest public utility, was able to protect its subscribers; and their bills averaged $50 a month, as compared to deregulated ones, which had shot up to as much as $138.

In 1996, as the deregulation bill was going for approval, energy expert Daniel M. Berman, co-author of *Who Owns the Sun?*, predicted what would happen.[29] He said that big industry would "come weeping to the public, as the savings and loan investors did," and that there would be a "massive ratepayers' revolt." When his prediction came true, he suggested that the state create, "an excess profits tax to get back the extorted revenues," and, most important of all, that it "ban utility money from any sort of politics." While they're at it, they should create new public power districts, set aside 5 percent of electric revenues for conservation, and in sunny California, mandate solar panels for all new buildings. There's a new activist coalition in California called PublicPowerNow that is calling for just that. It's not coincidence that the way that privately owned power gouged its consumers in California is so similar to what happened with water in Bolivia and Grenoble.

Whatever their faults, public utilities are by definition controllable by the public; and private ones have the overwhelming mandate to deliver profits. Add to that simple fact their records of political manipulation, fraud and lack of effort toward resource conservation and wise use, and it becomes clear that if we want a sustainable future, the *way* we manage our resources is just as important as our efforts to conserve them.

## The Power of Obstinacy

*This is what you do instead of gardening or cooking. My husband and I do this together. I'm the one for catastrophes; that makes me strong. He gets discouraged. But he's got the stamina.*
— URSULA SLADEK, THE SCHÖENAU ELECTRICITY CO-OP

In Germany, there are more than 900 utilities providing many kinds of power. Most of them are public, but some are large, private corporations. The country has been deregulated for some time. An essential aspect of the type of system they have developed is that a multitude of different utilities are allowed to sell their power to a central grid. That means that a small solar or wind company can sell anything it generates and use the money to expand. Therefore, in theory, renewable, "green" energy can gradually take over the grid. Nevertheless, in a tiny, picturesque village in Germany's Black Forest, a dedicated group of residents had to go through all the hoops that the average Canadian or American town with regulated, state power would have to deal with, in order to make their own energy revolution possible. It wasn't easy, but their fifteen-year saga is a quite amazing story of community, creativity and pure obstinacy.

Back in 1986, a group of ten parents in Schöenau, a little town of 2,500 souls, had become so alarmed by the events at Chernobyl that they decided, for the sake of their children, to do something to lessen their own, and eventually Germany's, dependence on nuclear power. So, they gave little courses on energy-saving techniques. One of the founders, Ursula Sladek, a mother of five in her late forties with very pink cheeks and dancing, crescent-shaped eyes, says they taught "simple things, like using a pot with a flat bottom to cook with, keeping it covered, doing the laundry only when the machine is really full, and other things like that." Then they started giving prizes for locals who achieved energy savings — half-price train tickets, coupons for department stores, a grand prize of a trip to Italy. In a very short time, a large proportion of the village was saving up to 50 percent of their electricity, and, says Ursula, "since there was no loss in their quality of life, we got more converts." But then they realized that their great strides in energy conservation weren't being matched by significantly lower bills, because, under a system similar to Canada's, they paid a base rate, which meant that conservation wasn't rewarded. The pricing system was set up to provide cheaper rates to big users and higher rates to small users, the opposite of a strategy to encourage conservation.

So Schöenau's activists began to demand a linear rate; the more you use, the more you pay. And in the meantime, they investigated cogeneration. Electrical generators, whether powered by gas, oil, nuclear or coal, create heat as a by-product. Ursula says, "we realized that with the heat our utilities throw away, we could heat all our houses and industries!" Cogeneration technologies are essentially little boxes that sit next to generators and capture their heat, which they then feed into a building or a town's heat supply. Although few Canadians or Americans have seen one, Germany is awash in cogenerators, usually sitting next to natural-gas-fired electrical generators. They're becoming extremely common in hotels, homes, bars, schools and government offices, and they eliminate one of the two usual energy-burning engines, one creating light and one for heat. Encouraged by the possibilities of expanding such technologies, thirty-one of the Schöenau energy activists decided to create their own utility, to produce renewable power. "It only took $1,000 each," says Ursula. "Money is never a problem, because if your idea is good, you'll find donors." They tracked down several closed small hydro power plants on nearby rivers and streams and leased them; they financed new cogenerators; and they got involved in the political process, so they could do something about getting their power onto the grid.

Like many towns in Germany, Schöenau had an energy contract with one utility — in this case a private one that had a monopoly in the area — and whose contact was coming up for renegotiation. The utility, called KWR, offered to award the town 100,000 DM for signing a new twenty-year concession, and naturally the town councilors were tempted to accept. So right away, the energy activists had to rush out and raise that amount themselves to match the utility's offer, so they wouldn't lose another twenty years of control over their energy supply. Ursula is a teacher, and her husband, Michael, a big man with a beard, a booming voice and the demeanor of a friendly bear, is the town's beloved doctor. Together with the other activists, they got to work and learned a great deal about electricity, putting together a 400-page study. Their Schöenau electricity cooperative, ESG (short for Elektrizitätswerk Schöenau GmbH) was immediately put to the test; they had to win a town referendum on where power would come from: the safe, reliable, but nuclear and oil-powered utility, or the untested, unprofessional but clean co-op. The co-op somehow won, much to the shock of the town councilors. But the co-op members then discovered that even though they could now supply clean electricity to feed into the utility's grid, they had to pay for the right to use KWR's delivery system: the wires, transformers and so forth. They did a study and determined that they would need a staggering 4 million DM to pay for it. They raised it by going door to door. "Old people would save 30 marks a year, then give us 100!" says Ursula Sladek. The local Protestant minister gave them his entire inheritance of 200,000 marks. And eventually, they got half: 2 million DM.

At that point, the GLS Bank, profiled in chapter one, knocked on their door. They started a Schöenau energy fund and gathered investors. The media had picked up the story, and little Schöenau became a national sensation. KWR, the private utility, was getting irritated, and said the co-op's study was all wrong: they needed 8.7 million DM to buy their services, "which would have been the highest price paid for a grid in all of German history!" says Ursula Sladek. She says that KWR's charges for cables, poles, transformers and other materials where higher than industry standards. This spooked the town council into calling a second referendum, "which was very hard," she says, because now the utility took them seriously, peppering the citizens with a blizzard of flyers and advertisements threatening power outages and poor delivery. They even claimed the green technology being offered by ESG wasn't clean. "Who do people believe?" Ursula asks. "All we had was going door to door on a very personal level. We were saying things like, 'I live here. My husband is the doctor. My children go to school here. If we're wrong, we'll all have to leave.'" Of course, there was gossip, intrigue, exhaustion — "six weeks of four to five hours of sleep a night," she says.

On referendum day, 85 percent of the voters turned out and gave the co-op a narrow 5 percent victory. But even then, the state ministry refused to reduce KWR's high delivery price. Ursula had an inspiration. She says, "I thought, there are at least a million opponents of nuclear power in Germany; if each one sent 5 marks, we'd have our 8.7 million!" Soon a national campaign was raging; one of the biggest PR companies in Germany offered Schöenau their services, for free. The GLS Bank got back to work. When the utility realized ESG would have the money to go to court, they panicked. They dropped their price to 6.5 million; by then, Schöenau had that much and more. And so, four years ago, the green co-op took over their own power supply. "We've had no shortages," say the Sladeks proudly. "Prices did not rise. Our cogenerators did not pollute." These days, nearly every person in the village is solidly behind them. The town's only factory and its largest employer, which recycles plastic and uses a good deal of electricity "was very afraid and against us before," says Ursula. But a year after they took over, she heard the owner interviewed on the radio, saying, "Everything is great! I'm content."

And once ESG was in charge of the village's power grid, what did they do? They changed the fees paid for cogenerating power. "We pay people more for doing that, so that they can make money," says Ursula. "If you want to change technology on a large scale, and you want that change to spread, you have to pay attractive rates for it." It's against the interest of large utilities, with investments in water, telecommunications and so forth, to encourage cogeneration, because they lose power that they could sell. In a scenario that should be becoming familiar by now, only the small, local, non-profit utilities have the right kind of incentives to conserve the resource. Today, the village has the highest amount of solar power of any town in the country. And best of all, they're off the nuclear grid. They even got an award for it, 18,000 DM that they're using to put solar panels on the school. And besides the 20 percent they produce on their own, they can buy from other clean co-ops in the country, or even from Austria. "We have an actual free market choice!" say the Sladeks. And then they got another idea.

ESG has now become middle-marketers for people all over Germany, finding them clean power at a good price. "We are known, people come to us, and we don't need any money to do this service," says Ursula. Indeed, ESG's fees for providing power are used simply to run their office, invest in wind and solar initiatives, and pay their ten employees, nine of whom are locals. They still depend on volunteers to stuff envelopes and help with their periodic celebrations and parties. Their 20,000 clients make this little village co-op the second-largest supplier of ecological energy in Germany. "If you compare our power grid to a lake," says Ursula Sladek, "all the energy flows in from two sources: one clean, one dirty. But gradually, we're decreasing the dirty water. The lake is getting cleaner."

We can all make the air, the water — and the earth — cleaner. We just have to get involved with one of the many organizations lobbying for energy change. The odd lesson of green energy is that you can have your cake and eat it too. Until recently, we've chosen the most damaging and primitive energy sources that exist. But there are many, many more — too many to even deal with in this chapter: tidal force, geothermal, hydrogen and plain old conservation. The damage wrestling with Pluto has done to our planet, and continues to do, sometimes beggars the imagination; we can't afford to let it chill our spirits. We have to call it quits, and leave Pluto and his hoard of underworld treasure alone.

# CHAPTER 9

# BREAKING OUT OF THE BOX
## New Ways to Think and to Learn

### When the Bullet Hits the Bone

*We were not suddenly captured by hunters and imprisoned in a room or a zoo, but over a period of several generations, our species has suffered a similar fate.*
— JERRY MANDER, INTERNATIONAL FORUM ON GLOBALIZATION[1]

Jerry Mander, the ex-ad man who wrote the seminal best-seller *Four Arguments for the Elimination of Television*, uses a story about a scientific experiment as a metaphor for the kind of life the First Industrial Revolution has brought us. Back in the 1970s, a team of scientists isolated several chimpanzees, one to a room, and taught them to communicate by means of buttons inscribed with symbols. If they wanted a banana, they pushed a button with a banana symbol on it, and one came down a chute. They could satisfy other needs in the same way; they could get water or changes in lighting, and there was even a button for physical affection. "When the chimp pushed it, a scientist would enter the room, hug and play with the chimp for a time, then go back out the door." Mander says that the chimpanzees' entire world was reduced to what they could ask for through the buttons, and was also limited by cost factors and what the scientists had thought to provide. The scientists had not, for example, attempted to duplicate the kinds of experiences the chimps had enjoyed in the forests in which they had evolved. There were twelve buttons in all.

The purpose of the experiment was to find out whether the animal would notice when the experimenters switched a symbol from one button to another, and would read the repositioned symbol correctly and request bananas not from button three, but from button ten. The chimps' almost immediate ability to do this was hailed as a scientific breakthrough, showing that these animals can understand and exploit abstractions, and can go through the same kinds of associative, symbolic mental processes that humans do. Mander has a different interpretation: "To me . . . the experiment only meant that the chimp in the lab was undergoing an accelerated version of human history . . . It meant that chimpanzees, like any other confined animals, will do whatever is necessary to survive and will make the best of a bad situation that is totally out of their control."[2] He goes on to note that when an animal, especially a higher mammal, is taken from its natural habitat and placed in an artificially rearranged world where its ordinary techniques for survival and satisfaction can no longer operate, it first of all becomes dependent on whoever controls the new environment, and "it will use its intelligence to learn whatever new tricks are necessary to fit that system." It will also become focused on, and even addicted to, the few experiences that remain available. Finally, it will reduce its mental and physical expectations to fit whatever it can actually get.

Mander's implied analogy between chimps in a lab and humans in modern society is, of course, far from exact, but it provides a useful perspective. We humans have also been removed from the three-dimensional natural surroundings in which we evolved — a complex environment that required us to regularly use all our musculature and all five of our senses. We now interact largely with manufactured commercial goods like books, papers, television and computer screens, which typically employ only two dimensions. We can operate them with no more than two of our senses and very few of our muscles. In fact, we are functioning in contexts as different from our evolutionary surroundings as that small room was to the experimental chimp, and, as with the chimp, human culture rather than nature is providing us with the limited choices we are typically given in our day-to-day lives.

Mander contrasts this environment with the conditions under which we humans evolved and survived for most of our several hundred thousand years on the planet. We then had to be constantly attuned to every change and detail in the activities and reactions of all the other life forms around us, and all the information brought to us by all five of our senses was essential to our survival.[3] A change in the behavior of the animals around us or "in wind or scent would arrive in everyone's awareness as a bucket of cold water thrown on the head might today arrive in ours," says Mander. But the talents that were so vital then are useless and even counterproductive in our busy lives today. If we could, as Mander says, identify fifty-six varieties of snowflakes, or hundreds of dream patterns or different altitude strata of flying insects, as various traditional peoples can or could until recently, it would do very little to help us get along in the modern world. "We have had to re-create ourselves to fit," Mander says. "We have had to reshape our very personalities to be competitive, aggressive, mentally fast, charming and manipulative. These qualities [are the ones that] succeed in today's world and offer survival and some measure of satisfaction within the cycle of work-consume, work-consume, work-consume."[4]

Mander also rather playfully compares our modern business and corporate offices to the chimps' little rooms; they at first seem soothing and unthreatening, but they are so featureless and disconnected that people eventually accept any kind of stimulus as a relief from their increasing feelings of alienation and lack of context. Although Mander admits it would be going too far to say that modern office buildings are sensory-deprivation tanks, "the elimination of sensory stimuli definitely increases focus on the task at hand, the work to be done, to the exclusion of all else. Modern offices were designed for that very purpose by people who knew what they were doing."[5] With the field of experience for office workers so drastically reduced, he says, "the stimuli which remain — paper work, mental work, business — loom larger and obtain an importance they would not have in a wider, more varied, more stimulating environment. The worker [like the chimp,] gets interested in them largely because that is what is available to get interested in." And of course, the worker has no real input into what is available for his interest; that is determined by others. Because this artificial environment is so unnatural and constrained, normal emotions and values that have been repressed often surface as aberrations, "like blades of grass popping up through a pavement" — the common office phenomena of fierce competitive drive, rage at small inconveniences, sexual escapades and intrigues over minor promotions or the number of windows in each office.

These observations are taken from a book written over twenty years ago, but they remain an apt description of the cubicle world of the office, satirized by *Dilbert* cartoons in the daily newspaper. Our world of business cubicles and high-rise apartment buildings is not so different from the little rooms in which the chimps had to live. It can often feel nearly as restricted, arbitrary, confining and sad. But we tolerate it because we keep getting bananas, and even some hugs. The thing is, we would probably all like a good deal more. What we'd like is to keep the bananas, the safety, the care — but also get out of that box. This may not be an impossible dream.

## Learning to Cut Through Barbed Wire

*The man who would exchange liberty for security deserves neither liberty nor security.*
— BENJAMIN FRANKLIN

By coming out of our "natural" habitat and learning to live as we do today, human beings have accomplished incredible things. We have greatly reduced the terrors of infectious diseases, and endemic warfare now affects only a fraction of the people it used to. It has been beaten back to a few areas on the globe, one of the reasons why the attack on the World Trade Center was so shocking, and continuing talk of war in Asia and the Middle East so destabilizing. In general, very large numbers of us have become accustomed to living out our lives in conditions of peace, food security and everyday comfort.

That doesn't mean, however, that even the most lucky among us have not lost many important components of life. Besides the decline of all the natural resources that are our lifeline to the future, many of us are worrying about the erosion of our communities, our sense of place and identity, as well as the steady loss of values that go beyond the material and lead to spiritual and emotional fulfillment. Too many of us feel like cogs in an enormous, cold machine, or like chimpanzees locked up in a box. When we raise these caveats, however, we are made to feel that we have no choice: it's all one, or all the other. Should we pause even momentarily in our search for greater material wealth and the support of continuous economic expansion, we're told we would soon find ourselves engulfed by war or dying of cholera.

Back in chapter one we met an idealistic couple, Dick and Jeanne Roy, who live by their environmental precepts and spend their time as "volunteers for the earth," trying to help as many people as possible in their search for sustainable, equitable and even joyful ways of living. They, and millions like them, do not believe that there are only two choices in life, and they feel that the one our society has made — modern, industrial, urban living — is too rigid and limited in the options it presents to us, especially in terms of how we make our livings and spend most of our time. They think it deprives us of the natural freedom we need in order to realize our individual goals in life. They feel that, in order to access the universal values of sharing and conservation, we need to stop emphasizing one value — material comfort — above all others. And they also feel that breaking out of the First Industrial Revolution box will not necessarily cause our doom.

Dick Roy says that, especially at times like these when people feel threatened by war or terrorism, they start to lose sight of their real values and to opt for safety above all things. He says, "The core of what we're trying to do in our courses, in our approach, is to help people align their conduct with a sense of their own highest purpose, no matter how difficult the situation." The question then becomes one of quality rather than quantity of life. Are we giving up the right to live life the way we would individually want, in exchange for much less fulfilling lives that may merely last a little longer? We also have to remember that the authorities who are in charge of keeping us in boxes and providing us with buttons to push may have a definition of freedom and happiness that doesn't coincide with our personal or local values. "The consumer society's overemphasis on economic and material goods," Roy says, "simply tries to take away a person's sense of purpose and instill [its own]. Modern society constantly tries to convince you that you have to buy to have a good life, that you should be spending dollars, and that you must stop thinking about things that don't have a commercial or money connection." He says we all need to learn how to "detach from all that; each of us has to figure out what our deepest, individual purpose really is."

The people and organizations we've been meeting in this book have broken out of the boxes designed by modern society to restrict human choices to whatever "the economy" may want or need. They've discovered their purpose, and are trying to make their innermost values a reality. Their goals are simple and straightforward: a respect for the natural systems that support us; the conservation of our resources; a wiser method of managing our local economies; and, especially, an ethic of sharing the world's goods in an equitable way. Diversified life goals of this nature would do more than simply reduce our personal, existential distress. They would probably protect all of us from hatred and terror more than any number of soldiers abroad or police at home brandishing high-tech devices for identification and control.

For example, it's interesting to speculate that Americans and the allied West in general would not have been a destabilizing military presence in Saudi Arabia or the Persian Gulf in the first place if the First World had taken the hint from the oil crisis back in the seventies and had diversified into solar, wind and other renewables. Every country would have its own sources of energy by now, and no one would have to fight for their share of a diminishing resource, co-opt governments in order to ensure supply, or destroy pristine wilderness in order to keep industry going. If the West hadn't heeded the siren call of material wealth and ever-increasing GDP, if we had a much stronger ethic of sharing and conserving, we might also be in a position to call ourselves a "free" society worth emulating. Activist Jaggi Singh, who we met back in chapter one, points out that "There's a huge difference between a society based on McDonald's and Coke and [one] that's solving the problems of polio, tuberculosis or tooth decay. Just because we don't want the first doesn't mean we don't want or can't figure out a way to continue to have the second!"

In Dick Roy's view, consumer culture masks a value system of selfishness that places our greed for individual comfort above any concept of community. "We live in a society that really can be related to prisons and boxes, even concentration camps. In our constant pursuit of wealth, it continuously challenges our inner moral purpose, it tries to force us to do things we know are wrong. [This means that] our dominant culture is abhorrent to many people on a deep, interior level. It encourages and rewards the best and brightest among us for doing things that they know are morally wrong, and this erodes their souls. The values of the economy become their only goals, their life's purpose. Their individual gifts and idealism are replaced by the corporate economy's needs and demands, and that is authenticated by their apparent material success. But they feel as if they have been taken over, and they have. It's the values of the corporate economy, not their own, that they're living for."

Roy sees his courses and methods of discussion as a way of "releasing people's individual energy, in order that they can become leaders for a change." He likes to use the example of the tobacco companies to illustrate his point. He spent thirty years as a successful corporate lawyer, so he knows what he's talking about when he says, "There is no other way for a publicly traded corporation, or even most private businesses, to survive in our current system, except this unnatural, unending growth." And when there are no alternatives in life, the nicest individuals become like the Capos, the prisoners selected for special favors in exchange for helping the SS guards in the Nazi death camps, or like the executives of the tobacco companies who, as Roy says, "hide facts, deny science and continue to push poisonous addictive substances to children, even though they know they can kill." Like the chimps in the little room, people caught in the modern business bind decide that their survival requires that they learn to push the right buttons, even buttons that downsize thousands of jobs and destroy once-thriving communities; buttons that continue to pump out dangerous substances from under the earth's crust; and buttons that require that basic science is ignored or co-opted to make sure that profits remain the one and only positive value. They do this not because they are bad people, but because they feel they have no choice. They don't have access to any other buttons.

There is a way out, however. Roy reminds us that "these corporate values that place material wealth at the pinnacle of human desire were introduced into our culture; they're not some instinct, some planetary 'given,' and they can progress to something else, in the same way. The early corporate powers back in the eighteenth century introduced the idea of ever-increasing wealth as the primary directive, and people, by and large, voluntarily accepted that ethic because they believed it would help everyone over the long term. We're trying to do the opposite, to create, individual by individual, voluntary communities with a sustainable sense of purpose, and a sense of human and environmental values." This is far from being an unattainable goal, especially now that the First World has so many reasons to rethink its underlying value system.

Roy also points out that not everyone has to become an advocate for the earth for things to change. What he and Jeanne and so many others are working to achieve is not as daunting as it may first appear; he notes that historically, only 10 or 15 percent of the human population has had to actively embrace new ideas for the world's culture to change, radically and very rapidly. And, as we have seen in this book, that's exactly what's happening, although not a moment too soon.

## Weavers of the Web

*This web must include strands connecting the youth to the elders, native to non-native, local indigenous people to international native cultures, and to the world beyond.*
— MEANING OF THE TSILHQOT'IN WORD "INTELILUYNI"[6]

Although the Roys' Northwest Earth Institute has chapters using their techniques to encourage sustainability in more than forty states, they don't extend all over the world. And yet, people and communities elsewhere are finding remarkably similar methodologies to get in touch with their individual and local core values. They want to build around these and not around values imposed by external models, like the cars and malls of the First World or the rigid religious or social mandates of oppressive regimes elsewhere.

In chapter six, "Listen for the Jaguar," we described how a coalition of native groups and environmentalists eventually got real policy changes on the provincial level to protect their forests. But when the David Suzuki Foundation (DSF) began reaching out to work with coastal communities in 1997, it quickly became apparent that the first thing they had to learn was how to stop trying to "help" and how to start listening. As we have seen, communities really are the experts on their own issues, and these ones in particular held strong beliefs that outside help would only be useful if it could support them in finding their own internal solutions.

The Suzuki Foundation had learned about a process called Participatory Action Research (PAR), developed by the Arctic Institute of North America in Calgary. Just like the Roys' methods and Allan Savory's holistic management techniques, PAR begins with the conviction that every community has its own values and talents. The challenge is to help the community articulate them and create a vision that will support their goals with their own untapped skills. If a community is open to such an approach, a person trained in these techniques can join it, not just to teach some courses, but to actually live in that place for at least three years, to help find their strengths and weaknesses.

The Xenigwet'in, a small Tsilhqot'in (Chilcotin) First Nations community in the remote Nemiah valley of southwestern British Columbia, were facing the problem of short-term logging jobs destroying their territory. When they heard that the Suzuki Foundation was interested in developing a joint project, they met together to undertake a road-mapping process, sometimes called a SWOT inventory (Strengths, Weaknesses, Opportunities and Threats), and asked basic questions designed to reach beyond the usual methods of community and management. They asked themselves: What do we want our community to be like in the next ten, fifteen, twenty years? Do we want to be employees or entrepreneurs? Is money the only answer, an end goal, or just a means to an end? Whichever way, what are we willing to exchange to get it? And what are we not willing to exchange?

Asking the right questions helped the Xeni community realize that if they could capitalize on the carving, baking, sewing and fishing skills of individual community members, the jobs they could create might eventually have enough impact that they wouldn't have to sacrifice the long-term health of their territory to the previously preceived "only" economic choice: logging. PAR facilitator Roberta Martell, also a DSF staff member, then arrived in Nemiah. She found a very isolated inland village, with no faxes or e-mail and only one radio phone line in and out of the band office. She helped establish a committee of four local women, Maryann Solomon, Francy Merritt, Bonnie Myers and Crystal William, who called themselves the Inteliluyni Team, the "Weavers of the Web." Their job was to try to figure out how the community's values could support them economically.

The Inteliluyni Team realized that before job creation could take place they needed an infrastructure for communications and power. So they helped bring a wireless phone system into the valley, got funding for seven computers, and built an internet café. They managed to get funding for a study of the feasibility of clean, alternate energy in Nemiah — micro-hydro, wind and solar — and met with Ballard Power to discuss installing fuel cells to harness the plentiful wind power available in the area. The team helped create two community gardens to curb the outflow of local cash for vegetables coming from hundreds of miles away. And they built a laundromat to save people the six-hour round trip over rough roads to Williams Lake. They even designed and built two straw bale houses, proving that the community could build comfortable housing with sustainable materials and local skills on a formerly inadequate budget of less than $30,000.

Since Tsilhqot'in culture is built around horses, the Community Economic Development Committee, which works closely with the Inteliluyni team, decided to organize trail rides for tourists. Horses that people already owned were enlisted to provide a livelihood for the locals and fun for outsiders, who were taken fishing, bird-watching and up to formerly inaccessible hiking spots. The Xenigwet'in are also exploring the sustainable harvesting of non-timber forest products — flowers, berries and so on — as a way of protecting their territory and providing income for their members. They're even building a traditional village, with careful input from the elders. Today, the energy, initiative and inspiration in this community are democratic and consensus-based. And maybe most significant of all, the people learning to build their own houses, grow their own fresh vegetables, sell their crafts and pies and take tourists on trail rides through their beloved forests, are enjoying life, and having a lot of fun.

The Xeni of the Nemiah valley are very aware that their struggle is symbolic of changing values around the world. Roberta Martell, who has now left a community well able to continue putting its agreed-upon values to work, says, "Why would anyone want to traditionally 'develop' this place? We'd be chasing the tail of a paradigm which thankfully is on its way out — the belief that we must have money at all costs, or that it's normal to live beyond our means. The Xeni have something money could never replace: a pristine home that can provide for nearly all of their needs, a sense of place — and a real future."

## Life's Expectations

*What is the good life? The good life is to be a good neighbor,*
*to consider your neighbor as yourself.*
— K. VISHWANATHAN, KERALA, INDIA[7]

There is one environmental problem most people can agree on; there are getting to be too many of us. For most of human existence, having children was necessary, to perpetuate our families and to ensure support for our old age. We are also physically programmed to enjoy reproduction, and most of us do find greeting the tiny, crumpled faces that come along to revitalize our families one of life's greatest rewards. But we now know that if we are to have any kind of a future to offer our new arrivals, we need to control two basic decisions: how big our families get, and how much and what kinds of things they can consume from the finite amount of resources still available on this planet. For most of the twentieth century, we believed that the way to achieve lower birth rates and stable social systems was to increase general prosperity. But if that approach seemed to solve the problem of our numbers, it merely adds to ecological degradation; because as we get richer, we accelerate our consumption of the world's resources, as well as the pollution that consumption causes. Twenty percent of the richest people on this planet, living largely in North America and Europe, are currently consuming 80 percent of all its goods, food, water, metals and fuel production, and there is little sign yet of that imbalance being reduced.

Decades of population studies have shown that people with greater income security have fewer children. FAO and UN demographic studies in the 1980s revealed something else, however: the higher the educational level and social status of women in a society, the fewer the children. This reverse correlation seemed to hold true across economic, cultural and religious barriers. So social services worldwide were mobilized in the 1980s and 1990s, not to increase male incomes, forcibly sterilize people as in India in the 1970s, or even spread large amounts of birth control paraphernalia around. Instead, efforts focused on getting little girls into school and on encouraging more female autonomy in terms of the rights to inherit or to work outside the home. Medical clinics that help children survive the first years of childhood were also discovered to have a high correlation with smaller families; women were having extra babies just to make sure that two or three would reach adulthood and be able to help take care of them. Accordingly, clinics for children under five were established in many of the world's poorest countries. These efforts have borne fruit, and female enrolment in primary school worldwide has jumped from 39 percent in 1980 to 57 percent in 1993, although in some countries it has dropped somewhat since, because IMF structural adjustment policies have forced countries like Tanzania to cut back on their health clinics and planned parenthood programs, as well as their schools.[8] Best of all, reproduction levels, as expected, are falling all over the world.

Even though this method is so successful, raising the status of females is not easy. In most of the developing world, boys are valued more than girls for long-standing cultural and economic reasons. In Moslem countries, boys traditionally look after their own parents and girls look after their husbands'; so a couple with no sons will be in serious trouble. Also, all across India and in many African countries as well, girls cannot be married without a dowry, which typically represents several years' income for the parents. Having more than one or two daughters can condemn an entire family to poverty; and if there are no sons, a couple will never have any return on their dowry investment. In the central Indian city of Bombay, for example, of 8,000 abortions performed at one clinic in 1990, all but one were female fetuses. And yet there are exceptions to the rule of undervaluing females, even in Hindu and Moslem countries. In the southern Indian state of Kerala, which is both Hindu and Moslem, the average number of women in the population is 1,036 to 1,000 males, approximately the First World average, and women have the longer life expectancies typical of the First World as well, proof that they are welcomed into their families, and are properly fed and cared for. But then, Kerala is a special place for many reasons.

In Kerala, although the per capita income is estimated at being between $298 and $350 (U.S.) a year (one seventieth the American average and lower than that of Cambodia or the Sudan), even the men can expect to live to be seventy, only two years less than the average North American male. Kerala has a 90-percent literacy rate (one of the highest on earth), affordable health care and birth control, an equitable land tenure system, free school lunches, subsidized foods and goods for the poor, and a child mortality rate that is less than half of the rest of India's. Perhaps most important of all, Kerala's fertility rate is just under 1.7 births per woman, lower than Sweden's and much lower than that of the United States, which at 2.3 is the highest in the industrialized world.[9] As Will Alexander of the Food First! Institute in San Francisco puts it, Kerala is a beacon for the world. It is "the one, single large human population on earth that currently meets the sustainability criteria of simultaneous small families and low consumption."

Kerala has a long history of proud, independent people and enlightened rulers. Unlike most of India, it also has water — rivers, streams, swamps and waterfalls — as well as the most biologically diverse mountains and forests in India, the Western Ghats. Although its religious community is 20 percent Christian added onto the often difficult mix of Hindu and Moslem, Kerala has managed to avoid bigger confrontations than the occasional bad-tempered clash, and is also more free of the caste system than any other place in the Hindu world. The state has a three-party political system; their communist party, the Left Democratic Front, takes turns with more moderate groups, generally holding power for only three or four years at a time. This means that one of Kerala's claims to fame is the fact that it has the first elected (and re-elected) communist government in the world. It is important to emphasize that its real political energy comes from thousands of community activist groups, organized around everything from trade unions and religious practices to sports enthusiasms and sewing circles.

It was this vast army of grassroots activists, rather than the government, that managed to boost the literacy rate to present levels. In a fascinating example of how active communities can change a society, the citizens of Kerala deployed more than 350,000 village-based volunteers to seek out the illiterate wherever they were, even providing them with donated eyeglasses. These volunteers worked until people could read at thirty words a minute, copy a text, add and subtract three-digit numbers, and multiply and divide two-digit numbers. The lessons were successful largely because they were centered around fun: village parades, songs, street theater and contests, festivals and sing-alongs. Similar campaigns for more equality for women and for every level of the caste society used the same methods of community participation, as well as billboards, school programs, newspaper articles and government policy changes. The social campaigns we see in the First World to encourage exercise or volunteer work need tax money to get off the ground, but in Kerala, there's so much voluntary citizen participation — and things are so cheap in general — that the literacy program is estimated to have cost only about $26 per person.[10]

Kerala has achieved an engaged, educated citizenry that feels empowered to demand and receive decent social services. The problems it retains are economic, rather than social. Akash Kapur, in a recent article in the *Atlantic*, says that the left-wing government has been "responsible for both the worst and best of Keralan development." Kerala has an abundance of natural resources but, Kapur says, industries have largely stayed away for fear of the state's difficult trade unions, pro-union courts and high minimum wages.[11] On a trip to Kerala a few years ago, journalist Bill McKibben recounted that "Strikes, agitations and 'stirs,' a sort of wildcat job action, are so common as to be almost unnoticeable."[12] But McKibben also thinks that such ferment, although inconvenient, may not be such a bad thing. "For the most part, the various campaigns and protests seem a sign of self-confidence and political vitality, a vast improvement over the apathy, powerlessness, ignorance or tribalism that governs many Third World communities."

Of course, what is a good thing for a local community may not fit in very well with the needs of global capital and a consumer society. Factory owners and multinational corporations in general dislike Kerala. Kapur tells the story of a Kerala tannery manager who cried, "the blood of the workers is polluted!" because his employees were always striking and demanding better working conditions. Tanneries are notorious and dangerous polluters, and this company director also complained that the state government inspected the water treatment facility next door too zealously, making things much harder for his tannery than when he worked in Tamil Nadu, China and Taiwan. When Kapur pressed the manager and asked if he really felt so unfortunate to be living in an educated state that cares about its environment, he "shrugged his shoulders . . . and uttered something between a laugh and a sigh. 'It's a good place to live,' he said, 'but a tough place to do business.'"

## The Keralan Model

*Kerala suggests a way out of two problems simultaneously.*
— BILL MCKIBBEN, JOURNALIST

Because of its politically active and informed populace, Kerala has remained outside the global economic free-for-all of international trade. Its high levels of unemployment (as much as 25 percent) affect even the highly educated segments of the populations, and thousands of Keralans have migrated across the Persian Gulf to find work in law, medicine and teaching. But, as McKibben points out, the emigration of the highly educated is a problem shared by countries like France and Canada. If the economy has remained largely stagnant, says Kapur, Keralans "have been singularly successful at implementing development through distribution. Perhaps more than anything else, the state's high standard of living is a story about *equal* standards of living." The land reform program of the 1960s abolished the landlordism that plagues northern India and makes virtual slavery common in Pakistan. Over 90 percent of people in Kerala own the land on which their home stands, and land ownership is limited to eight hectares (20 acres) per family.[13] Kapur says that food crops grown on redistributed land "ensure Keralans a basic income that shields them from absolute destitution." For the urban poor, there is also a system of rationing and Maveli, or "fair price" shops, that enables them to eat and light their kerosene lamps, if nothing else.

Kerala's poverty, the highest in India, may not be as detrimental to its people as we might think. Anthropologist Richard Franke of Montclair University in New Jersey points out that, despite global economic claims of increased GDP and income in India ever since the 1970s,[14] statistics from a highly respected Indian national survey show that between 1972 and 1994 the average caloric intake for all of India actually dropped 5 percent in rural areas, and declined slightly even in urban ones. "Despite the [seemingly] small percentage drops, this trend is important," Franke says, "because 21 percent of Indian children are already described as 'severely malnourished.'" Only two states on the entire subcontinent showed a caloric increase in both urban and rural areas over the same period: Kerala and West Bengal, which also has a progressive left-wing government. These figures are very significant, because they help illustrate the fact that a country that is performing well in terms of mainstream economic measurements, such as GDP and level of participation in the global economy, is not always one that is actually enriching its general population.[15]

For example, the Punjab, India's most prosperous state, is cited by globalization experts as an economic success story because of World Bank-inspired agricultural industrialization; and the Punjab does indeed boast a per capita income almost three (2.7) times Kerala's. But the Punjab experienced an incredible 31 percent per capita *decline* in caloric intake over the same period that unemployed Keralans were enjoying a 15 percent *increase*. In the rich, industrialized state of Punjab, 14 percent of the children are severely malnourished, compared to only 6 percent in Kerala. Franke believes that when poor people have the political power to demand a modicum of fair income distribution, they can ward off malnutrition even in a "poor" economy. But in places like the Punjab, where only the rich have that kind of power, only the rich can feed their children.

These policies have far-reaching ecological as well as social effects. In the Punjab, the mass adoption of industrial farming technologies has put tremendous pressure on their aquifers, which are being drained twice as fast as they can refill. Water tables have been dropping by one to three meters a year and more fossil fuels have to be used to run the pumps to bring up the water. Fossil fuels require cash, so the real costs of producing the food go up, and the poor naturally have less access. Industrial agriculture is generally controlled by big multinational chemical and seed companies and distributors, entities like the American-based giants Cargill and Monsanto, who are very present in the Punjab and noticeably absent in Kerala. In Kerala, people own little plots that are not suitable for industrial monocultures, so they are still the main beneficiaries of the food that is grown in their area. All these factors go toward explaining why Keralans eat far better than Punjabis, with only one-third as much money rolling around in the state economy.

Kerala's environment policies are also unusual. The people of Kerala have moved beyond literacy programs to what they call being "land literate." They want to understand more about keeping their land healthy by using it optimally, for instance by planting trees, stopping erosion and protecting watercourses. They also want to share more equitably and use the land more intelligently. In order to formulate local projects that would plant paddy land between floodings with vegetables, increase sanitation and clean drinking water, and build terraces and trenches to return over-grazed lands to polycultures, three million Keralans — that is, one out of every ten people — participated in mapping their communities. They made lists of community assets and deficits, interviewed locals, assessed land use, fertility and drainage, wrote up the data, and then tried, in very large groups, to turn all that information into project proposals. Today, Kerala is probably the only state on earth to have detailed self-study reports from every single one of its towns and villages.

In order for such programs to work over the long term, the users of a resource have to be nearly unanimous; their decisions have to express the wishes of the whole community, reached by honest consensus. For us to appreciate how deeply democratic the Kerala mapping program was, says Franke, we have to "imagine 1.8 million New Yorkers (10 percent of the state population, the same proportion of people involved in Kerala) meeting for hours, arguing, electing problem-solving working groups to plan strategies for overcoming local problems. Imagine thousands of them continuing to meet for weeks to hammer out local plans for which a massive portion of federal and state funds would be allocated. Imagine technically trained retired people in these communities forming associations of experts to help make the plans technically sound. Imagine all these people being compensated only with bus fare and lunch."[16] Imagine fun as well; sound trucks blaring music, street theater, school competitions, nighttime parades and processions of people singing and carrying smoking coconut-oil torches that light up the dark streets.

Yet another area in which the Keralan model is unusually consensus-based is in its people's protection of their wilderness ecosystems. Although Kerala has a population density of 747 people per square kilometer (compared to 234 in the UK and only 26 in the U.S.), almost a third of its land is still forested, and most of that forest is protected by government-established wildlife preserves and state and national parks. Like the Cores, Corridors and Carnivores concept exemplified by the Adirondack Park, four of these preserves have full protection and no people, but eleven others share the wild animal habitat with plantations and crop land, which means that people regularly intermingle with rare snakes and birds, elephants, crocodiles, tigers and guar, the Indian bison. The preserves are also sometimes connected, forming the corridors so vital to large ecosystem protection.

Keralans share their crowded environment with other forms of life apparently because they want to. Between 60 and 80 percent of all voters show up for each election, and the largest numbers turn out to participate in local initiatives such as park creation. So, despite the overwhelming amount of poverty and people's heavy dependence on exploiting the wealth of their natural systems, Kerala enjoys one of the highest levels of biodiversity in the world. It is the planet's only home for the Nelgiri Tahr, a beautiful brown and white mountain goat, and it protects many other creatures that are severely endangered elsewhere, such as lion-tailed macaques, guars, sloth bears, leopards, elephants, the masheer — the most endangered game fish in India — lake otters, civet cats, the Atlas — the largest moth in the world — the fairy bluebird, jungle nightjars, laughing thrushes, pangolins, wild boars, exotic crabs, monitor lizards — the list goes on and on. More than 150 endemic animals and birds can be found in the Neyyar Preserve alone.

Forest and plant diversity is also very high; in the Periyar wildlife sanctuary, for example, there are nearly two thousand flowering plants, as well as hundreds of grass and orchid species; elsewhere there are neem, bamboo and sandalwood forests, rare herbs, evergreens and rosewood. Plantations of tea, cardamom, cloves, vanilla, ginger, turmeric, nutmeg, cumin and star anise perfume the air in many of these parks, and a giant teak tree measuring 6.4 meters (19 feet) in diameter towers forty meters (120 feet) into the skies of the Pararnhikularn Wildlife Sanctuary in the Dhoni Hills. These preserves represent an amazing amount of natural, real wealth that so far we have never even thought of measuring. But it makes the water-guzzling, chemical-soaked monocultures of the Punjab — the "rich" state — look poor in comparison. The differences between the quality of life for every kind of creature, including humans, in the two states illustrates the fact that our globally accepted systems of wealth measurement, like export rates or GDP, do not reflect reality or measure the kinds of riches that lead to real human happiness and long-term well-being.[17]

### First We Take Berlin, Then We Take Manhattan

*Europeans only produce half the waste and use up half the fossil fuels as the average North American.*
— DAVID PIMENTEL, ECOLOGIST[18]

Research for this book led us not only to the palm trees and spice plantations of India, but also to the gray, dripping cities of Europe in the dead of winter. Berlin was particularly daunting, with miles of architecturally featureless and quickly constructed postwar apartment buildings filing past the train windows and a forest of cranes in the center of the city, where dozens of new complexes are going up. Architecturally speaking, the new Sony Center in the heart of downtown is a combination of Darth Vader and Walt Disney: IMAX theaters, sleek cafés, brand-name stores and video arcades glitter against shiny, black walls. Busy, headlight-swept highways cut through the conglomerations of familiar names — one Gap, McDonald's, Hollywood movie palace and Burger King after another. On a dark night in winter, it seemed a vision of a cyberpunk, corporate urban future.

And yet, there is also something organic, messy and indefinably exciting about Berlin; it has a vibrancy all its own, which changes pitch depending on whether you're in the old West or the old East. Holly stayed with some friends of her daughter's, Yvonne Hardt and Arno Hielscher, a young couple living in Kreuzberg, a largely Turkish neighborhood bordering old East Berlin and including the parks and no-man's lands the Berlin Wall used to snake through. It's a trendy district for young artists like Yvonne and Arno, with galleries, good restaurants and bars, but it's still cheap; they pay about $700 Canadian a month for a six-and-a-half-room apartment in a century-old building, with towering ceilings, wood floors and touches like a windowseat in the parlor and a dwarf door between Arno's study and the living room. Since these rooms belong to cash-poor owners, they are almost bare, with little more than one piece of furniture each: a bicycle, a bed, one couch, a rocker and an exercise bar. Yvonne is an accomplished modern dancer and choreographer, absorbed by the world of post-modern, urban art; Arno is just finishing his studies as an architect. These attractive young people are largely indifferent to nature and environmental issues, and are happy to live a stylish urban life. Yet their sensitivity about what happens to waste, what it means to use "dirty" transport, what constitutes pure food, where energy comes from and how much water is available for us all is light-years beyond that of a comparable Canadian or American couple.

As we drank coffee in their little kitchen, they said that the 80 million people in Germany have managed to reach a nearly unanimous social consensus, not unlike the Keralan unanimity about wildlife preserves and social assistance. German society firmly supports environmentally sustainable efforts that simply do not exist in North America. For example, there are tax breaks for installing water-conserving toilets like the one they have, put in by their landlord. Gas meters, also landlord-installed, are prominently displayed in the hall and the main room, so Yvonne and Arno can see just how much they're consuming. They're careful to keep unused rooms cool, confine their activities to just the kitchen or the parlor and monitor how they're doing. This is simple because their gas and electric meters are easy to read, unlike those used in the United States and Canada, which make no sense to a non-professional. Lighting is used judiciously as well, and every public hallway has lights that flick on when a person first enters the building and automatically turn off after a few minutes.

Although Yvonne and Arno have an efficient, front-loading washing machine with a good rating from Stiftung Warentest, the German consumer certification association discussed in chapter one, they have no dryer, but hang their wet clothes on a collapsible drying rack in the large bathroom. They have a little dishwasher that they run only when it's full to the brim. They wash other dishes in a basin, never under running water; Yvonne confesses she was horrified to see so many Canadians doing that. There is plenty of hot water available, but the meters have influenced the way they use it. Moreover, the gas water heater is activated only when it's turned on, so they don't waste money keeping a whole tank heated at all times as we do. The utility system in Germany is designed to help small and medium-sized providers get into the market. The one Yvonne and Arno subscribe to is moving into wind, bio-gas and other renewables, but their apartment heat is still natural gas, like many others in the country. In order to conserve natural gas there have been massive national insulation programs, with government incentives in the form of grants, tax rebates, and so on. The need to upgrade and retrofit the many old houses and buildings in former East Germany has frustrated some of the country's short-term goals to reduce greenhouse gas production, but Germany is still steadily reducing its use of fossil fuels. The grants policy has also resulted in the proliferation of super-efficient windows in the majority of structures, old and new, all over Germany. It is cold and windy in Berlin in late January, but no air gets in around their edges, and they also let in more sunlight for a bit of a passive solar kick.

Under their small kitchen counter, Yvonne and Arno have not one but four different colored containers for recyclables: paper, glass, biodegradables and every single kind of plastic. Although they are a busy couple, they are careful to follow guidelines, such as not putting orange peels, which have pesticides on them, in with the rest of the compost bucket, so that the city's compost will be organic. Organic produce and meat are readily available in German supermarkets, and the current government's goal is for 20 percent of all German farms to be free of agricultural chemicals by 2010; as we mentioned in chapter five, they will achieve this by gradually transferring existing farm subsidies to organic growers only, and Arno and Yvonne, who try to buy organic food as much as possible, are happy to hear it. They take their four garbage containers down to garages in the building courtyard, where the separation of material is strictly maintained. There are rows upon rows of color-coded garbage containers everywhere in Germany, with signs detailing the rules and pick-up times; they are obviously well integrated into urban life. One of the main bones of contention between Berliners and their large Turkish minority, incidentally, is the fact that some Turks are lackadaisical about their garbage separation; the Germans hope the young ones will be more adapted to the national environmental consensus.

On a pleasant walk around the neighborhood before dinner one evening, we spotted at least two dozen photovoltaic cells on slanted roofs, many passive solar windows and two green roofs, all in an economically depressed area that is considered disheveled and old-fashioned. At night, there were only enough streetlights to find one's way around and almost no neon signs, which these days are considered wasteful and gauche. And of course the streets were full of carbon-body Smart Cars and Lupos, but free of SUVs and enormous Jeeps. Public transport, as we have said, is so good that never for a moment did any of us need to take a taxi or long for a car; Arno and Yvonne prefer their bikes to even the highly efficient light rail and street cars that stop across the street from their door.

Berlin is not special; its policies and its citizens are typical of all big German cities — and Berlin lags behind others in countries like Sweden, the Netherlands, Switzerland and Denmark. In other words, even busy, urban creatures like Yvonne and Arno are willing to make these adjustments in their lives to benefit natural systems they are not particularly attracted to or passionate about. They are simply regular people who know that they need heat, light and water, that their garbage and wastes must be dealt with, and that the efforts they make will enable them to have decent lives for a long time into the future. But most important, perhaps, is the fact that efforts like theirs are causing neither personal suffering nor national economic problems. Despite or perhaps even because of them, Germany is one of the most prosperous nations on earth.

Keeping the heat down, riding bikes, dealing responsibly with wastes, paying for public transport and good insulation through taxes, increasing investment in renewable energy sources — these are all programs every single city on earth will have to deal with, if not this minute, then very, very soon. Painstaking studies undertaken by the Wüppertal Institute in Bonn in the mid-1990s made it clear that real, equitable sharing of the natural resources of the planet could enable every single starving, enslaved, sick human on earth to live just as well as middle-class Germans like Yvonne and Arno — without taking anything away from that comfortable young couple. We all need to think about that.

## Limits to Growth

*These were very poor people; subsistence farmers with a few cattle, living on crafts like cuckoo clocks and what game and fish they could get from the forest.*

— KONRAD OTTO-ZIMMERMAN, HEAD OF THE ICLEI, ON THE INHABITANTS OF THE BLACK FOREST

Berlin is a modern, busy city, full of big corporations, global aspirations and a belief in the ethic of economic expansion; that's one reason it makes such a good example of what any city can do. Berliners are not in the vanguard of any major social or environmental movement. And yet it's clear that somewhere in Germany, someone is. The widely accepted epicenter for the kind of environmental responsibility and deep love of nature that has even Berliners serenely buying special toilets and segregating orange peels is Germany's fairytale region of gingerbread cottages and pine-covered cliffs known as the Black Forest. Konrad Otto-Zimmerman is head of the International Center for Local Environmental Initiatives (ICLEI), an international NGO that tries to help people develop sustainable initiatives and implement the Agenda 21 principles that came out of the first Earth Summit of 1992. He's headquartered in Freiburg, the Black Forest's largest city, and is himself a newcomer from Swabia. We asked if he could explain what makes the Black Forest the birthplace of movements like the electricity cooperative in nearby Schöenau.

The revolution of 1848, the first movement toward democracy in Germany, found its most passionate adherents in this area, Otto-Zimmerman says, and "It's been a hotbed of democracy ever since." He explains that the concept of *Heimat* or *Heim* originated in this part of Germany. It means "home"; but it also implies everything that home can represent, all its culture, its natural surroundings like animals, plants and hills, its smells, its people and buildings, its spirit — everything. "You are part of it, and it is part of you," he says. And *Heim* also has to do with democracy, "being master of oneself, no king, no duke, no one from the outside telling you how to live."

Freiburg is one of the jewels of Germany, with much of its medieval town — the ancient walls, the cathedral, the surrounding squares and half-timbered houses — still intact. Five fingers of forest reach down into the town from the hills, and there is no urban sprawl, none of the spilling of tract homes and malls across the landscape that one sees in most of Germany and the rest of the modern world; the city fathers zoned against it. Much of the town is off-limits to cars, and is served by shiny electric trams that are constantly running to and fro. Even the crystalline mountain streams that used to flow through the city, filling horse troughs and feeding fountains, still sing merrily as they run along the meticulously constructed stone canals that line the pedestrian streets and walkways.

Freiburg sits on the Rhine, one of the most navigable rivers in the world, with France and Switzerland both within shouting distance, a perfect place for a port. Otto-Zimmerman worked for a year in Stuttgart, which is not very far away. He says that city is devoted to industrial development, always looking for more; "It's a survival mechanism for them — 'How can we let any opportunity pass by?' — and they're always focused on business, business." Stuttgart is the big port on the Rhine, "but if you look at the map, Freiburg is better located, right on a line of transportation that stretches from Scandinavia down to Spain. They could have gotten so much money to develop. Even Daimler-Benz, who comes from here — the city turned them down!" At first, Otto-Zimmerman wondered why the region had been so resistant to development for so long, but then, he says, "I discovered that people have a certain regional mentality which leads them to protect this home area — their *Heim*. It makes them very conservative and very cautious about changing what they already have, in the very best sense of those words."

The democratic expression of a region's social and political values is its smallest units, its municipalities; but in Canada, even if they're long established and well run, municipalities can be wiped off the map if the larger governing body, the province, suddenly wants them to amalgamate or disappear. Moreover, each Canadian municipality, however rural or tiny, must have an "industrial zone," and is forced to accept into it any industries deemed desirable by the province. In Germany, however, the state authority cannot override decisions made at the local level. If a town or village doesn't want a factory or dump to locate in their town, they don't have to take it. On the other hand, if a municipality does want to permit industrial development or investment, that has to be approved by the regional authorities. "It's a system of checks and balances that doesn't prevent all bad decisions," says Otto-Zimmerman, "but certainly helps avoid them. You can't supersede a democratic decision by a non-democratic, that is, an administrative one. Local self-government is pretty secure here." In other words, if the state in Germany had wanted to merge surrounding municipalities into megacities, the way Quebec and Ontario have done with Montreal and Toronto, they would have had to go through a public, democratic vote in Parliament. "And that," says Otto-Zimmerman, "would be very politically dangerous for the supporters of such a thing. Development, amalgamation, certain kinds of industry, they cannot be imposed."

The protection of local autonomy is only one way in which the citizens of the city of Freiburg show their expertise in conducting democracy. In fact, they practice it in much the same way native groups, holistic managers,

Keralans and anti-globalization activists do: through the extremely long and painstaking process of achieving unanimous consensus. Otto-Zimmerman says, "The no-car-zone idea first came up in 1975, ten years ahead of any other place in Germany. As it moved through all the studies and the committees, the city required every decision to be unanimous. There were visits from all the people affected, the city took every kind of complaint seriously, they talked to the neighbors, they made sure everyone on both sides of the issue understood everything — real participatory planning. It took *so long*, but when the decision to ban cars came, there was a real consensus. Everyone seems to love it now." He says these things are simple and they're subtle, but they work, and they work because the officials have the same kind of commitment to the area that the citizens do. "In city government," he says, "I noticed people from all the different offices talking to each other so carefully; they really understood the will of the developers, they understood both sides. But they would come up with every reason you can imagine *not* to develop. 'That's not the best place . . . maybe over here, or over there . . . maybe, you know, not here at all.' So they're very slow about it. Many developments came out not at all as the developers had wanted at first, but smaller, more adapted to the area."

Local, democratic power is the most fundamental and necessary requirement of sustainability; the two, as we have seen, almost always go together. Otto-Zimmerman says, "Globalists don't mind where they live, where they buy things, where those things come from. Borders, to them, just cause confusion, trouble, inefficiency. They are mentally torn down. But people who care about a certain place, they have real relations with it and with each other. This is the fundamental disconnect between the two approaches. And what we're learning now is that we really can have the best of both; internationalist populations that can see beyond local borders, and really care about what happens in other countries, but that also take care of their own homes, their *Heim*."

## Grading the School

*If you were a fish, the last thing you would discover is water.*
— OLD SAYING, QUOTED BY PETER BROWN, FORMER HEAD OF THE
   MCGILL SCHOOL OF THE ENVIRONMENT

As we've seen in Kerala, empowering people to participate fully in a demo-cratic society requires education, literacy and, especially, access to reliable information. But even a 100-percent literacy rate cannot empower intelligent, democratic societies if the information people are given — on the effects of toxins, the safety of food additives, the amount of habitat available to plant or animal species, the trustworthiness of a given politician, the legal rights available to a citizen — is in any way unreliable or tainted. Real democracy cannot survive the serious subversion of information. So if people really are concerned about preserving freedom and democracy, the solidity of information and the objectivity of our educational institutions must be prime areas of concern.

There was a time when scientists in Western universities, and David Suzuki was one of them, pursued their research interests in order to add to the global pool of knowledge. Along the way, these researchers might occasionally make discoveries that could be applied commercially, but knowledge for its own sake was the ideal for most academics. Not any more. With enormous profits to be made from private companies interested in medical, biotechnological or other scientific research, governments and industries are pressing for closer and closer links between university research and the private sector. But there is a serious cost involved in such a basic change in the Western educational environment. Allowing corporate interests to "own" information increases occasions for corruption, secrecy and greed in our society. On the research level, the profit motive also fuels the tendency to cut corners, to suppress failures, or to actively deceive the public, not just about the efficacy of this or that product, but about the nature of reality itself. We have referred to such effects earlier in this book — the many years that the oil lobby spent paying scientists to deny or belittle climate change; the continuing behavior of tobacco, chemical and pharmaceutical companies in manipulating studies to downplay the dangers of their products; the confusion of information about the effect our global economic institutions are having on local democratic rights.

Medical research is particularly liable to manipulation by scientists funded by profit-making bodies. Cases of corruption are costing people not just money, but their lives. In 1997, for example, the University of California at Irvine shut down a cancer research lab "after finding that scientists there had invested in a company that hoped to sell the drugs they were testing — and then failed to report side-effects."[19] The FDA recently reprimanded a Tufts University researcher for improperly treating a cancer patient with a gene therapy that may have doubled the size of his tumor. "Both the scientist and a Boston medical center held a large stake in the company developing the therapy."[20] In a very recent case, a blood-cancer experiment at a prestigious cancer research center in Seattle was allowed to drag on for years, even though patients were dying at a higher rate than with standard therapy. The deaths of at least twenty people were directly attributed to the treatment, the *Seattle Times* reported this year; and again, the cancer center and some of its physicians were found to have had a financial stake in the treatment.[21]

If it weren't for reliable, objective science, much of what we know about medicine and technology, as well as good environmentalism, would collapse. The safety of our machines, drugs and foods is continuously investigated by independent government and academic researchers who have documented the dangers of substances like PCBs, asbestos or DDT. Those of us who track this kind of research know that the studies that have enabled us to separate dangerous practices and products from safe ones have come almost exclusively from these "independent" sources — universities or government bodies — not from groups with vested commercial interests. If the independent studies that have alerted us to the facts of global warming, the dangers of radioactivity and industrial toxins and the alarming loss of species diversity worldwide had not been kept separate from industrial interests, it is doubtful that the information they provide would even exist. When the very foundations of scientific study at the university level are being corrupted by commercial concerns, how can we know that what we're teaching new generations of students isn't in the textbooks simply because some large corporation influenced the research on which the text is based through grants to the institutions that provided the information?

Fortunately, some of our universities and more prestigious publications, to say nothing of students themselves, have begun to deal with this problem. When the University of California at Berkeley struck a deal with Novartis, allowing the company first rights on any plant genetics discoveries in exchange for $25 million, students demonstrated vociferously, and ethicists got concerned. Sheldon Krimsky, a research watchdog at Tufts University, recommends a system that would require all scientists to acknowledge their corporate affiliations whenever they publish a study, speak at a conference or sit on a review panel. The peer-reviewed publications *Science* and *The New England Journal of Medicine* have just announced new rules that force disclosure of any author's financial ties to any company or institution. But seemingly the best solution comes from Richard Strohman, professor emeritus of microbiology at Berkeley itself. He suggests that professors shouldn't be allowed to have their cake and eat it too. "Tenure was established to enable academic researchers to speak the truth about their specialties without fear of reprisals, without being subject to any pressure commercial interests, governments or other outside interests could bring to bear on the university, that might damage their careers. If these people want to be free to work for private companies, they should have to give up tenure; it can be reserved for those who wish to remain relatively poor, but secure in their academic position. And it will be easy for interested parties to ascertain who is who."[23]

So far it's mostly students and NGOs who are pressing for disclosure and demanding that their schools get private money out of public research and private corporations, like Coke and Pepsi, out of their classrooms. But a growing number of mainstream institutions are trying to revamp themselves and are attempting to apply the kind of systemic changes to their accredited courses that we've been talking about throughout this book. McGill University in Montreal took a step in 1998 by founding the McGill School of the Environment, which offers both bachelor of science and arts degrees that cut across traditional disciplines. The School of Public Affairs of the University of Maryland has been offering a new view of economics through the famous ecological economists Herman Daly and Bob Constanza, and the Vermont Law School is trying to fit its values of defending social systems and the environment with its physical practices, including its buildings.

The former director of the McGill School, Peter Brown, says he tries to make it clear to his students that the first step people have to take in understanding the world around them is to get outside the unconscious assumptions of their own culture. These assumptions are so deeply embedded in our lives we aren't even aware they exist. "Just take some apparently simple ideas, like: What do we mean by 'development?' By 'cause and effect?' By 'the law of nature?' When you dissect such terms, you see how really complex these ideas are; when you go after them, they sort of disintegrate or get hard to formulate. So the point is to get people to think systematically about the structure of their own thinking so that they're not prisoners of their own history. And when they do, when they begin studying our culture from the outside, it doesn't take long before they realize that it's wildly dysfunctional."

The University of Texas at Austin has a similar school that extends to the graduate level and is even more committed. The Environmental Science Institute of the university comes right out and states that it was founded in direct response to the World Scientists' Warning to Humanity mentioned many times by David Suzuki in books, programs and lectures over the past ten years. In order to respond to these serious warnings, the institute (known as the ESI) has set up complex and impressive research efforts that crisscross traditional academic boundaries. Eight colleges, including law, pharmacy, mathematics, natural sciences, engineering and liberal arts, have united a score of departments, institutes, museums and bureaus to create a rapidly growing form of alternative professional training. One of ESI's founders, Dick Richardson, professor of integrative biology (what used to be termed zoology and botany), says of the program's success and growing reputation: "I think it's safe to say that we have established an academic beach head and are moving across the campus."

These courses are breaking away from the usual tunnel vision that accompanies isolated disciplines attempting to study whole systems. But they intend to go farther than their already revolutionary stated goals of teaching botanists to consider hydrology and history or making city planners look at toxicology and biology. They are also attempting to teach the students to understand the larger, interlocked systems in which their specialties are embedded, by forcing them to withdraw from all their presuppositions and to think for themselves. This move towards complexity and independence extends to the teachers themselves, who are learning as intensively as the students.

Dick Richardson and his wife, Pat, a laboratory chemist who works closely with him, described one of their summer courses. The students are taken out to a wetland and riverbank ecosystem that borders the desert outside Austin. The course's underlying goal is to enable the students to appreciate wholes instead of parts so that they can become more capable of understanding and protecting the natural systems that sustain ecosystems. But that goal isn't stated overtly; in fact, the first thing that happens is that they, not the teacher, have to divide into groups and determine what's worthy of study in the various ecosystems. All by themselves they have to come up with ideas like rates of biodiversity, water retention in the soils, hydrology, forest-edge ecology or level of pollutants. And then they have to decide how to construct such a study in the field.

In other words, they're not assigned methodologies or technologies or told what they're aiming for. Most undergraduate science courses state the desired outcome and use assigned equipment to duplicate a previous experiment. The students' grades depend on how perfectly what they do matches the predetermined template their professors have set up. These students, however, have to think up the right questions themselves; they even have to invent and develop their measurement technologies. The professor only assists by asking questions like: "Why did you choose a drip instead of an absorption method of measurement? Why did you divide your research area into quadrants instead of something else?" Such questions only alert the students to the choices that are available and to the many diverse avenues available to them when approaching a natural system; but they don't help them choose.

The results, of course, often do reproduce experiments done hundreds of times in the past, but the students don't know that. They've discovered how to construct an experiment and how to create the technologies of measurement — all on their own. The process is often frustrating. "Some of the students are outraged that the professor isn't telling them what to do. They don't know what's expected of them," says Dick Richardson.

"A certain number drop out," Pat Richardson agrees, "but the ones that are left gain intense confidence in their ability to work out problems on the spot." In short, they learn how to think in the context of the complicated and changing physical reality of the planet.

"All kinds of unexpected things happen that quicken their understanding of physics and the environment," says Dick. "One group this summer chose a xeric [desertified] area for their study. Then we had heavy rains, and their sandy spot with cacti and a few desert succulents suddenly became lush with greenery, all kinds of plants and flowers they had never seen before. That's when they realized that what they were dealing with isn't static! That's when they started to have fun."

Even grading is revolutionary. The students work in a system termed OLR (Online Learning Record) in which they evaluate their own progress. The thing is, they have to do this very closely with the professor, who's not impressed if they constantly evaluate themselves positively as "learning well" and doing things "right." "It's only when people make mistakes and start looking at how they're wrong that they begin to learn," say the Richardsons. Even the syllabus for this course prepares the student for a life observing natural systems when it warns: "A project rarely ends exactly as planned. Unexpected things happen, and…the earlier in the project the need for modification of activities is recognized, the better the chance for the project to be satisfactory." The emphasis is therefore on variability and complexity in the subject of study, humility and readiness to learn on the part of the students. They are being taught to look at the world not as reductionist scientists, but holistically, like the ranchers following the precepts of Allan

Savory's Holistic Management back in chapter three. And ironically, this apparently convoluted and imprecise approach often results in students volunteering to work even harder than they would in normal courses.

"Two of the groups asked to be allowed to go on monitoring their sites after the course was over," Dick says. "They were learning so much they didn't want to stop, even if they were no longer getting grades or credit, so they kept at it right into the fall. And, in fact, that's what's happening with these courses in general; we have a growing number of key faculty here noticing that the students coming out of our classes are not only knowledgeable, but enthusiastic." Dick thinks this is so because in his method of grading the students start with zero, so the teacher is an ally who helps them build their knowledge. Normal grading, he says, "starts with an A and then there's a race to erode it; the teacher has to try to catch you out, make you see you're wrong. If he doesn't, you won't learn. But in this system, I'm not trying to catch and punish them; I'm a resource and an ally."

Just like the old apprentice methods, and the way humans used to learn a long time ago. Patience, humility and observation have always been the keys to understanding nature and protecting its resilience, and these tools of the master hunter or amateur naturalist are now being offered to 21st-century scientists.

### Tracking Happiness

*Schools as we know them are not the only way to become educated. They were invented by the Industrial Revolution, so that people in the countryside would learn to be obedient factory workers. That's the model we now force upon our children, and we wonder why so many of them are unhappy there.*
— JON YOUNG, WILDERNESS AWARENESS SCHOOLS

An enormous amount of what young people learn about life comes not from the schools they go to, but from the values they're taught at home by parents and grandparents, friends and neighbors. These values had a lot of impact even just a generation ago, but these days a great deal of a child's time is spent at school, in what amounts to the same little box-like rooms with a limited number of buttons that Mander's chimpanzees experienced. School-age, middle-class children also typically spend several hours every day in places that are marginally more pleasant, but still a long way away from what might be called their natural habitat — in neon-lit, fossil fuel–heated gymnasiums or recreational centers, doing supervised activities like swimming, riding, skating, judo or dancing. And of course, whatever time they have left they spend in little rooms at home, pressing the biggest buttons of all on their TVs and computers.

Very young children are not very patient with little rooms. Most of them head straight for mud puddles, piles of leaves, unfortunate frogs and puppies, tools like sticks and boxes. When left to their own devices, children from every kind of culture, anywhere in the world, will spontaneously invent games like hide-and-seek and tag; they will explore every nook and cranny of a barn or a yard they can get into, they will chase each other, swing on trees, try to eat plants or bugs and figure out every possible thing they can do with a branch or a rock. These are natural habitat games and they are part of the hunting, stalking, self-defense and food-gathering survival skills every primate is born with. These days, however, we usually allow our children to practice these instinctive skills as little as possible. After all, they have another kind of survival they have to get on with. They have to settle down and behave in school.

Wilderness educator Jon Young remembers when he first realized how the modern world works. He was in second grade, staring out the window as kids do when they ought to be paying attention to the teacher, fascinated by a butterfly fluttering past the evergreens in the school yard and wishing with all his heart he was outside in the beautiful sunny day. The teacher, who had been trying to get his attention, finally broke into his consciousness by yelling at him. He says, "As I woke up from my dream of the outside world and looked at her, I suddenly realized for the first time that I wasn't free. The beautiful world outside was not for me; I couldn't go out and play. I was a prisoner. I actually felt my heart break."

Today, the Wilderness Awareness schools that Young founded exist in various forms in New Jersey, Vermont, New Hampshire, California and Washington. For the most part, they offer afternoon, summer and weekend programs for home-schooled and public-school children, but their facility in Washington State is a fully accredited high school. Their programs teach children traditional human activities, like stalking and observing wild animals, gathering wild foods and constructing shelters, learning how to interpret tracks and bird calls, and generally how to live in and move around a natural landscape. The cornerstone of their teaching is the "secret spot," a place in nature — even if it's just a park or a suburban back yard — where a person can go every single day and be fully present. There, these students learn to observe everything that is happening in the natural world, from the sounds of birds making alarm calls at cats or hawks, to the direction of the wind, the smell of coming rain or the path a mother weasel is taking under the bushes with her babies.

Young is in his early forties, vibrantly energetic, small and wiry. He says, "Put [children] on a computer, hook them up to an EEG, and you'll see there's a very localized little bit of the brain that's being used. Put them out in a yard, playing with a ball, catching frogs, climbing trees, and the electrical signals are moving all over the brain." The school's goals are based on the theory that our culture has become dangerously out of sync with the reality of how this planet functions on a physical level, largely because the things we now focus on are both artificial and limited. "We're using only one particular part of our brain very intensely, instead of all parts of it evenly," says Jon. "No wonder our culture has become unbalanced as well, and doesn't notice our actual three-dimensional reality, can't see how incredibly crazy it is to poison your own food or destroy your own air."

Young himself had a rather strange education. He has degrees in biology and ecology and studied under David Ehrenfeld, the famous founder of Conservation Biology, at Rutgers; but he seldom talks about that. Instead, he focuses on the seven years he spent roaming the New Jersey pine barrens as a child with a laconic young man named Tom Brown, who is known as a tracker and survivalist and is the author of many wildlife guides. People used to teach children by example. Every skill humans had, from tanning hides and carving stone to catching game and smoking meat, was learned by apprenticeship, by watching and helping. It took a very long time for people to become adept, but they usually chose their specialties out of personal inclination, and so the process was in some sense exciting and delightful. Tom Brown's fate was to became the apprentice of one of the last Apache trackers on earth, the famous Stalking Wolf, who lived out the last of his life at his son's house in New Jersey. Brown, now in his late fifties, was best friends with the old man's grandson, and for eleven years he was schooled every day in the pine barrens by an Apache elder who could literally track an ant across a mossy rock. Shortly before Grandfather, as Brown called him, died, he told the eighteen-year-old that he had to pass on the knowledge he had been given, because Stalking Wolf believed that people in the future would desperately need to know how to use all of their brains in this way. He said that Tom would be able to recognize his first student because the child would be holding Mother Earth on a string.

Brown knew that Jon Young would be that student when he spotted the ten-year-old three years later, all alone on a street corner, holding a fishing line attached to a big female snapping turtle. The turtle is the Indian symbol for the earth. Everything that Stalking Wolf had taught him he passed on to Young. And today, Young is trying to do the same thing, but for more people, much faster. The Wilderness School teachers — and there are hundreds of them now — concentrate on what they call "brain patterning." They believe that if at least some people — not even that magic 10 to 15 percent of the population; they'll settle for 1 to 5 percent — learn to think in three dimensions and a natural context again, they'll be able to help all of us apprehend the reality of the world around us and respond to it more appropriately.

There are measurable results of their methods that seem to bear out their beliefs. The first is that children diagnosed with "learning disabilities," from dyslexia and hyperactivity to Attention Deficit Disorder, not only learn quickly and normally under Young's methods; they actually do better than the others. They learn to spot and identify animals sooner, are able to read bent leaves or crumpled sand and reconstruct the passage of a deer or coyote more quickly; and these experiences ironically give them the confidence to do better in two-dimensional school projects as well. Research on dyslexic children especially has shown that they have concrete visual and perceptual problems in dealing with two-dimensional texts. Young thinks we shouldn't be surprised that a large number of people have brains that still function best in the three-dimensional world and react to stimuli from all five senses. These brains might well have trouble shrinking down to the two-dimensional world of books and computers. Jon says, "Such children are probably not under-endowed, which is the way we define them, but rather particularly *well-endowed* for survival in nature," and indeed studies have shown that outside the classroom context, dyslexics, for example, are often highly creative, natural leaders. In short, we may be so out of touch with reality that we're taking our best and brightest and calling them "disabled." We may even be doing the same thing in reverse, taking people who are culturally blind, neurotically greedy or otherwise tragically short-sighted or unbalanced, and elevating them to high political and business office.

There's toughness in this outdoor training, of course; students are taught to laugh about their three big complaints: "We're cold! We're tired! We're hungry!" There is a commitment to respect and to give thanks to the natural world, but this new type of education also encourages a tremendous amount of humor and horseplay. Young enjoys talking about how his stalkers often break ranks to jump into mud puddles and wrestle, chase each other up trees and laugh so hard they can hardly breathe. They employ what he calls "coyote teaching," which means the teachers act as tricksters. The children tend to learn the most when they think they're playing or on a break, the exact opposite of regular school. The teachers never lecture or pontificate. In fact, they often feign ignorance, so the child can inform them about what they saw and explain what it means — one of the best possible ways to sear a conversation into a human brain.

When Holly visited a fall session of one of the schools in southern Vermont, a group of about thirty children between the ages of six and twelve had arrived for a lesson. The teachers had prepared some improvised skits designed to teach the kids profound lessons about nature, like what happens to a young animal that doesn't learn to look beyond its own short-term needs and apprehend the nature of its reality. They played a game about hawks and robins. The grown-ups wore capes to impersonate sharp-shinned hawks; baby "robins," sporting red paper breasts, sat in a pile of twigs where they were to imitate hungry, chirping fledglings in their nest. Adult "robins" nearby were trying to warn their babies to leave their nests by flying to earth and keeping quiet. The "hawks" then swooped down and grabbed the breathless "baby robins" one by one; the children screeched with horrified delight as they were carried back to the hawk's "babies" (more caped kids) to be "eaten" and buried in a pile of leaves. Finally, the last of the five babies realized it should stop worrying about being fed, pay attention to external reality, and join mom and dad safely on the ground. The children were beside themselves with excitement and delight — and they had learned something profound about life. As they were being bundled off home, a little girl about eight years old, who had come to the school for the first time, went up to one of the teachers and said longingly, "Can I come back? Do you do this all the time?"

## Global Grizzlies

*If we would just go out and thank the animals and the birds and the trees and the clouds and really feel the wind and really touch the rain and really remember what it is to be a human being on this planet, we might realize that this is the only planet we have.*
— JON YOUNG

Jon Young is a good-humored, self-effacing person, who says that what happens to humans in the presence of nature is not mystical or spiritual, it's just normal life. But if you ask him why he got involved in the daunting task of trying to create a new educational system, he admits that back in 1983 he had what he can only term a vision. He had gone back to his beloved New Jersey pine barrens after graduate school, only to find that all the streams where he and Brown had fished were dead. The frogs and many of his favorite birds had vanished. The land was scarred with off-road vehicle tracks, the bushes full of beer bottles and old oil cans. He fell into despair out there alone by his campfire, and he asked for a way out. He had a vision that night of "all the holy men and women who had created the umbrella of culture that used to enable people to survive without destroying. They created a culture of unseen learning that taught, sustained and restrained the others."

Young felt this vision was telling him to teach. He says, "These schools weren't founded because we have to survive in hand-to-hand combat with wolves or find berries for sustenance any more. And I'm not saying we have to get rid of computers and cars and houses and go back to living in caves. I use those things, and I buy them for my kids. But we have to learn to recognize the other half of the world — nature — the one that we're completely ignoring, that also just happens to be our lifeline." He doesn't want to teach people to battle the elements or to make fires and build shelters in order to become paranoid survivalists prepared to cope with terrorist attacks or government conspiracies. He says, "It's not about personal or family survival any more. It's about the survival of the planet. We now have Global Grizzlies who are after us: global warming, horrible toxins that kill frogs and fish, greed that dries up streams and levels the forests. That's the reality of nature we have to survive in, and we'll need our entire brain to do it, not just one part."

Like so many other people in this book, Young thinks that local, democratic movements, which are exemplified by what is happening on holistically managed ranches and farms, at Shawn Endicott's Rebuilding Center in Portland, in Dick Roy's courses, at globalization protests, in Kerala and in German town meetings, will enable us to extend our time on the earth in a way that will benefit the greatest numbers of people, as well as the earth itself. "In history," he says, "the answers to our dilemmas never come from anywhere except the grassroots. The visionaries of the world today, who are working for environmental causes, world peace causes,

Native rights causes, human rights causes — these are the ones who will lock arms together in a treaty network, all around the planet." His school teaches three principles, which, as Paul Hawken described in chapter one, are very like all the others that are sprouting up to enrich the emerging shared vision of the world. One of these principles is Unity, and it was a pillar of Iroquois government, adapted but unfortunately watered down by the U.S. Constitution. The Unity principle in government required unanimous decisions from the people, complete consensus, the kind of agreement the demonstrators in Washington demanded of themselves before they would act; the principle under which the city of Freiburg makes its zoning laws. Young says, "They say the creator exists in all of us, so total consensus on very important issues is necessary; because if all our minds aren't as one, the creator isn't represented. Therefore we'll make mistakes."

This seems an impossibly idealistic rule, but it really isn't. The Iroquois confederacy existed under it for at least three hundred years, holding off the British and the French while they did so. Freiburg, Kerala and the new coalition established to save the B.C. coastal forest are examples that are functioning very well right now. People will complain, and rightly, that consensus takes time. In fact, sometimes it takes decades to come to a decision. Our response to that objection is: Why not? Why would we not take decades to make decisions that will affect our children for generations? Are we going anywhere? Are they? As Bill McDonough asks, "When do we decide we're native to this place, that we're not going to leave it?" If we wake up to that question, and realize that we're all "locals" as far as this planet is concerned, there are a lot of like-minded people we can start working with, who can share some pretty good ways to slowly reach consensus about how life could continue to be lived. Over the longest possible term.

# EPILOGUE

*Make your holistic goal 100 percent what you want and 0 percent
how it is going to be achieved.*
— ALLAN SAVORY IN *HOLISTIC MANAGEMENT*

Throughout this book, we have tried to present solutions that can save and
restore the natural environmental systems that are the physical basis of life
on this planet. It has always been hard to understand why creatures like us,
who evolved here and are capable of understanding cause and effect, would
continue to foul the water, destroy the soils and poison the air on which we
depend for our existence. The reason we have done all this has much to do
with the philosophical constructs of the 18th and 19th centuries in Europe.
The First Industrial Revolution really did seem like a good idea at the time,
but it hasn't taken that long for its flaws to manifest themselves. The major
premise of that revolution underlies most of the current forms of human
destructiveness to the planet and to our own societies: that history and
community are worth nothing compared to material comforts and money;
that much of nature is dead, or at least not of immediate value to us; that
we can break it down into separate components, and those components can
be altered, removed or interchanged without damaging any overarching
structure. As farmer Joel Salatin said in chapter five, once we begin to treat
"living, individual creatures as if they were dead things, numbers in our
profit margin," we will lose them. And so we have, in massive numbers.
What we hadn't realized is that treating the other lifeforms on the planet as
if they were expendable has made us expendable, too.

The good news is that millions of people in every country and every
walk of life have realized the problems inherent in our current social
and economic paradigm. The good news is that they are not only inventing

technologies, forming associations, agitating on the political level and altering their personal habits, they are also making the deep, philosophical changes we need to create a new way to live. At the beginning of chapter nine, we talked about chimpanzees trapped in little rooms. Even on that very level — the kinds of houses and offices we're building and that we now wish to inhabit — systemic change is taking place. But "green" architecture is not the only thing that's springing up around us. New ways of growing our food, of transporting goods, of protecting the natural systems around us have appeared suddenly, and all over the world.

Millions of people, who are discovering their deepest values, are starting to viscerally understand what Alan Savory tried to express when he said, "Make your holistic goal 100 percent *what* you want and 0 percent *how* it is going to be achieved." They are using their values to formulate lofty goals instead of settling for practicalities and worrying about obstacles. They are no longer thinking about how hard it would be to have clean energy in a little town like Schöenau or to save the lions of India; how hopeless it is to live in a native community in B.C. with no choice but to cut down the forest you love; how helpless a group of poor Keralan fishermen are in comparison to the power of the global market; how frightening it would be to face down teargas and clubs for your principles. All these people are simply going out and living the way they think they should, according to their deepest values, without worrying whether their goals are too high or impractical. They are even developing a few spontaneous "hows" along the way — new kinds of schools, new ways of teaching, managing and thinking. Organic farming, holistic management, wilderness schools and consensus-based urban development are a long way from being mainstream methodologies, yet the way they have developed is so spontaneous, their basic tools are all so similar, that we have to at least suspect that this is how truly revolutionary social movements begin.

For example, Boora, the firm of "green" architects we met in chapter one, were typically slow to embrace this revolution; but as they did, they took to heart studies showing that being confined in little rooms with artificial air and light is so unnatural for humans that it creates measurable physical problems, including mental strain, headaches and reduced productivity, not to mention the unmeasurable problems of boredom, alienation and depression. So besides using all natural light and air, when Boora designed Clackamas, a new high school in Portland, they did not treat the small, natural bog on the school property as if it were a mistake that had to be sanitized and filled in. Instead, they integrated it with the school's waste-water system so that "gray" water could be naturally purified and reused and the school's climate control system could benefit from the wetland's cooling properties. The water cycle function and the biodiversity of the bog remain intact, both as a learning tool for the students and as source of contact with their local, natural world.

The Vermont Law School, an educational institution specializing in ethical and environmental law, is trying not just to think outside the box, but to let their students out of it. The school's main classroom building was crumbling, so they built a "green" one that uses highly efficient insulation, natural light and air, and does not employ any solvents or other dangerous chemicals, all within a tight budget of only $3 million (U.S.). Like the Boora-designed buildings, it was slightly more expensive initially, but savings on operational costs made up for the additional outlay almost immediately, and the school now feels they got many features for free. It is a delightful place, with deep green linoleum flooring, huge windows opening out onto the mountains, a fireplace in the student lounge. Their pride and joy, composting toilets, which we had never seen before in a large, indoor public facility, allows them to use a mere 53 liters (14 gallons) of water to service 530 students a day, instead of the nearly 30,000 liters (8,000 gallons) they used to go through.

And it's not just small-scale projects that are expressing these new values. Chicago's enormous city hall now sports a "green roof" planted with grasses, ivy, mosses, sedges, crabapple and hawthorn trees. The plants are natural air conditioners, cooling the air by releasing water vapor through their leaves. This single roof will save the city more than $4,000 a year in heating and cooling bills — to say nothing of what it will do for staving off global warming. Of course, the soil and plant matter also insulates the building from the region's fiercely cold winters, and it absorbs rain water, a huge urban pollution problem as it sluices down asphalt roofs and streets and into storm drains.

These changes are very simple, and very typical of what we found — planting a roof with flowers, letting wastes decompose naturally instead of dumping them in watercourses, allowing people to work in fresh air and natural light, using the ecosystem services of a wetland. They're cheap; they're even obvious. But we have to realize that, at this point in time, they are also revolutionary. Like organic, biodiverse farming, like Cores, Corridors and Carnivores, like businesses that don't hurt the earth or hydro-gen-powered transport, all these new methodologies provide the double and quadruple dividends we have discussed in this book. They all work to purify and conserve water; they encourage habitat for diverse lifeforms; they avoid the use of toxins or fossil fuels; and they take advantage of the planet's ecosystem services, its natural energy sources and disposal services. And best of all, when compared to First Industrial Revolution methods, they require much smaller outlays of cash, much less complex and dangerous infrastruc-tures, and fewer subsidies to produce their benefits. Chicago plans to install more green roofs and solar panels on other buildings, and Mayor Daley has recently announced the city's ultimate goal: to be the greenest urban space in North America. Pure food is becoming more available and more desir-able; more Adirondack-like parks are springing up around the world. Even the corporate world is taking notice. Bill McDonough, the green architect so often mentioned in this book, together with his large staff, are redesign-ing the Ford Motor Company's 480 hectare (1,200-acre) River Rouge plant in a twenty-year project that he claims will formally auger in the Second Industrial Revolution. His clients, he says gleefully, have told him to go ahead and apply all the systems conditions of The Natural Step to this mammoth complex, "and to work — totally outside the box!"

Like the designers who came up with the cage-like offices in the first place, the people creating new designs for a sustainable future have a very good idea what they're doing; they understand the wider social implications of their designs. They realize that, for example, working and living in structures that take advantage of natural environments instead of destroying them will help people embark on paths that lead to greater physical health, freedom and creativity, and even enhanced emotional and spiritual responses to life. Swaying grasses and flowering trees pumping out oxygen and soaking up pollutants above congested, paved-over urban spaces, a group of kids witnessing the complete functioning of the planet's hydrological and toxin absorption cycle a few yards away from their class-room — these are the subtler aspects of a revolution that offers liberation from the sensory deprivation of an old system that sees Nature not only as dead, but as intrinsically separate from humans. Like the cubicles and assem-bly lines before them, such basic changes in methodology can lead towards a basic change in society.

Of course, the corporate executives who first commissioned green buildings, for the practical purposes of increased production and reduced costs, probably did not intend that they would help lead us towards more open and natural societies. And there are still many, many people, as well as powerful commercial interests, who not only do not understand this revolution, but will try hard to weaken and delay it. Nonetheless, if we really do want it, if we take the courses, read the books, join the groups, we can now, thanks to electronic communications if nothing else, reach a real global consensus. And once we start to feel the power of consensus, we may find that the walls of our boxes will simply fall away. We are starting to find these paths together, the occasional big corporation and government included; and that is what building sustainable environmental, economic and social structures is all about.

# LIST OF ORGANIZATIONS

For those of you ready to get involved, here's how to get started. There are so many activist groups and resources, all around the world, that are now available to help people save and expand their local natural and social systems that we could not begin to make a definitive list of them all. So, besides the organizations profiled in this book, we are simply including names and addresses of a selection of resources that we know, from personal experience, are effective; we are listing them by subject, that is, by chapter. Many more are just as remarkable, however, and to find them, we suggest consulting the various web sites and magazines listed below. We have tried to include resources such as *Yes!* magazine and the *Utne Reader*, which make it their business to put their readers in touch with local and national organizations working towards the kind of holistic revolution we have discussed in this book. The web addresses are particularly fertile because through their links to other sites you can reach literally hundreds more organizations. But we realize not everyone has Internet access, so we have also tried to provide, throughout this list, a core group of organizations and information sources that are accessible by regular mail and phone. Good hunting — the people already working hard to make life livable and beautiful for our children will be very glad to see you.

## GENERAL RESOURCES

### Council of Canadians
Maude Barlow, Chair
*Canadian citizens' watchdog group involved in water conservation, globalization, pure food, toxic waste and many other issues.*
502-151 Slater St, Ottawa, ON K1P 5H3 Canada
tel. (800) 387-7177 or (613) 233-2773    fax (613) 233-6226
e-mail: inquiries@canadians.org    www.canadians.org

### The Sierra Club of Canada
Elizabeth May, Director
*Perhaps the most active and effective general-issue environmental organization in the country, the Sierra Club of Canada campaigns on issues like biotechnology, toxic waste, pesticide reduction and global corporate rule. It is very different from its U.S. counterpart, operating on a shoestring and tackling issues in a more direct manner.*

1 Nicholas Street, Suite 412, Ottawa, ON K1N 7B7 Canada
tel. (613) 241-4611 toll-free: 1 (888) 810-4204
e-mail: sierra@web.net   www.sierraclub.ca/national

### Yes! A Journal of Positive Futures
David and Fran Korten
*An unfailing source of contacts and encouragement in the search for sustainability.*
PO Box 10818, Bainbridge Island, WA 98110 USA
tel. (206) 842-0216   fax (206) 842-5208
e-mail: yes@futurenet.org   www.yesmagazine.org

### Down to Earth
*Although this excellently written, entertaining magazine is published by the Center for Science and Environment in India, it also discusses many other issues affecting people in other countries around the world.*
Society for Environmental Communications
41 Tughlakabad Institutional Area, New Delhi 110 062 India
tel. 91 11 6981110 or 6981124   fax 91 11 6985879
e-mail: cse@cseindia.org   www.oneworld.org

### The Natural Step
*Discussed at length in chapter one; the list of conditions by which to live.*
In the US, contact:
The Presidio, Thoreau Center for Sustainability
PO Box 29372, San Francisco, CA 4125-0322 USA
tel. (415) 561-3344   fax (415) 561-3345
e-mail: tns@naturalstep.org
In Canada, contact:
Jamie MacDonald, National Coordinator
4010 Whistler Way, Whistler, BC V0N 1B4 Canada
e-mail: jmacdonald@naturalstep.ca   www.naturalstep.ca

### Greenpeace Canada
250 Dundas Street West, Suite 605, Toronto, ON M5T 2Z5 Canada
tel. (416) 597-8408 ext. 3030
www.greenpeacecanada.org

### Greenpeace U.S.A.
*Greenpeace has campaigns going on everything from global warming to genetic engineering. Sometimes they are on the main web site, like their Arctic Action, at www.greenpeace.org/~climate, sometimes they are listed separately, like their pure food campaign, www.truefoodnow.org; but there are always links from the main menu. Check their main web site for your major concern.*
1436 U Street NW, Washington D.C. 20009 USA
toll-free 1-800-326-0959   tel. (202) 462-1177   fax (202) 462-4507
www.greenpeaceusa.org

**Greenpeace International**
Keizersgracht 176, 1016 DW Amsterdam, the Netherlands
tel. 31 20 523 6222    fax 31 20 523 6200

**The Union of Concerned Scientists**
*A group of hundreds of eminent scientists who have banded together to investigate and publicize unimpeachable statements regarding global warming, deforestation and other issues.*
Two Brattle Square
Cambridge, MA 02238-9105 USA
tel. (617) 547-5552
www.ucsusa.org

**Adbusters and Media Foundation**
Kalle Lasn, editor
*The Media Foundation works to help people step back and analyze the role of public relations and advertising in the world of trade, culture and economics; its quarterly magazine is popular with designers and culture-jammers.*
1243 West 7th Avenue, Vancouver, BC V6H 1B7 Canada
tel. (604) 736-9401    fax (604) 737-6021
e-mail: adbusters@adbusters.org    www.adbusters.org

**Straight Goods**
*This is Canada's major source of non-corporate-funded news information.*
e-mail: ish@straightgoods.com    www.Straightgoods.com

**World Wildlife Fund**
*This organization has programs that vary enormously from country to country, and is particularly active and effective in the Third World.*
1250 24th St. NW, Washington D.C. 20037-1175 USA
tel. (202) 293-4800    fax (202) 293-9211
www.panda.org

**International Forum on Globalization**
*Headed by Jerry Mander, this is a San Francisco-based alliance of 60 leading activists, scholars, economists, etc. engaged in public education and popular conferences on all the issues dealt with in this book.*
1009 General Kennedy Ave. #2, San Francisco, CA 94109 USA
e-mail: ifg@ifg.org    www.ifg.org

**Utne Reader**
*Monthly magazine with selections from the best of the alternative press and many regular lists of contacts for sustainable activities.*
1624 Harmon Place, Minneapolis, MN 55403 USA
tel. (800) 736-UTNE; outside the US (515) 246-6952
www.utne.com

### International Development Research Centre (IDRC)
*A Canadian government agency that works on solutions to development problems through research. A very decent resource for citizen-activists with a bias for the local.*
PO Box 8500, Ottawa, ON K16 3H9 Canada
tel. (613) 236-6163
www.idrc.ca

### The Sacred Balance
*David's four-part television series on the magical and intimate links between all life and the environment, based on his and Amanda McConnell's book of the same name, was broadcast in the fall of 2002 and has its own interactive web site with many information links, games and ways to watch and contact David.*
www.sacredbalance.com

### Holly Dressel's Web Site
Go to www.goodnews.homedns.org for on-going stories of hope and sustainability and contacts for change.

CHAPTER 1
# MAKING MONEY LIKE THE BEE

### The National Center for Employee Ownership
*U.S. group provides information on details of employee stock ownership and other resources.*
3411 W. Diversey Ave., Suite 10, Chicago, IL 60607 USA
tel. (773) 278-5418
www.mcir.com

### Environmental Rights Action (ERA)
Friends of the Earth (Oronto Douglas, director)
*This Nigerian-based organization attempts to disseminate news of the human and environmental abuses by multinational oil companies like Shell Oil and Chevron in alliance with paramilitary and government groups in the Niger Delta. They help coordinate the worldwide Shell boycott, and can provide information on the activities of these corporations in the Third World.*
PO Box 10577, Ugbowo, Benin City, Nigeria
tel./fax (234) 8423 6365
e-mail: eluan@infoweb.abs.net or obebi@infoweb.abs.net or
oilwatch@infoweb.abs.net

### Development Alternatives
Ashok Khosla
*The highly effective Indian organization featured in chapters one and four. They also publish a newsletter by the same name.*
B-32, Tara Crescent, Qutal Institutional Area, Delhi 110-016 India
tel. 91-11-696-7938 or 91-11-685-1158 or 685-1509     fax 91-11-686-6021
e-mail: devalt@del3vsnt.net.in or tara@sdalt.ernet.in
www.tarahaat.com

**Redefining Progress**
*Finding alternative measures to the GNP, promoting the Tobin Tax and other economic innovations.*
1904 Franklin St., 6th floor, Oakland, CA 94612 USA
tel. (510) 444-3401
www.rprogress.org

**United for a Fair Economy**
*Provides data on the division between haves and have-nots; helps with living-wage campaigns.*
37 Temple Place, 2nd Floor, Boston, MA 02111 USA
tel. (617) 423-2148
www.ufenet.org

**The White Dog Café**
*The remarkable restaurant profiled in chapter one. Check the web site for the newsletter and list of speakers and activities.*
3420 Sansom St., Philadelphia, PA 19104 USA
tel. (215) 386-9224
www.whitedog.com

**The Social Venture Network**
*San Francisco-based association of business people trying to build a sustainable world through their businesses.*
PO Box 29221, San Francisco, CA 94129-0221 USA
tel. (415) 561-6501    fax (415) 561-6435
e-mail: svn@svn.org    www.svn.org

**The Rebuilding Center of Our United Villages**
*Shane Endicott, described in chapter one, is the director and founder of the Rebuilding Center of Our United Villages.*
3625 N. Mississippi Ave., Portland, OR 97227 USA
tel. (503) 331-9291    fax (503) 331-1873
www.rebuildingcenter.com

CHAPTER 2
## WITHDRAWING CONSENT

**PR Watch**
Center for Media and Democracy
*The Center for Media and Democracy, founded by Sheldon Rampton and John Stauber, keeps an eye on transnationals and their media manipulations. Their newsletter,* PR Watch, *is published quarterly.*
3318 Gregory Street, Madison, WI 53711, USA
tel. (608) 233-3346    fax (608) 238-2236
e-mail: 74250.735@compuserve.com    www.prwatch.org/

**The Transnational Resource and Action Center (TRAC)**
*Corporate Watch Internet magazine*
*This organization keeps track of corporate power and analyzes the dangers to democracy and to human rights. Their Internet magazine is a rich source of information about who is doing what and how to combat it.*
PO Box 29344, Presidio Station, San Francisco, CA 94129 USA
tel. (415) 561-6567
e-mail: trac@igc.org   www.corpwatch.org

**Institute for Policy Studies**
*The IPS is a Washington think-tank concerned with democracy, environmental and justice issues as they relate to trade.*
733 15th Street, NW, Suite 1020, Washington D.C. 10005-2112 USA
tel. (202) 234-9382   fax (202) 387-7915
www.netprogress.org

**Public Citizen**
*Founded by Ralph Nader, this organizations keeps people informed about globalization and its effects on their daily lives. They wage campaigns in the U.S. and publish books.*
tel. (202) 588-1000 or (202) 588-7742
e-mail: slittle@citizen.org   www.citizen.org

**Public Interest Research Groups**
**PIRGs**
*Ralph Nader's group has also inspired the formation of hundreds of local, grass-roots groups called PIRGs, mostly headquartered in universities across Canada and the U.S., which disseminate information and provide discussion areas for consumer, justice, environmental and globalization issues. Contact a local university or college.*
e-mail: webmaster@pirg.org   www.pirgs.org

**Ruckus Society**
*Trains activists to become effective at nonviolent civil disobedience.*
www.ruckus.org

**Third World Network**
*Malaysia-based network of academics and activists keeping the First World appraised of the Third.*
228 Macalister Road, 10400, Penang, Malaysia
tel. 60 4 2266728 / 2266159   fax 60 4 2264505
e-mail: twn@igc.apc.org   www.twnside.org.sg

**Association for the Taxation of Financial Transactions for the Aid of Citizens**
**ATTAC**
*French-founded, an active group working for the Tobin tax and other global reforms with branches across Europe, South America and in Quebec.*
124 avenue Philippe August, 75011 Paris, France

tel. 1 43-79-84-40
e-mail: jetin@club-internet.fr   www.attac.org

**Tobin Tax Initiative**
*U.S. Tobin tax group, working with CEED, the Center for Environmental Economic development.*
CEED/11RP, PO Box 4167, Arcata, CA 95518-4167 USA
tel. (707) 822-8347   fax (707) 822-4457
e-mail: ceciln@humboldt1.com   www.tobintax.org

**Ithaca Hours**
*Local currency group helping people start their own local money systems*
Box 365, Ithaca, NY 14851 USA
tel. (607) 272-4330
www.lightlink.com/hours/ithacahours

**Time Dollar Institute**
*American organization advocating a tax-exempt form of exchange allowing people to "bank" the hours they spend rebuilding family and community and to convert them into purchasing power.*
PO Box 42519, Washington D.C. 20015 USA
tel. (202) 686-5200
www.cfg.com/timedollar or www.timedollar.org

CHAPTER 3
## USING COYOTES TO GROW GRASS

**Natural Resources Defense Council**
*Fighting for natural ecosystems and species.*
40 West 20th St., New York, NY 10011 USA
tel. (212) 727-2700
e-mail: NRDCINFO@ NRDC.ORG   www.nrdc.org

**The World Wildlife Fund**
www.panda.org
*Their panda logo is known worldwide; their effects and politics vary from country to country, and are particularly active and effective in the Third World. The main web site or any office can provide you with local chapter information.*
In Canada:
245 Eglinton Ave. East # 410, Toronto, ON M4P 3J1 Canada
tel. (416) 489-8000   fax (416) 489-3611
In the U.S.:
1250 24th St. NW, Washington D.C. 20037-1175 USA
tel. (202) 293-4800   fax (202) 293-9211

**TRAFFIC India**
*We dealt with TRAFFIC, the WWF arm that tries to control illegal trade in animals.*
c/o WWF Secretariat, 172-B Lodi Rd., New Delhi 110003 India
e-mail: trfindia@del3.vsnl.net.in

**The Y-2-Y Conservation Initiative**
In Canada:
710 9th St., Studio B, Canmore, AB T1W 2V7 Canada
tel. (403) 609-2666    fax (403) 609-2667
In the U.S.:
114 West Pine, Missoula, MO 59802 USA
tel. (406) 327-8512
e-mail: hub@y2y.net    www.rockies.ca/y2y

**The Allan Savory Center for Holistic Management**
1010 Tijeras NW, Albuquerque, NM 87102
tel. (505) 842-5252   fax (505) 843-7900
www.holisticmanagement.org

**The Wildlands Project**
*Working with biodiversity projects like the Sky Islands and Y 2 Y across North America. Their online magazine is Wild Earth.*
PO Box 455, Richmond, VT 05477 USA
tel. (802) 434-4077
e-mail: infor@twp.org    www.wild-earth.org

*Conservation Ecology*
*Electronic peer-reviewed scientific journal on conservation themes quoted by us, with offices in five countries and 10,000 subscribers.*
e-mail: questions@consecol.org    www.consecol.org

**Canadian Parks and Wilderness Society (CPAWS)**
*Involved in everything from grizzly habitat protection to Marine Protected Areas, this "grassroots voice for wilderness," founded in 1963, has 20,000 active members fighting for new parks and nature-based management.*
800 Wellington St., Suite 506, Ottawa, ON K1R 6K7 Canada
tel. 1-800-333-WILD    fax (613) 569-7098
e-mail: info @cpaws.org or volunteer@cpaws.org    www.cpaws.org

**The Wilderness Society**
*Founded in 1935, this U.S. group has eight regional offices to champion the causes of wilderness habitat and conservation.*
1615 M St. NW, Washington D.C. 20036 USA
tel. 1 800-THE-WILDS
www.tws.org

**Oregon Country Beef**
*Doc and Connie Hatfield (profiled in chapter three).*
Box 50 Brothers, OR 97712 USA
tel. (541) 576-2455
e-mail: marketing@countrynaturalbeef.com   www.oregoncountrybeef.com

**Thirteen Mile Farm Lamb and Wool Co.**
Dave Tyler & Becky Weed
*Another predator-friendly holistic ranching business*
13000 Springhill Rd., Belgrade, MO 59714 USA
tel. (406) 388-4945
e-mail: becky@lambandwool.com   www.lambandwool.com

**Defenders of Wildlife**
*U.S. group finding solutions to wildlife problems, like their Wolf Compensation Trust, which reimburses losses of livestock at fair market prices; also helped create a 3,700- square mile marine sanctuary to protect the vaquita porpoise, the world's rarest marine mammal.*
tel. (406) 549-0761 (Hank Fisher)
www.defenders.org.

CHAPTER 4
# A RIVER RUNS THROUGH IT

See Council of Canadians, above.

**The International Rivers Network**
*Volunteer activists and water management professionals have formed a worldwide network fighting for policy changes and community-based river management. Provides project analysis and alternative technologies; the best of the river conservation groups we consulted, especially useful for news on mega-dams and decommissioning.*
1847 Berkeley Way, Berkeley, CA 94703 USA
(510) 848-1155   fax (510) 848-1008
e-mail: irn@irn.org   www.irn.org

**The Columbia River Inter-Tribal Fish Commission**
729 NE Oregon, Suite 200, Portland, OR 97232 USA
(503) 238-0667   fax (503) 235-4228
e-mail: croj@critfc.org   www.critfc.org

**British Columbia Institute of Technology**
*Active in the decommissioning of the Theodossia dam.*
3700 Willingdon Avenue, Burnaby, BC V5G 3H2 Canada
www.recovery.bcit.ca

**Public Services International**
*This NGO is a coalition of 500 trade unions in 400 countries representing 20 million people working in the public service — firefighters, health, public utilities and food inspection workers, judges and so on. Their web site and publications give information on a wide variety of environmental and justice issues.*
   www.world-psi.org

*Catch Water Newsletter*
*Put out monthly by Angil Agalwar's Center for Science and Environment mentioned in the text. Although the examples are all Indian, the easy availability of this interesting journal can make positive efforts to improve water supply available to a wide audience.*
   Center for Science and environment
   41 Tughlakabad Institutional Area, New Delhi 110062 India
   www.rainwaterharvesting.org

**Waterkeeper Alliance**
*An American and Canadian organization that keeps track of threats to waterways, especially organic pollution sources.*
   Neuse Station, 427 Boros Rd., New Bern, NC
   tel. (252) 447-8999   fax (252) 447-6464
   e-mail: riverlaw@ec.rr.com   www.waterkeeper.org

**The World Water Contract**
*This global movement can be contacted through a wide variety of NGOs already listed, notably the Council of Canadians, the International Forum on Globalization, the Institute for Agriculture and Trade Policy, Global Exchange, and Public Citizen.*
   www.citizen.org/cmep/Water

CHAPTER 5
**EATING HUMBLE PIE**

**Beyond Factory Farms**
*A national coalition recently formed to help Canadian citizens' groups fighting ILOs (Industrial Livestock Operations) across the country.*
   e-mails: gkoroluk@mb.aibn.com; Igerlach@canadians.org; or ccpasak@sask-tel.net

**Fair Trade and Organic Organizations**
*For those interested in obtaining foods that are organic and/or certified as delivering a fair price and decent growing conditions to the people and environments that produce them, contact your local Greenpeace or Oxfam office, or get in touch with: Global Exchange ([415] 255-7296, www.globalexchange.org), Transfair USA ([510] 663-5260, www.transfairusa.org) and Transfair Canada ([888] 663-FAIR, www.transfair.ca) or Equiterre, Quebec ([514] 522-2000, www.equiterre.qc.ca).*

**Institute for Agriculture and Trade Policy**
*Promotes family farms and healthy ecosystems world wide through education and advocacy.*

2105 First Avenue South, Minneapolis, MN 55404 USA
tel. (612) 870-3410    fax (612) 870-4846
e-mail: kdawkins@iatp.org   www.iatp.org

**The International Center for Technology Assessment and the
Center for Food Safety,** both headed by Andrew Kimbrell
*These two groups of Washington-based lawyers are energetic sources of information
and legal action that examine the social, environmental and political effects of new
technologies and undertake litigation where those technologies are doing damage.*
310 D Street NE, Washington D.C. 20002 USA
tel. (202) 547-9359
www.icta.org

**The Food Alliance**
*Certifying organization mentioned in chapters one and five.*
1829 Alberta, Suite 5, Portland, OR USA
tel. (503) 493-1066    fax (503) 493-1069
e-mail: dkane@thefoodalliance.org   www.foodalliance.org

**Seed Savers Exchange**
*This group grows, saves, distributes and sells organic and heritage seed. They also
fund workshops for Third World participants to increase their knowledge of
sustainable food cropping.*
Kent Whealy, RR 3, Box 239, Decorah, IA 53101 USA
tel. (319) 382-5990    fax (319) 382-5872

**SoilFoodWeb Inc.**
Elaine Ingham, President, SoilFoodWeb Inc.
*This organization advises, educates and provides the means for farmers to wean
their soils from agricultural chemicals and learn how to build soil for sustainable
agriculture.*
980 NW Circle Boulevard, Corvallis, OR 97330 USA
tel. (541) 752-5066    fax (541) 752-5142
e-mail: inghame@bcc.orst.edu

**NAVDANYA**
(National Program for Conservation of Native Seed Varieties)
Director, Vandana Shiva
*NAVDANYA is involved with actively saving the seeds of rural India from
patenting and industrial development.*
A-60, Hauz Khas, New Delhi 110 016 India
tel. 91 11 696 8077 or 91 11 651 5003
fax 91 11 685 6795 or 91 11 696 2589

**Food and Agriculture Organization of the UN (FAO)**
*A common source of statistics and information on forestry, fisheries, rural
development and especially agricultural and food security issues.*
www.fao.org

### The Chef's Collaborative 2000
*A network of chefs and other food professionals promoting sustainable cuisine through education, supporting farmers and spreading information. Their links page can put you in touch with everyone from the FDA to the Organic Trade Association.*
441 Stuart St., #712, Boston, MA 02116 USA
tel. (617) 236-5200
e-mail: cc2000@chefnet.com www.chefnet.com
A typical member is the Higgins restaurant and bar
1239 SW Broadway Portland, OR 97205 USA
tel. (503) 222-9070    fax (503) 222-1244
e-mail:higgins@europa.com

### The Edmonds Institute
*Its head, Beth Burrows, is a remarkable source of information about most subjects discussed in this book. Her Institute's focus is the economic impacts of technology and intellectual property policies, and women's issues in the Third World.*
20319 92nd Ave. W., Edmonds, WA 98030 USA
tel. (425) 775-5383
e-mail: beb@igc.org   www.edmonds-institute.org

### Food First!
*The poverty and food rights organization mentioned in chapter nine.*
398 60th St. Oakland, CA 94608 USA
tel. (510) 654-4400    fax (510) 654-4551
e-mail: foodfirst@foodfirst.org   www.foodfirst.org

### The Ram's Horn
*Brewster and Cathleen Kneen's monthly newsletter keeps subscribers abreast of crucial food issues in Canada and abroad. They also put people in touch with activist groups on biotech and other agricultural issues.*
S-12 C-11 RRRI Sorrento, BC Canada
tel./fax (250) 675-4866
e-mail: ramshorn@jetstream.net

CHAPTER 6
### LISTEN FOR THE JAGUAR

### Amazon Watch
*The main group keeping an eye on mining, drilling and other assaults to tropical rainforests.*
115 S. Topanga Canyon Blvd, Suite E, Topanga, CA 90210 USA
tel. (310) 455-0617 fax (310) 455-0619
e-mail: amazon@amazonwatch.org   www.amazonwatch.org

### Rainforest Action Network
*RAN is well known for working to protect the earth's forests and support the rights*

*of their inhabitants through education, grass-roots organizing and non-violent
direct action.*
   221 Pine Street, No. 500, San Francisco, CA 94702 USA
   tel. (415) 398-4404    fax (415) 398-2732
   e-mail: rainforest@ran.org   www.ran.org

**Yakama Forest**
   Box 151 401 Fort Road, Toppenish, WA 98948 USA
   (509) 865-5121    fax (509) 865-6850
   e-mail: cpalmer@yakama.com

CHAPTER 7
## SONG OF THE ALBATROSS

**Sea Shepherd Conservation Society**
Paul Watson, Director
*A famous direct-action group created by the most gutsy founder of Greenpeace that
fights over-fishing and oil spills and protects sea mammals in news-making
confrontations and legal actions around the world.*
   22774 Pacific Coast Highway, Malibu, CA 90265
   tel. (310) 456-1141    fax (310) 456-2488 or (800) WHALES
   www.seashepherd.org

**National Fishworkers Forum (NFF)**
Father Thomas Kocherry
Sister Cicely Plathottam, Sister Philomen Mary
*This incredible organization cannot be overpraised for the work it does constantly
protecting the lives and environment of the poorest people of Kerala.*
   KSMTF/CHERVRESMI
   Velankeanny Junction, Valiathura
   Thiruvananthapuram, Kerala 695008 India
   tel. 011-91 471-501-376 or 011-91 471 505-216
   e-mail: fishers@eth.net or delforum@vsnl.com

**Marine Stewardship Council**
*This body certifies sustainably caught wild and raised fish and supports market
incentives for sustainable fishing with its "Fish Forever" eco-label.*
   119 Altenburg Gardens, London, SW11 1JQ England
   44 171 350-4000 fax 44 171 350-1231
   e-mail: 106335.77@compuserve.com   www.panda.org

**The Seafood Guide**
*Sustainable eating, complete with recipes, available at*
   www.audubon.org/seafood/guide
The organization has also published a book by Carl Safina: *The Seafoodlover's
Almanac* (Audubon's Living Oceans, 2000). See also:
   www.seafoodchoices.com and www.conservefish.com

**Ecofish**
*The company providing sustainably raised fish to the market mentioned in chapter nine.*
78 Market St., Portsmouth, NH 03801 USA
tel. (603) 430-0101 fax (603) 430-9929
e-mail: consumerservice@ecofish.ca   www.ecofish.com

**Audubon's Living Oceans Project**
*Probably the most active of the large environmental groups in marine preservation issues.*
550 South Bay Ave., Islip, NY 11751 USA
e-mail: livingoceans@audubon.org   www.audubon.org

**Marine Fish Conservation Network**
*A coalition of U.S. national and regional commercial and recreational fishing groups and environmental organizations.*
660 Pennsylvania Ave. SE, Suite 302B, Washington D.C. USA
tel. (202) 543-5509 or 1-866-823-8552   fax (202) 543-5774
www.conservefish.org

Note: Nearly all the big environmental organizations like Greenpeace, the NRDC and WWF are also involved in marine conservation.

CHAPTER 8
## WRESTLING WITH PLUTO

**Rocky Mountain Institute**
Amory and Hunter Lovins
*Profiled in chapters one and two, the institute invents and promotes the nuts and bolts of the sustainability technology revolution.*
1739 Snowmass Creek Rd., Snowmass, CO 81654-9199 USA
tel. (970) 927-3851 fax (970) 927-3420
www.rmi.org

**Center for Environment, Health and Justice, CCHW**
Lois Gibbs, Executive Director
*This grassroots U.S. group, supported by blue-collar workers, low-income families, farmers and people of color, fights toxic dumps and works for victims of contamination. They have their own toxicologist and can do much to help frightened citizens get a handle on suspected industrial poisons.*
PO Box 6806, Falls Church, VA 22040-6806 USA
tel. (703) 237-2249   fax (703) 237-8389
e-mail: cchw@essential.org or noharm@iatp.org
www.essential.org/cchw or www.noharm.org

**Pesticide Action Network**
*The Pesticide Action Network is a scientifically reliable source of information on what compounds your food and environment contains, how dangerous they are and how to organize to limit or eliminate pesticide use in your area.*

49 Powell St., Suite 500, San Francisco, CA 94102 USA
tel. (415) 981-1771    fax (415) 981-1991
e-mail: panna@panna.org    www.panna.org

**Project Underground**
*Fights the toxic pollution and human rights violations of the current worldwide gold rush on metals, led in large part by Canadian corporations. They provide information, legal help and outside research to people suffering the effects of the world land-grab for minerals.*
1916a Martin Luther King Jr. Way, Berkeley, CA 94703 USA
tel. (510) 705-8981    fax (510) 705-8983
e-mail: project_underground@moles.org    www.moles.org

**Mining Watch Canada**
Joan Kuyek, National Coordinator
*Keeps an eye on the environmental degradation and human misery caused by mining around the world.*
tel. (613) 569-3439
e-mail: joan@miningwatch.ca    www.miningwatch.ca

CHAPTER 9
# BREAKING OUT OF THE BOX

**Northwest Earth Institute (NWEI)**
Dick and Jeanne Roy
*Rapidly spreading courses, as described in chapters one and nine, that teach a new way to live, with hundreds of communities now participating in 40 states and Canada.*
Suite 1100 506 SW Sixth Ave., Portland, OR 97204 USA
tel. (503) 227-2807
e-mail: info@nwei.org    www.nwei.org
The same office also runs the Oregon Natural Step, and publishes the
*Oregon Natural Step News.*

**Sustainable Northwest**
*A key group working towards the definition of sustainability; they help ranchers, farmers, and urban business people focus on their goals, and publish a yearly celebration of success,* Founders of a New Northwest, *which is now expanding beyond the original Pacific coast.*
620 SW Main, Suite 112, Portland, OR 97205-3037 USA
tel. (503) 221-6911    fax (503) 221-4495
e-mail: sustnw@teleport.com    www.sustainablenorthwest.org

**International Council for Local Environmental Initiatives (ICLEI)**
*A worldwide group trying to implement Agenda 21 principles drafted at the first environmental summit. Their main office is in Canada.*
www.iclei.org

**New America Foundation**
*Nitty-gritty economic solutions and methods by which to change the current sequestering of finances in a few hands into a broad-based, democratic monetary system.*
  1630 Connecticut Avenue NW, 7th floor, Washington D.C. 20009 USA
  tel. (202) 986-2700
  www.newamerica.net

**New Road Map Foundation**
*Part of the growing frugality movement, founded by Vicki Robin, they help people rediscover simple, sustainable lifestyles.*
  PO Box 15981, Seattle, WA 98115 USA
  tel. (206) 527-0437   fax (206) 528-1120
  www.newroadmap.org

**Center for a New American Dream**
*A wonderful resource for ideas and exchanges on how to live more rewarding lives.*
  6930 Carroll Ave., Suite 900, Takoma Park, MD 20912 USA
  tel. (301) 891-3683   fax (301) 891-3684
  e-mail: newdream@newdream.org   www.newdream.org

**Wilderness Awareness School**
Jon Young
  26311 NE Valley St. #5-137, P.O. Box 5000 Duvall, WA 98109 USA
  or 26331 NE Valley St. PMB 137, Duvall, WA USA
  Wilderness Awareness School in New Jersey
  tel.(425) 788-1301, ext. 38 or contact John Gallagher at (425) 788-6155 for
  the locations of schools in four other states, including Battleboro, Vermont.
  e-mail: Yakewin@aol.com or steve@VermontWildernessSchool.com
  www.natureoutlet.com or www.WildernessAwareness.org

**McGill School of the Environment**
Pete Barry, Program Coordinator
  3534 University St., 2nd Floor, Room 23, Montreal, PQ H3A 2A7 Canada
  e-mail: info@mse.mcgill.ca   www.mcgill.ca/mse

**Environmental Science Institute**
*Fosters environmental research and education across disciplines.*
  ESI, University of Texas, Austin, TX 78712
  www.geo.utexas.edu/esi

# NOTES

CHAPTER 1
## MAKING MONEY LIKE THE BEE

1 Social Ventures Network, PO Box 29221, San Francisco, 94129-0221 USA; (415) 561-6501; fax (415) 561-6535; e-mail svn@svn.org; web site www.svn.org

2 For many such examples, look up Founders of a New Northwest publications by Sustainable Northwest, 1020 SW Taylor, Suite 200 Portland, OR 97205 USA; (503) 221-6911; email sustnnw@teleport.com; web site www.sustainablenorthwest.org

3 The Natural Step now has offices in eight countries. For more details, see www.naturalstep.org

4 In terms of accepting the reality of climate change and looking for alternative energy initiatives, BP and Shell are the best; but even Shell is about to get busy in Alberta's tar sands, as well as expanding its interests both offshore and in the Niger Delta. As for Chevron-Texaco, Occidental, Mobil and the other big oil corporations that have not admitted that climate change is a reality, they are definitely not switching to sustainable energy sources. They are all increasing their drilling activities, especially in remote, untouched and aboriginal areas in Africa and South America. For details, contact Project Underground, an NGO monitoring oil and mining activities (address at the back of this book). See especially their Oil Campaign Fact Sheets. Contact the Rainforest Action Network (also listed at the back). See also Stephen Kretzmann and Shannon Wright, *Drilling to the Ends of the Earth: The Ecological, Social and Climate Imperative for Ending Petroleum Exploration*, Project Underground and Rainforest Action Network, 1998, and Greenpeace's Climate Change campaign, www.greenpeace.org.

5 The Union of Concerned Scientists (UCS) point out that Ford's green initiatives will improve its ranking as one of the most polluting automakers on the planet only slightly. "Their SUVs and other light trucks have the poorest fuel economy in the industry," and phase-out dates are far in the future. This basically means that without legislation, like strong federal emission standards applicable to trucks as well as cars, even well-intentioned corporations will continue to drag their feet. See www.ucsusa.org/vehicles, or contact UCS at the address listed at the back of this book. See also Margot Roosevelt, "How Green Was My SUV," *Time* magazine, August 14, 2000. Contact Jerry Scott at the David Suzuki Foundation for even

more details. And see especially "Ford Reaches Out to Environmentalists, *Wall Street Journal,* May 15, 2000, and David Booth, "Ford Pulls the Plug on Explorer Hybrid," *The Journal,* November 27, 2001.

6 Occidental Petroleum and Mobil are extremely active in ecologically pristine areas of South and Central America. See "Visit the World of Chevron" and "Drillbits and Tailings" at the www.moles.org web site, or write them for copies. The Rainforest Action Network also has much information on the activities of these companies. See also the most active NGO in this field at the moment, www.amazonwatch.org. The Institute for Policy Studies in Washington (see address at the back of this book) has a Sustainable Energy and Economy Network, www.seen.org, where good information is available on the activity of the big oil corporations and especially their links with World Bank funding.

7 See the new book by Ike Okonta and Oronto Douglas, *Where Vultures Feast: Shell, Human Rights and Oil in the Niger Delta* (San Francisco: Sierra Club Books, 2001), especially chapters 4 and 5. We documented interviews with Owans Wiwa and Oronto Douglas, who are eyewitnesses to the types of situation encountered by Roddick on her Nigerian tour in August 2000 and November 2001 respectively. See also Shannon Wright and Stephen Kretzmann, *Independent Annual Report: Human Rights and Environmental Operations Information on the Royal Dutch/Shell Group of Companies 1996–97,* Project Underground, Rainforest Action Network and Oilwatch, 1997. For Roddick's personal experience, contact Thorsons Publishing, publishers of her recent book *Business As Unusual* (London: Thorsons Publishing, 2001).

CHAPTER 2
## WITHDRAWING CONSENT

1 Sarah van Gelder, "Corporate Futures," an interview with David Korten and Paul Hawken, *Yes! Magazine,* Summer, 1999.

2 S. Jacob Scherr, "Conservation Advocacy and the Internet: The Campaign to Save Laguna San Ignacio," NRDC, 2001.

3 PR Newswire release, August 27, 1999; see also Scherr, "Conservation Advocacy."

4 Bernard Lietaer, "Beyond Greed and Scarcity, dialogue with Sarah van Gelder," *Yes! Magazine,* Spring, 1997; Bernard Lietaer is the author of *The Future of Money.*

5 David Korten, "Money vs. Wealth," *Yes! Magazine,* Spring, 1997.

6 Lietaer, "Beyond Greed and Scarcity."

7 See http://www.ceres.org for more details.

8 Bill McDonough, "How do you love ALL the children?" *Yes! Magazine,* Fall 2000.

9 See F.M. Lappé, J. Collins and P. Rosset, *World Hunger: Twelve Myths* (New York: Grover Press, 1998) 270; Frances Moore Lappé, "People, not technology, are the key to ending hunger," *Los Angeles Times,* June 27, 2001; FAO, quoted by Peter Rosset in reference above; Vandana Shiva, *Yoked to Death,* (New Delhi: Research Foundation for Science, Technology and Ecology, January 2001), 8; *Staying Alive,* (New Delhi: Research Foundation for Science, Technology and Ecology).

10 Miguel Altieri, "Ten reasons why biotechnology will not ensure food security, protect the environment and reduce poverty in the developing world," University of California, Oct. 15, 1999, in www.gene.ch/; and Lori Ann Thrupp, "New Partnerships for Sustainable Agriculture," 1997 World Resources Institute; and the UNDP Agroecology project, "Creating the Synergism for a Sustainable Agriculture," 1995.

11 See "RE: William McDonough," interview by Amanda Griscom, *FEED*, June 12, 2000; www.feedmag.com.

12 See Murray Dobbin, "NAFTA's Big Brother," at www.canadians.org/campaigns-tradepub.

13 Maude Barlow and Tony Clarke, *Global Showdown* (Toronto: Stoddart, 2001), 55.

14 Ibid., 56.

15 Irwin Block, "Singh trial postponed," *The Montreal Gazette*, Nov. 2, 2001.

16 Gwynne Dyer, "Genoa: The Recession Summit," syndicated column, July 17, 2001.

17 David Korten, *When Corporations Rule the World*, (San Francisco and West Hartford: Kumarian Press, Inc. and Berrett-Koehler Publishers, Inc. 1995), 232.

18 Taken from the "Statements of the IMF Missions for 1993/94/95," including correspondence related to "Article IV, Reviews and Consultations with Canada," obtained by the Halifax Initiative and the Sierra Club of Canada through the Access to Information Act, September 30, 1999.

19 Ed Ayres, "Why Are We Not Astonished?" adapted in *World Watch*, May/June, 1999, 26.

20 T. Rajamoorthy, "Financial crisis and Capital Controls: the Malaysian Experience," presented at the New International Financial Architecture Seminar, Lima, 6–8 Sept., 2000. Rajamoorthy is echoed by other economic analysts, such as Yilmaz Akyuz, the director of the Division on Globalization and Development Strategies at the United Nations Conference on Trade and Development (UNCTAD). Subsequent events bear them out. Yilmaz Akyuz, "Causes and Sources of the Asian Financial Crisis," TWN Series on the Global Economy, 2000.

21 UNCTAD Trade and Development Report, 1999.

22 Rodney Schmidt, "Efficient Capital Controls," International Development Research Centre, Government of Canada, April, 2000; see the following Web sites: www.ceedweb.org; www.halifaxinitiative.org; www.attac.org; www.waronwant.org for a great deal of information on a movement that stretches from Canada to Senegal, from India to South America.

23 Paul Hawken with Amory and L. Hunter Lovins, in *Natural Capitalism: creating the next industrial revolution* (NY, Little, Brown & Co., 1999), 9.

24 This entire section is taken from Sarah van Gelden, "Corporate Futures," interview with David Korten and Paul Hawkin, *Yes! Magazine*, Summer 1999.

CHAPTER 3
## USING COYOTES TO GROW GRASS

1 William Cronon, *Changes in the Land* (New York: Hill and Wang, 1983), 22, 107.

2 "A Political History of the Adirondack Park and Forest Preserve" www.adirondack-park.net.

3 Ibid., 101–2.

4 Ibid.

5 Verplanck Colvin, from www.adirondack-park.net.

6 Philip Terrie, *Contested Terrain: A New History of Nature and People in the Adirondacks* (Syracuse, NY: Syracuse University Press, 1997).

7 See also Terrie, "Behind the Blue Line," and "The Adirondack Paradigm," *Adirondack Life*, January/February 1992; and "Collector's Issue, 1999." See also Paul Schneider, *The Adirondacks: A History of America's First Wilderness* (New York: Henry Holt & Co., 1997).

8 Kevin Kelly, *Out of Control* (New York: Addison-Wesley, 1994) chap. 4: "Assembling Complexity"; see also www.well.com/user/kk/Out of Control; and Catherine Bell, "Biodiversity" in *Conscious Choice*, May, 1995, www.consciouschoice.com; and "Major Forces in the Loss and Decline of Biodiversity in the Plains," Nature Conservancy Great Plains Program, www.greatplains.org.

9 See Bermuda Biological Station for Research, Inc., "A Brief Guide to Nonsuch Island Nature Reserve," www.bbsr.edu; also "The 1999–2000 Cahow nesting season," by David Wingate, at www.audubon.org; Island Resources Foundation and BirdLife International, "Threatened and Endangered Birds of the Insular Caribbean," www.irf.org; and Kelly, "How to do everything at once" in his *Out of Control*.

10 Richard Conif, *Every Creeping Thing* (New York: Henry Holt & Co., 1998), pp. 31–40.

11 Ibid.

12 Allan Savory with Jody Butterfield, *Holistic Management: A New Framework for Decision Making* (Washington D.C.: Island Press, 1999), especially pp. 195–215.

13 John Acocks, "Non-selective grazing as a means of veld reclamation," *Proceedings of the annual conference of the Grassland Association of South Africa*, vol. 1: 33–39, 1966.

14 See also Thirteen Mile Lamb & Wool Company, Belgrade, Montana, "Predator Friendly" wool and meat, www.lambandwool.com and becky@lamgandwool.com.

15 Other resources: John P. Kretzmann and John McKnight, *Building Community from the Inside Out* (ACTA Publications, 1997); also John McKnight, *Careless Society: Community and its Counterfeits* (New York: Basic Books, 1996); Jan Christiaan Smuts, *Holism and Evolution* (Highland, NY: The Gestalt Journal Press, 1996); André Voisin, *Grass Productivity* (Washington D.C.: Island Press, 1959)

16 See "Current Projects: Rewilding and Biodiversity, Complementary Goals For Continental Conservation in www.twp.org. Michael Soulé is professor of environmental studies at the University of California at Santa Cruz and founder of the Society for Conservation Biology. Reed Noss is editor of *Wild Earth* and co-director of the Conservation Biology Institute.

17 Michael Soulé, "Does Sustainable Development Help Nature?" in *Wild Earth*, www.ecoworld.com/Animals/archives.

18  See Janna Bialek, "Conference Explores East's 'Wild' Possibilities," *Audubon Naturalist News*, May 2001.

CHAPTER 4
## A RIVER RUNS THROUGH IT

1  See the quoted works by Sandra Postel, author of *The Last Oasis* and head of the Global Water Policy Project, as well as officials of the World Health Organization, the Ford Foundation and UNICEF; also Michael S. Serrill, "Wells Running Dry," *Time Magazine Special Issue, Our Precious Planet*, November, 1997, vol. 150, no. 17A; and Marq de Villiers, *Water* (Toronto: Stoddart, 1999), "Water in Peril," 1–21.

2  Allerd Sikker, "Water Today and Tomorrow: Prospects for Overcoming Scarcity," *Futures*, vol. 30, no. 1 (Great Britain: Elsevier Science Ltd., 1998); quoted in Maude Barlow, "Blue Gold," June 1999; Special Report by the International Forum on Globalization, 5.

3  Barlow, "Blue Gold."

4  Quoted in "Communities do have an answer," in *Catchwater*, the CSE Campaign for People's Water Management, vol. 3, no. 1, Feb. 2001 at www.rainwaterharvestin.org/catchwater.

5  Stories other than those from DA are from Anil Agarwal's monthly, published by the Centre for Science and the Environment, New Delhi; the Neemi story is from Press Release of April 25, 2001, at www.cseindia.org; "Jal Biradari Launches Movement to Drought-Proof Villages," "Harvest of Hope," Centre for Science and Environment, January, 2000 *Down to Earth*; www.cseindia.org, or email cse@cseindia.org; see also *Catchwater*, Feb. 2000–Feb. 2001.

6  From Priit J. Vesilind, "The Middle East's Water: Critical Resource," *National Geographic*, May 1993.

7  Vesilind, "Middle East's Water."

8  Wendy Elliman, Jewish Telegraphic Agency, Jan. 29, 2001, at www.zipple.com.

9  De Villiers, *Water*, 171.

10  See David Pimental, "Rapid Population Growth in California," at www.diversityalliance.org.

11  Elliman, Jewish Telegraphic Agency.

12  De Villiers, especially chap. 16; and Vesilind, "Middle East's Water."

13  Mona Grieser, Barbara Rawlins and Khulood Tubaishat, "Water Conservation in Jordan," at zipple.com.

14  Postel, "Troubled Waters," *The Sciences*, March/April 2000.

15  See Ish Theilheimer, "Downsized water expert finds no profit in protecting Walkerton residents," *Straight Goods*, May 31, 2000; see also two *Toronto Star* articles: Roberta Avery, "Chlorine would not have saved lives, water inquiry told," January 12, 2001; and Caroline Mallan, "Half of Ontario water plants flawed," Jan. 2, 2001.

16  Barlow, "Blue Gold."

17  Roberta Avery and Kate Harris, "Stories of Walkerton," *Toronto Star*, May 20, 2001.

18  Arundhati Roy, "The Art of Spinning: How Uncle Sam Turns Indian Gold into Straw," in *Art India, Inc.*, 2001.

19  Patrick McCully, *Silenced Rivers: The Energy and Politics of Large Dams* (London: Zed Books, 1996).
20  See Roy, "The Art of Spinning."
21  International Rivers Network, "Questions and Answers on Large Dams," paper, www.irn.org
22  International Rivers Network, "the Environmental Impacts of Large Dams," www.irn.org
23  See www.recovery.bcit.ca
24  Robert Sullivan, "River, Interrupted," *Mother Jones*, January, 2001. See also Postel, "Where Have All the Rivers Gone?" *World Watch*, May/June, 1995.
25  See Postel, "Where Have All the Rivers Gone?" See also her "Troubled Waters."
26  Postel, "Where Have All the Rivers Gone?"
27  Emanuele Lobina, "Water Privateers, Out!" in *Focus On the Public Services*, February, 2000.
28  Lobina, "Water Privateers, Out!"
29  Shawn Tully, "Water, Water Everywhere," *Fortune Magazine*, May 15, 2000, 55.
30  Barlow, "Blue Gold," 15.
31  The Public Services International Research Unit, under the auspices of the University of Greenwich.
32  Public Services International Research Unit.
33  See "The Way Forward: Public Sector Water and Sanitation," PSI briefing to the World Water Forum, The Hague, March 17–22, 2000.
34  Postel, "Where Have All the Rivers Gone?"
35  Barlow, "Blue Gold."
36  Ibid.

CHAPTER 5
**EATING HUMBLE PIE**

1  J. Stephen Lansing, *The Balinese: Case Studies in Cultural Anthropology* (New York: Harcourt Brace, 1995).
2  Ibid.
3  Quoted in Lansing, *The Balinese*.
4  Lansing, *The Balinese*, 99.
5  Ibid., 93.
6  Lansing, *Priests and Programmers*, (New Jersey: Princeton University Press, 1991), 112–14.
7  Lansing, *The Balinese*, 100–1.
8  Cited in Lansing, *The Balinese*, 101.
9  Miguel Altieri, "Ten reasons why biotechnology will not ensure food security, protect the environment and reduce poverty in the developing world," University of California, Oct. 15, 1999; in www.gene.ch/; see also Frances Moore Lappé, Joseph Collins and Peter Rosset, *World Hunger: Twelve Myths* (New York: Grover Press, 1998), 270. See also chapter 9, the comparison between caloric intake in Kerala and the Punjab, India.
10  Frances Moore Lappé, "People, not technology, are the key to ending hunger," *Los Angeles Times*, June 27, 2001.

11  Ibid.

12  FAO, quoted in Rosset, *World Hunger.*

13  Vandana Shiva, *Yoked to Death* (New Delhi: Research Foundation for Science, Technology and Ecology, January, 2001), 8.

14  Vandana Shiva, *Staying Alive: Women, Ecology, and Survival in India* (London: Zed Books, 1989), 129.

15  Shiva, *Yoked to Death* (New Delhi: Research Foundation for Science, Technology and Ecology), 19.

16  Lori Ann Thrupp, "New Partnerships for Sustainable Agriculture," 1997 World Resources Institute; and the UNDP Agroecology project, "Creating the Synergism for a Sustainable Agriculture," 1995.

17  Ibid.

18  John Ikerd, "Sustainable Agriculture: a Positive Alternative to Industrial Agriculture," University of Missouri, April 7, 2001; www.ssu.missouri.edu. Presented at the Heartland Roundup Conference, December 7, 1996. See other papers by Ikerd, such as "The Coming Renaissance of Rural America" and "Towards an Economics of Sustainability," at www.ssu.missouri.edu, or contact the University of Missouri.

19  Ibid.

20  Ibid.

21  Ibid.

22  See David Suzuki and Holly Dressel, *From Naked Ape to Superspecies.* (Toronto: Stoddart, 1999), 163–66.

23  See also, *Sustainable Agriculture . . . Continuing to Grow,* published by Sustainable Northwest, an Oregon NGO, the Western Sustainable Agriculture Research and Education Program of the University of California and the U.S. Department of Agriculture.

24  See also the Report of the Auditor General, Feb., 2001, www.oag-bvg.gc.ca.

25  See www.panna.org/resources, appendix 2, "Trends in pesticide use by chemical crop in California." All stats from the California Department of Pesticide Regulations 1999, Pesticide Use Reports. For sales data, the state's Pesticides Sold in California, 1991–97. See the U.S. EPA definition of carcinogens, as well as chemicals listed as "Reproductive and Developmental Toxicants" under California's Property 65, the Safe Drinking Water and Toxic Enforcement Act of 1986.

26  See Canadian Health Coalition "Overview of Hormones Used in Canada," *Straight Goods,* June 27, 2001.

27  See healthcoalition.ca, "Consumers advised to stop eating pork until Carbodox taken off the market," April 11, 2001, and "Raising valid beefs about meat testing," November 21, 2000.

28  Brad Duplisea, "What Canadians need to know about Mad Cow disease," *Straight Goods,* June 29, 2001.

29  Interview with Steve Suppan of the Institute of Agriculture and Trade Policy, May 2001.

30  Lawrence Alderson, *Rare Breeds* (New York: Little, Brown & Co., 1994), 79; all breeds described here are in Alderson's book.

31  Ibid. 16.

32   See "Regulations on Labeling and Production of Genetically Engineered foods, " True Food Network, GMO facts, www.truefoodnow.org/gmo.

33   See, among many other such stories, Tom Spears, "'Superweeds' invade farm fields," *The Ottawa Citizen*, Feb. 6, 2001. In Mexico, gene contamination became a national crisis when the purest wild form in the Mexican highlands was found to be contaminated with GE characteristics. First brought to light in late 2001 in the peer-reviewed magazine *Nature*, the GE industry responded with such fury that a scandal developed that threatened the magazine as well as the plants. See, among many others, Mark Schapiro, "Sowing Disaster?" *The Nation*, USA, October 28, 2002; Angelica Enciso, "Problem Confirmed in the Juarez Sierra of Oaxaca, Warns the Researcher," *La Jornada*, Mexico, Feb. 21, 2002; and Ariel Alvarez-Morales, "Transgenes in Maize Landraces in Oaxaca: Official Report on the Extent and Implications," *7th International Symposium on the Biosafety of Genetically Modified Organisms*, Oct. 2002.

34   See "Food Scandal Exposed," Michael Sean Gillard, Laurie Flynn and Andy Powell, *The Guardian*, February 12, 1998. The so-called mild herbicide, glyphosate, which is poured on plants throughout the growing season, has also been linked to human health problems. See Drs. Lennart Hardell and Mikael Eriksson in the *Journal of the American Cancer Society*, March 15, 1999. See also "Diabetics not told of insulin risk," *The Guardian*, March 9, 1999, and the Edmonds Institute, whose director, Beth Burrows, says, "I think . . . we don't know the effects of the GG consumption because we were/are unwilling to bear the costs of finding out. Long-term human health consumption research is expensive and takes a long time to do. It will only be done by a society that feels a responsibility to the future and feels comfortable enough to accept the fact that its descendants may not be able to correct every mistake they have made."

35   John Chalmers, "Scientists champion drought-resistant crops in India," Reuters, May 2, 2000.

36   "The sisters of nutrition," IRRI Press Release, April 3, 2000, www.irri.org/Hunger/Nutrition.

37   See David Suzuki and Holly Dressel, *From Naked Ape to Superspecies*, (Toronto: Stoddart, 1999), 98–126.

38   "Biotech brokers penetrate Asia," GRAIN news release, October 30, 2000.

39   Paul Brown, "GM rice promoters 'have gone too far,'" *The Guardian*, Feb. 10, 2001.

40   "ICIPE announces safe new methods for controlling stemborers . . . and Striga," ICIPE press release, Nairobi, Kenya, June 15, 2000.

41   Ibid.

42   See F. Gould, "Potential and Problems with High-Dose Strategies for Pesticidal Engineered Crops." *Biocontrol Science and Technology* 4, 1994, 451–61.

43   Quoted in Carl Frankel, "Food, Health and Still Hopeful," in Tomorrow: *Global Environment Business*, March–April 2000, 6. 44 Wendell Berry, "The Pleasures of Eating," in *What Are People For?* North Point, 1990.

45   See Laura J. Enriquez, "Cuba's New Agricultural Revolution," Development Report No. 14, Department of Sociology, University of California, Berkeley,

May 2000. See David Pimentel et al, "Environmental and Economic Effects of Reducing Pesticide Use, *Bioscience*, vol. 41, no. 6, 1991, 402–9, which states, "Although pesticide use has increased during the past four decades, crop losses have not shown a concurrent decline . . . The share of crop yields lost to insects has nearly doubled during the last 40 years, despite more than a ten-fold increase in both the amount and toxicity of synthetic insecticide used" (p. 403).

46  See Scott G. Chaplowe, "Havana's Popular Gardens: Sustainable Urban Agriculture," from the *WSAA Newsletter*, a publication of the World Sustainable Agriculture Association, Fall, 1996, vol. 5, no. 22; see also wwww.foodfirst.org/cuba; and www.cityfarmer.org/cuba.

47  The U.S. practice of dumping unsaleable corn and soy on desperate populations as "food aid" has increased dramatically in recent years. See especially the most recent famine crisis, where the Zambian government turned back GE grain for fear it would find its way into the ground and contaminate native varieties. Rory Carroll, "Zambians Starve as Food Aid Lies Rejected," *The Guardian*, UK, Oct. 17, 2002; "GM Crops in Africa—Better Dead than GM-Fed?" *The Economist*, Sept. 19, 2002; Manoah Esipiser, "Top US Official Says Starving Africa Should Accept GMO Food," Reuters, Aug. 2002; "Why Africa SHOULD Reject GE-Contaminated Food Aid," *WSSD/Earth Summit Press Release of African Government and Cvil Society Representatives*, Aug. 30, 2002; see also, Agence French Presse, "U.S. Withdraws Genetically Engineered Animal Food Donations After Bosnia's Hesitation," Jan. 30, 2001, at www.centraleurope.com/bosniatoday/news.

CHAPTER 6
## LISTEN FOR THE JAGUAR

1  In American Association for the Advancement of Science, *ScienceNOW*, Aug. 7, 1997.

2  Ibid., David Perry of Oregon University.

3  See Suzanne W. Simard, *Nature*, Aug. 7, 1997; Evelyn Strauss, *Science News*, Aug. 9, 1997, 87; also Carl Zimmer, "The Web Below," in *Discover*, November, 1997.

4  See Garrett Hardin, "The Tragedy of the Commons," *Science*, 162, 1968, 1243–48; see also the remarkable Web site, www.egroups.com/group/dieoff.

5  Quoted in Scott Atran, "Itza Maya Tropical Agro-Forestry," *Current Anthropology*, vol. 34, 1993, 633–700.

6  See Susan Zwinger, "The Wisdom of an Eco-forester," interview with Merv Wilkinson, April 12, 1994 at www.realnews.org. All quotations by Merv Wilkinson are taken from this reported interview.

7  Brad Knickerbocker, "Forest Managers Learn How to Grow 'Green' Lumber," *The Christian Science Monitor*, Nov. 29, 1993.

8  See David Malin Roodman, *The Natural Wealth of Nations* (New York: W.W. Norton and Worldwatch, 1998), 52–53.

9  See Thomas Michael Power, *Lost Landscapes and Failed Economies* (Washington D.C.: Island Press, 1996), 165.

10  Timothy Egan, "Oregon, Foiling Forecasters, Thrives as It Protects Owls," *New York Times*, October 11, 1994.

11  See Klemens Laschefski and Nicole Freris, "Saving the Wood from the

Trees," *The Ecologist*, July/August, 2001, 40–3.

12   See Brad Knickerbocker, "Timber! (tenderly)," *The Christian Science Monitor*, (c) 2000, The Christian Science Publishing Society.

13   Available on the David Suzuki Foundation web site; see www.davidsuzuki.org

14   See Northern Forest Press Release, Doris Duke Charitable Foundation: "Industry, Environmentalists, Land Owners and Wood Buyers All Benefit under New Forest Conservation Initiative," May, 2000, contact Molly Lovett, 202 822-5200; also, The Nature Conservancy Press Releases, May 17, 2000, "The Nature Conservancy to permanently protect more than 18,000 acres of key forest habitat in Northern New Hampshire," wwww.nature.org

CHAPTER 7
## SONG OF THE ALBATROSS

1   Private correspondence between David Suzuki and Carl Safina, 2001.

2   E. Pinkerton and M. Weinstein. "Fisheries That Work: Sustainability through Community-Based Management". (Vancouver, BC, The David Suzuki Foundation, 1995).

3   Christopher Dyer and Richard Leard (1994), in Pinkerton and Weinstein, "Fisheries that Work."

4   Ibid., 101.

5   These figures are from the June 23, 1993 Indian Supreme Court Judgment of Justices S.C. Agarwal and Jeevan Reddy.

6   See David Roodman, *The Natural Wealth of Nations* (New York, W.W. Norton, 1998), 69.

7   Carl Safina, "Empty Oceans, Empty Nets," interview in the film series of the same name; habitatmedia.org

8   Tracey C. Rembert, "Swearing off Swordfish," *E/The Environmental Magazine*, Environmental Research Foundation, June 1998, www.emagazine.com

9   Callum Roberts and Julie Hawkins, *Fully Protected Marine Reserves: A Guide* (University of York, England, 2000); quoted in Larry Pynn "Special Edition," *Vancouver Sun*, a 5-part series on marine conservation, April 30–May 4, 2001; see specialedition.net/cgi.

10   "Tortugas Marine Reserve Now Largest in U.S."; see www.ens.lycos.com, July 6, 2001

11   Ibid.

12   Carl Safina, "Cry of the ancient mariner," *Time* magazine, Earth Day, 2000.

13   Cited in Pynn, "Special Edition" series *Vancouver Sun.*

14   Carl Safina, "Cry of the ancient mariner."

15   Ibid.

16   Press release, National Fisheries Forum, Jan. 2000.

17   Ross Gelbspan from his web site, www.heatisonline.org

18   Safina, "Empty Oceans, Empty Nets."

19   Ibid. And for those interested in directly combating this excess, look into the activities of the Sea Shepherd Conservation Society, p. 369.

20   The "Guide to Seafood" is available from the Audubon offices in Washington D.C. or online at www.magazine.audubon.org.

21   Jennifer Bogo "Brain Food; Choose your Seafood with Tomorrow in

Mind," *E/The Environmental Magazine*, July/August 2000; also www.ecofish.com.
22 William McDonough, interviewed by Amanda Griscom in *FEED Magazine*, June 12, 2000.
23 Cited in Pynn, "Special Edition" series, *Vancouver Sun*.

CHAPTER 8
## WRESTLING WITH PLUTO
1 That is, from 280 ppm to 360 ppm.
2 Andrew Weaver, *Vancouver Sun*, Feb. 8, 2001.
3 www.ems.psu.edu/~radovic/env fossil.html
4 William McDonough, interview by Amanda Griscom, *FEED Magazine*, December 6, 2001.
5 Guy Dauncey and Patrick Mazza, *Stormy Weather: 101 Solutions to Global Climate Change* (British Columbia: New Society Publishers, 2000); see also "What's next after fossil fuel?" *Yes! Magazine*, fall 2001.
6 "California Solar Plant Is a Success," *Climate Change Gazette*, www.e5.org, and www.edisonnews.com
7 Alan Thien Durning, *The Car and the City* (Seattle WA: Northwest Environment Watch, 1996).
8 Amory B. Lovins, L. Hunter Lovins, Ernst von Weizsacker, *FACTOR 4: Doubling Wealth — Halving Resource Use 1997* (London: Earthscan Publications Ltd., 1997).
9 J.H. Crawford, *Carfree Cities* (Utrecht: International Books, 2000).
10 Jay Walljasper, "Going Places," *Utne Reader*, July 1993.
11 www.greenspiration.org
12 There is a great deal of evidence available; see especially Ross Gelbspan, *The Heat Is On: the Climate Crisis, the Cover-up, the Prescription* (Cambridge MA: Perseus Books, 1998).
13 Speech by Lester Brown of the Worldwatch Institute, in Hungary, Feb. 5, 1999
14 See the many articles and programs addressing this issue, especially Rick Moore's article, "GM Super Salmon and the Wisdom of Tinkering with Fish," posted at the University of Minnesota's online publication, www1.umn.edu/urelate/kiosk. See also an interview with Dr. Anne Kapuscinski at www.habitatmedia.org/tran-kapuscinski, and articles at www.centerforfoodsafety.org and www.ems.org/biotech/fish
15 Ross Gelbspan, "Bush's Withdrawal from Kyoto Protocol," *Christian Science Monitor*, April 2, 2001.
16 http://www.igc.org/icc370/bp.htm
17 "Dirty Dozen," *Globe and Mail*, May 23, 2001.
18 Please go to www.pbs.org and read the transcripts and the internal memos from the corporations. Absolutely spine-chilling.
19 *The Ottawa Citizen*, Editorial, February 19, 1999.
20 See www.oecd.org/env/outlook/outlook.htm.
21 Ibid.
22 From Hanno Beck, Brian Dunkiel and Gawain Kripke, *Citizens' Guide to Environmental Tax Shifting*; Introduction by Paul Hawken (Washington D.C.: Friends of the Earth, June 1998).

23  James MacKenzie, Roger Dower and Chen, "The Going Rate: What it Really Costs to Drive," World Resources Institute.

24  From Beck, Dunkiel and Kripke, *Citizens' Guide.*

25  See the special edition of *The Ecologist* on Monsanto's history and corporate behavior, vol. 28, no. 5, Sept.Oct. 1998, Brian Tokar, "Monsanto: A Checkered History"; Cate Jenkens, "Criminal Investigations of Monsanto Corporation — Cover-up of Dioxin Contamination in Products — Falsification of Dioxin Health Studies," USEPA Regulatory Development Branch, Nov. 1990; Peter Schuck, *Agent Orange on Trial: Mass Toxic Disasters in the Courts* (Cambridge, MA: Harvard University Press, 1987); Dr. Samuel S. Epstein, "Unlabelled Milk from Cows Treated with Biosynthetic Growth Hormones: A Case of Regulatory Abdication," *International Journal of Health Sciences,* vol. 26, no. 1, 1996; Jed Greer and Kenny Bruno, *Greenwash* (Penang, Malasia: Third World Network, 1996) on many chemical companies; see also www.pbs.org, "Trade Secrets" for internal memos and documents from all the companies in the Chemical Manufacturers Association (CMA).

26  Rachel Brahinsky, *San Francisco Bay Chronicle,* "California State Crisis," June 2001.

27  Quoted from "A Tale of Three Cities," in *Yes! Magazine,* Summer 2001

28  See Brahinsky, above; also *Public Citizen's Critical Mass Energy and Environment Program* report, January 2001. The Province of Ontario, after a brief and disastrous experiment with deregulation in 2002, in which rates also skyrocketed, by 2002 was promising to reimburse consumers and is seeking a return to a public system.

29  Daniel M. Berman and John T. O'Connor, *Who Owns the Sun?* (Vermont: Chelsea Green Publishing Company, 1997).

CHAPTER 9
## BREAKING OUT OF THE BOX

1  Jerry Mander, *Four Arguments for the Elimination of Television* (New York: Quill, 1978).

2  Ibid., 121–22.

3  Ibid., 76–77.

4  Ibid., 123.

5  Ibid., 63–64

6  Interpretation provided by Roberta Martell.

7  K. Vishwanathan, quoted in Bill McKibben "The Enigma of Kerala," excerpted by the *Utne Reader,* March–April, 1996.

8  Statistics from the Population Reference Bureau, www.prb.org.

9  Akash Kapur, "Poor but Prosperous," *The Atlantic Online,* September 1998, www.theatlantic.com.

10  Govindan Parayil, ed., *The Kerala Model of development: perspectives on development and sustainability* (London: Zed Books, 1999); Shekhar Gupta, "Kerala: the literacy war," *India Today,* Aug. 31, 1991: 77 and 80; Jean Dreze and Amartya Sen, eds., *Indian Development: selected regional perspectives* (Delhi: Oxford University Press, 1998).

11  Kapur, *The Atlantic Online.*

12  McKibben, "The Enigma of Kerala."

13  "Kerala — the Facts," *New Internationalist*, issue 241, March, 1993.

14  Figures based on India's National Sample Survey (NSS).

15  Richard W. Franke, "Lessons in Democracy from Kerala State, India, 1999 University Lecture," http://chss.montclair.edu/anthropology; see also Madhura Swaminathan and V.K. Ramachadran, "New data on calorie intakes," Frontline 16 (5), March 12, 1999.

16  Franke, "Lessons in Democracy."

17  For statistics, see: United Nations List of National Parks and Protected areas: India, 1993, at www.wcmc.org.uk; www.expert-eyes.org/parks; and www.mysticindia.com/tourism/kerala.

18  See "Sustainability: the Global Challenge," ZPG Backgrounder, Washington D.C.; "All-Consuming Passion," published by the New Roadmap Foundation, zpgseattle.org/roadmap.

19  Ibid.

20  Douglas Birch and Gary Cohn, "Of Patients and Profits: How a cancer trial ended in betrayal," *The Baltimore Sun*, June 24, 2001.

21  Ibid.

22  Tinker Ready, "Science for sale," *The Boston Phoenix*, April 29, 1999.

23  Part of a CBC radio interview for the series *From Naked Ape to Super-species*.

# BIBLIOGRAPHY

Because the revolution towards managing the planet sustainably is new and still evolving, much of the information about it we obtained from interviews, magazines and the Internet. Nonetheless, besides the books mentioned in the footnotes, there are a few others available that will serve as serious food for thought for anyone interested in the subjects covered in *Good News for a Change*. We have listed our favorites below.

Barlow, Maude, and Elizabeth May. *Frederick Street: Life and Death on Canada's Love Canal* (Toronto: Harper Collins, 2000).

Barlow, Maude, and Tony Clarke. *Global Showdown: How the New Activists Are Fighting Global Corporate Rule* (Toronto: Stoddart, 2001).

Benyus, Janine M. *Biomimicry: Innovation Inspired by Nature* (New York: William Morrow & Co., 1997).

Brouwer, Steve. *Sharing the Pie: A Citizen's Guide to Wealth and Power in America* (New York: Henry Holt & Co., 1998).

Brown, Lester. *The State of the World* series, published yearly by the Worldwatch Institute.

Costanza, Robert, et al. *An Introduction to Ecological Economics* (Boca Raton, FL: St. Lucie Press, 1997).

Cronon, William. *Changes in the Land: Indians, Colonists and the Ecology of New England* (New York: Hill and Wang, 1983).

Durning, Alan. *How Much is Enough? The Consumer Society and the Future of the Earth* (New York: W.W. Norton & Co., 1992).

Goodall, Jane, with Phillip Berman. *Reason for Hope: A Spiritual Journey* (New York: Warner Books, 1999).

Hawken, Paul, and Amory and Hunter Lovins. *Natural Capitalism: Creating the Next Industrial Revolution* (New York: Little, Brown & Co., 1999).

Korten, David C. *The Post-Corporate World* (San Francisco: Berrett-Koehler Publishers, and West Hartford, CT: Kumarian Press, 1999).

Mander, Jerry. *Four Arguments for the Elimination of Television* (New York: Quill, 1978).

Mander, Jerry, and Edward Goldsmith, eds. *The Case Against the Global Economy and for a Turn Toward the Local* (San Francisco: Sierra Club Books, 1996).

Roodman, David Malin. *The Natural Wealth of Nations: Harnessing the Market for the Environment* (New York: W.W. Norton & Co., 1998).

Savory, Allan, with Jody Butterfield. *Holistic Management: A New Framework for Decision Making* (Washington D.C.: Island Press, 1999).

Sustainable Northwest; any of the *Founders of a New Northwest* series.

Suzuki, David, and Amanda McConnell. *The Sacred Balance: Rediscovering Our Place in Nature* (Vancouver: Greystone Books, 1997).

Suzuki, David, and Holly Dressel. *From Naked Ape to Superspecies: A Personal Perspective on Humanity and the Growing Eco-Crisis* (Toronto: Stoddart, 1999); soon to be republished by Greystone Books.

Wackernagel, Mathis, and William Rees. *Our Ecological Footprint: Reducing Human Impact on the Earth* (Gabriola Island: New Society Publishers, 1996).

Wessels, Tom. *Reading the Forested Landscape* (Woodstock, VT: The Countryman's Press, 1997).

Wilcove, David S. *The Condor's Shadow: The Loss and Recovery of Wildlife in America* (New York: W.H. Freeman & Company, 1997).

There are also myriad practical guides, such as *The Official Earth Day Guide to Planet Repair*, by Denis Hayes (Washington D.C.: Island Press, 2000). Good hunting!

# INDEX

secondary forest, 208
Second Industrial Revolution, 62–64
  values of, 64–68
  vision for future, 85–88
seeds, genetically engineered, 190,
  191
self-provisioning gardens, 203
Sen, Amartya, 73
Severn, Sarah, 23–24
sewage, 141–42
shareholders, as obstacles to
  sustainability, 47–49
Shell Oil, 45–46, 290
Shelton, Gilbert, 178
Shiva, Vandana, 9, 170–71, 186–88,
  195, 198
Shorebank, 34
Sieber, Peter, 28–31
Sierra Club, 296–97
*Silenced Rivers* (McCully), 149
Simard, Suzanne, 206–7
Singh, Jaggi, 70, 73–75, 321
Sky Islands Wilderness Network, 118
Sladek, Ursula, 311–15
SmartCar (MCC), 31, 284
SmartWood certification program,
  232
Soares, Mario, 160
Social Venture Network, 10
"solar income," 66
solar power, 281–82
Solenium, 26–27
Solomon, Maryann, 324
Soros, George, 41
Soulé, Michael, 116–18
South Africa, 159, 260
Southern California Edison, 309
Spain, 302, 307
Springfield (Oregon), 228–29
Sri Lanka, 199
Starr, Joyce, 137
State Land Master Plan, 93
State of the World forum, 9–10, 26,
  46
Stauber, John, 142
Sten, Eric, 141
Sterritt, Art, 241
Stiftung Warentest, 27–30
Stikker, Allerd, 129
striped bass, 242–46
Suez, 155, 156
Superfund, 294

sustainability
  in architecture, 21–22
  in business, 9–50
  as long-term goal, 20, 22, 24
  as marketing decision, 25
sustainable development, 323–32
sustainable energy sources, 281–84
sustainable forestry, 16–18, 215–32
  principles, 239
sustainable jobs, 37–41
Sweden, 19–20
  green taxes, 302
Swoope (Virginia), 176–78
SWOT inventory, 323
Sydney (Australia), 156
Sydney (Nova Scotia), 296–98, 301–2
Sydney Steel Corporation (SYSCO),
  297

Tahawus Club, 93
TARA Center, 133
Tarbela Dam, 148
tar ponds, 296–98
Tarun Bharat Sang, 136
Technion-Israel Institute of
  Technology, 139
Technology and Action for Rural
  Advancement (TARA), 38–41
temperate rainforests, 233–41
Tennessee Valley Authority (TVA),
  148, 149
"terminator" gene, 191
terrace ecosystems, 163–64
Terrie, Philip, 93
Texaco, 290
Texas, 103–4
Thailand, 150–51, 199
Theodosia River, 151–52
thermodynamics, laws of, 20
Thompson, Tommy, 111
timber industry, 92. *See also* forestry
tobacco companies, 321–22
Tobin, James, 84
Tobin Tax, 84
Tobin Tax Initiative, 84
Toronto, 283–84
Toronto Catholic District School
  Board, 283–84
Toronto Dominion Centre, 283
Tortugas Marine Reserve, 265
*Toxic Sludge Is Good for You*
  (Rampton & Stauber), 142

The David Suzuki Foundation works through
science and education to protect the balance of nature and our
quality of life, now and for future generations.

To find out how you can become a
Friend of the Foundation, or to make a donation, contact:

The David Suzuki Foundation
2211 West 4th Avenue, Suite 219
Vancouver, B.C. V6K 4S2
Tel.: 604-732-4228
Fax: 604-732-0752
e-mail: solutions@davidsuzuki.org
www.davidsuzuki.org